W9-AGU-317

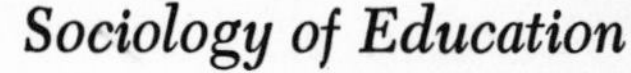

Sociology of Education

THE DORSEY SERIES IN SOCIOLOGY

Editor ROBIN M. WILLIAMS, JR.
Cornell University

Sociology of Education

WILBUR B. BROOKOVER
Michigan State University

EDSEL L. ERICKSON
Western Michigan University

1975

The Dorsey Press *Homewood, Illinois 60430*

Irwin-Dorsey Limited Georgetown, Ontario L7G 4B3

First Printing, February 1975
Second Printing, July 1977

ISBN 0-256-01674-7
Library of Congress Catalog Card No. 74–24459

Printed in the United States of America

Dedicated
to
Edna Brookover
Ruth Erickson

Preface

This is the third book by the senior author entitled *Sociology of Education.* Although it may be viewed as the third edition, this volume is almost completely new. The first *Sociology of Education* appeared 20 years ago, in the spring of 1955. In the preface to that edition, he indicated that since the *Sociology of Education* was new the author could do little more than raise questions and state hypotheses. Research evidence upon which to base generalizations or conclusions was almost nonexistent. When the second *Sociology of Education* was published in 1964, in collaboration with David Gottlieb, there was considerably more research upon which to draw. Although the general frame of reference of the second volume was essentially the same as the first, considerable new material was available for analysis. There were, of course, still many areas in which only limited knowledge was available. In the last decade research on the social aspects of education has increased to a level that required a new and expanded treatment. For this reason, the current version of *Sociology of Education* is almost completely new.

Readers of the previous volumes, however, will still find the general frame of reference which emphasizes interactionist theory present, but other theoretical perspectives have been added. Consequently, several chapters are decidedly different and the content is greatly benefitted by the extensive research which has occurred.

The senior author takes great pleasure in having Edsel Erickson join in the preparation of this edition. Although some chapters are more directly the product of one or the other authors, both have contributed significantly to all chapters. Although we have sought to examine the available research in the various areas and to reflect objective analysis of contemporary knowledge, we have not hesitated to express policy positions in which we reflect our own values at various points in this volume. When this has occurred we have sought to provide evidence in support of our positions and recognize where the evidence is inadequate.

No book is the exclusive product of the authors. Our associations over the years with colleagues, including teachers and students, have been the source of many ideas and much information in this book. We can not, of course, thank all those colleagues and friends whose ideas permeate the volume. We wish, however, to mention a few who, in recent years, have contributed significantly to our efforts. Among the many are Shailer Thomas, Richard Morse, Carl Couch, Lee Joiner, Michael Walizer, William Bennett, Paul Green, Herbert Smith, Jeffery Schneider, Ronald Henderson, Grace Gist Henderson, Richard Gigliotti, Lawrence Lezotte, and Robert L. Green. To these and all the unnamed who have contributed to our understanding, we express our thanks.

We also wish to express our thanks to Robin Williams and Blaine Mercer for their numerous suggestions and editorial assistance in the preparation of this manuscript. Ruth Park and Judith Brawer have also made significant contributions in the editing and preparation of the manuscript for publication. Our secretaries, Barbara McFadden, Lois Carl, Betty White, and Holly Mikel, have provided assistance far beyond the call of duty. To all these and many others, we express our thanks and appreciation; and to our wives, Edna Brookover and Ruth Erickson, we dedicate this volume in appreciation of their continued support and assistance.

January 1975

WILBUR B. BROOKOVER
EDSEL L. ERICKSON

Contents

part one

Introduction

1

The Sociology of Education

DURING the two decades since the original edition of this volume first outlined the emerging field of sociology of education, a number of important changes have occurred.[1] Twenty-five years ago there were only about a dozen sociologists in North America and only a few more in Great Britain and continental Europe who were identified by their research and publications as sociologists of education. Consequently, the research available for preparation of the first edition was extremely limited. In contrast with the situation at mid-century, there are now several hundred sociologists in the American Sociological Association and the American Educational Research Association who are examining the social nature and function of education. In addition, a large proportion of these scholars in North America are actively engaged in research of great significance to education and to the society in general. During the last decade sociological research on education has received national and indeed international attention in the popular communication media. The pictures of very few social scientists have appeared on the front pages of the *New York Times* in recent decades. James Coleman was one of these. His direction of the Equality of Educational Opportunity[2] study made him the personal symbol of many sociological contributions to our understanding of the educational system and the processes of teaching and learning. These contributions indicate both the enhanced interest in the sociology of education and the recognition that sociological analyses may explain much of what occurs in the educational system.

The sociological concern with education has not been limited to the

[1] Wilbur B. Brookover, *A Sociology of Education* (New York: American Book Company, 1955).

[2] James Coleman et al., *Equality of Educational Opportunity* (Washington, D.C.: U.S. Government Printing Office, 1966).

Western Hemisphere. Extensive research and theorizing on education are currently being conducted by sociologists and educators in Great Britain, Australia, Japan, Yugoslavia, New Zealand, and other nations of the world. The rapid growth in the field of sociology of education since World War II has resulted in a rather dramatic expansion of our knowledge about the social functions and context of education. We have gained considerable awareness of the economic, political, ideological, religious, and, yes, the military functions of education. We now know a great deal about how our educational systems socialize us and how the internal dynamics of educational organizations and systems work.

However, we hasten to add that not all of our recent insights are the result of studying only education. We have also gained a knowledge of education from developments in other areas of sociology and from the extensive development of research on social systems, organizations, conflict resolution, socialization, and learning which are useful in understanding our schools and their functions. On the other hand, numerous in-depth sociological studies of education have added immeasurably to our knowledge of human conduct in general.

The recent rapid expansion of the sociological analysis of education contrasts sharply with the previous, almost exclusive, dependence on psychology for explanations of the educational process. The dominance of educational psychology was based on the assumption that all explanation of the teaching-learning process is to be found within the individuals involved. The teacher's effectiveness and the students' learning were affected only by physical traits, intelligence, or other personal characteristics of the individual teacher or student. The psychological study of individuals alone has helped us understand much human behavior, but a comprehensive knowledge of the educational process requires an examination of the interaction of the teachers and learners in the social context wherein such interaction occurs. Knowledge of the school as a social system and of the social nature of man is essential for an understanding of education. Other reasons for the sociological study of education will become apparent in succeeding discussions. Before we proceed, however, it is necessary to consider certain historical developments in the sociological study of education.

Historical Background

It is generally agreed among sociologists that Emile Durkheim, in the late 1800s, first clearly indicated the need for a "sociological" approach to the study of education. During the whole of his teaching life at the Universities of Bordeaux and Paris, Durkheim taught educational theory and practice as well as sociology. In his lectures at the

Sorbonne, Durkheim began by saying that he viewed education as a sociologist, and that he considered education "to be something essentially social in character, in its origins and its function, and that as a result the theory of education relates more clearly to sociology than to any other science."[3] Durkheim was emphatic in pointing out that there was no single or ideal type of education for all men. He expressed the opinion that differences in sociocultural needs would play a major role in the type of educational programs which are established in various societies. He noted that education is not a static phenomenon but a dynamic and ever-changing process. We have only to note a few of the many current efforts organized around implementing open schools, changing admission criteria, desegregation proposals, preschool programs, and community education to note the accuracy of Durkheim's observation.

It should be noted that Durkheim made a sharp distinction between the educator and the social scientist. He thought the educator should be occupied with bringing about changes within the educational system; on the other hand, he saw the sociologist as an analyst of human behavior and considered it the sociologist's function to explain current social phenomena. In order to better explain the social phenomena of education, Durkheim made explicit the following research areas which he considered appropriate for sociologists:

1. Identification of the current social facts of education and their sociological function.
2. Identification of the relationships between education and social and cultural change.
3. Cross-cultural and comparative research in various types of educational systems.
4. Investigation of the classroom and school as an ongoing social system.

Despite the clarity of Durkheim's position, it was many years before many sociologists accepted his research direction. Perhaps this was due to the lack of scientific sophistication and the nature of human concerns among intellectuals during Durkheim's time. Similar to today, at the turn of the century educators were faced with numerous social problems. For example, in the United States and Canada, the large influx of immigrants, the shift to a younger and more urban population, and the increased complexity and demands imposed by increased industrialization presented a series of dilemmas.

In the first half of this century social analysts of education were asked: What are the most effective means by which immigrants can be integrated into the school and community? What types of educational pro-

[3] Emile Durkheim, *Education and Sociology* (New York: The Free Press, 1956).

grams are best for the majority of children who are rural children and are embarking on their first formal educational experiences? In what ways are differences in European language, ethnic identity, and religious affiliation influencing patterns of learning and behavior? It is clear that the "social problems" of education were among the first concerns of the sociologists as well as of educators. There was a growing need to comprehend the social tasks and problems of education.

Educational Sociology

As acceptance of the need for a sociocultural understanding of school problems grew, colleges of education introduced courses which attempted to give the prospective teacher a sociological approach to the dynamics of the classroom. However, an analysis of the content of teacher education courses in 1927 showed that these courses had little in common and were, for the most part, a hodgepodge of views about educational problems which instructors had put together for students.[4] Similarly, educational sociology courses in sociology departments were characterized by a diverse conglomeration of speculative orientations about the functions of education. Of course in the early part of the century there was a wide range of beliefs among both sociologists and educators about what the purpose of sociology should be in relation to education—a situation that still exists.

As we have implied, one of the predominant early themes in the sociological study of education was that sociology should provide a basis for organizing education in such a manner that social problems would be resolved and social progress would be attained. The use of sociology to assist education in solving social problems we refer to as an *educational sociology* orientation or theme and was in large part initiated in 1922 by one of the early leaders of sociology in the United States, Lester F. Ward.[5] The problem-solving theme was, for the next 25 years, the major orientation of sociologists in general as well as those concerned with education in particular. Educational sociologists, be they sociologists or educators by formal training, emphasized the application of sociological principles to help solve educational problems.

Closely related to the problem-solving approach was the belief that educational sociology should also provide the goals or objectives of the educational system. The educational sociology view held that educational

---

[4] H. Lee, *Status of Educational Sociology* (New York: New York University Press Bookstore, 1927).

[5] Lester F. Ward, "Education as the Proximate Means of Progress," *Dynamic Sociology*, 1924 edition (New York: Appleton-Century-Crofts), vol. 2, ch. 14. (Original edition: 1883.)

sociology in schools of education should include any and all aspects of sociology which would assist teachers and others in understanding and controlling those social processes which influence education. This attitude about the use of sociology to assist education also prevailed in sociology departments and led to the establishment of a variety of sociology courses that were believed desirable for the education of teachers. The most common of these courses were those which focused on socialization processes in families, communities, and schools and on the most appropriate purposes of education. In other words, sociology courses in both schools of education and departments of sociology were concerned with the development of educational goals and the identification of principles of social behavior that might be applied to the resolution of educational and social problems.

In the 1940s, a somewhat different emphasis among sociologists began to emerge. It involved the analysis of the community in society as it related to the functioning of the educational system. Here the emphasis was on relationships occurring between the school and its community. The emphasis on school and community relationships provided for a shift away from merely applying sociology to the alleviation of educational problems to include the use of sociological theories and methods to enhance our knowledge about education in particular and social behavior in general. This orientation toward the acquisition of knowledge we refer to as the *sociology of education* theme in contrast to the earlier educational sociology theme. However, before we elaborate on the sociology of education era, certain concerns and interests among sociologists during the earlier educational sociology period need to be further clarified.

During the first half of the present century there was little consensus among sociologists with regard to the proper functions for sociologists in relation to education. The process of classifying almost everything and anything under the rubric of educational sociology may have led many competent sociologists to avoid the study of education. There was, to be sure, a decline in the number of educational sociology courses taught in both colleges of education and departments of sociology during the latter part of the first half century. But it is also true that the increased interest in education by sociologists during the 50s and early 60s was characterized by a shift away from concerns for problem resolution. For 20 years after World War II, much of the interest of sociologists who studied education was limited to describing and explaining the socialization process and structures of educational systems without particular concern for resolving social problems. This era was also characterized by considerable research activity. The emphasis on acquiring knowledge without regard to the resolution of social problems characterized the emerging sociology of education era following World War II. Of course, during this era considerable discussion was given to what exactly should be included in the sociology of education. This discussion continues today, but sociologists have returned to investigations of major social issues such as segregation, busing, and related concerns relevant to the quality of education.

Sociology of Education

To be sure, attempts to make clear what should be included in the sociology of education are not new. We mentioned Durkheim's position in the late 1800s. Following Durkheim's lead, an American sociologist, Robert C. Angell, in 1928 maintained that an educational sociologist should be a sociologist specializing in research in the educational process. "Educational sociology," he said, "is merely a branch of the pure science of sociology."[6] He preferred to call the application of sociological knowledge to the study of education "the sociology of education," indicating the school as a source of data which could be analyzed. For him the traditional use of the phrase "educational sociology" implied that the school was an object of social action, and he believed that an applied science of educational sociology was impossible. According to Angell, the application of sociology alone to the educational process does not supply all that is necessary to administer and determine educational policy. The school administrator faced with the necessity of both organizing and directing an educational system must draw on information provided by psychology, political science, economics, and many other disciplines. For this reason, Angell contended that the problems of school administration involve a broad technology.

In 1935, a position similar to Angell's was stated by another leading sociologist, E. B. Reuter, who wrote: "the interests of the educational sociologist differ from those of the general sociologist only in the fact that he works with a specially selected set of materials . . . He is interested in understanding education's forms, functions and developments in diverse situations, in understanding the behavior and ideologies of school men, in discovering the effects of school on existing institutions and its influence on personality."[7]

Reuter believed that his definition of educational sociology eliminated much which had been identified by that name. Reuter continued: "Educational sociologists have, for the most part, been concerned with other than sociological materials . . . Even that labeled sociological com-

[6] Robert Angell, "Science, Sociology and Education," *Journal of Educational Sociology*, vol. 1 (1928), pp. 406–13.

[7] E. B. Reuter, "The Problem of Educational Sociology," *Journal of Educational Sociology*, vol. 9 (1935), pp. 15–22. Reprinted by permission.

monly deals with social, practical and moral topics or with questions of educational objectives and curricular content rather than with sociological problems."[8]

Unfortunately, neither Angell nor Reuter followed this delineation of the sociological study of education with an extensive analysis of the field. However, at about this time another sociologist wrote what might be considered the forerunner of contemporary sociology of education. Willard Waller's book, *The Sociology of Teaching*, published in 1932, was the first major attempt to analyze the role of teachers in relation to their students and their communities.[9] Waller provided what is still a useful analysis of the social structure and culture of the school. Although limited by the theoretical and methodological state of the field at that time, Waller's work is a classic analysis of a school system in one era in relation to its community and culture. Waller's scholarly achievement was a forerunner of much of modern sociology of education.

However, several years were to pass before Waller's views and the dictums of Angell and Reuter were to be taken up by most sociologists interested in the study of education as a substantive field. From the 1930s to mid-century, only a few research sociologists or educators made significant contributions to our knowledge of the social aspects of education. The senior author undertook this research and first published his conception of the field during this period.[10] As we previously stated, when the first edition of the book was in preparation in the early 50s, there was very little sociological research or sociological publications on education from which one could draw.

A number of sociologists have tried to identify the reasons for this lack of sociological study of education up to World War II. Ronald Corwin, among others, believes that the earlier educational sociology promised too much with regard to the improvement of education, that many people became disillusioned, and that sociologists in general were not too impressed with the emphasis on moral philosophy which often characterized educational sociology.[11] There has also been some belief that the mixture of educators and sociologists working together in the early days impeded the development of methodological and theoretical skills which supposedly would have produced more substantive sociological knowledge. Olive Banks notes that the sociological study of education fell into disrepute and recognizes that for some the separation of educa-

[8] Ibid.

[9] Willard Waller, *The Sociology of Teaching* (New York: John Wiley and Sons, Inc., 1932).

[10] Wilbur B. Brookover, "Sociology of Education: A Definition," *American Sociological Review*, vol. 14 (1949), pp. 407–15.

[11] Ronald Corwin, *A Sociology of Education* (New York: Appleton-Century-Crofts, 1965), pp. 56–64.

tional sociology from the mainstream of sociology prior to World War II was a primary source of this disrepute.[12] It should be clear, however, that the rapid increase in research and quality of the field during the 60s and 70s has also been accompanied by a high degree of interaction and joint effort between sociologists and educators. Today there are many prominent sociologists who hold appointments in both sociology and education, as did Emile Durkheim. In addition, it should be recognized that sociology was never firmly established in teacher-training institutions prior to World War II, as was psychology; and when sociology did appear in schools of education, it was often taught by persons who were not trained as sociologists.

We suspect that the explanations of both the decline and the subsequent rapid development of sociological interest in education must be found in forces other than association with educators. However, it is true that, in the social status "pecking order" of the liberal arts tradition in Western culture, the physical sciences are at the top while the natural and social sciences and the applied areas of education follow in descending order. Education has not attained the professional eminence of such occupations as law and medicine, and the study of education has less prestige in the university than the natural and social sciences. Some sociologists may be guided by these perceived status rankings in their choice of specific research interests. How much such status striving has affected the slow emergence of education as a field of study we are not certain, but many other conditions are surely operative.

It is likely that an increasing mass public concern for education and its functions in society is one of the more important reasons for the changing interest of sociologists. National and local awards and money are now given to those sociologists who offer insights into educational problems. A few years ago there were few national politicians who found it necessary to develop positions on education. Now political campaigns depend very heavily on educational platforms. And, like all sciences, sociology is partly shaped by common cultural concerns. World War II caused many sociologists to study propaganda and communications processes; struggles for racial and ethnic equality in Western cultures produced sociologists of minority relations; and the recent "war on poverty" in the United States and Canada has helped to shape a rebirth in the sociology of poverty similar to that which occurred during the depression years of the 30s.

Another reason for the expanding interest in the sociological study of education may be the simple recognition by many sociologists that education in both its formal and informal aspects has a crucial role to play in both personal and societal conduct; to understand individual

[12] Olive Banks, *The Sociology of Education* (London: B. T. Batsford, Ltd., 1968), pp. 7–8.

behavior or collective acts requires an implied or explicit understanding of the nature of education. This latter appears to be the more rational explanation for the recent interest of many sociologists in education. Whatever the case, sociologists, along with economists, political scientists, historians, philosophers, lawyers, and many others, are in the business of seriously studying education. Like the other disciplines, sociology is a social enterprise as well as a discipline and is guided by all of the quirks and principles which shape any human fad or fashion. With these guidelines in mind, a brief overview of differences and trends among sociologists of education of recent years is in order.

Trends within the Sociology of Education[13]

The first and predominant trend in the sociological study of education since World War II has been social-psychological in character, where individual attitudes and conduct are explained by reference to the influence of others. Sociologists of education, reflecting an emphasis on contributing to the development of sociological knowledge, have spent the greatest proportion of their time studying the development and outcomes of student values and conceptions of self and world. The impact of family, friends, and teachers upon student views and values has characterized a considerable proportion of this effort. Similarly, there has been a very heavy concern for the impact of the families, neighborhood, race, and socioeconomic status on student performance and attitudes. This also reflects a concern for the social and psychological context. There have also been a significant but lesser number of studies on the social-psychological effects of differing types of school environments.

Among the more important studies on student attitudes have been those on students' self-images and self-concepts. Sociologists of education have conducted literally scores of studies of the development and functions of students' self-concepts. But over all, the largest proportion of social-psychological studies of students have dealt with students' educa-

---

[13] There are a number of very interesting and more detailed analytical reviews of trends in the sociology of education. Among these are the works of B. Y. Card, J. G. T. Kelsey, and Julia Wong, "The Development of Educational Sociology as Reflected in Its English-Language Textbooks Published from 1912 to 1970," a paper presented to the History and Historiography Division of American Educational Research Association Annual Meeting 1971; Neal Gross, "Sociology of Education," in R. K. Merton (ed.), *Sociology Today* (New York: Basic Books, 1959); J. Floud and A. H. Halsey, "The Sociology of Education: A Trend Report and Bibliography," *Current Sociology,* vol. 8, no. 3 (1958); Eldon E. Snyder, "Sociology of Education: A Description of the Field," *Sociology and Social Research,* vol. 52, no. 2 (January 1968), pp. 237–48; and Charles Bidwell, "The School as a Formal Organization," in J. G. March (ed.), *Handbook of Social Organizations* (Chicago: Rand McNally, 1965).

tional and occupational aspirations and plans. This trend was also followed by psychologists and educators. As reviews of the research literature will attest, two of the most frequently studied variables in social science have been students' aspirations and their socioeconomic status level.

A second major trend of writing and research in the sociology of education has been the development of studies of the functions of education in the larger society. Various types of research and writing may be identified here. The most extensive work on school and community has been and continues to be on the reciprocal effects of education on economic and social developments in "emerging" countries. This effort, of course, is closely related to questions of the effects of various types and levels of education on social change in general. In the more highly industrialized nations, studies of the relationships of education to society have centered on the functions of education in the stratification of society. Other studies relating society to education have looked at the political functions of education, particularly at how schools act as agencies for governmental institutions. Sociologists have also become interested in relating education to culture. Recently a number of sociologists in the United States, Canada, and Great Britain have given their attention to the functions of education in the perpetuation or the alleviation of poverty, and to the role of education in integrating or in maintaining a segregated pluralistic society. In this respect many current sociologists of education, like sociologists in general, have returned to some of the concerns of the earlier educational sociologists who wished to use education as an ameliorative agency for dealing with social problems. For example, there have been hundreds of recent studies by sociologists on the particular problems of urban education faced by minorities and how the problems may be overcome.

A third trend in the sociology of education may be grouped under the terms "organizational" and "social systems" analyses. Among these analyses are found studies of patterned relationships between teachers and administrators and sometimes between teachers and students. Most organizational or systems studies of education have dealt with the social roles of elementary and secondary school administrators and teachers. Recent developments, however, are shifting focus to include students and to do more studies of higher education. Examination of the differences among college academic and social climates and of the effects of these differences on student rebellion, attitudes, and learning has expanded. It should be noted that, while sociologists have directed their attention to a conceptual analysis of schools as complex organizations and as bureaucracies and while considerable theoretical work has been done on systems analyses, a very limited list of empirical studies of schools as complex organizations or systems can be presented at this time. However, we anticipate that considerable research will be forthcoming on the organizational structures of schools and on the nature of social systems, emphasizing the role of education.

Frequently presented in relation to the organization or social structure of the school is an analysis of the school culture. Much research has involved the study of roles, norms, and values attached to school systems and to variations in roles, norms, and values within school subcultures. Much of the focus in this work has involved the identification of the cultural norms and values in the secondary school and in higher education and has given rise to considerable discussion concerning the reality of a distinguishable adolescent subculture. Some observers have maintained that the school has characteristics of a closed society and thus generates distinct cultural settings in which adolescents behave quite differently from adult members of the society. Others maintain that the distinctions are not nearly as great as implied in some of the literature. In later discussions we will treat this issue more thoroughly. At this point, it is merely necessary to recognize that this issue is likely to be present in the sociology of education and in general sociology for some time to come.

In summary, we would like to reiterate that trends within the sociology of education tend to reflect the full range of sociological concerns. Since schools and educational systems represent a wide spectrum of social phenomena for analysis and since sociologists are not of one mind, it is only reasonable to expect that education will be examined from several sociological points of view. In other words, sociologists may and often do employ a combination of perspectives and purposes in analyzing a particular educational phenomenon. Furthermore, different sociologists may quite legitimately look at the same data about a school from entirely different frames of reference. Thus a school classroom may be described as a group with a number of individual members as well as a system of interrelated roles such as teacher, good student, average student, or poor student. The norms and expectations which characterize this classroom may also be examined. And certainly the individual behavior of students including their attitudes, cognitions, and senses of identity in a school classroom may be described in terms of the social environment. The composition and size of classroom populations may also be studied from a demographic or ecological frame of reference. Throughout this volume we will refer to sociologists and their research which reflect each of these areas of activity and in some cases two or more areas in the same context. To be sure, the sociology of education is not a distinct branch of sociology with its own theoretical perspectives, but rather a division of sociological activity in which sociologists of many skills, views, and interests analyze educational phenomena from several frames of reference.

An Overview

Three distinguishable and important types of social relationships of current concern to sociologists of education provide a basis for organizing our subsequent discussions. These are (1) relationships between the schools and other aspects of the society; (2) relationships among managers, teachers, and clients in school organizations; and (3) the effect of the school social system and culture on learning.

We will not consider all relevant sociological viewpoints in each area of analysis. We will, however, discuss a large number of current social issues concerning education. In Part Two, we will use contributions of economists and political scientists as well as of sociologists to examine the relation of the educational system to the larger society. This analysis includes an examination of several of the crucial relations between education and other aspects of society under the general headings of education as an open system, social control of education, education and social change, and education and social stratification.

Our analysis of the school as a social organization in Part Three is largely sociological, but the contributions of other social scientists will occasionally be recognized. We discuss some general and basic concepts concerning the internal functioning of school organizations and focus our attention on the informal as well as formal managerial roles in many school settings, on teaching as a career and profession, and on the nature of many student social structures.

In Part Four, both macro and micro levels of sociological analyses are employed in conjunction with social psychology. In this section we draw heavily on theory relevant to student self-concept development and the influence of others, particularly parents, peers, and teachers. This is followed by reviews of research and theory pertaining to the influence of types of school organization, educational climates, and cultural forces on student learning.

In the final chapter, identified as Part Five, we examine what we consider the major issues relevant to education in American society in the last quarter of the 20th century.

Suggested Readings

Charles S. Benson, "Economics and Education," *Review of Educational Research,* 37, no. 1 (February 1967).

William M. Cave and Marc A. Chesler, eds., *Sociology of Education: An Anthology of Issues and Problems* (Riverside, N.J.: Macmillan Co., 1974).

William M. Cave and Donald L. Halsted, "Sociology of Education," *Review of Educational Research,* 37, no. 1 (February 1967).

W. W. Charters, Jr. "Social Psychology and Education: An Essay Review of Lindsey and Aronson," *The Handbook of Social Psychology, American Educational Research Journal,* 10, no. 1 (Winter 1973), pp. 69–73.

Burton R. Clark, "Development of the Sociology of Higher Education," *Sociology of Education,* 46, no. 1 (Winter 1973), pp. 2–14.

Ronald G. Corwin, "The Sociological Study of Education," chapter 3 and "Out of the Past: Sociological Perspectives on the History of Education," chapter 4 in *A Sociology of Education* (New York: Appleton-Century-Crofts, 1965).

Bernice M. Fisher, "Education in the Big Picture," *Sociology of Education,* 45, no. 3 (Summer 1972).

Wayne C. Gordon, ed., *Uses of the Sociology of Education,* The Seventy-third Yearbook of the Society for the Study of Education, part 2 (Chicago: National Society for the Study of Education, 1974).

Jack L. Nelson and Frank P. Besag, *Sociological Perspectives in Education* (New York: Pitman Publishing Corporation, 1970), chapters 1 and 2. In addition to defining sociology of education and educational sociology, it examines the relation of sociology to education.

Harry Wolcott, "Anthropology and Education," *Review of Educational Research,* 37, no. 1 (February 1967).

part two

School and Society

2

Education: In an Open System

ALTHOUGH ". . . education in an industrial society concerns those formal and systematic approaches to social life that were once the exclusive province of family and community,"[1] the family and other institutions have not given up the attempt to influence education. Although much education occurs elsewhere, our primary concern is with the formal system—the schools. Conduct within the school is still very dependent upon the school's social cultural environment. On the other hand, many events which occur in the community are influenced by what is going on within that community's schools. Through the teaching of values, skills, and knowledge, the expenditure of vast sums of money, the employment of an increasing proportion of the community, control over who gets into many occupations, provision of training and of spawning grounds of political debate, and many other functions, the schools influence changes in our society.

Some of these social changes may be purposively sought and recognized—they are *manifest* functions of the schools—while other social consequences of school education may be unintended and unrecognized—they are *latent* functions of such education. Sociologists of education are particularly interested in the unintended consequences of school activities. Occasionally, just the opposite of what is intended results, as in the case of some compensatory educational programs which were designed to reduce inequality but which may sometimes actually aggravate the disparities in educational outcomes by labeling students as slow or inferior. Such reverses in outcome can be dramatic.

[1] John Harp and Stephen Richer, "Sociology of Education," *Review of Educational Research*, vol. 39, no. 5 (December 1969), p. 673.

School-community relations are further dramatized by their almost constant turmoil. In Great Britain and Canada there have been spirited debates in parliament over student demonstrations. The Yugoslavian government promised several educational reforms and granted amnesty to students who had protested the actions of university administrators. Throughout Europe, Asia, and Africa, as well as the Americas, local police and national troops have frequently been used to quell student demonstrators. We have watched student upheavals spread from one country to the next, from the universities down through the junior high schools, from the predominantly black inner-city schools to the all-white suburban schools, from the urban to the rural areas, and from one region to another. Depending upon the views of the particular communities, charges regarding student unrest may be directed at the political left or the political right, at royalty or anarchy, against affluence or poverty or towards parental laxity or rigidity. Regardless of where blame or praise is placed, one inescapable fact remains: student unrest has been a fact in countries of nearly every political, economic, and social complexion.

The turmoil within the schools and society is not limited to student unrest. A broad range of educational issues has provided conflict within the communities. Busing, sex education in the schools, court orders to change methods of financing, legislative and administrative battles over tracking and ability grouping, the use of personality and intelligence tests, the desegregation of students, and the decentralization of school districts are but a few of the many issues which have recently wracked U.S. and Canadian communities. Wherever one looks, in whatever country, the society is involved with education. And if a rapidly changing pluralistic society is composed of diverse political, economic, and religious social strata and subcultures striving for existence and power, strife is typical. Such cultural strife almost inevitably finds its way into education.

The sudent unrest in the last decade may lead some to think that the educational involvement in cultural conflict is of recent origin. A review of the history of any society will reveal considerable conflict involving education. At times, the school has been at odds with other social institutions, but nearly always the school has reflected the social problems of its community. At times, the school itself has precipitated conflict in the larger society.

It seems reasonable to suspect that those people who abhor conflict in general will also abhor conflict within the school or between the school and other social institutions. However, conflict at varying levels of intensity is nearly inevitable. If groups in a community are at odds, it is quite likely that their differences will affect attitudes on educational issues. Even such concerns as types of fire and police protection, questions of war and peace, transportation needs, health facilities, and bonding and taxation issues which are normally within the jurisdictional perogatives of other community and government groups find their expression in the schools. In a similar fashion, issues which originate within the school often provide the basis for conflict within the larger society. Furthermore, should the community become embroiled in conflict with another community, the schools of the respective communities somehow become involved, for the school is part of its larger social context.

While it is generally recognized that the school carries out various tasks for the family, it must also be acknowledged that the school is the agent of economic, religious, political, and military complexes. The schools train people for industry, churches, and government positions. The schools are also used by various groups to affect family sizes, to wage war, to sell more and more modern products, and to fight pollution. The schools are used by all institutions to achieve their objectives, and the schools, in turn, use these institutions for their own purposes. The military, for example, depends on the university for personnel and research, from which the university sometimes receives resources which may be used for other purposes. The military also may reimburse local communities for providing educational services. There is nothing strange in the idea that our schools exchange services with other social institutions. In fact, should there fail to be an exchange of services, the schools would soon cease to exist.

The function of providing services, however, raises several fundamental questions. With whom will the schools exchange services? In an urban west coast community where one of the authors taught school, a political pressure group was nearly successful in having a teacher fired for using educational materials provided by a trade union. A short time later, in this same school district, another teacher nearly lost his job because another political pressure group disliked his using material provided by the local Chamber of Commerce. Interestingly, the materials provided by the union and business groups were almost identical.

Educators often feel that they are caught in the middle of community pressures, that no matter what they do they will be in trouble. The dilemmas of education are complicated by the fact that our schools are often dependent on support from competing institutions which recognize that their own strengths and jurisdiction are affected by the schools. For example, some parent and religious groups have sought to stop the increasing role of the school in matters of sex education because they believe this to be an intrusion on their own rights. Indeed, the contacts between schools and their surrounding institutions are often intense.

In matters of school policy, can the school ignore its community? While our schools often follow the lead of various community groups and on occasion assume leadership roles, one thing is fairly certain about school-community contacts: schools rarely ignore their cultural environments. Some will mistakenly believe that the schools are apathetic to certain community needs when they do not appear to be responding to some favored demand or another. However, what appears as apathy is often a condition of the school's accommodating itself to the felt needs of another segment of its environment. This leads to questions of whose will and whose values shall prevail in the area of education.

One objective in this and subsequent discussions is to examine several of the relationships which exist between the school and various segments of a pluralistic culture under conditions of rapid social change, especially in those areas which have relevance for what goes on within our schools and within our society. We will use several perspectives in examining these relationships, focusing on such questions as: Who shall control education? What are the conditions under which social change shapes and is shaped by education? How do the schools function to allocate persons and resources to various social classes and positions in society? How are subcultural struggles for equality and supremacy, integration and pluralism influenced by educational processes? Each of these questions can be approached on a number of levels and from a variety of perspectives. A psychologist, for example, might emphasize the importance of personality traits among leaders in education and society or point to behavioral modification principles as important to questions of who controls whom. On the other hand, an economist may employ concepts of supply and demand and other economic principles. A political scientist might approach issues of social control with ideas about the nature of power and conflict. Sociology also offers a number of perspectives for examining and explaining social events. Our emphasis in this discussion does not deny the utility of other disciplines or other levels of analysis. On the contrary, the perspectives offered here can be seen as part of a large number of social science tools for understanding the nature of relationships which occur between education and society.

Unfortunately, there has been a common tendency in Western society to explain social conditions by looking only to the rhetoric, values, and conduct of involved individuals. Emphasizing the role of individuals in explaining social events, while often valid, may also result in important social forces' being ignored. For example, a president of a given university may be blamed for a student rebellion when in fact a number of other cultural forces have culminated in the campus turmoil and it really would not have made any difference who was president.

The intricate interdependence that exists between schools and other social institutions is often disregarded in explanations of educational issues. From one perspective schools have been viewed as total[2] social institutions or closed social systems which are quite independent of the outside world. Like hospitals, prisons, and some factories, the participants in schools interact with each other for all or a large portion of the day much more than they do with persons outside the school. The degree of external interaction varies greatly from one type of school to another. Students and teachers in residential schools for the deaf, for example, have far less parental contact on a day-to-day basis than do those in neighborhood elementary schools. But even in the latter there is only limited interaction with parents or others in the community during school hours. Although such variation between schools exists, the boundaries within which (rather than across which) greater interaction occurs can readily be identified. Analysis of the educational system from the closed system frame of reference focuses attention on the roles, statuses, and patterns of interaction within the school boundaries. Such analyses contribute significantly to an understanding of the internal characteristics of the school social system. At the same time, examination of the school as a closed system may ignore the dependence of all schools on external social cultural forces. A clearer understanding of both the nature and the weakness of contemporary schools may be achieved by viewing formal education as a social cultural system *open* to influence from the larger society.[3] Such a perspective helps to explain the fact that family, community, and other factors outside the school strongly affect the behavior outcomes of the educational systems. Both the behavior of teachers and what children learn in school are largely determined by the interaction of school and society.

As we mentioned earlier, nearly every major issue which plagues a community sooner or later, in one way or another, extends into its schools. Reciprocally, many conflicts which first occur within school settings emerge to become major community issues. By focusing our attention on the interrelationships between education and other social institutions we will be able to understand some of the kinds of influence that the school and other community components exert upon each other. However, if we are to understand the impact of education on other community components as well as its contribution to the total society

---

[2] See Erving Goffman, *Asylums* (Chicago: Aldine Publishing Company, 1961), for a description of the total institution concept. Charles G. Bidwell, "The School as a Formal Organization," in *Handbook of Organization,* ed. James G. March (Skokie, Ill.: Rand McNally and Company, 1965), pp. 972–1022, reviews the organization research on schools.

[3] A more comprehensive treatment of education as an open system can be found in Robert E. Herriott and Benjamin J. Hodgkins, *The Environment of Schooling: Formal Education as an Open Social System* (Englewood Cliffs, N.J.: Prentice-Hall, 1973). Our comments here draw heavily on pp. 15–16.

we need to be as clear as possible about the boundaries which separate education from its social environment. Implicit in this view is that we can recognize what constitutes an educational subsystem as distinct from the other social subsystems of society; that we can discern who is a part of the educational system and who is acting upon this system identified as schools; that we can examine the changing nature of educational system boundaries; that we can investigate the extent to which these boundaries can be penetrated and the nature of this penetration; and that we can study how educators strive to protect the boundaries of their authority.

The Boundaries of Education

The concept "educational system" is well established, in English-speaking countries at least. The usage is quite well understood as referring to a set of relationships with a high degree of stability and focused in the school. This implies the existence of boundaries which distinguish education from other systems, subsystems, or organizations. We do not here refer to the walls of the school or the fence which surrounds the school grounds, but the conceptual boundary that encompasses the social processes and the personnel formally and informally related to the school system. Boundaries are identified by the difference in rate and types of interaction occurring between participants within the educational system and those occurring between education and its environment. In a completely closed system the latter would not occur. It is not an easy task to discern just where the boundaries of a school's jurisdiction or the boundaries of a school's interaction with economic, political, religious, and family institutions occur. If the boundaries of education refer to areas of jurisdiction or control by educators, then of course there are many gray areas. Obviously, there have been and will continue to be many disputes over the rights of educational systems. Depending on our perspectives, our community, and our legal systems we may grant to educators certain rights, privileges, and obligations while withholding others. For example, teachers may almost completely determine the English curriculum but be narrowly restricted in teaching about sex or religion. Certainly there is no total consensus on all of the rights of educational institutions in modern society.

When educational boundaries are discussed in terms of areas of the school's obligations there is also little agreement. This is one reason for so much court involvement in education.

From another perspective, school boundaries may refer to points of exchange between schools and other organizations. Unfortunately, the concept of boundary is often used only in terms of occupying space or land area such as the boundaries of nations, cities, or private homes. The boundaries of social subsystems are comparable to those of subsystems operating within the human body in that they cannot be adequately described on the basis of clearly distinct physical locations, as is the case of national political boundaries. For example, consider the respiratory and motor subsystems of a human organism. Through the mouth, lungs, heart, legs, and every other part of the body where blood vessels are found, the respiratory system functions together with the motor system to take in oxygen and remove waste. The human motor and respiratory systems actually surround and permeate each other. In a similar way, many educational, governmental, economic, and community organizations function around and through each other. Territory, in the sense of occupying so much space, is an inappropriate term for designating the boundaries of either the respiratory system or the motor system, and yet physiologists and physicians find it useful to think in terms of distinct subsystems in order to understand and describe the functioning of the total organism. Similarly, social scientists have found it useful to consider the educational system as separate from but interdependent with other economic, political, and religious subsystems when they attempt to understand the functions of each in the larger society.

Herriott and Hodgkins have shown a relationship between indicators of modernity such as percent urban, income, availability of physicians, and use of telephones and several indexes of education in the several regions, states, and communities of the United States. For example, the correlation between the median years of school completed in the several states and the index of modernity was more than .50 each decade from 1940 to 1970.[4]

Such interrelationship complicates the task of distinguishing the major activities and functions of educational systems from those of other social systems. For example, there are problems in specifying the many educational activities of a society that are produced in military, government, and family institutions. From our perspective, an educational subsystem is not restricted to what goes on in formally designated schools. For example, just as legal activities may occur within schools or military organizations, educational activities may operate within the military and court systems. Thus, there are problems in describing the points of intersection between educational, political, religious, legal, and other societal systems. However, it is clear that there are a number of conditions or characteristics of organizational boundaries that we may wish to examine when we attempt to classify people, roles, norms, values, and activities as operating within or external to the boundaries of an educa-

[4] Ibid., p. 134.

tional organization. By limiting our discussion to formal educational organizations commonly identified as school systems rather than to the total system of education in society, we simplify our task.

One of our first tasks, if we are to distinguish an educational organization from government, family, religious, or other social organizations is to indicate the major roles involved. We will want to know who the participants are and what forces are impinging upon schools from outside sources. We have already pointed out that one person's suggestions as to what is or should be included or excluded from education may be considered by others as arbitrary and subject to debate. This is especially so since sophisticated skills and knowledge for analyzing organizations are far from a highly developed science. However, there is no need to be completely arbitrary since a number of scholars are in agreement about what we should be examining as we study school boundaries; they are: (1) the extent to which areas of jurisdiction and points of contact with other organizations and institutions, such as the family and industry, are subject to change; (2) the criteria for being included within the educational system; (3) the openness of education to information, constraints, resources and other inputs from its environment; and (4) the procedures and practices within society for controlling the boundaries of education, e.g., court actions opening the schools to minorities or preventing certain types of research or religious practices.

The Flexibility of School Systems

The boundaries of a school organization should never be considered permanent or fixed. Nearly always the boundaries of such educational systems show some change over time, no matter how subtle. As in economic organizations, educational organizations grow in quantity and complexity. Some absorb other educational organizations and some are absorbed. According to recent studies, between 1960 and 1970 the number of school districts, grades kindergarten through 12, in the United States was reduced by 53 percent (from 28,000 to 18,000 districts).[5] The school districts got bigger. The total enrollment in grades kindergarten through twelve increased by 22 percent.

The school also grew in other ways. Specialized noninstructional staff increased 121 percent. New programs were offered for the handicapped and adults. Retraining programs for the unemployed were initiated. Community educational activities of all sorts were initiated. The numbers who graduated from high school increased by 54 percent between 1960 and 1970. Seventy-seven percent of those persons 18 years old were gradu-

[5] *Statistics of Trends in Education: 1960–61—1980–81* (Washington, D.C.: National Center for Educational Statistics, 1972), DHEW pub. no. (OE) 72–97, Fed. 1972.

ated from high school in 1970, up from 66 percent in 1960. By 1980 it is estimated that 84 percent of the 18-year-olds will graduate from high schools. In 1970, 62 percent of the high school graduates went to college. At all levels of administration and instruction specializations have developed.

One outcome of all this growth is that the boundaries of educational jurisdiction and interaction with society have been modified considerably in only a ten-year period. Of course in societies characterized by rapid technological developments and social change the boundaries of education change very rapidly. However, even in societies of rapid change the boundaries of an educational system must have some permanence for their existence to be recognized and accorded legitimacy by the larger society. If the boundaries of education were in too great a flux, it would be meaningless to speak of boundaries or of educational organizations. In the following discussions considerable emphasis will center on changes in educational jurisdiction and those circumstances which precipitate change.

Criteria for Membership

The question of whom to consider inside or outside an educational system is difficult to answer; depending upon the circumstances, one may be considered both a member of an educational organization and at the same time an outsider. It is generally helpful to view the boundaries of education in relation to those events which we wish to explain. For example, if we wish to account for the production of reading skills among children in a school which involves parents as assistant teachers, the boundaries of the formal system for teaching of reading will include the parents in their roles as assistant teachers. When the parents have an authorized teaching role to perform as part of the school's general role, they are operating within the educational system. In other instances parents would be considered as operating outside of the school even though they may be influencing the schools. For example, parents may exert power to determine whether Latin is taught in school without occupying a recognized role in the school itself. In this latter case, we recognize that the parents are social forces impinging on an educational subsystem per se. Similarly, parents may sometimes be viewed as learners who are products of an educational subsystem, but are not members of that subsystem as if they were taking classes at school. What they learn in school may be considered a product of the educational system in much the same way that automobiles may be considered one of the products of an economic subsystem.

By considering the parents to be inside the educational system when they are formally involved in a school's teaching assignments, we are recognizing that the parents are subject to certain educational values and authority structures. On the other hand, parents often exert influence on education when they are not subject to the norms, values, and authority structures governing the educational subsystem. One implication of this approach is that we may consider persons or groups as simultaneously influencing education both from within and outside of a school organization. From this perspective several important questions follow: How can we best characterize students? When are they and when are they not members of the educational organization? From our perspective, it is apparent that students are, on occasion, members of their school organizational systems, but more often than not they are best viewed as "human material" to be processed by schools. Under some conditions students may function as participants in running their schools, but in most cases they function as recipients or clients to be taught. Occasionally students actively assist educators in teaching, maintaining order, promoting school programs, or resisting outside influence on school domains. When, under school authority, students engage in public relations activities, assist in teaching, or provide student control functions they are a part of the school organization. When students are given roles such as hall monitors, crossing guards, or members of school committees with responsibilities for establishing policy, particularly in the areas of student conduct, they are considered as members of the school organization whose task it is to treat themselves and other students as clients of the educational system. An interesting question with which we will deal is: Can students and parents exert influence over their schools by operating within or outside of the educational system? Before we examine those conditions for maximizing student or parent power over education, however, we shall examine what it means for boundaries to be open or closed to outside information and resources.

Open and Closed Boundaries

It is evident that governmental, political, economic, educational, and other societal organizations have some means of exchanging information and products. It is also evident that complex information rarely, if ever, flows freely and completely without distortion across social boundaries. There are many reasons for this. Many people in government, in education, in factories, and elsewhere work at keeping a certain amount of their activities shielded from public view. Legitimately or otherwise, information is frequently kept from those who are perceived to be in a position to apply negative sanctions should they become aware of such information. Authorities may withhold data, garble their messages, or even send out false information. It is not uncommon for authorities in any institution, democratic or authoritarian, to screen or distort information coming from the outside. Not everyone wants to know the truth about their environment or wants to have it known. In addition, some organizations are restricted in their ability to send or receive information by their relative social or physical isolation. Whatever the case, it is common for information between schools and other community groups to be incomplete and distorted. One important question to which answers are sought by sociologists of education is: Under what conditions is information exchange within education, and between education and the rest of society, likely to be complete and accurate?

Obviously, there is considerable variation among schools and between schools and other political, religious, and family groups in the openness with which information is exchanged. As an illustration, recent research has demonstrated that residential school systems for the deaf are more closed to information from the families of their students than are public schools.[6] Of course parents with children in community schools have greater access to school information through their children, their neighbors, and the school personnel than have parents who may be a hundred miles from their child's school.

There are many other less obvious circumstances which create differences among schools and between educational organizations and other groups in the openness with which information is passed. Some schools simply do not have the ability to accurately interpret all the phenomena impinging upon their activities. For example, they may not be able to predict with accuracy the number of students they will receive in succeeding years, or changes in political and legal climates. To the extent that a school cannot receive accurate information, particularly feedback, regardless of the reason, boundaries for information exchange are closed. To the extent that schools do not receive resources to operate, such as money and students, or provide resources to others, such as skilled manpower, we may also view the boundaries as closed. If boundaries stay closed in all areas, the schools will eventually cease to exist.

A totally closed and a totally open school system are, of course, abstract ideas. A relatively closed school system is one whose boundary is impervious to certain information transactions with other social systems. All schools are open to interaction with their environments in some areas. An open school system is recognized as being relatively open to particular types of information exchange and to the reception of certain resources. No school organization is completely open or completely closed, but some certainly interact with external organizations, persons, or social systems more often than others.

[6] Michael Walizer, "Boundary Openness and Interpersonal Outcomes in Schools," paper presented at Southern Sociological Society meetings, 1971.

Another difficulty in characterizing boundary openness is that information rarely flows with the same clarity in both directions between the schools and other social units. Some schools might be open to receiving certain information from their community while closed with reference to transmitting some information about school matters outside the educational arena. Awareness of the openness of a school's boundaries to matters affecting school policy is important for several reasons. The openness of educational institutions is an important factor in understanding the social control of education, its relation to social change, its involvement in social conflict, and even the continued existence of particular educational insitutions. These points will be more fully treated in later discussions.

Boundary Protection Activities

When people perceive that their social institutions are at stake, they tend to engage in activities designed to justify and protect those institutions. In this regard educators are like people in other institutions in that they often lay claim to a "turf" or sphere of influence and exert considerable effort to protect and justify what they believe to be their rightful jurisdiction. All roles and activities of a social system which function to protect and legitimize the system's membership, possessions, and spheres of influence are referred to as the *boundaries subsystem.* A school's boundary maintenance subsystem is illustrated by its public relations activities designed to legitimize certain features of the school in the eyes of people both inside and outside of education. Within some school districts both an administrative staff and volunteer parents spend much time justifying the existence of one school program or another. An administrator's efforts to maintain the boundaries of his school's jurisdiction may be expended in such low-key activities as speaking to parent conferences, participating in local community organizations, maintaining friendships with community leaders, or fostering winning football teams. All these and other activities may serve to enhance or maintain the school's good image. In a more aggressive manner, educators may employ court suits, power politics, economic pressures, and other tactics to maintain what they believe to be the rightful area of school jurisdiction.

The importance of being sensitive to the idea of boundary subsystems is at least threefold. First, we are likely to be more sensitive to education's role in the larger society's efforts to maintain its boundaries. The schools often play important roles in helping society defend its borders. Training military and foreign service personnel, serving as a pool for consultant services to the government, providing a vehicle for international cultural exchange, and supporting and fostering inventions for war and peace are but a few ways that educational institutions are involved in helping the larger society to control its boundaries. Second, to be sensitive to the existence of boundary subsystems is to be sensitive to those activities within education which not only preserve and protect education's jurisdiction but strive to extend the school's activity; the area of sex education is an example of boundary expansion. Third, when we are aware of the phenomenon of boundary subsystems we may also better understand the conflict between competing groups within education. The pressure exerted by school psychologists on school administrators and legislators to allow only certified school psychologists to do student adjustment and intelligence testing and provide personal therapy, and their pressure to prevent teachers, counselors, social workers, and others from providing such service illustrate internal boundary modification. The struggle between unions and administrative personnel and school boards over the rights to set standards of conduct demonstrates the effort to redefine areas of activity.

The operation of internal boundaries between vocational education and special education, and between counseling and teaching, will be discussed in Part 3, Chapters 7 through 10. Here our emphasis centers on the boundary maintenance activities of education with respect to the larger society.

Adaptation to Culture

When demands are placed on schools as a result of shifts in economic priorities, political struggles, religious pressures, family needs, or military objectives, it is reasonable to expect that there will be those in education who will attempt to adapt their school to these outside pressures. All of the efforts by educators to deal with current or anticipated pressures from the school's environment are referred to as the *adaptive functions* of education.

The shift in science and mathematics education in the United States after "Sputnik," the mass training programs for teachers of lower-class children after the "war-on-poverty" was begun in the 1960s, and the recent cutbacks in teacher-training programs for elementary and secondary teachers following the decrease in jobs available in the early 1970s illustrate the schools adaptation to their social environment. In a more subtle fashion the schools adapt every day to subtle shifts in the culture and society; innumerable changes in law, government, public attitudes, financial resources, and centers of power occur continuously. Numerous changes in educational activities are made to help the schools adapt to the external changes. Schools are constantly being reorganized. Many, perhaps 30 or 40, different patterns of decentralized school districts have been developed in recent years to accommodate to pressures for more community control.

Many people and groups in education are charged with responsibilities for helping society to be aware of itself, so to speak. Universities have played a major role in this regard. For instance, much of the current awareness of and interest in the damages, real and anticipated, of pollution are the result of university organizations and researchers who gathered and disseminated information on pollutants in our air, water, and land. Currently education is providing pools of manpower for a number of governmental agencies, industrial organizations, and ecology groups involved with pollution problems. On the other hand, the added immediate costs of pollution control have also caused some industrial groups to pressure the schools to refrain from aiding the cause of ecology. Universities in particular get involved in conflicts between competing economic and ecological interests. Recently a professor in a large American land-grant university gained a national scientific reputation fighting against what he believed to be the pollutant effects of certain farm chemicals which had been developed by other scientists. Agricultural interests in turn pressured his university to fire or silence the scientist. In some universities the various colleges of agriculture, ecology, medicine, education, law, engineering, social work, and business may seriously contend with one another in their attempts to adapt the university to different cultural and economic interests. Indeed, vested-interest groups can be very powerful forces in the environments of schools.

In each of our succeeding discussions, the adaptive responses of educational organizations to inputs from their environment and the societal adaptations to changes in education will be of special concern. For example, we will examine some of the adaptive responses of schools to court orders designed to reduce civil inequality, and in return we will examine how the courts have been influenced by changes in education. We will also be interested in how educational groups and organizations within the larger educational system adapt to one another. And, of course, we will note how individuals, particularly students, adapt to various educational structures.

One of the interesting, though sometimes frustrating, features of the way individuals and their organizations adapt to pressures is to create images of change without making any real change. In particular, we will observe how school systems are constantly reorganizing with little change in outcome. It might be more correct to contend that sometimes organizational change is superficial, with little more changed than titles and organizational charts. Perhaps such change should not be called change at all, but merely a coping or adaptive response to conflicting pressures.

Recently one of the authors entered an elementary school in which the traditional grades kindergarten through three were supposedly abolished. In district brochures and speeches by local administrators, including the principal of this elementary school, the school was identified as a "non-graded" or "continuous progress" school. Theoretically, "non-graded" or "continuous progress" schools do not have grades, each student moving at his own individualized pace. Several years after the announced change, one of the authors entered this so-called non-graded school and asked a child standing in the hall where the third-grade teacher's room was. The child pointed to a particular room and said Mrs. Jones was the third-grade teacher. Down the hall another child was asked the same question, and again the same teacher's name and room were pointed out. The same inquiry was made of a teacher walking in the hall, and she too stated that the same Mrs. Jones was the third-grade teacher. When the author walked into the "third-grade teacher's" room and asked if she was indeed the third grade teacher, she concurred that she was the third-grade teacher. Discussing her materials and what she was covering in class, along with the common age level (eight years) of her students, it became readily apparent that this teacher in this so-called "non-graded, continuous progress" school was functioning in the same fashion and at the same level as another third-grade teacher in a graded school which was visited by the author only a few hours earlier. Out of curiosity, on the way out of the school the author stopped into the principal's office and asked the principal who the third-grade teacher was; she said, "We don't have teachers assigned by grade levels. This is a continuous progress, non-graded elementary school." The author thanked the principal for being helpful and went away wondering.

Why, in spite of the nongraded school rhetoric did this in fact remain a graded school just as it had been at its inception many years before? Many other changes in educational organization have supposedly occurred in recent years. After much pressure from one midwestern community, the school board directed the junior high school be replaced by a "middle-school" organization. Teachers were sent to orientation and in-service training programs, and the community was notified in a multitude of ways that they now had a middle school in philosophy and organization. An evaluation team was employed to evaluate the new program. One of their main conclusions was that, in spite of the descriptions of the school in public relations releases, the school was in fact functioning just as most junior high schools did. The point is that schools, as well as individuals, engage in *norms of evasion.*

Schools evade pressures sometimes by indicating that they have changed when in fact it is business as usual. Schools cope or adapt themselves to their environments sometimes by making "real" changes and sometimes merely by giving illusions of change. Sometimes people think that the school has tried but failed to achieve some community ideal when in fact the school has not tried. On such occasions one may ask, Why has the school not been modified? How can old roles be maintained in spite of all kinds of pressure?

Maintaining the System

The failure of the educational system to change under both internal and external pressure is not unique. All social systems develop patterns of behavior and organizational arrangements which serve to maintain the status quo. Such activities may be identified as the *maintenance subsystem* within traditional patterns of interaction and methods of achieving the goals of an organization tend to persist in spite of changing expectations. The resistance of teachers to the demands for teacher accountability illustrate the maintenance subsystem. The school system has functioned for many years without assumption by the teachers and other staff personnel of full responsibility for the students' learning specified patterns of behavior. The teachers define this as proper and wish to maintain their traditional roles and the expectations associated with them. Much energy is expended by large numbers of people engaged in maintaining the teachers' role as it has been. Other evidences of maintenance activities in education can be readily identified. The schools may be more successful in maintaining a given organizational pattern than some other social systems because of their openness and the public interest in their effectiveness.

Some of a school's maintenance efforts may be attained through the selective recruiting of new staff with similar needs and qualities. Other maintenance efforts may involve recruitment of staff through friendship cliques where desired actions and attitudes can be more readily reinforced. In addition, new members are readily socialized into traditional modes of operation. School systems also use various committees to provide an illusion of change to staff members while resisting pressures to change. On the other hand, committees can sometimes initiate changes while giving the illusion that nothing much is happening. However, committees are but one way of organizing to protect and advance group needs. Teachers and others within the school are likely to continue their efforts to maintain a preferred order of conduct through the organization of strong and sometimes militant maintenance activities. In addition, many students and community members may aid the school staff in maintaining old norms in spite of demands from other segments of the community.

The school staff, however, will not always be able to resist pressures to accommodate themselves to community demands, even when counter to staff needs. The pressures of other groups and organizations on education can be powerful indeed. In our next chapter, particular attention is given to various religious, political, and economic groups in a pluralistic society and how these groups can sometimes overcome the *maintenance subsystems* within education.

Suggested Readings

Frank W. Banghart, *Educational Systems Analyses* (New York: The Macmillian Company, 1969). While this text does not present a sociological analysis of education systems it does illustrate how educators are attempting to use social systems concepts to develop a management technology for educational administrators.

Norman R. Bernier and Jack Williams, *Beyond Beliefs: Idealogical Foundations of American Education* (Englewood Cliffs, N.J.: Prentice-Hall, 1973).

G. Black, *The Application of Systems Analysis to Government Operations* (New York: Praeger, 1968).

W. Buckley, *Sociology and Modern Systems Theory* (Englewood Cliffs, N.J.: Prentice-Hall, 1967).

Burton R. Clark, *The Open Door College: A Case Study* (New York: McGraw-Hill, 1960). This is an interesting, easily read book on the functions of the junior or community college which employs an open-systems perspective.

Donald P. Eckman and Mihojlo Messrovic, "On Some Basic Concepts of the General Systems Theory," *Third International Congress on Cybernetics* (Namor: Association Internationale de Cybernetique, 1963). For the advanced student this is an excellent discussion of systems theory traditions emerging from biology, cybernetics, and engineering systems.

Susan Ferge, "Some Relations Between Social Structure and the School System," *Sociological Review Monographs*, Monograph 17, 1970.

Erving J. Goffman et al., *The Concept of Education as an Investment* (ERIC Document Reproduction ED 058476). Reports on how economic benefits and investment in education is related to other societal resources.

Robert E. Herriott and Benjamin J. Hodgkins, *The Environment of Schooling: Formal Education As An Open Social System* (Englewood Cliffs, N.J.: Prentice-Hall, 1973).

Talcott Parsons and Gerald M. Platt, *The American University* (Cambridge, Mass.: Harvard University Press, 1973).

Richard Pratte, *The Public School Movement* (New York: David McKay Co., 1973).

Patricia Cayo Sexton, *School Policy and Issues in a Changing Society* (Boston: Allyn and Bacon, 1971).

Arthur G. Wirth, *Education in the Technological Society* (Scranton, Pa.: Intext, 1972). An historical presentation of the development of schools in relation to economic, political, and social forces.

3

The Control of Education

WHO SHALL have the power to control education is a continually recurring issue in nearly every socially complex nation. Put quite simply, people of many diverse perspectives are concerned about their schools and want to determine the objectives and conduct of education in accordance with their own values. They do not want the education of their children to be in the hands of those who hold values different from their own or who exhibit behavioral patterns they dislike. Furthermore, people of diverse political, economic, religious, and social perspectives often want their objectives attained in a certain manner. A contest over whose desires shall prevail is common. It is not surprising that nations sometimes experience very intense internal struggles over the control of education.

Not all subsocieties are equally able to exert power, and so some turn to the creation of their own private or parochial schools or to the provision of formal training after regular school hours, only to find that disagreements again emerge within their subculture over curriculum matters and objectives. In addition, forces in the larger society are constantly attempting, in various ways, to influence what goes on within the private schools. In the United States and Canada, there is no dearth of regulations and laws governing all schools, public and private. Similarly, the various religious, ethnic, and social subcultures continue their efforts to influence the public schools, even though they have created private schools of their own. Nearly all social forces attempt to exert some power over education.

It sometimes appears that people are more desirous of controlling education than they are of any other aspect of the public sector. Whatever the case, most poeple who try to influence education seem to recognize that to influence education is to influence society. A myth has grown up, however, that education should be and is free of politics. Educators and other citizens often recite the familiar notion that politics and education are separate worlds and should not be involved with one another. As Larry Iannaccone has stated: "It is easy enough to document the continuing existence of politics in education and of educationists in politics at every level of government . . ."[1] The establishment of nonpartisan school boards elected separately from political party elections or the appointment of school boards is evidence of the attempt to insulate the system of school control from formal partisan political processes. However, so called nonpartison school boards sometimes enhance the influence of special political interests. There is merely a shift from formal public political processes' influencing educational decisions to more informal, less observable political activities. Thus, the separation of educational control from public partisan political activity does not insure the elimination of politics from education. Rather, it simply changes the arena within which educational politics is played.[2]

Before we examine more fully the politics of education, however, it is necessary to distinguish three key concepts involved in the management of social behavior: authority, power, and social control. *Authority* is the legitimate or formal right to exercise control, and *power* refers to the ability to control with or without authority. *Social control,* defined by Tannenbaum, is ". . . any process in which a person or group of persons or organization of persons determines, that is, intentionally affects the behavior of another person, group, or organization."[3]

The control of education is exercised in numerous ways and through a variety of social processes. School-community norms and role expectations for educators are obvious means of informal control. More formal mechanisms include laws of the federal, state, or local units, school board policy guides, administrative regulations, and individual or collective teacher contracts. In addition to control by applying rewards and sanctions, control is achieved by socializing people to certain values and habits. As we internalize certain social norms so that they become our own norms of behavior, the control may be identified as a form of self-control.

It is sometimes difficult to distinguish between the control exercised by other persons, groups, or organizations through sanctions and rewards and that behavior controlled by the individual's acceptance of social norms as his own. Although such self-directed behavior may have de-

---

[1] Laurence Iannaccone, *Politics in Education* (New York: The Center for Applied Research in Education, 1967), p. 6.

[2] Ibid.

[3] Arnold Tannenbaum (ed.) *Control in Organization* (New York: McGraw Hill, 1968), p. 5.

rived, in part at least, from external forms of control, we do not usually identify such processes as social control. Our concern in this chapter is primarily with the external system of social control as it affects the educational organization. However, external societal pressures should be viewed in the context of efforts by educators to insulate themselves from their communities.

Education's Efforts to Achieve Autonomy

Countering the various political forces impinging on education from society are the many obvious and not so obvious efforts of educators and their supporters to keep the school systems free of outside influence. Teachers in the United States, for example, strike to prevent direct community and parental involvement in matters of tenure and of the day-to-day operation of their schools. In a less obtrusive manner, some educators have sought to prevent parental and community pressure from developing by controlling the kinds of information made available to others. For example, many school systems have resisted the publication of school assessment or other evaluation that reflects unfavorably on the quality of education provided. The creation of a positive public image for a school may involve the publication of positive reports or suppression of unfavorable information on achievement levels, costs, delinquency rates, and teacher deficiencies. On another level, some educators have sought to diminish community influence by influencing who gets elected to school boards and other governmental units. Educators also participate actively in many of the groups and institutions upon which the schools depend, from parent-teacher groups and service clubs to political parties. Research has shown that teachers are more likely to contribute to political campaigns, support lobbying forces at state, provincial, and national levels, and run for and occupy public offices at all levels of government than are people in most other occupational groups.[4]

The concept of "academic freedom" has been promoted, particularly by college and university professors, to minimize outside interference. The assumption that the schools can function as independent agencies apart from the rest of society and that self-control by educators can replace external control are basic to the concept of academic freedom. Such beliefs are to some extent unrealistic; as we have noted, education is essentially an open social system and can never be totally insulated from other aspects of society. Nonetheless, the case is usually made

---

[4] William S. Bennett and Edsel L. Erickson, "Teacher Profile," *Encyclopedia of Education* (New York: The Macmillan Company and The Free Press, 1971), vol. 9.

that academic freedom is essential for a free and democratic society. The issue is further complicated by the argument that a complete definition of democracy includes the right of the citizenry to control their social institutions, including education. Of course, there are numerous dilemmas and paradoxes associated with all political belief systems. Whatever the case, no institution in any society, regardless of political orientation, is completely free of control by other segments of the social order. The school system in every society is created and sustained by religious, social, economic, family, and political forces which will not leave school personnel totally free to determine their own objectives and conduct. Notwithstanding the rhetoric which favors academic freedom and the efforts to insulate education from external societal control, one may be assured that every major social institution will reflect the view that it has a vested interest in education as a vehicle for imposing its values.

Groups of educators and individual teachers do attain varying degrees of freedom from outside influence. It should be recognized, however, that impeding parents and other community forces from shaping education does not necessarily produce academic freedom for individual teachers. Nor does the academic freedom of individual teachers to inquire or to teach necessarily follow from having the power over education vested solely in the hands of educators. Many teachers have had their professional and constitutional freedoms restricted by their colleagues. While threats of outside pressure may be a valid reason for imposing cultural values on their peers, educators sometimes use such threats merely as an excuse for limiting the freedom of individual teachers. As a matter of fact, there have been in the United States many court cases seeking academic freedom and constitutional rights for teachers and students that have been initiated and sustained by persons and groups outside of the educational establishment, and many of these cases have involved educators as defendents. Our point is that the school is subject to diverse societal pressures and is itself composed of diverse groups and ideologies, some of which represent outside forces striving to maximize control over education, while other groups both within and outside the school attempt to insulate education from society. Generally speaking, however, most persons within education probably favor both academic freedom for themselves and control over education by educators, even though one does not necessarily follow from the other.

Another source of confusion is the absence of a clear distinction between (1) external control in shaping priorities and allocations among subjects taught and (2) external control in shaping substantive content (and the criteria of validity) within the educational processes. Many educators accept the legitimacy of their community's right to set priorities as to subjects offered and other goals for education, but regard as interference any attempt to tell them how to teach or what constitutes the criteria of teaching excellence.

While the values of academic freedom and collective self-control are important issues in struggles over who controls education, such factors as social status and economic concerns may be even more important. Economic interests guide the actions of most parents, other members of the community, and educators alike. Many lower-class and politically disenfranchised parents, along with many middle- and upper-class persons who identify with the plight of poor people, are beginning to recognize that the schools must be pressed to respond equally to all segments of the community as is implied in the concept of equality of educational opportunity.

In succeeding discussions, information will be presented documenting the unequal distribution of educational resources and training related to social and economic status. The more affluent have always recognized the economic stake they have in education, and the schools have generally reflected their needs. Increasingly, the poor are pursuing their economic stake and are simultaneously finding ways of pressing their interests on education. This change in the environment of the schools has resulted in considerable discussion and some action on the part of educators to adapt to these new pressures from and on behalf of the poor.

Although social systems commonly adapt to their environment, it does not follow that all social systems inevitably accommodate themselves to those who exert pressure. It should also be noted that, while many groups frequently attempt to use education as a vehicle for imposing their values, it does not follow that educators *should* capitulate. Perhaps, the question of accommodation or capitulation should depend upon which values or principles are at stake. Even so, and generally regardless of the values in question, schools, like other organizations, have a tendency to maintain their traditional norms and boundaries of authority. For example, one of the authors recently listened to a discussion by a group of educational administrators on how they might "get around" government requirements for parent and community participation and still receive federal aid that is dependent on involving parents. One method suggested was to be very selective in placing only those known to be "friends" of the school on committees. In one case a trusted principal from a middle-class suburb was placed on a parent committee representing a very poor city neighborhood, even though he did not live in the school district. The argument was made that since the principal was also a parent and had once been poor, he would know what poor parents wanted and needed. In other cases, school administrators have placed trusted middle- and upper-class parents in positions which, according to government guidelines, were supposed to be occupied by lower-income parents. Our emphasis here is on the fact that school systems, as well as other social systems, engage in coping or adaptive responses to pressures from their environment. Even when a subsystem of a society attempts to meet the needs of a new force in its environment, it is unlikely to surrender willingly the power to control its own existence. This also illustrates the open nature of the school system as it responds to outside influences but tries to maintain closed boundaries.

Information Control

Placement of friends on committees is only one method of managing outside pressure. One of the methods most utilized by educational systems for preventing encroachment on its powers of self-control is the management of public information. People who control the information input into a system, who channel information through the system and manage the information output of a system, have considerable power over that system.[5] In essence, control of information often represents power over the lives of others.

While we are all familiar with the policies in totalitarian societies which seek to control the information flow in, through, and out of their countries, we are seldom aware of how the same processes occur in all social systems. Small organizations such as academic departments or disciplines in colleges and universities, as well as nations, seek to control information flow. For example, psychology, history, sociology, chemistry, physics, biology, education, and engineering each represents an academic social organization within most higher educational institutions. Psychologists, for example, process their information in, through, and out of their professional group. Perhaps the bulk of psychological information output is through what teachers of psychology teach and write for their students. Much of the information circulates through a limited range of fellow psychologists and their advanced students. Sometimes, however, their books are received by a more general lay audience. Indeed, when this occurs, the impact of a discipline on its societal environment can be very dramatic. In psychology the writings of Freud, Skinner, and others have provided us with many of the words and concepts we use to describe ourselves and others. From the writings of professional psychologists and psychiatrists we have learned to use such terms as "ego," "self-concept," "retarded," "defense mechanisms," and "reinforcement." Sociologists, economists, educators, historians, and

[5] A distinction is usually made by systems theorists between "control" and "communication." Cybernetics is the science of control and communication. See Norbert Wiener, *The Human Use of Human Beings* (New York: Doubleday Anchor Books, 1956), pp. 15–17. In this section we are primarily concerned with the control of information.

other academic specialists have made similar contributions. Phrases and ideas such as "organization man," "socioeconomic status," "recession," and "educationally disadvantaged" are so extensively used today that we may overlook the fact that their origins were in various academic subsystems.

Another way in which educational subsystems like sociology may have an impact on their environment is by the limited special audiences they serve. The government often contracts with universities to provide research for military, political, and social purposes. There have been thousands of government-supported studies by sociologists on race, poverty, and education. Some of these studies, obviously, have had greater impact on public policies than others. The Coleman Report is one of the more recent sociological studies which have influenced government responses toward busing and racial integration.[6]

Another mode of information output for education subsystems is through expert service to particular institutions. Nearly all major banking institutions have on their payrolls as consultants economists from various universities. The courts also recognize expert witnesses. In the United States, social scientists from universities have played a major role as expert witnesses in the racial desegregation court cases in recent decades. Mental and physical health organizations such as the Veterans Administration in the United States and child guidance clinics have long been customers of academic disciplines housed in university departments. They hire their students, they utilize their faculty as consultants, and they subscribe to their journals and other writings. The reader may think of many other ways that educational subsystems affect their community's environment. But how, one may ask, is the information output of an educational subsystem like psychology or sociology controlled?

Control of Output. One type of control which both individuals and organizations employ is to focus attention on certain message sources and avoid others. Schools may refuse to hire persons trained in certain universities or departments. Various groups may refuse to bring in consultants from certain academic disciplines. And, of course, university research project funding often depends on the credibility of the university in question.

The funding of research shapes the output of academic disciplines in other ways. When the federal government in the United States started funding proposals to investigate poverty and education, this influenced the universities in the kinds of problems they selected for research and the kinds of skills they demanded of their new faculty, as well as the

[6] James Coleman et al., *Equality of Educational Opportunity*, U.S. Department of Health, Education and Welfare (Washington, D.C.: U.S. Government Printing Office, 1966).

courses they offered. For example, the poor and the handicapped have always been present in America in great numbers. While a few lonely voices have always asked for greater allocation of educational resources for persons of poverty, it was not until the advent of government and large foundation funding in this area that disciplines in the social sciences and education began to shift their attention accordingly. Should the funding agencies shift their support for social research away from concerns for inequality, racism, and poverty, perhaps the academic disciplines would similarly shift their concerns.

Another way that the society shapes the messages of its institutions and members is by reserving and granting official authority to speak on certain matters to selected groups and individuals. Just as one may not practice medicine without passing government-administered examinations, psychologists, marriage counselors, engineers, lawyers, and many others must be officially certified to practice in many communities.

Local and national governments also exert control on message output of universities by their willingness to fund the universities themselves. Unpopular expressions of the faculty seriously affect the responses of legislators, congressmen, governors, presidents, and others for university support. Simply put, the academic freedom of teachers to publish their views when their cause is distrusted by the community is sometimes nominal.

Control of Input. In the same way that the information output of a school is in part controlled by other institutions and people in its social environment, the school often attempts to control information input. For example, psychology departments may hire only psychologists who have gone through training programs similar to theirs and are likely to screen professional candidates to make sure that the recruits believe in the "right kind" of psychology. Some psychology departments are therefore primarily Freudian in orientation while others are reinforcement oriented and, rightly or wrongly, men and women are hired on the basis of the image of the department in which they were trained. Other departments may seek a range of interests and competence. Anyone interested in the sociology of education gains plenty of material to interest him or her simply by watching how each university department attempts to control the kinds of beliefs it allows to enter. Input is also controlled by the kind of messages each discipline allows to be published in its journals and at its meetings.

Control Within. Within the school, messages are controlled in a variety of ways. Sometimes only certain professors are allowed to teach a given course regardless of their abilities, credentials, or interests. Some professors may be encouraged to do research and write while others are not. Similarly, some professors may be encouraged to write for certain professional journals and not for others. And, of course, one way of managing communications is to test students and grant degrees only to those who know and profess the views valued by the instructor.

We are sure the reader is well aware of many other ways in which communications are controlled within schools. One common vehicle for control is the restriction of information to certain persons and groups. Information is often guarded within school systems as it is in government agencies. By keeping parents, students, teachers, and others from a complete awareness of the circumstances of their condition it is usually easier to manage them.

Our interest in information control lies in the recognition that the behavior and attitudes of people are managed, to a large extent, through a command of the information they are given. In other words, social control is largely a communication process. But one important point should be remembered. No school or individual can totally manage or control the information it will receive, how it will process that information (e.g., what students will be taught and what they will learn), or what information it will communicate to others. Control of information can never be complete, for no one belongs to exactly the same social groups as another and, to that extent, while being dependent for information upon others in a given group, each person will have some autonomy of thought from that group through his contact with others outside the group. Similarly, no discipline such as psychology, history, education, or sociology can be totally shaped to meet the norms of its university setting; each department has contact with individuals and groups outside the university. Similarly, no given school, college, or university will totally reflect the norms of its community. Universities are also connected to social forces beyond their local community settings. And so too, no man, who is a social psychological system in his own right, will ever be exactly like his neighbors. However, every social system does try to reduce dissonance among its members by shaping people to a common set of values. It is for this reason that the first question in the minds of those concerned with school community relations is: Who is going to control education? A close examination of the various issues of education, whether they involve sex education, vocational preparation, open enrollments, decentralization, desegregation, or other issues, reveals that they largely reflect the concern over which group's view is to prevail.

Why should there be this constant effort by educators to keep their system closed to outside influence? We have noted that many place a high value on academic freedom and its role in a democratic society. We have also mentioned the importance of social status and economic concerns. The range and importance of external influences vary from time to time and from one country to another. The primary external control is generally vested in some government agency. An examination of some of the official and informal agents and means of control follows.

External Control of Education

Various governmental units and officials are the most obvious educational control agencies and generally are identified with the "educational establishment." Such units range from the highest level of the central government to small local governmental units. Numerous informal communities are associated with official government agents in establishing school policy and practice. In many communities, school administrators and school boards have initiated various systems of advisory committees and other semiformal groups to consult with the school administration and advise them on policy matters. Occasionally, such committees exert a great deal of influence upon educational programs. In addition to these relatively formal community agencies, there are frequently groups and individuals less readily identified who exert considrable influence on educational decisions. An understanding of the control of education must include all of these external groups and influential persons.

Concentration of Political Power

One of the most significant forces shaping a school's responses to its environment is direct political action. If a school must cater to a range of different government agencies and social institutions, it is likely to have more independence than when it must be responsible to a limited number of powers. As power in the society becomes centralized in one segment, such as in business, labor, the military, church, or government, increasingly the school is likely to act in the interests of that institution. As increased power has been exercised by the federal government in the United States, national governmental jurisdiction over the schools has also increased. The judicial, congressional, and executive branches of government are giving and can be expected to give more and more of their time and attention to schools in order to attain national objectives.

It is obvious, however, that the government in any society is, in one sense, an arena within which many different forces are contesting for power. Forces representing business, labor, the military, medicine, bureaucratic groups, and others with vested interests in government often do not agree on how education should be conducted, but to the extent that there is consensus the school will probably reflect the common view. However, as long as there are competing forces jockeying for political power, schools can usually attain some added measure of influence over themselves, just as competing religious forces have given the schools some measure of freedom from any one religious group. Although schools will never be totally free of external forces, they are likely to be freer to shape their own destinies in societies where there is a multitude of divergent political forces than they will be in nations where the power is concentrated in one group. The dilemma this creates for thoughtful citizens is that often desired changes in education and society are impeded by the possession of veto power by many subgroups in the society. On the other hand, centralization of political power may mean that school personnel will lose many rights to shape their curriculum. For education, as for other social institutions, the problem is to find that ideal balance of political power for community and professional persons to enjoy.

Of course, the rhetoric in struggles for power over education generally incorporates the idea that this or that program will more effectively produce quality education. Special interest groups, however, have often argued for quality education in terms of their own concerns. For instance, groups opposing the use of alcohol and drugs have exerted pressure on schools to institute drug education programs. Insurance companies have promoted driver education courses. Agricultural interests have pressed for agricultural courses and research, and for farm-oriented-curricular clubs such as the 4H Clubs and Future Farmers of America. Some groups are demanding more sex education, others less. The following represent some of the more generalized vested-interest areas which have shaped and are continuing to shape educational outcomes in every society.

Religious and Ethnic Interests

Historically, religious bodies have operated more schools than other nongovernmental organizations. There are widespread systems of parochial and private schools in many parts of the world. In some societies, government agencies have provided extensive subsidy for parochial schools under religious group control. In some Canadian provinces, for example, public schools are either Catholic or Protestant. In Ireland, all schools are church schools with public support but with very little public control. In much of the Judaeo-Christian world, sectarian religious groups have been instrumental in developing the larger community educational system. Catholic and Jewish groups in New York City, the Christian Reformed in western Michigan, the Baptists in Tennessee are influential forces on the public school programs of their communities. Other examples can be cited for nearly every region. In France, some provinces in Canada, and various other areas, schools directly organized and controlled by religious bodies are subsidized by public funds. In other instances, the religious influence may be entirely informal or indirect. In still other instances, such as the United States, a separate system of schools is maintained by religious bodies relatively independent of the public educational system and with relatively little support from public funds.

In societies in which religious beliefs are relatively homogeneous, opposition to sectarian religious influence over education is less likely to occur than in societies with many different religious beliefs. Divergent religious influences often produce conflict and multiple patterns of education and learning. For example, in order to maintain their distinct culture, the Amish in the United States maintain their own elementary schools and resist compulsory public education in certain worldly skills and knowledge. Other religious groups who desire a more common culture for all members of society pursue their perceived interest by insisting that the Amish children attend high school and learn the skills and attitudes of the larger community. Although United States courts have permitted some variation of enforcement of the compulsory education laws in Amish communities, some conflicts persist. Nearly every society attempts to indoctrinate and force its members to abide by its ways. The schools in the United States and Canada have been a major agency in the assimilation of immigrants. However, some cultural groups prefer to retain their own identities, languages, skills, and attitudes rather than adopt the dominant culture. When they do not wish to change, conflict is likely to occur.

Religious or other groups may exercise varying strategies to maintain themselves.[7] They may isolate themselves and provide for their own educational programs, or they may attempt to influence the conduct of the schools serving the larger community. For example, some religious groups have put pressure on schools to have certain types of prayers recited in the classrooms, while other religious groups have opposed such efforts.

A common strategy among groups who exert control over school matters and who wish to impose their value system is to hire public school teachers and administrators who reflect the desired religious or ethnic cultural values. Another is to instill preferred religious ceremonies and instruction into the school program. Some states and communities in the United States exclude or control the teaching of evolutionary theory in public schools because of religious views. In other communities children from families opposed to theories of evolution are required to learn such theories in order to stay in school.

---

[7] See, for examples: James A. Banks, Chapter 4, "Curricular Models for an Open Society," pp. 43–64; Dan W. Dodson, Chapter 7, "Authority, Power and Education," pp. 99–108, and Barbara A. Sizemore, "Community, Power and Education," pp. 109–136, in *Education for an Open Society, ASCD 1974 Yearbook* (Washington, D.C.: Association for Supervision and Development, 1974). Also, S. Weinman, "Local Control over Formal Education in Two American-Indian Communities: A Preliminary Step toward Cultural Survival," *Review of Educational Research,* vol. 42, no. 4 (Fall 1972), p. 533.

Minorities

The civil rights movement in the United States during the third quarter of the 20th century has been heavily focused on the educational system. The efforts of Blacks, Chicanos, Puerto Ricans, American Indians, and their colleagues in the movement to reduce discrimination and inequality have made these minorities a significant factor in educational decision making. As we shall note in Chapter 6, educational policy has been effected by court decisions and legislative actions largely initiated by minority groups. Although previously ignored in educational policy making, these minorities now have some voice in educational policy at all levels of government. In many instances it is only a token representation, but in other situations minorities may have an important impact on the educational system.

Occupational Interests

Particular forms of domination by particular occupational groups are illustrated by management, trade, and labor interests. Traditionally, public school systems have been more influenced by managerial and professional groups than by labor. Communities have frequently resisted any attempts by labor groups to assume greater influence in educational matters. This is apparently based on the assumption that labor would use its influence to modify the nature of the educational program drastically and through it the structure of the society. There is little evidence on which to base such a conclusion, particularly in the 1970s. Some have maintained that labor control would result in increased emphasis on vocationally oriented education designed to increase labor's skill and marketability. Others have hypothesized that the labor influence on public education would result in less emphasis on vocational education and more on the type of education that would increase mobility in the social structure. Evidence on which to verify either contention must await a careful analysis of the types of schools maintained under conditions in which labor has acquired the dominant voice.

While differences between labor and business on how they would influence schools may be difficult to distinguish, control exerted by specific vocational and professional groups can easily be discerned. The medical profession's control over medical schools is very extensive as compared to the control of most other professions. Teachers and other school personnel, for instance, have had very little control over the conduct of teacher-training institutions. However, contemporary events may modify this condition. Government subsidies are being offered to teacher-training institutions in the United States to encourage the involvement of public school teachers in training programs. In some areas in Canada and other countries teacher-training institutions have advisory boards composed of teachers. As teachers become better organized and more militant, they may extend their control. Teachers now frequently indicate that they should have a major voice in teacher education. Teachers have also developed powerful lobbies at state and national levels to affect legislation and policies on school matters. In later chapters we will elaborate on the emerging role of teachers' unions and associations in controlling schools.

The skilled trades exert considerable authority in educating their membership. The electricians, plumbers, and other trade groups provide their own educational programs. One may be trained as an electrician in the military, hold a masters' degree in electrical engineering, and be otherwise competent, but if he has not been through the electrician's training program, a permit to wire a single socket will not be granted in many communities. In other words, many occupations hold monopolies over the education and certification of their members.

Political Parties

It is not unusual for political parties to be active in school affairs, despite the efforts of many to insulate education from formal partisan politics. Politicians are concerned with maintaining and creating social conditions, and, certainly, those interested in shaping the activities and attitudes of a community can hardly be expected to overlook one of the main institutions charged with that responsibility. However, political parties vary in the extent to which the educational system receives their attention. When major reforms or a revolution in societal conditions is sought, as was the case in Nazi Germany and the People's Republic of China, the schools are the recipients of more political attention than in societies in which major social changes are not immediate political objectives.

Educational institutions are also called upon from time to time to help perpetuate political power. Children are often taught in schools to honor certain political figures and parties. It is also common practice in many communities to appoint persons to educational posts for political patronage reasons. Persons with little experience in education sometimes become college presidents or superintendents of public instruction.

Although there is some distaste for the politicalization of educational decision-making, school issues are often used as vehicles for attaining political power. Neal Gross pointed out that some school board members in Massachusetts in the 1950s sought such positions as a stepping stone to other political careers. There is no reason to suspect that conditions have changed in the 1970s. In many countries and districts school boards and school officials are selected on a nonpartisan basis. In several nations—e.g., France, Australia, the United States, and England—educational posts at very high levels are placed under administration of a civil service type. One should not conclude from this, however, that political parties are not influential in the operation of so-called nonpartisan school systems. Widely held beliefs that political control of education is undesirable primarily function to keep such patterns of influence at unofficial levels.

The Socially Elite

In various societies special educational elite groups have dominated the control of educational systems. In many, elite groups have used the educational systems to maintain their high status by limiting access to education to a relatively small proportion of the society. This is clearly exemplified by past conditions in India and the United States. The high castes of India often monopolized higher education to the exclusion of the "untouchables" and other lower-caste groups. In the United States blacks were even officially denied instruction in reading during slavery days. Often, however, this control is more subtle. Whatever the case, the argument that accompanies such monopolization by elite groups is usually the same. The elite groups tend to maintain that the masses are not qualified to exercise decision-making power with regard to the educational process and that the welfare of the society as a whole is therefore best served by maintaining a limited control group. Remnants of such a system may be found where participation in school elections and bond issues is limited to property holders who pay a major portion of the school taxes. College admission standards, tracking children into college-bound and vocation-bound lanes, vocational schools, and special education programs are other examples of programs which have functioned at times for the benefit of the socially elite and at the expense of the masses of working-class children. Other informal systems of influence have had a similar impact in many communities. It is commonly assumed that such monopolization of the school by the elite strata of society tends to maintain the status quo of the social structure. Although this may generally be true, there is some evidence that monopolization of educational control by the upper strata of society has not always resulted in conservative educational policies. It has frequently been assumed that the predominance of business managers and other middle-class school and college board members guaranteed that the educational system would support the dominant social class of their communities. Some years ago, Charters[8] challenged the contention that school board

[8] W. W. Charters, Jr., "Social Class Analysis and the Control of Public Education," *Harvard Educational Review*, vol. 23 (Fall 1953), pp. 268–83.

composition determined school policy. He suggested rather that numerous forces influence the values and policies of the school. The elite members of boards certainly have some influence, but school administrators, legislators, labor leaders, organized parent groups, and other groups discussed above also contribute to educational policy making.[9] Some discussion of the way in which such groups merged into a functional control system follows.

The Educational Establishment

The identification of diverse groups that play some part in the control of education is only a beginning in the analysis of the control system. Although some groups have decidedly more power than others, it would be inaccurate to assume that an identifiable elite group controls the educational system without constraints from other forces. Useem and Useem emphasize that "the sector most likely to have a major voice in school policies is the local economic elite,"[10] but such control is far from absolute. "It is constrained by the pressures of a variety of groups and organizations centrally concerned with the educational process."[11] The interaction, cooperation, and sometimes conflict between the various persons and groups concerned with and primarily controlling the educational system have generated the concept *educational establishment.* The composition of the complex of organizations, officials, informal groups, and persons that control education varies from one level to another and from one community to another. A brief examination of educational establishments follows, but the results of the control system are considered in subsequent chapters, particularly Chapters 5 and 6.

The Public School Establishment

The control of elementary and secondary education in the United States as well as in some other countries is officially divided between state and local agencies. Primary responsibility is lodged in the states, but all have delegated much of this responsibility to local school districts. Educational establishments have developed at both levels. Both result in part at least in keeping the schools free of partisan political influence and other forces considered detrimental to the educational system. In

[9] See Neal Gross, *Who Runs Our Schools* (New York: John Wiley and Sons, Inc., 1958), for an examination of the various influences on school boards in one state.

[10] Elizabeth L. and Michael Useem, *The Education Establishment* (Englewood Cliffs, N.J.: Prentice-Hall, 1974), p. 5.

[11] Ibid., p. 6.

their analysis of the state educational system, Pinner, Collins, and Sederberg maintain that the state educational establishment developed both alongside of and within the political system of the United States.

> This Establishment is vulnerable because it must rely on the state for both the means of forcible constraint (e.g., the enforcement of compulsory attendance laws) and for its financial resources. However, the earmarking for education of a portion of governmental taxes gives the educational establishment a modicum of independence. Having economic resources gives the Establishment some power to use and to protect its independence.[12]

The continued existence of an educational establishment depends, according to Pinner and associates, on three conditions: the maintenance of public credibility, the defense of inviolacy, and the propagation of the faith. The concept of inviolacy has particular relevance to this discussion of the open versus the closed nature of educational systems. Inviolacy refers to the freedom of an organization or social structure from external and internal disturbances. Internal inviolacy calls for the avoidance of threats to the establishment from within education. External inviolacy requires a monopoly position and a degree of autonomy in relation to society. Autonomy means that the educational establishment must be able to make its own policy decisions. This is accomplished by arrangements which guarantee that there is minimal interference from outside institutions in the formulation of educational policy.

A definition of the establishment is extremely difficult because it has no precise membership of organizations or people and no clearly defined boundaries. In delineating the educational establishment in Michigan, Pinner and others identify a complex of educational organizations and associations, State Board of Education, State Department of Education, and a number of other organizations and individuals who are formally or informally in charge of education.[13] The identification of such organizations and persons does not, however, fully define the concept of establishment. The concept also involves the belief that there is a legal base and some professional expertise which establishes the right of these organizations and persons to assume the major role of operating the schools in contrast to outside groups which might wish to interfere with or destroy this educational system. It requires the existence of a civil body of "friends of education" who propagate a faith in the establishment and thereby provide the energy the schools need to function: money, students, and legitimacy. The State Department of Education

[12] Frank Pinner, John Collins, and William Sederberg, "The State and Education: A Report to the Urban Institute," mimeographed (East Lansing: Michigan State University, 1971), p. 18.

[13] Ibid., passim.

operates in continuous interaction with other aspects of the establishment.[14]

Educators, as we previously emphasize, generally attempt to maintain decision-making within the educational system, even though they are dependent upon outside sources for financial support. Iannaccone has indicated that the educational system is designed to protect the schools from corruption by removing them from the mainstream of political life.[15] The educational establishment develops and maintains the boundaries of the educational system and the status quo of education and society.[16] In other words, the educational establishment seeks to maintain the boundaries of the system and protect it from periodic, if not continuous, invasion by the political system which provides some financial support. The independent taxing powers given to school boards in many states or the extensive capital assets of some private universities illustrate how some schools achieve independence even in the area of funding and thereby are able to restrict outside influence. For most schools, however, the necessity to seek financial support from governmental agencies provides an avenue by which the governmental system can exert pressure on the educational system. Still, even where the school is dependent on government funds, considerable effort will be expended to reduce influence by the source of such funds. The zeal with which the educational system seeks to protect its boundaries from external political influence may be illustrated by the comment of a school superintendent to a member of a city council when suggesting support. When the superintendent was asked by a council member how the school system arrived at particular budget figures, the superintendent remarked, "You tend to your business and we'll tend to ours."[17] Although various persons, groups, and segments of the educational establishment may disagree on a variety of issues concerning education, they tend to close ranks in their efforts to maximize the financial support obtained from the state or federal government and to protect their internal decision-making power in those areas they consider inviolate. This is illustrated in the United States by the strong opposition to the introduction of voucher plans which supposedly provide parents with a choice in program selection for their children.[18] Regardless of the merits or lack of merits of a voucher plan, such a program would drastically modify the decision-making process in the education system and would be strongly

[14] See Frederick M. Wirt and Michael W. Kirst, *The Political Web of American Schools* (Boston: Little, Brown & Co., 1972), pp. 111–24, and James B. Conant, *Shaping Educational Policy* (New York: McGraw Hill, 1964), pp. 37–38.

[15] Iannaccone, *Politics in Education*, passim.

[16] Ibid.

[17] Personal experience of the senior author while serving as a city councilman.

[18] Pinner et al., *The State and Education*, pp. 71–72.

opposed by educational lobbyists and school district officials, and more moderately so by other friends of the current educational establishment.

Another feature of the educational establishment which helps it to maintain itself is its tendency to avoid certain public issues and thereby elude the creation of powerful enemies. There is considerable evidence that educational administrators and others responsible for schools, with rare exception, avoid taking positions on political issues in which there is intense involvement by powerful publics. The school establishment would jeopardize its own interests by taking strong positions without broad public support. It appears that the maintenance of an educational establishment with its powers of internal control depends, in part, on the avoidance of public statements by establishment members or their charges which threaten outside political forces. If powerful cultural forces perceive the functioning of a school system to be unsatisfactory, political pressure is very likely to open that system to increased outside control; the consequence is a modification in the internal power of the establishment. In addition, a change in the "line-up" of the establishment membership is a strong possibility. The average length of occupancy in the position of school superintendent in the United States is five years or less.[19] This may be indicative of the extent to which the educational establishment is no longer able to set itself apart and avoid public positions on matters of intense public concern by contesting political forces. Even a rarely expressed position on a matter of controversy can cause upheaval in education. The educational establishment of today is caught in the middle of an internal struggle for control and many of the former boundaries of education are breaking down. Schools in such conflict situations become increasingly open to changing community powers.

The school board, by whatever name, has usually been identified as the primary controlling agency in local school districts. The predominance of business and professional members representing elite and middle-class parents and other organizations was presumed to reflect the educational establishment views and desires. Recent research, particularly in large urban school systems, casts some doubt on the school boards' power to control. An analysis of the New York City school system's efforts to desegregate and of their failure to do so indicates that the administrative bureaucracy played a major role in blocking any significant change.[20] "Various organizations of principals, district superintendents, and other administrators in the New York system banded together . . . [and] engaged in open rebellion . . . against policies of

---

[19] Iannaccone, *Politics in Education*, p. 26.

[20] See David Rogers, *One Ten Livingston Street* (New York: Vintage Book, a Division of Random House, 1969), for a fascinating analysis of politics and bureaucracy in the New York City school system.

their own chief administrator [the superintendent of schools] and the board of education."[21] This illustrates that the school administrators are a powerful force in the large urban school district establishments. The local school establishment must involve such administrative groups as well as school boards and other groups if it is to exert effective control over the schools.

The role of the teachers in both state and local school control has become a major one in recent years. The educational establishment has involved organized teacher groups to some degree for many years, but the National Educational Association, its state, and local affiliates were often dominated by administrators. The teachers representation, if any, was likely to be lodged in superintendents, principals, or other administrators. The teachers themselves have now emerged as leaders of these organizations as well as the locals of the American Federation of Teachers. Through these organizations, the teachers exert much greater power in educational decision-making at local, state and national levels than formerly.

Advocates of more authority for teachers base their arguments on the professional competence of educators to determine what is appropriate for the educational program. Few would doubt the superior competence and ability of teachers to shape, to a considerable extent, the nature of their schools. It is doubtful, however, that complete control by a faculty will result in harmonious efforts to change the school or its function in society. Teachers who have themselves been educated in a particular discipline and subculture, like other people, tend to promote their own biases. They are likely to promote the programs traditional in their backgrounds. There are exceptions, of course. Teachers have fostered some educational changes as programs for the handicapped and other diversified educational opportunities. On the whole, however, teachers have not been promoters of liberal causes or educational changes designed to improve educational quality for the masses. Rather, they have used their power to protect and extend their interests.[22] On the whole, educators are a relatively conservative group who will tend to support the kinds of education they themselves have experienced.

Students at the college and high school level are beginning to see that they can exercise considerable control over educational, social, political, and military matters when they act collectively. This movement is occurring in societies of varying political persuasion and levels of technological development. China, Yugoslavia, and the U.S.S.R., as well as Canada, France, and the United States, have witnessed various forms

[21] Mario Fantani, Marilyn Gittell, and Richard Magat, "Local School Governance," Chapter 5 in Useem and Useem, *The Education Establishment,* p. 91.

[22] See Myron Brenton, *What's Happened to Teacher?* (New York: Coward, McCann and George Hagen, Inc., 1969; Avon Book 1970), pp. 116–26.

of student rebellion. The pressure for student influences on the controlling boards now frequently involves student participation with or without vote on public school and university boards of trustees.

Students are not likely to exercise as much control over education as teachers, professors, and administrators. Students are less permanent; by the time they are sufficiently organized to mobilize some power, they graduate or leave school. Also, most students are dependent for their support on their parents or the government and have less access to other sources of community power than older groups. Educators, on the other hand, are often active and influential members of political parties and vested interest groups which can mobilize on their behalf. Since the voting age in the United States has been lowered to 18 years, a significant shift of power to college and senior high school students may occur.

It should be recognized that the focus of control within education has been diffused considerably by the emergence of faculty and student power pressures. As a result, school administrators have lost considerable control over matters of hiring and firing, teaching methods, course content, and general policy, and it is to be expected that they will lose even more.

Higher Education Establishments

The higher education establishments in the United States overlap those of the public schools to a limited extent. At the state level some segment, such as the state board of education, some legislators, and some education organizations may participate in the decision making relevant to both public elementary-secondary school systems and public higher education institutions. Community or junior colleges are sometimes extensions of the public school system. As such, decisions concerning them may be largely made by the public school establishment. The complex of persons, groups, and organizations that influence colleges and universities are largely independent of the elementary school establishment. Furthermore, establishments identified with each institution of higher education are usually quite separate from those of other institutions. State systems of higher education with several colleges and/or universities may have common establishments but some independent influences are also likely to occur.

The nature of a university or college establishment may vary from one institution to another, but the following components are generally common: The board of trustees, faculty, alumni, university administrators, legislative committees (if public institutions), educational organizations, various friends of the university, and, increasingly, the students. The locus of control is officially and legally (if a public institution) in the board of trustees, overseers, regents, or whatever the board of directors may be called. In most colleges and universities in the United States and other western nations, the faculty has either been delegated or has assumed considerable power over curricula, academic policies, and student affairs. This provides a setting for a continuing contest for power between the faculty and the board. Since higher education is dependent on the legislative appropriations, gifts, or grants from foundations, government, industry, or individuals for much of its financial support, all segments of the college or university establishment must join in encouraging and promoting such support. The boards of colleges or universities, like school boards, are predominately business and professional people who are presumed to be conservative in their attitudes toward academic freedom for the faculty, educational programs, and public issues. A study of 5,000 board members revealed considerable variation in their views, with most quite willing to give faculty, administration, and students much decision-making power in various campus matters. Only in the appointment of a president did the majority reserve the power exclusively to the board.[23] These findings reflect the fact that control is dispersed through various persons and groups in the establishment. The specific amount of power or influence that each group—board, administration, faculty, alumni, students, friends of the university—has in decision or policy making varies with the issues involved and with time. Students currently exert much greater influence on housing patterns than they do on graduation requirements, but more on both than a score of years ago. In general, college and university decisions involve the interaction of several persons and groups recognized as part of the institution's establishment. Rarely does a single group completely determine a policy or make a decision.

Educational Establishment and the Social Structure

The "establishment" refers to the existing power structure or authority in the society. As such it connotes a tendency to preserve the status quo and maintain the social structure. At least establishments generally do not knowingly destroy their power and authority. Several social scientists have examined the educational system from this perspective and concluded that the educational establishment tends to prevent change and maintain the inequalities in the stratification of societies.[24] The three following chapters will further examine these and related

[23] Rodney T. Hartnett, *College and University Trustees: Backgrounds, Roles, and Educational Attitudes* (Princeton, N.J.: Educational Testing Service 1969), pp. 19–40; Useem and Useem, *The Education Establishment,* p. 156.

[24] See Useem and Useem, *The Education Establishment,* for a sample of these analyses and an extensive bibliography of this literature.

issues. At this point we only suggest that, although the educational establishments do tend to maintain the social structure through control of the schools, the educational system also promotes some changes and provides some mobility in the social structure.

Centralization or Decentralization of Educational Control

Several levels of power and authority operate in the educational system. We have noted that state, local district, and even single school establishments have varying degrees of power. The degree of concentration or dispersion of control in a single locus or throughout many subunits of society varies greatly from one society to another. The nature of these varying systems and their relation to educational outcomes require some examination.

Traditionally, centralization of education has been viewed in terms of state, provincal, or national educational authorities. Obviously, from such a perspective various degrees of centralization occur, ranging from highly centralized national educational systems where there is little local control over policy to highly decentralized systems where policy is determined primarily at the local level. Generally speaking, there are few societies, if any, where official power over education is completely centralized in regional or national bureaus and establishments or where it is completely decentralized. However, it is quite appropriate to recognize that some societies have a greater centralization of educational control than others. In France, for example, authority over education is concentrated in the national government much more than it is in Canada or the United States. The degree of centralization is somewhat related to the homogeneity of religious, ethnic, and other cultural groups in the society. Diverse social-cultural groups try to preserve some identity and resist centralized control of education by a dominant group. Of course concentrated economic and political power may overcome such resistence even in pluralistic societies.

Before we proceed with an elaboration of the relationship of systems of control to various outcomes in the society, it may be helpful to further characterize variations in centralization as they appear in a number of countries.

United States

The United States, with a federal system in which power is distributed between national government and the states, illustrates the situation in which the national government exercises less control over education than state and local agencies. The federal government, however, increasingly provides financial and other assistance. The United States Supreme Court, Congress, and the President now determine more and more school policy issues than in years past. Furthermore, there are numerous national educational organizations and other forces which function on a national scale to produce a nation-wide program of education. Under the federal constitution the states have extensive legal authority to control the schools but they are influenced by the national organizations and agencies. The states in turn delegate the exercise of much of their authority to local school districts. The local school districts have developed strong participation in school administration control and financial support. In addition to authority over public education, the states also have considerable authority over private schools. All states have some elementary and secondary schools controlled by religious bodies which operate with very little direct financial assistance from government. The states generally exercise only limited legal authority over the religious schools so that they are almost autonomous.

England

England represents an interesting division of responsibility between national government and local units. The local units are larger than the average local school district in the United States or Canada. In fact, the population of some of these districts exceeds that of some provinces and states in North America.

A great deal of freedom is enjoyed by local school authorities in the administration of their school programs, even though the national government provides a large part of the financial support. In addition to the primary and secondary schools directly controlled by the governmental agencies, there are "public" schools which are similar to private schools in the United States and Canada. Some of these receive no financial assistance; others have direct grants from the ministry of education. The number of public schools is relatively small, but they exert tremendous influence on British education. They have traditionally existed for the socially and economically elite. Recently, however, there has been a press in government to close down such schools and thereby diminish the power of schools for the socially elite and traditional ruling classes.

France

In contrast to England and the United States, the French system of education involves little or no local participation in either major policy formulation or administrative arrangements. However, some local taxes are levied to support both the public and parochial schools. The pattern of educational control follows closely the centralized pattern of government. There has been a long struggle between clerical and anticlerical forces in France concerning the control and financing of the extensive system of Catholic schools. Recently the government has provided subsidy for students in Catholic as well as public schools. The centrally controlled public schools and the Catholic schools, subsidized by the government, operate in parallel fashion.

Australia

In Australia, the national, state, and local governmental organizations are similar to those of the United States. The national government exercises little direct control over education, though it makes some financial contributions. Various states in Australia, as in the United States, are constitutionally responsible for education. Unlike the United States, however, the Australians have not created local school districts or authorities to operate the schools. The educational system of Australia is a state system as completely centralized within the state as is the French system in the nation as a whole.

U.S.S.R.

The Union of Soviet Socialist Republics has developed a pattern of federated government in which the federal government has wide powers and responsibilities for education. It has, however, delegated many of these powers to the constituent republics which make up the union. In each of these republics, a decentralized system of organization and control gives authority to smaller local government units. Financial support comes from all three levels of government. Overlying the decentralized plan of organization, however, is a pattern of control by the Communist party. Since government officials are selected from the party, the educational system is under the authority of the party organization. Private sectarian schools are not encouraged.

Some Issues in Centralization

Obviously, any attempt to increase or decrease centralization of educational control is going to create conflict. The issues centering on the manner of financial support, community control, providing for manpower needs, democratic political participation, and equal educational opportunity are seemingly recurring issues in every modernizing, multi-ethnic society. All of these issues in one way or another complicate the larger issue of whether to centralize education at the national level or to place the authority over schools in smaller units of society or at lower levels of government. Furthermore, each of these issues is characterized by considerable myth about the functioning of both education and government.

Bases of Financial Support

Related to the centralization of political power and the centralization of education within national governmental agencies—but by no means perfectly correlated with it—are the sources of financial support. Although we commonly assume that the control of education is located with those who provide the funds for education, a number of qualifications must be made. In the United States there are many schools near military bases or defense factories which depend very heavily on federal funds to run their programs. In these schools, decisions about curriculum matters, hiring, firing, discipline, and so forth, tend to be made by local school boards and school personnel in much the same way as is done in neighboring schools not receiving federal funds. It may also be noted that legislators sometimes complain that while they provide the funds they do not have sufficient control over what goes on in schools and colleges. Of course, those who pay the bill often exert some control through the amount of money provided, but, in many instances, the educational system is subsidized by governmental units and private sources which are prevented by law or custom from controlling certain aspects of education. Although certain provisions are usually made for conditions under which financial assistance may be received, the extent of control over education has not shifted from local to national levels to the same degree that the financial support has shifted.

Community Control

There are two mistaken assumptions that are commonly made when considering centralization of schools. One concerns the placement of schools under the control of their own boards of education. Many have mistakenly equated such school board control with community control. In the United States, school boards may not always reflect the views of major communities within the region they serve. For example, it has not been uncommon to have entire ethnic and religious populations, both intentionally, and unintentionally, excluded from control. Recently, native American, Black, and Mexican-American parents in the United States have attempted to gain some authority over the schools serving their children. These groups have urged the decentralization of large city school systems in order to enhance their chances of making decisions concerning the education of their children. This movement for local community control has resulted in the implementation of numerous different plans for school decentralization in cities throughout the United States.

Although local community school boards have been given significant power there is little evidence of major improvement in the education of minority children. Such decentralization, however, gives us little reason to believe that the schools will be governed by all segments of the community. Groups in power are not likely to willingly give over their powers to others. In addition, the complex, bureaucratic structure of urban societies and their educational systems often renders citizens powerless when dealing with their schools. The immigrant, the very poor, the rural migrant, the urban migrant, and those handicapped by inability to use the language of the school may be served by the school, but they are not likely to exert authority over it. In some large city schools with 50 percent to 75 percent student turnover during the school year there is little opportunity to establish patterns of influence. Furthermore, there is no reason to believe that simply because one is elected from a given community he will reflect that community's preferences. Sometimes school boards reflect the interests of their school administrations far more than of the publics which elected them.

A second erroneous belief associated with discussions over community control concerns the notion that centralization inevitably removes power from the local level. This points up one of the major issues long dominant in education. Any analysis of the relation between the degree of centralization and the nature of the educational system should be made in relation to specific goals of purposes. For example, we will examine briefly the question of centralized versus decentralized control in relation to three specific issues: (1) the effectiveness in supplying needed manpower and allocating personnel within the society; (2) the degree of democratic control; and (3) the provision for equality of opportunity.

Manpower Needs

In societies with relatively little geographic mobility, the local control of education is likely to result in training programs which supply the necessary manpower and allocate people to various positions reasonably well. Local leaders know the particular types of training necessary for the various positions in their community. They are also likely to be qualified to determine the kind of education that will prepare young people for their future roles in society.

Although systematic analysis is not available, it seems that in highly mobile societies centralized systems of controlling education are more likely to facilitate national goals than are local control systems. Local educational authorities may be too provincial or unaware to view the needs of the total society. The post-Sputnik concern in the United States with effective training of needed scientific and engineering personnel has been followed by an extensive reexamination of local control of education. The Congress, the President, and federal agencies have given considerable effort to implementing national goals for education. It seems unlikely that thousands of local school authorities can respond efficiently to the national need for highly educated personnel in a variety of fields. Governmental programs which encourage local agencies to provide better education in science, mathematics, and languages, and better guidance services are reflections of national concerns not being met at local levels. The federal financial aid to education in the United States, the willingness of the courts to be concerned with educational issues, and executive orders detailing educational goals are indicative of an increase in centralized influence on the educational system. Historically, national educational programs in England, Australia, the United States, Russia, Canada, and elsewhere have developed, in part, from a concern about the effectiveness of education for groups such as the physically handicapped, and for developing nationally needed human resources. Although the limited experiences of these few nations is not a sound basis from which to generalize, it suggests the hypothesis that the training and allocation of personnel resources for national needs is more effectively achieved by a centralized system of control.

Democracy

Much of the opposition to centralized control of education in the United States is based on the assummption that centralized control is undemocratic—that it is removed from the people, so that the vote of the electorate is ineffective. This assumption arises from the recognition that centralized systems of control involve an extensive bureaucratic organization and the belief that bureaucracies are not responsive to the will of the people. The more remote locus of administrative decision-making and legislative policy-making provides some foundation for this belief. The informal patterns of influence which exist in a local school district are less likely to be operative in a centralized school system.

However, in the past both locally administered and centrally controlled systems have been readily influenced by small pressure groups that do not represent the interests of the majority of the people. One important point here is that minority groups, whether racial, ethnic, or political, can sometimes wield power on the national level but not on the local level.

An examination of the proportion of electorate voting in local school elections as compared with the proportion voting in state and national elections may also suggest an hypothesis concerning centralized control. In the typical school board election in the United States, a small proportion of the eligible voters participate. Participation of more than 20 percent of qualified voters is unusual. In recent national elections, in contrast, more than 50 percent of the voters have participated. If the test of democratic control is participation in the election process, the United States experience suggests that centralized systems of government are likely to be more democratic. However, there are countries with 90 percent or more of the people voting in elections. The complex of issues involved in such elections may dilute the importance of an educational issue in the electorate's decisions. In general, however, centralized government officials are chosen by a broader electoral base than are local school boards.

On the other hand, the question of community representation is not that simple. Sometimes governments do not effectively represent many of their communities even though they represent most people in their districts. School districts are often much broader than communities, and, when this is the case, some communities may not be represented at all. The centralization of schools, in fact, is sometimes employed to do just that—keep certain communities from exercising their will. Centralized control can be and has been used to the advantage and the disadvantage of both minority and majority groups. Since centralized powers can be used on the behalf of both minority and majority interests, no clear statement about whom centralized school districts will inevitably represent is possible.

Equality of Opportunity

One of the most universally held goals for education in Canada, the United States, and many other countries is the maintenance of some degree of equality of educational opportunity. If this purpose is generalized throughout a nation, one finds it difficult to justify the variations in educational programs from one local district to another and from school to school within the same district. The widespread variation in teaching qualifications and educational facilities found in school districts in the United States obviates the possibility of equal educational opportunities, even though one recognizes that such factors are not adequate criteria for measuring the quality of education. Several states and provinces in the United States and Canada have recognized this inequality and have sought to equalize educational opportunities through various governmental aid programs. In both situations an attempt has been made to maintain the maximum degree of local control with centralized systems of financing. Although differences in quality of education are frequently present in systems with more centralized control, it seems likely that such differences will be minimized when a centralized system exists.

However, the issue of equal opportunity is much too complex to be more than tentative in our generalizations at this point. In Chapter 5, differing definitions of equal educational opportunity will be examined in greater detail for their particular implications.

Suggested Readings

Kenneth E. Boulding, "The Schooling Industry," *Review of Educational Research,* 42, no. 1 (Winter 1972), pp. 129–43.

Lesley Browder, ed., *Emerging Patterns of Administrative Accountability* (Berkeley, Calif.: McCutchan, 1971).

Joseph N. Cronin, *Control of Urban Schools* (New York: The Free Press, 1973).

Edsel L. Erickson, Clifford E. Bryan, and Lewis Walker, *Social Change, Conflict and Education* (Columbus, Ohio: Charles Merrill Publishing Co., 1972).

Marilyn Gittel, *Participants and Participation: A Study of School Policy in New York City* (New York: Praeger Publishers, 1967).

Marcia Guttentag, "Children in Harlem's Community Controlled Schools," *The Journal of Social Issues,* 28, no. 4 (1972).

George R. LaNoue and Bruce L. R. Smith, *The Politics of School Decentralization* (Lexington, Mass: D. C. Heath and Co., 1973).

Henry Levin, "The Case for Community Control of Schools," in Martin Carnoy, ed., *Schooling in a Corporate Society* (New York: David McKay Co., 1972).

Philip M. Marcus and Dora Marcus, "Control in Modern Organizations," in Merlin B. Brinkerhoff and Phillip R. Kunz, eds., *Complex Organizations and Their Environments* (Dubuque, Iowa: William C. Brown Co., 1972).

Nicolaus C. Mills, "Community Control in Perspective," *Information Retrieval Center on the Disadvantaged Bulletin,* 8, no. 5 (November 1972).

Douglas Mitchell, "Ideology and Public School Policy Making," *Urban Education,* 9, no. 1 (April 1974) pp. 35–59.

David Rogers, *One Ten Livingston Street: Politics and Bureaucracy in the New York City Schools* (New York: Random House, 1968).

Harry Summerfield, *Power in Process: The Formulation and Limits of Federal Education, Policy* (Berkeley, Calif.: McCutchan Publishing Co., 1974).

Elizabeth L. Useem and Michael Useem, *The Education Establishment* (Englewood Cliffs, N.J.: Prentice-Hall, 1974).

Edward Wynne, *The Politics of School Accountability: Public Information about the Schools* (Berkeley, Calif.: McCutchan Publishing Co., 1972).

"Education for an Open Society," ASCD Yearbook (Washington, D.C.: Association for Supervision and Curriculum Development, 1974), pp. 1–216.

4

Education and Social Change

ALMOST any discussion of the means for attaining a major change in society is likely to include education. To many, education is a panacea, a solution to the problems of the world. Such assumptions are, however, clearly oversimplified and exaggerate the potency of education as a vehicle for achieving social change. Indeed, education sometimes acts as an impediment to social change; and when education does cause change, its influence is often complex and very subtle.

On the other hand, a view emphasizing the importance of education is not totally without foundation and has been a significant motivator of economic, political, and social programs everywhere. The widespread belief that education is a major means of achieving industrialization permeates the world, and both technologically developed and developing countries attempt to design educational programs to achieve their economic goals. The enhanced education of its population has been a major goal of every country seeking to enhance the productivity of its people. Education has therefore become one of the major areas of investment for economic development. Preliminary evidence indicates that the return on investment in education is often greater than the return on investment in other capital goods.

It is important to recognize, however, that the relationship of education to social change is not exclusively concerned with economic development. Education is intimately related to all facets of the social structure. The political, religious, and family institutions of our society, our systems of stratification of people into social classes, mobility, and our opportunity structures are clearly related to our educational system. Paradoxically, the educational system can concurrently function both to preserve and modify all aspects of the social structure.

Before we proceed further with an examination of the effects of education, we should note two important principles concerning the nature of social change. First is the principle that rates of social change vary greatly from one society to the next. In highly isolated societies the rate of social or cultural change is relatively slow because there is little opportunity to receive information and resources from other cultures. In contrast, those societies having ready access to the ideas and materials of others through trade, travel, and rapid communication change more rapidly.

A second principle concerns the differential rates of change of various segments within a society. Differential rates are more likely to be found in rapidly developing societies. As a rule, material things such as tools and machinery and the techniques associated with them are discarded more rapidly than the nonmaterial, such as family structure, religion, government, and other aspects of social relations. This is exemplified in such countries as Australia, Canada, and the United States, where considerable value is placed on new mechanical devices. The new automobile, washing machine, or hay baler is better than the old. In fact, the salesperson of material devices finds it very profitable to emphasize that the model being promoted is the very latest, just off the assembly line. On the other hand, there is not only a great reluctance to accept the new in family, religious, and government institutions, but there is pressure against doing so. Thus, in our society there is a tendency to foster differences by accelerating change in some areas and retarding change in other areas.

On the other hand, efforts to prevent change in one area of the culture or society and foster change in another have not been entirely successful because of the interrelatedness of all institutions. For instance, new modes of transportation may be related to the rising divorce rate. Although such changes in the family may not be a direct result of changes in transportation, the complex of cultural changes generated by new transportation may involve the family. We cannot speed up changes in tools, machines, and gadgets without producing related modifications in the structure of our social order and our beliefs and values. All features of society are functionally interrelated, and this includes education. The school is part of the total social system, and we must examine the educational system within the context of the total society. It is not an extrasocietal agency, but is embedded in the social system. Education is affected by society and acts within, as well as upon, the social system.

Education as an Agency of Change

Although we have a vast commitment to the belief that education can and does serve as a change agent, we have limited knowledge of how or under what conditions it serves this function. The complexity of the relationship between education and change in other aspects of the society makes it extremely difficult to analyze the precise nature of the relationship. As we have emphasized, the educational system is constantly interacting with all other aspects of the society. Education is therefore only one of several variables which interact to produce social change. As Olive Banks has said, "it is possible that at least part of the problem lies in the way the question is framed. The concept of education as producing or impeding social change is enormously complicated by the fact that the educational system is itself a part of the society which it is changing. Consequently, the real issue is one of the actual interrelationship between educational institutions and other aspects of the society."[1] It is obvious that we do not yet have all of the tools for analyzing how education facilitates or impedes social change. We can, however, identify several conditions which are important to our understanding.

Government, Education, and Change

Many have speculated on the relative impact of government action and education in the process of social reform. This has been strikingly illustrated in recent years by the discussions concerning the role of education in overcoming discrimination and segregation in the society in comparison to legislation and court orders. We believe that arguments over whether education or legislation is more important are relatively fruitless. The educational system is unlikely to initiate activities to force change in a society in which the system of governmental control is opposed to such activities. In fact, it is extremely difficult to find cases where the schools have initiated and carried out programs to educate for changes in the government, the family, the military, the religions, or the systems of entertainment without active pressure or at least acceptance by the established governmental agencies. In many ways, formal education is an extension or agent of governments everywhere.

The complex interaction of the educational system with sources of control both informal and governmental is illustrated by two recent studies at different governmental levels. David Rogers analyzed the failure of the New York City public schools to desegregate.[2] Although numerous community groups, government agencies, and even the school board were seeking change, the necessary ingredients were not present in New York to produce significant desegregation. There were counter-

[1] Olive Banks, *The Sociology of Education* (London: B. T. Batsford, Ltd., 1968), p. 217.

[2] David Rogers, *One Hundred and Ten Livingston Street* (New York: Vintage Books, A Division of Random House, 1969).

vailing power groups and government agencies as well as the resistance of a large and unmanageable educational bureaucracy. Organizational conditions and the pressures of various groups combined to prevent any significant change in either the educational system or the patterns of segregation in the city.

Gary Orfield analyzed the impact of the United States Office of Education, the Justice Department, and other federal, state, and local efforts to prevent or cause the desegregation of school systems in the South.[3] The balance of power, particularly veto power, existing among the various governmental agencies, community groups, and educational systems is clearly demonstrated in Orfield's analysis. The process of desegregation was delayed for some time by the counter forces of several governmental agencies.

Education, Technology, and Social Change

Much has been written about the role of technology in the process of economic and industrial development, while little attention has been given to the role of education in this process. However, there is no doubt that the schools' training in science and technology has contributed much to the development of new methods and materials which made a major impact on our standards and styles of living. To a large extent, agriculture, engineering, and much of science training have been devoted to the short-term goals of economic profits and meeting immediate social needs. This is not an articulated goal of the elementary and secondary schools, but the widespread teaching of the value of technological change for immediate needs with little critical evaluation permeates the entire educational system.

The effect of education as a whole, therefore, is to increase the speed with which technological and material changes are diffused throughout the society. The more extensive the education in science and in communication skill, the more willing the citizen is to accept improved methods of production, tools, and machines. The more educated citizens are also likely to develop an awareness of many more ways for spending their resources; and, indirectly, advanced education, through its association with greater power and affluence, increases the ability of individuals, groups, and societies to experiment with new ways of doing things. In this way, the educational system contributes to a better world for some in the areas of health, labor-saving devices, and related fields. On the other hand, education and technology contribute to pollution, the maintenance of inequitable and freedom-restricting governments, vehicles for waging war, propaganda strategies, and delinquency.

[3] Gary Orfield, *The Reconstruction of Southern Education* (New York: Wiley Interscience, A Division of John Wiley & Sons, Inc., 1969).

The extent to which education in the scientific and technological aspects of life can contribute to the solution or creation of such problems as war, crime, poverty, intergroup conflict, labor-management conflict, and other social questions is not clear. However, there are problems which many persons have in mind when they call on education to make a better world. The physical and biological sciences or other areas in which the schools are free to stimulate change may produce some desired modification in the conditions causing these problems. However, the overall or by-product effects of the scientific and technological changes to which the schools contribute probably also serve to complicate the social problems of a given time.

It is precisely here that one of the major difficulties of education occurs. Education in every society of every political, economic, and value persuasion is expected to stimulate change in the material and technological realm and at the same time to preserve the current economic system, to demonstrate that the enemy is always to blame for war, to maintain permanent patterns of family relations, to teach respect for societal views on property, and to protect the elite classes. In some societies this is done by perpetuating the belief that the poor are inherently lazy, "no account" people for whom nothing can be done. In other words, the educational system is expected to prevent change in the sentiments and beliefs concerned with human values, at the same time that it teaches a science and technology almost certain to make some forms of human relations obsolete.[4]

Education, Values, and Social Change

In many respects, the transmission of the values of the society as defined by adults is an extremely important and basically conservative function of the educational system. However, the schools tend, as Banks suggests, to create a mental set for change by introducing new needs and expectations.[5] As we noted, the teaching of science and technology serves to bring about change. In Western industrialized societies, the transmission of scientific and technological knowledge is highly valued and certainly a part of the social norms. The effect of education may be greatly modified by the value which the society places on change and stability. In the industrialized nations, society values change in technology very highly, and such values are related to the whole notion of progress or retardation in our affluence and comfort of living. In these circumstances education is valued as a means of promoting pro-

[4] See Robert and Helen Lynd, *Middletown in Transition* (New York: Harcourt, Brace, 1937), pp. 204–41, for an excellent illustration of the dilemma in one American city.

[5] Banks, *The Sociology of Education.*

gress. In other societies the norms relevant to the processes of change are drastically different. Many South Asians commonly accept hardships and inconveniences with a belief, often fostered in schools, that one should "make do" with what is available. Obviously, if an educational system transmits the norms and values of accepting a situation as it is, the status quo is more likely to be maintained than if progress is promoted. In short, education affects and is affected by the whole complex of norms and values associated with change in the society.[6]

Religion, Education, and Social Change

There is some evidence that the social effects of education vary with religious sponsorship or control of schooling. In societies with strong and socially dominant religious forces operating to control education there is a tendency to use the schools to maintain the status quo. If the educational program is designed to maintain a religious order that opposes significant social and economic changes, and increase in such education is unlikely to produce such changes. Armer and Youtz found, for example, that years of education in Muslim schools were negatively associated with individual modernity in Northern Nigeria.[7] In underdeveloped societies, the traditional religions play an important role in maintaining the social order. The intended education provided by religious leaders of the established and dominant religions is likely to be conservative rather than liberal or radical.

We hasten to add, however, that religious groups are not always conservative in their use of education. Many religious groups in both Eastern and Western hemispheres have sponsored educational programs to foster major changes in their society. Myrdal maintains that Buddhism encouraged revolt against the caste system which was supported by Hinduism in India.[8] A Buddist educational system may be a major force in changing the social structure, while education in Hindism may serve to maintain the stratification system. To further complicate matters, religious groups may not agree among themselves on political, economic, military, governmental, or educational values. A consequence is that often there are differing and contesting pressures put on the schools which emanate from the same religious organization. For example, the Catholic schools in New Orleans were desegregated before the public schools. On the other hand, Catholics in outlying parishes were able to

[6] See Gunnar Myrdal, *The Asian Drama*, vol. 3 (New York: Pantheon, A Division of Random House, 1968), Chapter 31.

[7] Michael Armer and Robert Youtz, "Formal Education and Individual Modernity in African Society," *American Journal of Sociology*, vol. 76, no. 4 (January 1971), pp. 604–26.

[8] Myrdal, *The Asian Drama.*

resist desegregation for a longer period. The interrelationship of religious agencies and education in the change process may vary in different situations. Religion-sponsored education may enhance or retard social change.

Communication, Education, and Social Change

The discovery and invention of new knowledge and its dissemination throughout society are major functions of the educational system. The educational dissemination process is inextricably related to the various means of communication systems.

Institutions of higher education dedicate a significant portion of their resources to research programs designed to discover and develop new knowledge. But education at all levels is dedicated to the diffusion and dissemination of both old and new knowledge, throughout the society. At all levels, but particularly in higher education, the media—publications, radio, television, films—are utilized in this process. As a disseminator, education is a part of the mass communication system. The discoverer or inventor of a new idea is not likely to initiate significant change unless relevant related ideas are available for him or her to combine it with. Furthermore, new inventions are much more likely to occur if the inventor has access to a wide range of related knowledge which may be combined in new ways. The institutions producing scholarly lectures, discussions, journals, books, and other mass communications all contribute to the creation and diffusion of new ideas.

Educational institutions are expected to preserve the old by teaching it to new members of the society, but they are also expected to communicate new ideas. New ideas often subvert old traditions. In addition, the transmission of old ideas at times serves an innovative function. Also, old ideas in new combinations often produce new knowledge and thereby produce change. Thus education designed to prevent change may unintentionally serve a contrary function. Actually it is impossible for the educational institutions to function so as to prevent change. Either old or new knowledge communicated to students diffuses knowledge, and widespread diffusion of knowledge results in changes in political, economic, family, religious, and governing institutions. The media by which both old and new knowledge are disseminated are clearly involved in the interaction of forces related to the processes of social change.

The relevance of communication and related transportation is illustrated by the international or cross-cultural diffusion of knowledge. Rapid transportation and instantaneous communication through modern electronic media have facilitated the dissemination of knowledge enormously. The continual communication between scholars and educators in various parts of the world has facilitated the development of new knowledge at a rapid pace. Personnel in the institutions of higher education are in continual and instantaneous communication with their colleagues in all parts of the world. This international diffusion is certainly a factor in the processes of social change throughout the world. Any understanding of the role of education in this process must therefore recognize the relation of education to the mass communications system.

Multiple Causes and Interaction in Change

In the preceding paragraphs we have briefly identified some of the other components of a social system which interact with education to facilitate or impede social change. Only a few conditions have been identified, but they serve to illustrate the complex patterns of interaction which are involved. Just as the forces which produce change are many and often subtle, so are the consequences of these forces. Although educators have tended to concentrate on industrialization and related economic changes, it must be recognized that a wide range of cultural and social structure variables may be affected by the changes that occur. Any change in one unit of society is felt in the other units.

Efforts to determine which institution is the most important in social change may be fruitless. Hydrogen is not twice as important as oxygen in the existence of water simply because H_2O has two parts of hydrogen to one part of oxygen. Without oxygen, water would not exist. Without some type of educational system, an industrialized society would not exist. An examination of the reciprocal nature of the relationships between education and other aspects of the social environment will assist in understanding the process of social change. The subtle and obvious contributions of education to manpower, income, conditions of production, life styles, attitudes, institutional organizations, and norms require elaboration. The linkage of social systems involved in the maintenance or change of the total society is a complex one. Education is a part of that process.

In the next section, we turn our attention to an analysis of the role of education in relation to other forces in modernizing societies.

Education and Modernization

Much of the discussion about how to achieve social change in recent decades has focused on educational and economic developments in Asian, Middle-Eastern, African, and Latin-American societies. Systematic attempts to change the nations of these areas from "traditional" to "modern" societies have involved extensive educational programs. Canada, the United States, China, the Soviet Union, Japan, and the nations of

Western Europe have all contributed in varying degrees to the modernization of the less developed nations. Both the contributors and the recipients of such efforts have perceived education as a major instrument for modernization. In doing so, these nations place great emphasis upon education's role in the development of modern society. To a large extent this has been a matter of faith. We simply do not know the precise manner by which education initiates, impedes, or facilitates social change in general, let alone the modernization process in particular. We do know, however, about some of the possible contributions of education to modernization, and scholars are rapidly adding to our knowledge.

The Process of Modernization

Various terms have been used to characterize the economic and technological developments of industrialized nations. One commonly used symbol for such developments is the term "modernization" or "modern." Nations which are identified as *emerging* or *developing* are commonly and synonomously referred to as "modernizing" nations. Presumably, the idea behind the typical application of the term "modernization" to a developing society is the belief that the society is emerging from a more traditional society into a more valued "modern" society. The idea that all new economic, political, and social developments are progressive is not easily agreed upon by most scholars of social change. What is progress to one may not be progress to another.

Further analysis of modernization also reveals that the concept is often applied and limited to economic developments. The notion that progress is attached to certain economic developments may be appropriate, particularly when they are viewed as a society's achievement of planned economic goals. In this way, the increased production of goods and services to satisfy the rising felt needs or wants of a society may be viewed as progress. By the same token, any increases in pollution and health hazards which may be undesired outcomes of the same increased production would not be considered progress. Perhaps it would be best to consider progress as an evaluation of the outcomes of productivity or modernization, which may or may not be appropriate depending upon one's focus.

Concerning the question of what leads to the achievement of economic goals, a number of generalizations have been made. An important one is that the level of productivity in traditional and sacred societies is decidedly lower than in rapidly changing and secular societies.[9] It

[9] See, for example, Paul Green, "Towards a Theory of the Social Bond," mimeographed (Kalamazoo, Mich.: Western Michigan University, 1973), and Everett Rogers, "Communications in Development," *The Annals*, vol. 412 (March 1974), pp. 44–53, for a treatment of the concept of modernization as society's ability to reflect upon and modify itself.

is contended that the process of modernization involves agencies or institutions which plan and work for the achievement of economic goals. Furthermore, these agencies have the ability to obtain feedback information concerning the consequences of their efforts. Skill in the area of communications management is as important as technological skill in the production of goods and services in modern societies. In one sense, the ability of a society to reflect on and modify itself to achieve planned goals is an index of modern society.

A more commonly used index of productivity is the gross national product per capita. This reflects the level of income and the production of food and shelter and other goods as priced in the market system. The processes of economic development are generally associated with the industrial revolution, including the change from village handicraft production to factory-type production with power-driven machinery. Such production requires capital investment in the expanded technology essential to an industrialized society. Although economic aspects have been emphasized in the characterization of the development or modernization processes, several other characteristics are integral parts of the process.[10]

The first of these is the spatial mobility of population, the associated willingness to move and appreciation of life in other locations. Traditional societies have been characterized by residence in relatively isolated villages with a local sphere of knowledge and communication. Such people have seldom migrated far beyond the local community boundaries. Modern societies, in contrast, have people with high mobility rates and knowledge of the world outside their local communities of residence. Mobility in highly industrialized societies involves movement from one industrialized center to another; in the modernization process it is characterized by mobility from rural villages to urban centers. The patterns of mobility and industrialization, of course, are highly associated with the process of urbanization, since sources of power, patterns of trade, and the factory mass-production system concentrate population in urban centers.

Closely associated with the whole movement to urban centers and knowledge of the other societies is the use of communication media other than that of face-to-face or primary group interaction. In a traditional society the communication is almost exclusively based on face-to-face personal relationships. Modernization is much more dependent on the mass media for communication with those outside the immediate primary group. Communication through a printed language, of course, involves literacy. The modernization process therefore is generally associated with

[10] See David Lerner, *The Passing of Traditional Society* (New York: The Free Press, 1958), Chapter 2, for an elaboration of the interrelated aspects of modernization.

an increase in literacy. At this point the educational system makes a major contribution to the modernization process.

The process of modernization also involves changes in political and governmental organization. Traditional societies have commonly been controlled through feudal or tribal types of government or colonial domination. On the other hand, modernization is associated with more citizen participation in the political processes.

There are other concomitants of modernization. For example, as people have become more urbanized and mobile and as their communication and knowledge of the outside world have increased, changes in the traditional family structure also occur. Women are more likely to participate in economic and political activities and numerous social groups outside the family system. Some economic functions of the family may be transferred to other production units as urbanization occurs. The stratification system in the modernized society is also likely to provide more opportunities for status mobility as well as geographic mobility than in traditional societies. The attitude of people toward change and their ability to see themselves in new roles and new situations develop through the expanded interactions which people have. Certainly one of education's main functions is training people to perform new roles.

The characteristics of a modern society are highly interrelated and the process of modernization probably involves concurrent changes in all those characteristics. The function of education in modernization is not easily segregated from mobility, industrialization, mass communication, or political changes. Although the process is a complex one, involving many factors, some indicators of the correlation between education and other factors in modernization are available. A brief examination of these follows.

Education and Economic Development

Clearly, the extent to which the population is educated is associated with the productivity of the nations of the world. While levels of education and economic productivity are clearly correlated, the reasons for this correlation are not clear. Drawing on an earlier study, economist Mary Jean Bowman[11] indicates that economic productivity in an earlier period may be a better predictor of the level of education than the reverse. However, she maintains that "the world-wide emphasis on education both as an instrumental variable in public policy oriented to

[11] Mary Jean Bowman, "The Human Investment Revolution in Economic Thought," *Sociology of Education*, vol. 39, no. 2 (1966), pp. 111–37. This is an analysis of the research on economics of education with particular emphasis on the investment in human resources through education.

growth and as a national prestige symbol is a situation in which schooling must almost inevitably lead economic development rather than following upon it."[12] The emphasis upon education in developing nations may therefore create a situation in which the educational level increases before changes occur in economic productivity. There may be several intervening variables, or both the development of education and productivity may result from a common set of variables which are characteristic of developing societies.

Although there have been many studies of the relationship of investment in education to economic growth, this has all occurred in the last couple of decades, and most of these studies have been made in highly developed nations. It is impossible, therefore, to indicate in which manner the investment in education will produce economic growth or change in the less industrialized nations. Furthermore, most of these studies have focused on identification of manpower needs and have not given much attention to the education necessary to produce needed manpower. On the other hand, some recent cost-benefit analyses have attempted to identify the contribution of various types of education to economic returns for both the individual and for society, and are giving promising results. Such studies demonstrate the complexity of the question and indicate that there are various factors in both the educational system and society generally which may affect the contribution of education to economic development. Myrdal, for example, emphasizes the importance of health and energy of the people in relation to the educational investment.[13] Bowman also emphasized the "extreme complexity of the web of interdependencies" in analyzing the relationships between the educational institutions.[14]

Education and Social Development

When one examines the relation of education to other aspects of the modernization process the data available are decidedly more limited than those concerning education and economic development. Most of the less industrialized nations have placed a great emphasis upon basic education and how it facilitates the processes of social change.

We have noted that a whole complex of interrelated social factors are involved in the development or modernization process. Education of various types is clearly associated with many of these: urbanization, vertical and geographic mobility, birth rates, status of women, political participation, and other social variables as well as the economic output.

[12] Ibid., p. 130.

[13] Myrdal, *The Asian Drama,* pp. 1533–58.

[14] Bowman, "Human Investment Revolution," p. 136.

We cannot say with assurance, however, that increases in education in all circumstances will automatically bring about changes in the other aspects of society. The particular contribution of education to other social change may vary with the level of economic development and other social conditions.

In several nations there apparently has been an overinvestment in education when allocation of resources to other capital investment might have resulted in greater development. The education of personnel for jobs that are not yet available produces some unemployment problems and possible wastage of resources in certain stages of development. Numerous people have pointed out the dangers to individuals and social institutions of a level of education which exceeds the ability of the society to absorb educated personnel. However, some degree of overeducation may be a desirable motivator for modernization. Although there is no hard research evidence to substantiate such a hypothesis, it seems reasonable that the education of a significant number of people beyond the ability of the economy to fully utilize their skills may frustrate these people and motivate them to demand more rapid social change than might otherwise occur. This hypothesis develops out of the notion that a population dissatisfied with the situation as it is may be motivated to act in a manner that produces change. As we pointed out earlier, a society that accepts the situation as it is and makes do with whatever is available is not likely to change rapidly. We have no basis upon which to suggest the degree of discontent and dissatisfaction desirable for the maximization of social and economic development. It does seem, however, that education beyond the level of full utilization may produce such dissatisfaction.

Education, Social Mobility, and Modernization

One of the complications in analyzing the relation of education to social and economic development is its function in social mobility and status determination. Education is highly valued in most societies for reasons that may or may not be associated with economic productivity or other changes in the society. Education is perceived as intrinsically good or valuable both for the individual and for the society as a whole. In addition to this, education generally provides prestige in the social structure roughly commensurate with the level of education obtained. This symbolic value of education, however, may not be directly correlated with occupational status or economic productivity. In numerous societies the acquisition of elementary or higher levels of education provides a symbolic status that makes it inappropriate for a person with a higher education to work in occupations that are considered demeaning or of lower status.

Although there is a general idea that vertical mobility is closely related and dependent upon formal education, such a conclusion must be made very cautiously. Anderson has pointed out that although the school exerts a strong influence on an individual's chances to move upward or downward, only a modest part of all mobility is linked to education.[15] The popular image, however, serves to motivate large numbers of people in many societies to acquire an education. It seems likely therefore that the level of educational demand may be somewhat in advance of the ability of the society to absorb people with given levels of training in maximally productive capacities. Many manpower specialists looking at the specific occupational needs of society have been disturbed by this tendency to have a surplus of educated personnel, at various levels or stages of development. Since education has a symbolic value in the status system, it is likely to be used as a means of social mobility in such manner that it creates some overeducation for the maximum economic productivity. Although the effect of this surplus has not been systematically analyzed, it may tend to speed up the change process because of dissatisfaction with economic development.

Types of Education and Economic Development

A surplus of highly educated personnel with advanced degrees in social science or law, for example, along with a shortage of agricultural and industrial technicians has led manpower specialists to be highly critical of the types of education emphasized in traditional societies. The assumption is that if the proper number of people were given appropriate types of education, a maximum level of employment and productivity could be achieved. This has generally resulted in the advocacy of more vocational and technical education and less higher education in the nontechnical fields. It has also been assumed that people educated in specific vocational or technical fields will be employed in these needed occupations. Foster's study of Ghanian education led to a widespread questioning of this assumption.[16] He found that many vocationally trained students were not engaged in the specific occupations for which they were trained but rather were employed in clerical and commercial jobs where there was great demand and higher pay. Academically educated persons were somewhat more advantageously placed in similar jobs. This increased the demand for such academic education. Other

[15] C. Arnold Anderson, "A Skeptical Note on Education and Mobility," in Halsey, Floud and Anderson, *Education, Economy, and Society* (New York: The Free Press, 1961).

[16] Phillips Foster, "The Vocational School Fallacy in Development Planning," in Anderson and Bowman, *Education and Economic Development* (Chicago: Aldine Press, 1966).

studies using cost-benefit analysis as well as some manpower planning methods have tended to confirm Foster's findings.[17] In both Argentina and Nigeria the contribution of vocational and technical education to economic development was not commensurate with the cost of such education. Perhaps, at the elementary and secondary levels a general and nontechnical education may contribute as much to economic development as the technically specific vocational education which has been advocated by manpower planners.[18]

Whatever the focus, it does appear that a significant proportion of society must have an elementary education as a necessary, if not sufficient condition for economic productivity beyond a certain level. The appropriate balance of secondary and higher education for the maximization of productivity is not, however, clear.

It is very probable that some types of education serve to preserve or maintain the status quo rather than stimulate social change. The education of a limited elite group in traditional patterns of education at various levels may serve to maintain the status quo.[19] Schools that are designed to teach the traditional attitudes and beliefs which maintain the society as it has been are not as likely to produce change as those which are designed to motivate students for the kinds of activities that would be associated with a different future. This outcome, of course, involved the nature of the curriculum and the characteristics of the teachers. Differences in curriculum and the quality of teacher preparations may both be associated with the degree of social change, but the precise manner in which these occur is certainly not known at this time. It seems reasonable to hypothesize that a school with teachers who are educated to function as change agents in the community and who exhibit behavior and attitudes conducive to change will produce more change than one in which teachers are oriented toward the maintenance of the society. Some theorize that the amount of prior education and quality of teacher training may be associated with the degree to which the schools contribute to social change. We know of no evidence, however, which indicates that level or type of teacher preparation is associated with social change.

Education and Modern Attitudes and Values

The role of education in the development of modern nations involves changing individual behavior, attitudes, and values, as well as the economic and social institutions of the society. As we have noted in earlier discussions, various scholars concerned with the modernization process

[17] See Bowman, "Human Investment Revolution," pp. 135–36.

[18] Anderson and Bowman, *Education and Economic Development.*

[19] Myrdal, *The Asian Drama,* pp. 1687–1828.

recognize the importance of the individual attitudes and values.[20] The exact nature of the personal qualities which characterize modern man have not been fully identified, but Inkles has identified a set of personal qualities that fit a theoretical conception of modern man and is typical of such individuals in six countries.

> Central to this syndrome are: (1) openness to new experience, both with people and with new ways of doing things such as attempting to control births; (2) the assertion of increasing independence from the authority of traditional figures like parents and priests and a shift of allegiance to leaders of government, public affairs, trade unions, cooperatives, and the like; (3) belief in the efficacy of science and medicine, and a general abandonment of passivity and fatalism in the face of life's difficulties; and (4) ambition for oneself and one's children to achieve high occupational and educational goals. Men who manifest these characteristics (5) like people to be on time and show an interest in carefully planning their affairs in advance. It is also part of this syndrome to (6) show strong interest and take an active part in civic and community affairs and local politics; and (7) to strive energetically to keep up with the news, and within this effort to prefer news of national and international import over items dealing with sports, religion, or purely local affairs.[21]

The personal characteristics of modern man are certainly associated with related characteristics of modern societies. Although various social scientists have emphasized different aspects of society they are clearly interrelated and associated with the attitudes, values, and behavior of the people in the society.[22]

Our concern is the extent to which education may produce the individual attitudes and values essential for modernization. It has frequently been assumed that education in general has the effect of producing such attitudes as openness for experience, belief in the possibility of change, progress, independence from traditional family and village ties, and similar attitudes. There is limited evidence concerning the actual effect of education on such attitudes and value orientations. One hypothesis concerning this relationship that has guided educational planning holds that different types of education differentially affect such attitudes and values. Education programs designed to perpetuate the traditional beliefs and attitudes in traditional societies are not likely to produce modern societies. In contrast, many have hypothesized that education

---

[20] See Armer and Youtz, "Formal Education and Individual Modernity"; Myrdal, *The Asian Drama;* and Alex Inkles, "Making Men Modern: On the Causes and Consequences of Individual Change in Six Developing Countries," *American Journal of Sociology,* vol. 75, no. 2 (1969), pp. 208–25.

[21] Ibid., p. 210.

[22] See Lerner, *Passing of Traditional Society.*

characteristic of modern western societies will produce such results. It has also been hypothesized that some traditional values, attitudes, or behavior patterns may be more amenable to change than others. These questions have been examined by Armer and Youtz[23] in an analysis of the effects of education on Nigerian students' value orientation as measured by a scale designed for use in the developing countries. A factor analysis of the responses of over 500 young men interviewed in a Northern Nigerian city indicated that the principal components of modernity were (1) independence from family, (2) ethnic equality, (3) empiricism, (4) mastery of efficacy, (5) receptivity to change, and (6) a future orientation.

The value orientations of the young men in this sample were clearly correlated with the amount of Western-type education they had received. It is important to recognize that the type of education is a relevant factor. Northern Nigeria has a number of well organized religious schools whose curriculum is primarily focused on teaching the Koran. The extent of education in these schools was not positively related to individual modernity. In fact, there is a low, but significant, negative correlation between the amount of schooling in the Koranic schools and the individual scores on the modernity scale. There mere presence in organized schools therefore does not guarantee that individual values related to modern society will be achieved. Although there are some differences among the Western secondary schools in Northern Nigeria, all seem to have a significant effect on the individual's modernity. The more academically oriented secondary schools are more highly related to production of modern attitudes than are the craft, technical, or clerical schools, but the latter as well as the teacher-training schools have a significant impact on the individual's value orientation.

Armer and Youtz sought to determine whether the relationship between Western education and modernity might be explained by other factors which are likely to effect such value orientations. They found that exposure to mass media, membership in voluntary associations, father's occupation, father's formal education or knowledge of English, the parent's ethnic background, or family income did not explain the association between level of Western education and modernity. Although these background factors as well as individual intelligence test scores are related to modernity scores, the correlation between individual value orientations and level of Western-type education clearly persisted when each of these factors was controlled. It seems apparent, therefore, that Western-type education does have an effect on these youths' value orientations as identified in the scale used.

Although we do not have extensive data, the research available indicates that some types of education at least are related to the values,

[23] Armer and Youtz, "Formal Education and Individual Modernity."

attitudes, and beliefs of individuals in some developing nations. It would appear to be essential that individual attitudes, values, and behavior of students as well as social institutions and organizations change if a society is to develop into modern-type society. The limited evidence available suggests that education contributes to both such types of changes under certain conditions. The particular type of education necessary for such changes may vary from one society to another and from one period to another. It should be recognized, however, that education may be designed to perpetuate the status quo and orient people to the traditional society as well as toward a modern society.

Education and Diffusion

We should not overlook the fact that the concept of modernization of society is derived from a variety of societies with differing economic and social conditions. If Asian and African nations were still completely isolated from European and American societies, the whole issue of modernization would probably be irrelevant. We know that the diffusion of knowledge is a major factor in the processes of social change. Education certainly plays a significant role in this diffusion process. Literacy is perhaps of primary significance in providing the base for the diffusion of knowledge across cultures. Media other than the printed word are of course becoming increasingly important, but the level of education in a society is related to the degree of cross-cultural diffusion into that society.

Of particular significance in the cross-cultural diffusion is the process of foreign education and exchange of educated persons. Many societies have sent significant numbers to other countries for higher education. This serves to provide highly educated personnel in the professions and other fields and no doubt contributes to the modernization process. The individuals educated in universities abroad acquire much more than particular competence in engineering or science or agriculture. Such persons also acquire a knowledge of a different culture and return with many new beliefs and attitudes which may contribute to the processes of change in their native society.

Nations wishing to modernize have also frequently imported educators from more industrialized societies to assist in developing modern economic and social systems. This exchange of persons, which is associated with rapid transportation and communication systems, has greatly facilitated the diffusion of knowledge and culture throughout the world.

In recent years, several international organizations of educators and scholars in various fields have been formed. These organizations foster the exchange of knowledge and the motivation to seek new knowledge on a world wide basis. Such organizations would not exist without a significant number of highly educated people in the various societies. The role of organized higher education in diffusion and its concomitant condition—social change—is clear. The international or third culture of educated scientists and professional personnel makes a definite contribution to the process of modernization throughout the world.[24]

Change in Educational System

We have noted in Chapter 2 that the educational system is not an isolated social system, but rather one that is open to interaction with other social forces. Just as education may have some impact on other aspects of the society, so the other aspects of society affect the processes of change within the educational institutions. Significant research on this process has occurred in the past few decades.[25] Much of this research has focused on the adoption of new educational practices with particular reference to the diffusion and adoption of new media in the schools. Relatively less analysis of the process of changing school organization or the basic school curriculum is available.

Like other segments of society, schools are more likely to adopt technological changes than they are new organizations of authority, power, and purpose. The adoption of new buildings, textbooks, new media materials, and new equipment is likely to occur rather readily. This is no doubt associated with the belief system that new machines like automobiles or radios are better than old ones. The changes in school buildings in the last 25 years would certainly suggest considerable acceptance of new modes of educational plant construction. Such changes have some impact on other aspects of the educational institution. The installation of a language laboratory, for example, may modify the pattern of foreign language instruction significantly and also the time schedule within the school system.

Changes in educational institutions are, of course, strongly related to the other social forces impinging on the schools. Changes in the curriculum are likely to occur with concomitant changes in other aspects of the society. This is well illustrated by the significant changes in the science and mathematics curricula in the schools which resulted, in part at least, from concern about national defense generated by the first Russian Sputnik launching in the late 1950s. The extensive consolidation and reorganization of school districts in recent decades has been gener-

[24] John Useem, "The Study of Cultures," *Sociological Focus*, vol. 4, no. 4 (1971), and *Reconstituting the Human Community, A Report of Inquiries Concerning Cultural Relations for the Future* (New Haven, Conn.: Hazen Foundation, 1972).

[25] See Matthew B. Miles, ed., *Innovation in Education* (New York: Bureau of Publications, Teachers College, Columbia University, 1964), for an analysis of the early research in this area.

ated to considerable degree by changes in population, transportation patterns, and urbanization. Changes in school organization generated by other forces in the society may set in motion other changes within the educational institution. For example, the change in the science and mathematics curricula generated by national defense concerns has had a significant impact on curricula in other fields such as social studies.

Resistance to Educational Change

Resistance to change in educational practice is also related to beliefs and practices in the society generally, but resistance also results from the forces tending to maintain the established educational system and structure.[26] Changes in some practices would require a major restructuring of the entire system. This is illustrated by the persistent practice of "aptitude" testing as a basis for college or graduate school admission and assignment to various educational programs, even though we know that these tests add little to the prediction of which students will acquire the knowledge indicated or complete the educational program. It is also common in some communities to assign children identified as retarded to special classes, although research has shown some would benefit more if placed in regular classrooms.[27] It is entirely possible that these practices serve other functions desired by the teachers and the community. The general feeling among teachers that it is more convenient or easier to teach a class with only certain kinds of students tends to perpetuate the practice and the assumptions which justify it.

In a similar manner we continue types of curricula or educational programs which have been highly functional at one period but cease to serve a significant purpose. Certain secondary school vocational education curricula served a very useful role several decades ago when only a small proportion of the population went beyond high school for vocational or technical training. It is doubtful, however, that many of these programs serve a useful function at a time when the majority of students are taking some kind of post-high-school training for a wide range of occupational roles. However, the establishment of programs with special equipment, specialized personnel and an organization which is designed to perpetuate itself makes change difficult. Change will not occur on the basis of scientific knowledge alone.[28]

Many other illustrations could be cited to indicate the persistence of educational patterns and practices beyond a time when they are

[26] See Rogers, *One Ten Livingston Street,* and Orfield, *Reconstruction of Southern Education.*

[27] Floyd M. Dunn, "Special Education for the Mildly Retarded—Is Much of It Justifiable?" *Exceptional Children,* vol. 35, no. 1 (1968), pp. 5–22.

[28] See Sam Sieber, "Images of the Practitioner and Strategies of Educational Change," *Sociology of Education,* Fall 1972, vol. 45, no. 4, pp. 362–385.

functional in the society. In this regard, education is not different from other social institutions and organizations. There is an extensive body of data which indicates that many features of society persist beyond the time for which they were appropriate. Such institutional resistence to change is characteristic of many institutions, including our schools. Although farmers have been considered rather conservative, Eicholz and Rogers found that innovation in agriculture came much easier than educational innovation.[29] They concluded that the lack of economic incentives for change hindered the development of educational change agents. They noted that the salaries of teachers are not generally affected by the innovations adopted in the classroom.

In spite of the relatively slow adoption of new practices, it is clear that many changes have occurred in education over recent decades. Some practices, of course, have been adopted much more readily than others. Considerable attention has been given to research designed to explain the differences in these rates. Although there may be many factors affecting the rate at which new practices are adopted, we should recognize the possibility that educators reject new practices because they believe such practices will not improve the quality of learning. The emphasis upon the adoption of new practices has been so great in recent decades that some seem to assume that anything new is better and therefore should be adopted. Many new techniques and materials have not been thoroughly tested and it is quite possible that students are better educated if the new devices are not used. It is also quite possible that new practices or techniques have been adopted which contribute little or nothing to the quality of education. The difficulties of thoroughly evaluating new practices are much greater in education than in evaluating new practices to increase the yield of corn. It is therefore understandable that educators are not easily convinced of the desirability of new techniques. On the other hand, it is quite possible that factors other than the improvement of education significantly affect the adoption of new practices.

Fads and Fashions

Observation of school systems over an extended period of time suggests that educational changes occur in patterns similar to styles or fashions in clothing. For example, the recent adoption of team teaching, ungraded classrooms, and middle school organizations occurred with

[29] Gerhard Eicholz and Everett M. Rogers, "Resistance to the Adoption of Audio-Visual Aids by Elementary School Teachers: Contrasts and Similarities to Agricultural Innovation," in Miles, ed., *Innovation in Education.*

little evidence to justify such changes. It is possible that they may be temporary styles or fads in education that have little long-range persistence or impact. A couple of decades ago the core curriculum type of organization was very popular; it has apparently gone out of style in most school systems. These illustrations suggest that schools are characterized by educational fashions or fads. A school system that had not adopted some team teaching or nongraded classrooms in the early 70s was not likely to be considered modern or up to date by many educators. Such patterns of instruction may persist over a long period and be demonstrated to have superior educational value, but they may also become as outmoded as the core curriculum in the not too distant future. We suggest, therefore, that the adoption or failure to adopt new practices may, in some instances, be little affected by objective evaluation—rather they are the result of relatively nonrational conditions.

The fads or styles in educational practice may result from the fact that the new practice is never fully incorporated into the school organization. The adaption is initiated and partially implemented, but the community may turn to the initiation of new innovations before the old one is routinized.[30]

Economic Resources

Among the various factors that may affect change in education, the level of expenditures is probably mentioned more frequently than any other. Educators frequently claim that they would be able to adopt new practices and thus improve the schools if they had sufficient resources to do so. Evidence concerning the relationship between expenditure per pupil and innovation, however, is not conclusive. Helfiker found no correlation between expenditures and innovation in a study of Wisconsin school districts.[31] In contrast, however, Christie and Schribner found that expenditures may be a significant variable in innovation.[32] Furthermore, Johnston found that the most highly innovative school districts spend more money per child than do less innovative school

[30] Joseph B. Giacquinta, "The Process of Organizational Change in Schools," in Fred Kerlinger, ed., *Review of Research in Education* (Itasca, Ill.: F. E. Peacock Publishers, A publication of the American Educational Research Association, 1974), p. 200.

[31] Leo R. Helfiker, *The Relationship of School System Innovativeness to Selected Dimensions of Interpersonal Behavior in Eight School Systems. Report from the Models for Planned Educational Change Project. Technical Report No. 70.* (Washington, D.C.: U.S. Department of Health, Education and Welfare, January, 1969).

[32] Samuel G. Christie and Jay D. Schribner, "A Social System Analysis of Innovation in Sixteen School Districts," a paper presented at the American Educational Research Association Annual Meeting, Los Angeles, 1969.

districts.[33] This variation in research findings suggests that other factors which are associated with the expenditures per child are more related to innovation or change in practice than the sheer expenditures; it is not safe to assume that more money per pupil will produce improved educational practice or the acceptance of innovation generally.

Relevance of Personnel

Research on the relationship of various personnel factors to the initiation and the acceptance of change in the educational system indicates that the school principal is probably the most likely change agent in the school setting. Eicholz and Rogers found that the principal's position was the one in which change is most likely to be initiated.[34] This does not mean, however, that all principals are change agents, for Eicholz had earlier found that only one in five principals acted as a change agent.[35] Teachers apparently perceive the principal as the most likely initiator of change.[36] They ranked subject supervisors, department heads, teachers, district superintendents, school boards, central office personnel, and parents in that order after the principal. Since many principals are not perceived as innovators, there has been some effort to determine under what conditions the principal is a change agent. Research in this area has not provided any conclusive findings. It would appear, however, that principals will not be initiators of change unless there is a readiness to accept change on the part of the teachers. In any case, the school climate and interpersonal relations are important factors affecting the principal's role as an initiator of change. This is further supported by Gottlieb and Brookover, who found that teachers who are highly committed to the values of the school administration are likely to follow the administrator's lead in innovation.[37] If the administrator is perceived as desiring innovation the teachers are likely to be supportive unless the teachers differ with their administrators over important social and educational values.

[33] Homer M. Johnson, *Organizational Climate and the Climate of Educational Innovation.* (Washington, D.C.; Office of Education, Department of Health, Education and Welfare, 1969).

[34] Eicholz and Rogers, "Resistance to Adoption of Audio-Visual Aids."

[35] Gerhard Eicholz, "Development of a Rejection Classification for Newer Educational Media," (Ph.D. diss., Ohio State University, 1961).

[36] James M. Mahan, "The Teacher's View of the Principal's Role in Innovation," *The Elementary School Journal* (April 1970), pp. 359–65.

[37] David Gottlieb and Wilbur B. Brookover, *Acceptance of New Educational Practices by Elementary School Teachers: Social Factors in the Adoption of New Teaching-Learning Techniques in Elementary Schools* (East Lansing: Educational Publication Services, College of Education, Michigan State University, 1966).

There is little evidence to indicate that teachers are often leaders in innovation. In an attempt to determine whether or not teachers perceived innovation as a significant part of their job, Gottlieb and Brookover found that only three percent of the teachers in eight schools studied considered the opportunity to be creative and original as important in their role.[38] The factors which they considered important, such as a stable and secure future and an opportunity to be helpful to others, are not necessarily incompatible with the initiation of new practices, but they do suggest that innovation is not a major function of their teaching roles.

There are some areas, of course, within which the teacher can initiate change with little or no involvement of other personnel. Slight changes in classroom instructional procedure or the arrangement of curricula content within a course can be carried out with little or no cooperation or interference by other personnel.[39]

There has been much discussion about the relation of age and length of tenure of school personnel to the adoption of new practices. The evidence on this question is far from conclusive. Some studies, such as those by Pafford[40] and Helfiker,[41] found no relationship between age or length of tenure and criteria of innovation. The study by Eicholz and Rogers confirmed these findings.[42] Johnston, on the other hand, found that the innovative teachers were more likely to be younger and have shorter periods of experience than the noninnovative teachers.[43] Brookover and Gottlieb found the same situation.[44] The confused results on the question of age and experience again suggest that other variables may intervene between these factors and change or innovation.

There is some evidence that teachers who come from higher social-economic status and from urban backgrounds are somewhat more predisposed to accept change than teachers from lower status and rural backgrounds. There is also some evidence that teachers who are highly committed to professional associations are less willing to accept change than those not so committed. The increasing unionization and power of professional organizations among teachers may therefore have the effect of reducing the rates of change in education.

---

[38] Ibid.

[39] Henry M. Brickell, "State Organization for Educational Change: A Case Study and a Proposal," in Miles, ed., *Innovation in Education.*

[40] William N. Pafford, "Relationship Between Innovation and Some School Factors in Kentucky," *School and Society,* vol. 96, no. 23 (1968), pp. 438–440.

[41] Helfiker, *Relationship of School System Innovativeness to Interpersonal Behavior.*

[42] Eicholz and Rogers, "Resistance to Adoption of Audio-Visual Aids."

[43] Johnston, *Organizational Climate.*

[44] Gottlieb and Brookover, *Acceptance of New Educational Practices.*

Community Climate

We believe that variations in the rate of school adoption of new practices are related to the local community norms with regard to their schools as innovators or educational leaders. Two studies have indicated that a "climate" or norm variable is related to educational change.[45] We believe that there are schools and communities in which the adoption of new practices is widely accepted by both teachers and parents. In such communities, the failure to try new educational technology or new classroom and school organization will be perceived as evidence that the quality of the school is deteriorating. In other communities and school systems the adoption of new practices would be perceived as undesirable unless they had been well tested and accepted in other schools and communities. Such a pattern of community norms regarding the practices would explain the cycles of initiation and acceptance of various school practices in the manner of fashion or styles discussed earlier. The schools in which educational change is a valued norm are early adopters and only after these have set the style do the other schools adopt the practice. By the time the latter accept the current fad, the innovative schools may have dropped it and started a new one.

Organizational Change

The empirical analysis of the processes of change in school organization has not yet provided verified conclusions concerning the factors affecting such change.[46] One of the most widely held theories is that the participation of the members of the organization in the decision-making process is essential. Research evidence to support this "law" of change is very spotty and inadequate. The empirical evidence provides little basis for any conclusion about the effect of participation process in comparison with strategies in which the administrators initiate change without rank and file involvement in the decisions.[47] Other factors such as the characteristics of the proposed changes and of the school organization in which they are introduced may affect the extent to which changes in school organization are adopted. There is neither adequate theory or empirical research evidence to make any generalizations concerning such changes in schools.

Although considerable research on changes in educational practice has occurred, most has involved the adaption of a new technology such as television or other media with only limited attention to the organiza-

[45] Johnston, *Organizational Climate,* and Brickell, "State Organization for Educational Change."

[46] Giacquinta, "Organizational Change in Schools," pp. 178–208.

[47] Ibid., p. 188.

tional changes involved. An explanation of the failure of the Midwest Airborne educational television experiment may lie in the failure to recognize the changes in school organization that were necessary to incorporate Airborne televised instruction in the school social system. Changes in the teacher's classroom role, the instructional schedule, and numerous other aspects of the organization were necessary for this innovation to be adapted. Although the instruction provided on the air may have been superior to the instruction given by local teachers, the organization of schools were not changed sufficiently to use this instruction except on an occasional basis in a part of their classes. An analysis of the organizational changes necessary for use of this television instruction might have given a basis for predicting its failure. Mere exposure to a new product, even though it is superior, does not change social organization. Until we have better theory and more comprehensive knowledge of school organizational changes we will not be able to predict the outcome of proposed changes in education.

After a careful analysis of organizational change research in relation to school organizations, Johnson states:

> First, in order to achieve change there should be coordinated changes in the organization's norms and role expectations and in the values and attitudes of the members. Second, the successful introduction of change within an organization depends upon the commitment to the change of the organization's members at all levels of the authority structure.
>
> Most change programs in schools appear to be triggered and nurtured by some active person or group, either external to or within the school. Within the organization, those individuals who are most likely to be sources of constructive proposals for change typically are intelligent, cosmopolitan, high in risk-taking and autonomy, and base their proposals upon rational, objective evidence as opposed to subjective feelings.
>
> The advocates of change, when faced with rational opposition, have a choice of dealing with the resistance in a productive or unproductive way. The unproductive use of opposition entails either ignoring or submitting to the opposition. A more productive approach involves an awareness and respect for a rational opposition's position, since they have certain legitimate interests which must be taken into account and are frequently more apt to perceive the unanticipated dysfunctional consequences of the proposed changes.
>
> There are also organizational factors that influence the introduction of change. The literature emphasizes that innovative organizations are those that create conditions that allow individuals to operate in a facilitating setting. They not only tolerate divergent behavior and other forms of originality, but encourage and reward it. They promote contact with outsiders, are flexible with regard to long-range planning, and experiment with new ideas.
>
> Whether or not an innovation in a school improves its functioning is an empirical question that can be answered only by rigorous evaluation procedures. It is unfortunate, however, that educational innovations are

almost never evaluated systematically and in the absence of evaluatory evidence, educators must use inferior, substitute bases for judgment such as educational ideology, sentiment, or persuasive claims by salesmen."[48]

We would only add that changes within educational organizations are affected by changes in other aspects of the society.

Suggested Readings

Don Adams and Gerald Regan, *Schooling and Social Change in Modern America* (New York: David McKay, 1972).

Joel S. Berke, "The Role of Federal Aid in the Post-Rodriquez Period," *Education and Urban Society*, 5, no. 2 (February 1973).

Daniel Callahan and Dale C. Lake, "Changing a Community College," *Education and Urban Society*, 6, no. 1 (November 1973), pp. 22–48.

Martin Carnoy, *Education as Cultural Imperialism* (New York: David McKay, 1974).

Michael Fullan and Jan J. Loubser, "Education and Adaptive Capacity," *Sociology of Education*, 45, no. 3 (Summer 1972).

Joseph B. Giacquinta, "The Process of Change in Schools," pp. 178–208 in Fred Kerlinger, ed., *Review of Research in Education*, vol. 1 (Itasca, Ill.: F. E. Peacock Publishers, 1973).

Michael Katz, *The Irony of Early School Reform* (Cambridge, Mass.: Harvard University Press, 1968).

Henry M. Levin, "Equal Educational Opportunity and the Distribution of Educational Expenditures," *Education and Urban Society*, 5, no. 2 (February 1973).

R. I. Miller, ed., *Perspectives on Educational Change*, (New York: Appleton-Century-Crofts, 1967).

George Psacharopoulos, *Returns to Education: An International Comparison* (San Francisco: Jossey-Bass Publishers, 1973).

Ingo Richter, "Educational Innovation and the Constitution," *Education and Urban Society*, 6, no. 1 (November 1973), pp. 5–21.

Theodore W. Schultz, ed., "Investment in Education: The Equity-Efficiency Quandary," Committee on Basic Research in Education Workshop, *Journal of Political Economy*, 80, no. 3, part 2 (May/June 1972).

Guy E. Swanson, *Social Change* (Glenview, Ill.: Scott Foresman & Co., 1971), p. 183.

Martin Trow, "The Expansion and Transformation of Higher Education," (New York: General Learning Press, 1972).

Michalina Vaughan and Margaret Scotford Archer, *Social Conflict and Educational Change in England and France 1789–1848* (New York: Cambridge University Press, 1972.)

[48] David W. Johnson, *The Social Psychology of Education*, (New York: Holt, Rinehart and Winston, 1970), pp. 283–84. Reprinted by permission of Holt, Rinehart and Winston and David Johnson.

5

Education and Social Stratification

THE CONCEPT of social equality has been a cherished but elusive goal in many societies. Revolutions have been inspired by this desire to eliminate social inequities. In spite of its elusive nature and the massive efforts to achieve the goal of equality, every society has maintained various degrees of inequality and stratification throughout the centuries. Governmental, economic, and numerous other social institutions have operated in ways that maintain unequal strata in America as well as in other societies. The educational institutions are no exception. The schools of most nations in varying degrees are organized so that students from different social strata are frequently provided different education. This may serve to maintain or sometimes even enhance the differences.

The relation of the school to the stratification of American society is the focus of our attention in this and the following chapter. This relationship has been the subject of more research and scholarly writing than any other topic in the sociology of education. It is also a major issue in nearly all societies. National, state, and local governmental elections have been decided on issues relevant to the segregation of schools and the stratifications of American society. Although somewhat less obvious, similar issues have pervaded recent public discussions and social policies in Canada. Similarly, sociologists and other social scientists have turned their attention to the relation of the educational system to the social stratification of the society. They are interested in how social stratification affects schooling and how schooling affects social stratification.

It is impossible to examine all of the ramifications of the relationship of education to the stratification system. The focus of our attention here is on the nature of the social stratification system and the role of the educational system in maintaining or modifying the social structure. Although there are some common aspects in the relation of education to social stratification in various societies, each society is unique in some respects as well. Our analysis will be based primarily on America, but many of the forces operating there have application in other societies. One of the major factors distinguishing the American situation from that of other countries is the conflict between two sets of highly valued beliefs; the belief in equality of opportunity on one hand and the belief in individual differences and recognition of achievement on the other. It is our contention that the interaction of the educational system and the social stratification system of American society occurs within the context of highly valued beliefs which to some extent, at least, conflict with each other.

The struggle for political equality in the American Revolution reflected only a portion of a broader vision expressed in the Declaration of Independence, which held it "self-evident" that "all men are created equal." Although this ideal is rarely achieved and frequently denied, the value expressed is a potent influence in American society. Few Americans would deny a belief in the values of equal opportunity even though they may not be convinced that all men are created equal. The belief that American schools would serve to maximize the degree of equality of opportunity is nearly as universal as the belief in the value itself. The development of the concept of equality of opportunity in the United States was primarily a question of political equality derived from the British political experience. Americans, however, extended the British concept to eliminate the acceptance of an aristocracy. A belief in equal rights was the firm foundation for the practice that one man's vote is no greater than another's vote. The history of the English-speaking societies and other countries describes various steps to expand the voting rights to all citizens. This trend is punctuated by various hesitancies and stops and starts. But, overall, it has expanded voting rights among those who held no property, the poor, different racial groups, women, and, most recently, younger adults.

The belief in equal rights for all people has been associated with a high positive evaluation on an open society in which one's status is acquired through his own achievement. Although many barriers have been placed on social mobility, as we shall see, the belief that opportunity for mobility is not only desirable but essential is held by most citizens in many societies.

In contrast, of course, to the belief in equal rights and that one person is as good as another is a belief in the inherent differences among people. The concept of mobility in an open society is based on the perception that the people in some strata in the society are superior in abilities, motivation, or other characteristics to those in other strata. Differentially evaluated strata are possible only when there is a conception that people differ in merit and that position is at least partly based on such differences in capacity and performance. Mobility from one neighborhood to another and from one social group to another as well as from one occupation to another are all highly desired in American society. This reflects the differences that are believed to characterize people in these different strata.

The different values placed on equality and differential characteristics of people in American society are reflected in our differences in beliefs concerning the processes of mobility. The complex division of labor in a highly industrialized society requires some system of selection of people for various positions. Associated with our belief in an open society is the encouragement of upward mobility and a recognition of achievement which results from this striving for higher positions. This was idealized in earlier decades by the Horatio Alger stories. The process of recognizing achievement and rewarding the high achievers with higher status positions is identified by Turner as "contest mobility."[1] Rewards of higher status in an open society are received by those who have demonstrated the achievement necessary to perform in such positions.

Parallel to the open or contest mobility system which functions to some degree in American society are a number of barriers to such processes. Basic to these barriers is the belief that there are vast differences in human ability. It is therefore considered desirable to develop an efficient system of selecting those with particular abilities for various positions in the complex social and economic system. The process of identifying as early as possible those individuals who will be trained for particular positions is highly valued. Although this process of sponsored mobility[2] is perhaps more characteristic of Western European societies than American, it also characterizes much of the allocation process in the American status system. Since much of this allocation function has been assumed by educational institutions, it is essential that we understand both the stratification system and the processes by which the schools assist in allocating people to different positions.

Social Stratification

Although some Americans seem to deny the existence of social strata it is clearly established that there are ranked differences in prestige, power, and other characteristics of status among people in all societies.

[1] Ralph H. Turner, "Sponsored and Contest Mobility," *American Sociological Review,* no. 25, 1960, pp. 855–67.

[2] Ibid.

The bases for these strata are somewhat different from society to society. A brief examination of social stratification in the United States will give a foundation for our analysis of the questions of education in relation to stratification.

The system of stratification in America involves several different factors, including race, ethnic identification, occupation, income, educational level, place and type of residence, and other related variables. Racial and some ethnic categories are established by birth or family classification over which the individual has no control. In the United States these factors interact with other factors in determining what has been identified as achieved status.[3] Although other factors affect their status, the position and mobility of racial and ethnic groups such as Black, Chicano, Puerto Rican, and native American is clearly affected by categories.

Other criteria of social stratification in industrialized societies have been identified in several ways. Max Weber referred to such factors as "class, status, and party."[4] Lenski identified these aspects as privilege, prestige, and power.[5] Both refer to differentiations among social positions according to economic, honorific, and political characteristics. These three dimensions are highly interrelated and commonly identified as socioeconomic status or social class. Individuals with great wealth also are highly honored and have great power, while poor people are weak politically and have little prestige. There are exceptions to this generalization, however. School teachers may have higher prestige than plumbers or members of other occupational groups whose income is generally higher than that of teachers. The proper identification of a person in the social class system may be very complex and involve several different indexes of his or her position in society. Occupation, however, is probably the most valid single indicator of the position one occupies in the American stratification system. Occupation reflects better than any other measure the three dimensions of stratification. Blau and Duncan describe the situation as follows:

> The occupational structure in modern industrial society not only constitutes an important foundation for the main dimensions of social stratification, but also serves as the connecting link between different institutions and spheres of social life, and therein lies its great significance. The hierarachy of prestige strata and the hierarachy of economic classes have their roots in the occupational structure.[6]

[3] Ralph Linton, *The Study of Man: An Introduction* (New York and London: D. Appleton, Century Co., Inc., 1936).

[4] Hans Gerth and C. W. Mills, *From Max Weber: Essays in Sociology* (New York: Oxford University Press, 1946).

[5] G. Lenski, *Power and Privilege: A Theory of Social Stratification* (New York: McGraw-Hill Co., 1966).

[6] Peter M. Blau and Otis Dudley Duncan, *The American Occupational Structure* (New York: John Wiley & Sons, 1967).

Although the level of education which persons have acquired is quite highly correlated with occupation, the latter is more commonly used as a basis for classifying Americans in social status categories. As we shall see, education provides the means for entering some strata and a channel for mobility from one stratum to another. Indexes combining occupational level and educational level have sometimes been used as measures of social stratification, but the most widely used method is the rating of occupations.

Many studies have demonstrated that Americans identify different occupations as superior and inferior to one another. Perhaps the most commonly used rating of occupations is that first created by North and Hatt in 1947. In that study a sample of respondents were given a list of occupations with instructions "for each job mentioned, please pick out the statement that best gives your personal opinion of and general standing that such a job has."[7] The alternatives provided were "*excellent*", "*good*", "*average*", "*somewhat below average*", and "*poor*." By assigning a score of *100, 80, 60, 40,* and *20* to each of these alternatives respectively, an average rating was computed for each occupation. The result was a distribution of occupations by prestige scores such as shown in Table 5–1. Subsequent studies have resulted in slight modifications of the North-Hatt rating but the ratings have remained quite constant during the past three decades. Furthermore, the analysis of the ratings indicate that there is great similarity in occupational prestige ratings made by persons occupying widely different positions in the stratification system.

TABLE 5–1
Prestige Scores of Selected Occupations

Occupation	*Score*	*Occupation*	*Score*
Physician	93	Policeman	67
College professor	89	Mail carrier	66
Banker	88	Plumber	63
Minister	87	Garage mechanic	62
Dentist	86	Machine operator in a factory	60
Lawyer	86	Barber	59
Civil engineer	84	Clerk in a store	58
Building contractor	80	Truck driver	54
Public school teacher	78	Filling station attendant	52
Radio announcer	75	Bartender	44
Electrician	73	Janitor	44
Undertaker	72	Garbage collector	35
Bookkeeper	68		

Source: Adapted from Albert J. Reiss, Jr. et al., *Occupations and Social Status* (New York: The Free Press, 1961), pp. 54–57.

[7] Albert J. Reiss, Jr., et al., *Occupations and Social Status* (New York and Glencoe, Ill.: Free Press, 1961).

Although other factors may and do affect one's position in the stratification system, our primary reference in our discussion of social status and stratification will be to the system of occupational differences. We do this with the understanding, however, that the level of educational attainment is highly correlated with the occupation as an index of socioeconomic status. We will sometimes use broad categories of strata such as the middle class, lower class and occasionally upper class to refer to rankings in socieoconomic status. The middle class can be distinguished roughly from the lower class by the fact that they are either white collar occupations or higher skilled manual working class occupations. Lower class, in turn, refers to the lower income and less skilled manual occupations and other poor people with less education and little power or prestige. The concept lower class or lower socioeconomic status has no moral connotation or reference to such personal characteristics in our usage.

Although farming is frequently identified as a lower-level occupation, it should be recognized that the rural farm stratification system varies considerably from the urban industrial occupations. Some farmers with large farm businesses and extensive holdings are comparable to persons in managerial occupations. Smaller farm operators have somewhat lower status and farm laborers have status roughly equivalent to semiskilled or unskilled laborers.

It should also be recognized that the exact status of a particular occupation may vary somewhat from one region of the country or one community to another. The place in which one lives, whether central-city or suburban area or open country-rural, may affect somewhat the classification of one's position in society. Extensive evidence indicates, however, that there are quite consistent and clearly identifiable differences associated with occupations which provide the foundation for American stratification system.

Stratification within Education. The significance of the relation between stratification and education is readily reflected in the current literature of the sociology of education. Olive Banks devotes a major portion of her analysis to various aspects of this relationship in both Great Britain and the United States.[8] Similar reviews can be found in various American sources on sociology of education.[9]

The relationship between the stratification system and educational programs has many ramifications. At this point we are primarily concerned with the interaction between stratification in the larger society

[8] Olive Banks, *The Sociology of Education* (London: B. T. Balsford Ltd., 1968).

[9] Robert Perrucci, "Education, Stratification and Mobility," Chapter 4 in Donald Hansen and Joel Gerstl, *On Education: Sociological Perspectives* (New York: John Wiley and Sons, 1967), and W. B. Brookover and David Gottlieb, "Social Class and Education," in W. W. Charters, Jr., and N. L. Gage, *Readings in Social Psychology of Education* (Boston: Allyn and Bacon, 1963).

and the stratification, segregation, and differentiation within the school. In Chapter 13, we shall examine more carefully the impact of such school stratification on the performance of students.

Although much has changed since the earlier studies of social stratification in education, some reference to the earlier research which has influenced contemporary analyses is desirable.

One of the first studies to focus attention on education and class was the classic Middletown study during the 1920s.[10] This analysis of the Muncie, Indiana, community included social process of educating the younger generation. The Lynds found that the people of Middletown were much concerned about education. Their concern was not limited to elementary and secondary schools, but the parents wanted their children to go to college. One important factor in determining the extent of education in Middletown was the economic status of the child's family. The Lynds found that, although education was viewed by a large section of the working class as a means of salvation for their children, the school drop-out rate and the level of education achieved were clearly affected by the socioeconomic position of the family. They concluded that the lower-class children are often penalized within the school system because they do not possess the symbols, attitude, and behavior characteristics valued by the dominant social class segment of the society.

A decade later, W. Lloyd Warner and his associates carried on a series of studies of the social system in contemporary communities which analyzed the relation of social stratification to education.[11] Warner and his associates summarized the relationship of education to the stratification system in *Who Shall Be Educated?*[12] A major conclusion of this work was that schools provide a social class screening system which generally keeps upward mobility to a minimum. They found that "our schools functioning in the society with basic inequalities, facilitate the rise of a few from lower to higher levels, but continue to serve the social system by keeping down many people who try for higher places. The teacher, the school administrator, the school board, as well as the students themselves play their roles to hold people in their places in our structure."[13] Although the studies on which this conclusion was based were made three or four decades ago, there is no evidence to indicate that the conclusions are not applicable to the contemporary American schools. The differentiated curricula, particularly in the high school,

[10] Robert S. Lynd and Helen M. Lynd, *Middletown: A Study in American Culture* (New York: Harcourt, Brace, 1929).

[11] W. Lloyd Warner and Paul S. Lunt, *The Social Life of a Modern Community* (New Haven: Yale University Press, 1941).

[12] W. Lloyd Warner, Robert J. Havinghurst, and Martin B. Loeb, *Who Shall Be Educated?* (New York: Harper, 1944).

[13] Ibid., page 49.

function to differentiate children from upper-social strata from children from lower strata in much the same way today as is described in *Who Shall Be Educated.* The details of the relation of the school to the social allocation for differential status have no doubt changed since the studies of Warner and his associates, but the contribution of these analyses to understanding of the relationship of education to social stratification is a major one.

In *Elmtown's Youth,* Hollingshead analyzed the adolescent social structure of a Midwestern community, including both high school and out-of-school youth.[14] He focused on the relationship of social-class level to patterns of school attendance, school attrition, dating, school activities, employment, career expectations, and peer associations. He found significant differences in social class for each of the variables studied. These data, supplemented by case histories, provided the foundation for the conclusion that opportunities for attainment of the desired goods and values in society vary positively with the individual's position in the social-class ladder. Although other forces operate in the Elmtown community, it was clear from Hollingshead's analysis that the social system of the school reflected the community stratification system and functioned to allocate people to various social strata.

Since the early studies of social class and education a wide range of research has been devoted to various aspects of this relationship. One of these aspects is the processes by which the school affects the educational and occupational choices made by and for their students.

The Allocation Function

In addition to teaching the common cultural aspects of behavior every society has some system of allocating people to various positions in society. In industrialized societies, with extensive divisions of labor, the process is complex. People must fill the many occupational positions ranging from garbage collector to physician as well as learn to behave like females and males. This process of socializing or educating the young people for different statuses is achieved by a complex of social agencies and institutions beginning almost from the moment of birth. In technologically developed societies the educational system is one of the major agents performing this function. The level of schooling achieved, the grades assigned to students by teachers, the kinds of curricula to which students are exposed, and numerous other devices within the educational system function to determine whether the student will acquire the prerequisites required for professional, skilled, or unskilled occupations. There is hardly any position in modern society which does

[14] August Hollingshead, *Elmtown's Youth* (New York: John Wiley & Sons, 1949).

not now have associated with it some kind of certification or educational prerequisites. Therefore the type of education and of evaluation of students helps determine the positions in which young people will find themselves. Many educators do not recognize this function, but it is a major one of formal education with important implications for the social structure of society. Education cannot escape its allocation function unless a new institution is developed to implement the allocation process.

The assignment of allocation function to the educational system has had a long history in both the United States and other societies. Early in the present century, the president of Harvard University is reported to have expressed this function as follows: "Here we come to a new function for the teachers in our elementary schools, and in my judgment they have no function more important. The teachers of the elementary schools ought to sort the people and sort them by their evident or probable destinies."[15] This clearly states the belief that the schools should serve to differentiate students, classify them, and label them for future positions. In doing this, it is clear that the schools give students classified in different categories somewhat different educational programs. The superintendent of schools in Boston in 1908 expressed the need for differentiated education to achieve this purpose as follows: "Until recently [the schools] have offered equal opportunity for all to receive one kind of education, but what will make them democratic is to provide opportunity for all to receive such education as will fit them *equally* well for their particular work."[16]

This description of the school's function clearly indicates that it should develop different educational programs rather than common ones for the various categories of students in order to prepare each child for his particular life work and station in society.

The process of classification and allocation to different positions in society involves a number of decisions by the school system and a variety of organizational techniques. Evidence also indicates that the process is initiated almost at the outset of the educational career and continues throughout the educational system. Observation and systematic studies of kindergarten and early elementary grades clearly indicate that teachers classify and label children as fast or slow learners as early as the beginning of kindergarten. Rist[17] found, for example, in an all-black ghetto school a kindergarten teacher had classified her students into three

[15] Henry J. Perkinson, *The Imperfect Panacea: The American Faith in Education, 1865–1965* (New York: Random House, 1968), p. 145.

[16] Samuel Bowles, "Getting Nowhere: Programmed Class Stagnation," *Society* June 1972.

[17] Ray C. Rist, "Student Social Class and Teacher Expectations: The Self-Fulfilling Prophecy in Ghetto Schools," *Harvard Educational Review,* 40 (August 1970), pp. 411–50.

groups as early as the eighth day of kindergarten. The one group which received most favorable attention from the teacher was identified as the fast learners. These children were more likely to come from homes where one or both parents had higher levels of education and somewhat higher incomes than the children in the second and third group. Continued observation of the children in this same school as they moved through the first and second grades indicated that the fast learners remained identified and classified in separate groups and that the children who had been originally classified as slow learners did not succeed in achieving the more favorable label in either the first or the second grade class with a different teacher. The teacher's assessment of the child's presumed ability to learn, her knowledge of the family background and general reaction to the behavior of the children are primary bases for the classifications made in the early school years.

The process becomes more formalized and defined as a part of the bureaucratic system in the later secondary school years. At the high school level this is commonly identified as classification into college-bound and non-college-bound students. Analysis of the secondary school clearly demonstrates the existence of the allocation system at this level.[18] The allocation function continues in the community colleges, post-high-school technical schools, colleges, and universities.[19] The classification of students and their assignment to the particular curricula at the secondary and post-high-school levels are based on a number of factors. The teachers' assessments and recommendations are still relevant in this decision but tests of past achievement and their presumed aptitude for the academic college subjects become a significant consideration in the classification.[20] A staff of test experts and counselors may play a major role in the decision-making process. The parents are frequently consulted, and the degree to which their recommendations are determinant depends on the teacher's and counselor's perception of the parents' status and their perceived knowledge of what is "best" for their children.

The exact nature of the process as well as the outcomes of the allocation procedures varies from school to school. In secondary schools composed of students from highly educated families, essentially all students will be found in the college-bound program. The distinctions in such schools are largely based on whether there are special programs for

[18] Aaron A. Cicourel and John I. Kitsuse, *The Educational Decision-Makers*, (Indianapolis and New York: the Bobbs-Merrill Co., 1963) and Walter E. Schafer and Carol Olexa, *Tracking and Opportunity* (Scranton, Pa.: Chandler Publishing Co., 1971).

[19] Burton R. Clark, *The Open Door College: A Case Study*, (New York: McGraw-Hill, 1960).

[20] W. B. Brookover, Richard Gigliotti, Ronald Henderson, Bradley Niles, and Jeffrey Schneider, "Quality of Educational Attainment, Standardized Testing, Assessment and Accountability," *The Seventy-third Yearbook of the Society for the Study of Education*, 1974, pp. 161–91.

the "gifted" or not. Classifications may, therefore, be simply general academic or college-bound curriculum versus the enriched curriculum for a select group of students. In schools with students from lower socioeconomic-status families, the gifted curriculum is less likely to exist and in some cases the college preparatory curriculum may not be present. The allocation system thus may be facilitated in part by the segregation of students on the basis of socioeconomic status, race, or other criteria. The range and type of classifications found will commonly depend upon the range of the socioeconomic status of the student body.

Factors in Allocation Decisions. The importance of the system of allocating young people to different positions in society has focused much attention on the factors involved in this process. Most schools have some process of classification, labeling, and allocating students to different educational programs and through this to future education and/or occupational careers, but we have no systematic longitudinal studies of students from kindergarten to twelfth grade or into post-high-school education analyzing the continuing process of classification and labeling and its association with educational careers. The process generally starts early and is increasingly based upon some presumably objective classification. Cicourel and Kitsuse indicated:

> Our material suggest that the counselor's achievement-type classifications of students is a product of a subtle fusion of "rational" and common sense judgment. Belonging to the "in-group" may be given greater weight than grade point average in classifying a student as an "excellent student," or "getting into a lot of trouble" may be more important than "performing up to ability level" in deciding that a student is an "underachiever."[21]

Regardless of the exact procedure or the factors considered, it is clear that, by the junior high school years, students in most schools have been classified according to some measures of ability and achievement, behavior in school, family social status, and a variety of other variables. By high school the grouping is linked to career-oriented curricula. In the context of our beliefs about human abilities and the institutionalized processes of allocation, a complex of factors affect the decisions which teachers and students make in the allocation system.

An underlying factor in all of the allocation decisions is the assumption that children have a wide range of abilities, aptitudes, and interests which are relatively permanent factors. Assuming such wide differences in qualifications for various types of behavior—the belief in a vast range of abilities, aptitudes, and interests—it is not only appropriate but highly important that the school prepare the individual for the place where he will be most productive and most likely to be happy. It is necessary to identify the individual's abilities and interests in order to design an

[21] Cicourel and Kitsuse, *Educational Decision-Makers,* p. 71.

educational program that fits these abilities. Although we may assess the abilities in many ways, we should not lose sight of the fact that the assumption regarding differences in abilities underlies the process and justifies the differentiated programs and assignment to them.

Associated to some extent with ability, but also independently affecting allocation decisions is the social background or status of the child's family. Although the school personnel seldom say Johnny comes from a poor family, they may nevertheless assign him to a lower achievement section or the non-college-bound curriculum because of his family's social status. Children from families with low levels of education and different language and cultural styles generally do not do well on formal tests of ability and aptitude and behave in ways that the school personnel identify as characteristic of poor students. The correlation between family status and the level of education or the educational programs to which assigned[22] demonstrate that family SES and other family factors affect educational decisions. It is clear, however, that the relationship is by no means a perfect one. The system of allocation provides the means by which some students from low-status families achieve higher educational levels and high levels of occupational achievement.[23] Some students, however, do not achieve the level expected because of their presumed ability or family background, while others' school achievement is higher than would be expected as a result of these variables. Furthermore, achievement in school is not strictly limited to performance in the curricula or subject matter. Teachers and other school personnel are constantly classifying students and labeling them on the basis of this complex of interacting of variables: presumed ability, school achievement in the formal curriculum, family background, and other aspects of the student's behavior.

On the basis of these evaluations of the student, the expectations of what they will do in later school careers and in the adult world are formulated. The evaluations and expectations of the teachers are communicated to the students themselves and usually to their parents. Through their interaction with the school staff, parents, peers, and others, students come to formulate their own self-evaluations and identify their educational and occupational aspirations and plans. The students' evaluations and plans are often in accord with the plans formulated by the decision-makers in the school social system. Rehberg and Hotchkiss found that high school sophomores' educational expecta-

[22] Hobson, Julius, *vs.* Carl Hansen, 269 F. Supp. 401 (1967). Also *Congressional Record,* 90th Congress, 1st session, vol. 113, part 13, House, June 21, 1967, pp. 16721–762, and Richard Rehberg and Laurence Hotchkiss, "Educational Decision-Makers: The School Guidance Counselor and Social Mobility," *Sociology of Education,* vol. 45, no. 4 (Fall 1972), pp. 339–61.

[23] Bruce K. Eckland, "Academic Ability, Higher Education and Occupational Mobility," *American Sociological Review,* vol. 30, October 1965, pp. 735–46.

tions or plans for further education are significantly related to their intelligence scores, family SES status, parents' educational encouragement, the teacher's educational advice, the counselor's previous advice, and their previous educational plans. No single factor is the sole determinant of educational and career decisions. It is clear, however, that the school does not produce students with equal chances of choosing any occupation or status with which they might identify. It is also clear that the educational system does more than convey students from lower-class to lower-class positions or from middle-class to middle-class positions. There is some possibility of mobility in the social status system and the school also contributes to that.

Differentiation versus Equality in Education

One of the major issues among educators derives from conflicting values in the society. Educators, like others, generally believe that schools should enhance equality of opportunity among their students, but they also believe that students are inherently different in ability and the schools should efficiently prepare them for different positions in the social structure. These divergent goals for education derive from parallel goals in society: (1) the maintenance of an open society in which social class barriers are minimized and mobility within the social structure is facilitated; (2) the efficient selection of people to fill the many positions in a society with complex division of labor associated with various levels of power, wealth, and prestige. When applied to individual students these conflicting goals are characterized by degree of equality of educational attainment sought versus the enhancement of individual differences among students. The maximization of educational attainment for all students with an emphasis on equality of opportunity to achieve is associated with the goals of an open society. The enhancement of individual differences with identification, classification, and placement of students in different educational categories and programs is associated with an emphasis upon stratification and allocation to different positions in the society. The promotion of the latter goals for individual students under a policy of individualized instruction and the enhancement of differences is frequently pursued without recognition of its potential for stratification of the society.[24] Differentiated educational programs based upon race, social class, special abilities, or ethnic differences generate much feeling and ambivalence among Americans. This ambivalence reflects the conflicting values that undergird attempts to solve the dilemma between differentiated education and equality of educational opportunity. Different education for different students has sometimes

[24] See Brookover et al., "Quality of Educational Attainment."

been defined as equal education because it prepares each equally well for different statuses. A clarification of the meaning of equality of educational opportunity is therefore necessary.

Although equality of educational opportunity is highly valued in many societies there is not a universally accepted definition of its meaning. Ideas of equality of educational opportunity were essentially foreign to 19th century England. Differentiated educational opportunity was provided by the Education Act of 1870 in England. This differentiated system in England has survived to a large extent and has provided a basis for continuation of such a system in North America. Differentiated education in Britain, Canada, and the United States clearly provides unequal educational opportunity appropriate to one's presumed station in life and the maintenance of a stratified social order. The segregated black-white school system illustrates this process in the United States.

There is much confusion among both scholars and the general public in the use of the term equality in reference to education. In the United States it has included the following elements: (*a*) providing a free education up to a given level which constitutes the principal entry point to the labor force; (*b*) providing a common curriculum for all children regardless of background; (*c*) partly by design and partly because of low population density, providing that children from diverse backgrounds attend the same school; (*d*) providing an equality within a given locality, since local taxes provided the resources for schools.[25] These conceptions of equality of opportunity in education developed in a predominantly rural society. It assumed that the provision of common curricula in local schools provided equal opportunity. The obligation to use this opportunity was on the individual student and his family and no one assumed that the outcomes were appropriate criteria for defining equality. This assumption that equality is provided by relatively equivalent school facilities and curriculum inputs has continued until recent decades. Many educators and public officials still maintain that educational equality is provided by equal financial and other inputs.

The conception of differentiated educational programs for a different group of children developed early in American cities.[26] These differentiated programs were rationalized on the basis that different types of education should be provided for students destined for different future statuses in the society. It maintained that providing equal or the same educational curricula to students with different future roles was a denial of equal opportunity. Therefore, different students should be equally well prepared for the different statuses which they were going to have as adults.

[25] James S. Coleman, "The Concept of Equality of Educational Opportunity," *Harvard Educational Review*, vol. 38, no. 1, 1968, pp. 7–22.

[26] Michael B. Katz, *Class, Bureaucracy and Schools* (New York: Praeger, 1971).

Since the 1954 Supreme Court decision, the concept of equality of educational opportunity has shifted to encompass the results of the educational program. The court in that decision indicated that racially segregated schools could not be equal because the effects of such separate schools were almost certain to be different. This emphasis upon equality of results may involve two different sets of assumptions. As Coleman[27] points out, under one conception equality of educational opportunity is measured by the results of the educational program when the individual students come to school with equal backgrounds and abilities. The alternate conception of equal educational opportunity suggests that the results of the school program should be relatively equal for students with different individual inputs. Although few assume that this can be completely achieved, this latter conception of equality would indicate that equal educational quality is reached only when the results of schooling in achievement, attitudes, and other outcomes are the same for disadvantaged minorities as they are for the dominant group.

Both semantic differences and value differences produce misunderstandings regarding a reasonable conception of equality of opportunity. Komisar and Coombs[28] point out that equality has been semantically used in two distinctly different ways: "same as equal" and "equal as fitting." In the former, "equal" has a precise and singular meaning in all contexts as in the same weight, same books, or same teaching methods. Equality in the "fitting" sense has a much more indefinite meaning; one which shifts from one context to another. When equality or equal opportunity is used in the latter sense it is impossible to give a definitive interpretation without a knowledge of the ethical standards involved.

The sameness concept of equality is illustrated by: (1) the government gave equal (the same) amounts of monies to each school district on the basis of the number of students in the district and; (2) the university set equal (the same) standards for admission regardless of race by using the same criteria with all students. The "fitting" concept of equality on the other hand is illustrated by: (1) it is "fitting" for the government to give additional funds to school districts with greater numbers of educationally handicapped students in accord with the equality of opportunity principle, and (2) it is fitting for the university to give blacks and whites an equal chance to attend by taking into account differences in income, the appropriateness of tests for students from different cultures, and past exclusionary practices in accord with the principle of

[27] Coleman, "Concept of Equality of Educational Opportunity."

[28] B. Paul Komisar and Jerrold R. Coombs, "The Concept of Equality in Education," *Studies in Philosophy and Education*, vol. 3, no. 3 (Fall, 1964), reprinted in C. Tesconi, Jr., and Emanuel Hurwitz, Jr. (eds.), *Education for Whom?* (New York: Dodd, Mead and Co., 1974), p. 68.

equality of opportunity. As Komisar and Coombs note, the latter assertions of equality have the force of judgments of appropriateness rather than reports of sameness. They go on to point out that to assert that certain treatment is equal treatment when not the same is to say that it is fitting to the subjects exposed to the treatment.

Green provides a similar approach which emphasizes an analysis of inequality or equality from principles of injustice or justice based on merit and need and not on sameness.[29] Green points out the importance of our value systems for judging what is equal and what is not.

> The charge of injustice cannot be lodged against every unequal distribution. . . . We do not worry, for example, if people come out of the educational system with different abilities or competencies or knowing different things or even with different honors and awards. We expect the educational system to make discriminations of these sorts. We do not require that different people should know the same things. Neither would we be upset if it turned out that on the whole philosophers are paid more than those who know a lot about English literature or if physicists are paid more than those that know a lot about mathematics. These are inequalities in the results of the educational system and in subsequent economic "chances" related to those educational results. But such differential results present no serious problems of equality or inequality.
>
> On the other hand, we would probably regard it as a serious problem if we found that certain social groups taken as aggregates are differentially treated by the system. For example, it could be regarded as a serious social problem if the educational system, on the whole, teaches whites more than blacks, the rich more than the poor, males more than females, or the middle class more than the lower class. It can be legitimately asked, however, why the existence of this distributive inequality is more serious than the existence of the other. Both have to do with the same goods and benefits—knowledge at specifiable levels in specific areas together with the subsequent opportunities associated with possession of that knowledge.[30]

The concept of equality of educational opportunity as equal or the same has been quite acceptable when applied to availability of schools, reasonably similar facilities, or the same expenditures, but widely rejected when applied to outcomes. Green, for example, finds it quite appropriate or fitting for the educational system to produce some people with different abilities and competencies, but rejects as inappropriate such unequal outcomes if whites are taught more than blacks or the

[29] Thomas Green, "Equal Educational Opportunity: Durable Injustice," *Studies in Philosophy and Education*, 1971, pp. 121–143, and reprinted in Tesconi and Hurwitz (eds.) *Education for Whom?* (New York: Dodd, Mead and Co., 1974), pp. 78–100.

[30] Ibid., p. 126.

rich more than the poor. This indefinite conception of "equal" educational outcomes gives wide latitude for someone, presumably the educator, to judge what are appropriate or fitting outcomes for different students. At another time it was, and for many it still is, quite appropriate for blacks and poor whites to receive less than wealthy whites. Many also judge it fitting that students with presumably less intelligence be taught less in school than those with higher I.Q. scores and call the outcomes equal. The contemporary emphasis on individual differences in ability and anticipated need defines a wide range of educational outcomes as appropriate and thus "equal." We find it difficult to accept this judgment of educational equality when we reject lower outcomes for poor as unequal. The fitting concept of equal educational opportunity provides a basis for justifying many inequalities in educational outcomes. Presumed differences in ability to learn have long been used to justify inferior education. The inequalities in educational outcomes are not likely to be reduced if the appropriate or fitting conception of equality prevails.

Edmund Gordon[31] attempting to make the principle of equal results reasonably attainable in our time, suggests that equality of outcomes should refer to a minimal or basic set of behavioral goals which are essential for political and economic participation, with the provision that added optional areas of learning and specialization be available to all regardless of socioeconomic status. In essence, Gordon's idea of equality of opportunity is that everyone possible must be taught certain common skills in order that they may perform effectively in society and exercise their civil rights. This view of minimal needs is also supported by Green:

> Just as our sense of injustice may demand the creation of a minimum level of income, so it may also demand establishment of a minimum level in the receipt of educational benefits. It certainly must be true in principle that there are levels of educational achievement and points in the system of schooling where educational benefits should be distributed on grounds of need. . . . Here, need is defined not as resources needed to attain an equalization of distribution between social groups, but as minimum educational benefits needed for life in a particular society.[32]

When the U.S. Department of Health, Education and Welfare reports that in 1974 there were about one million children in the United States, aged 12–17 years, who would end formal schooling without being able to read a simple paragraph, even at the fourth-grade level, the concept

[31] Edmund Gordon, "Toward Defining Equality of Educational Opportunity," in Mosteller and Moynihan (eds.), *On Equality of Educational Opportunity* (New York: Vantage Press, 1972), Chapter 10.

[32] Green, "Equal Educational Opportunity," p. 141.

of minimal needs takes on an urgent meaning. The problem was found to be most severe among low-income black males, of whom one out of five would end their schooling without being able to read at a fourth-grade level. Among poor whites with family incomes of less than $3,000, one in ten would not be able to read a simple paragraph. But the problem crosses income boundaries. There are, according to the report, 4.7 percent of the youth in families earning $10,000 or more who would also be as deficient in reading.[33] Given such low reading skills it is difficult to imagine how these people will be able to receive much of the instruction which is usually in printed form, about their civil rights or obligations, let alone about job skills or opportunities. Surely, equal opportunity is meaningless rhetoric to such persons living in our literacy oriented society. A basic education in the knowledge and skills essential for successful performance in the society is certainly a minimum criterion for equality of educational opportunity.

Although the definition of educational equality has varied from time to time, there has always been a strong belief in the value of education as a means of providing a measure of equality of opportunity in many societies. It is apparent, however, that the high value placed on the concept of equality in many societies and in their educational systems diverges greatly from the belief that individuals are unique and different and that each individual's ability differs greatly from others. These divergent beliefs and values underline much of the parallel emphasis upon open society, mobility and equality on one hand, and stratification, segregation, and allocation to fixed strata on the other hand in American society. Similarly, these conflicting value systems and the associated educational norms are the basis for much of the conflict over differentiated and equal education in American society. An examination of the assumptions, policies, and practice derived from these two sets of beliefs follows.

Alternate Models of School Policies, Practices, and Effects on Social Structure

The conflicting goals of equality of educational opportunity, which enhances an open social structure, and individually differentiated outcomes, which efficiently allocate people to different social strata, can be identified with models of school social systems. There is much confusion with regard to the type of education and student processing that is likely to achieve the different social goals. The enhancement of individual differences through individualized instruction, identification, classification, and placement of students in different educational categories and programs has frequently been advocated as a means of promoting

[33] Associated Press, *Kalamazoo Gazette,* May 5, 1974, p. 16.

maximum quality of education and perhaps equality of opportunity. It seems unlikely that highly differentiated educational programs for students identified as having different abilities is likely to reduce the differences and increase the degree of equality of opportunity or freedom of choice in the social system. The maximization of differentiation of educational programs for different children is commonly advocated without regard to the effect of such education on the social structure or the opportunities for mobility. These programs and policies do not recognize that equality of opportunity is not facilitated by highly differentiated educational programs based upon the presumed differences between lower- and middle-class children. One does not achieve equality by enhancing the differences in children and thus allocating them to different social strata.

Some understanding of the relationship between the assumptions, practices, and outcomes of the educational system may be facilitated by identifying two types of educational systems.[34] Figure 5–1 identifies

FIGURE 5–1
Ideal Types of School Systems

Type "A" Differentiation Oriented		*Type "B" Equality Oriented*
Vast differences in innate ability Differences are identifiable and unchangeable	Ability Assumptions	Innate differences slight and unidentifiable Observed differences largely environmental and changeable
Systematic identification of differences Aptitude testing used for placement and prediction Formal classification and labeling of students Homogeneous grouping and tracking Emphasis on individualized instruction Differentiated instructional programs with different goals	School Policies and Practices	No formal identification of differences Criterion based testing used to assess extent of learning No formal classification and labeling of students Random or systematically mixed grouping Common achievement norms for all students Common basic curriculum with mastery goal for all students
Little mobility between groups and educational programs Formal allocation to future careers (College, Non-College) Preparation of students for specific statuses Limited status mobility through education	Hypothesized Outcomes	Mobility between groups and school classes frequent Basic education for any careers for all students Prepared so student is able to choose position on basis of desires and costs Open opportunity for mobility through education

Source: Adapted from W. B. Brookover, Richard Gigliotti, Ronald Henderson, Bradley Niles, and Jeffrey Schneider, "Quality of Educational Attainment, Standardized Testing, Asssesment and Accountability," *The Seventy-third Yearbook of the Society for the Study of Education,* 1974.

[34] Brookover et al., "Quality of Educational Attainment."

two ideal types or models of school assumptions, policies, practices and outcomes. We identify these as ideal types because neither is likely to be found in a completely pure form in any school. A school may exhibit characteristics of both models or types. Schools characterized by the ability assumptions identified in model "A" are more likely to exhibit the policies and practices identified with Type "A" and to produce student outcomes associated with Type "A." Type "B" schools, if any exist, are more likely to exhibit the combination of assumptions, policies, practices and outcome identified in Figure 5–1. Each model could be elaborated by more detailed specification of each item, but each is designed to identify the types in sharp contrast rather than to describe in qualified terms the common policies or practices found in schools which approach one or the other model.

Although most schools exhibit mixtures of Type "A" and Type "B" characteristics, it is our contention that most American educational systems are closer to the differentiated Type "A" model than to the equality-oriented Type "B" model. In spite of our belief in equality most educational systems operate on the assumption that there are vast differences in innate ability to learn and that educators can identify these unchangeable differences in ability. On the basis of these assumptions, the school then sets up a formal system of identification of the differences in learning ability and a formal classification and labeling of students. Homogeneous grouping and tracking with differentiated instructional programs frequently characterized as individualized instruction result from these classification and labeling processes. These practices tend to allocate students to educational programs which clearly identify them with future careers, largely predetermine such chances, and limit the range of opportunity available to students. Such a system limits the mobility between educational programs and through educational programs mobility in the social system is likewise limited. Most schools therefore serve to process students in such a manner that their future status in the social structure is identifiable from the type and level of education with which they are identified.

Although few elementary and secondary schools demonstrate the characteristics of Type "B," we contend that such a school could be designed and that a few approach this model. Such a school would clearly be in harmony with our fundamental beliefs in equal human rights and equality of opportunity. If we operated on the assumption that innate differences in ability to learn are slight and that whatever differences may be observed are changeable, we could develop a school in which there is little formal identification of differences and little formal classification and labeling of students as innately inferior. Such a school would operate on the assumption that common mastery of basic curricula is possible. It seems likely that such a school would provide a relatively common basic education for all students so that they might have reasonably similar opportunities to choose careers requiring specific types of preparation. With such a school system, it is hypothesized that there would be reasonable equality of opportunity for individuals to choose their status in the social system regardless of race, income, or other group labels.

If we continue to operate our schools as we have in the past, we think that a stratified society based on race, ethnicity, and the social status of one's parents will continue. Some changes, however, are taking place. Minority group members are developing political skills and demanding education equal to that of the dominant white middle class. Courts are increasingly identifying and defining educational inequality. Educators and some middle-class clients are reexamining educational policies and practices. The educational system may therefore move toward the equality-oriented model for at least a basic elementary and secondary education.

Education and Mobility

In our discussion of the process of social allocation, we have indicated that some students achieve higher or lower status positions through the educational system. A belief in equality of opportunity through education implies that educational systems should facilitate such movement in the status system. The belief that upward mobility is achievable through education has been an extremely important factor in the expansion of the educational system and the rapidly increasing level of educational achievement in society. Perhaps this belief in the possibility of upward mobility is more important for educational motivation than the actual amount of mobility achieved through education. Although it is generally recognized that considerable mobility occurs in American society as well as other Western societies, some argue that education contributes little to this process.[35] Some analysis of the relation of education to mobility is therefore essential.

There are two general types of social mobility—horizontal and vertical. Horizontal mobility refers to the process of moving from one location or position in the society without significant change in prestige, power, or other measures of social status. In this context school teachers move from one school to another or from one educational system to another in essentially the same type of position without modifying their status in the society. Vertical mobility refers to movement from lower to higher

[35] C. Arnold Anderson, "A Skeptical Note on Education and Mobility," *American Journal of Sociology*, vol. 66, no. 1, May 1961. Also in A. H. Halsey, Jean Floud, and C. Arnold Anderson, *Education, Economy and Society* (New York: Free Press, 1961).

status positions or vice versa. Such vertical mobility also may be of two types. One is career mobility in which an individual starts his career at one status and moves to a higher or lower status position during his lifetime. An individual who starts his career as a bank teller and becomes the president of the bank would illustrate such upward career mobility. A significant amount of such mobility occurs in the society but there is little evidence on which to base any conclusion on the contribution of education to this type of vertical mobility. Much more attention has been given to what is termed intergenerational mobility. This refers to the process by which sons or daughters move to higher or lower positions in the status structure than their parents.

Intergenerational mobility occurs in part because of the changing occupational structure in American society. Concurrent with the industrialization process and the development of technology a decreasing proportion of American working force are engaged in unskilled and semiskilled occupations. As noted in Table 5–2, there has been a significant change in the proportion of professional service employees in the labor force in the past decades. This changing occupational structure has been associated with rising educational requirements within the labor force. The exact mechanism by which the changing occupational structure and the educational level interact is not clear. One theory is that the educational requirements reflect the demand for greater skills on the job because of technological change. Another is that employment requirements reflect the efforts of competing status groups to monopolize or dominate jobs by imposing their cultural standards on the selection process.[36] Collins maintains that the "main dynamic of rising educational requirements in the United States has been primarily the expansion of mobility opportunities through the school system rather than the autonomous changes in the structure of employment." This is in contrast to the position that education has responded to the increasing demands for higher-skilled positions. In either case, education is significantly related to the changing stratification in modern societies. The mobility that results from this changing occupational structure is reflected in data showing mobility patterns between generations and makes the analysis of factors associated with mobility somewhat more complicated than it otherwise would be.

The extent of mobility from one generation to another is demonstrated in Table 5–3. Although we tend to emphasize the lack of mobility out of the lower class, there is still an enormous amount of economic mobility from one generation to the next.[37] We note from Table 5–3 that more

[36] Randall Collins, "Functional and Conflict Theories of Educational Stratification," *American Sociological Review*, vol. 36, no. 6, December 1971, pp. 1002–1019.

[37] Mary Jo Bane and Christopher Jencks, "The Schools and Equal Opportunity," *Saturday Review of Education*, September 16, 1972, pp. 37–42.

TABLE 5–2
Employed Persons, by Major Occupation Group and Sex: 1950–1973 (in thousands of persons, 14 years old and over, through 1955; 16 years old and over, thereafter; annual averages, except as indicated. Beginning 1971, not strictly comparable with previous years.

OCCUPATION GROUP AND SEX	1950 [1]	1955 [1]	1960	1965	1970	1971 [2]	1972 [2]	1973,[2] Apr.
Total	**59,648**	**62,997**	**65,778**	**71,088**	**78,627**	**79,120**	**81,702**	**83,299**
White-collar workers	22,373	24,585	28,522	31,852	37,997	38,252	39,092	39,859
Percent of total	37.5	39.0	43.4	44.8	48.3	48.3	47.8	47.9
Professional and technical workers	4,490	5,792	7,469	8,872	11,140	11,070	11,459	11,634
Managers and administrators, exc. farm	6,429	6,450	7,067	7,340	8,289	8,675	8,032	8,456
Salesworkers	3,822	3,976	4,224	4,499	4,854	5,066	5,354	5,398
Clerical workers	7,632	8,367	9,762	11,141	13,714	13,440	14,247	14,372
Blue-collar workers	23,336	24,771	24,057	26,247	27,791	27,184	28,576	29,362
Craftsmen and kindred workers	7,670	8,328	8,554	9,216	10,158	10,178	10,810	11,057
Operatives	12,146	12,762	11,950	13,345	13,909	12,983	13,549	14,151
Operatives, except transport	(NA)	(NA)	(NA)	(NA)	(NA)	(NA)	10,340	10,823
Transport equipment operatives	(NA)	(NA)	(NA)	(NA)	(NA)	(NA)	3,209	3,328
Nonfarm laborers	3,520	3,681	3,553	3,686	3,724	4,022	4,217	4,154
Service workers	6,535	7,106	8,023	8,936	9,712	10,676	10,966	11,178
Farmworkers	7,408	6,537	5,176	4,053	3,126	3,008	3,069	2,900
Male	**42,156**	**43,191**	**43,904**	**46,340**	**48,960**	**49,245**	**50,630**	**51,203**
White-collar workers	13,549	14,305	16,423	17,746	20,054	20,138	20,176	20,333
Percent of total	32.1	33.1	37.4	38.3	41.0	40.9	39.8	39.7
Professional and technical workers	2,696	3,608	4,766	5,596	6,842	6,737	6,957	6,860
Managers and administrators, exc. farm	5,439	5,454	5,968	6,230	6,968	7,182	6,621	6,878
Salesworkers	2,379	2,451	2,544	2,641	2,763	2,911	3,127	3,228
Clerical workers	3,035	2,792	3,145	3,279	3,481	3,308	3,470	3,367
Blue-collar workers	19,727	20,925	20,420	22,107	23,020	22,579	23,800	24,286
Craftsmen and kindred workers	7,482	8,114	8,332	8,947	9,826	9,792	10,424	10,583
Operatives	8,810	9,235	8,617	9,581	9,605	9,015	9,426	9,821
Operatives, except transport	(NA)	(NA)	(NA)	(NA)	(NA)	(NA)	6,351	6,643
Transport equipment operatives	(NA)	(NA)	(NA)	(NA)	(NA)	(NA)	3,075	3,178
Nonfarm laborers	3,435	3,576	3,471	3,579	3,589	3,772	3,950	3,883
Service workers	2,685	2,657	2,844	3,194	3,285	4,034	4,128	4,134
Farmworkers	6,196	5,305	4,219	3,295	2,601	2,494	2,526	2,450
Female	**17,493**	**19,807**	**21,874**	**24,748**	**29,667**	**29,875**	**31,072**	**32,096**
White-collar workers	8,824	10,280	12,099	14,106	17,943	18,114	18,915	19,526
Percent of total	50.4	51.9	55.3	57.0	60.5	60.6	60.9	60.8
Professional and technical workers	1,794	2,183	2,703	3,276	4,298	4,334	4,502	4,773
Managers and administrators, exc. farm	990	997	1,099	1,110	1,321	1,493	1,410	1,578
Salesworkers	1,443	1,525	1,680	1,858	2,091	2,155	2,226	2,170
Clerical workers	4,597	5,575	6,617	7,862	10,233	10,132	10,777	11,005
Blue-collar workers	3,608	3,847	3,637	4,140	4,771	4,605	4,776	5,075
Craftsmen and kindred workers	188	215	222	269	332	387	386	473
Operatives	3,336	3,527	3,333	3,764	4,303	3,968	4,123	4,330
Operatives, except transport	(NA)	(NA)	(NA)	(NA)	(NA)	(NA)	3,989	4,180
Transport equipment operatives	(NA)	(NA)	(NA)	(NA)	(NA)	(NA)	134	150
Nonfarm laborers	84	105	82	107	136	250	267	271
Service workers	3,850	4,449	5,179	5,742	6,427	6,642	6,838	7,044
Farmworkers	1,212	1,233	957	758	525	514	543	450

NA: Not available.
[1] Based on first month in each quarter.
[2] Data not strictly comparable with earlier years due to reclassification of census occupations.
Source: 1950 and 1955, U.S. Bureau of the Census, *Current Population Reports,* series P–50. Beginning 1960, U.S. Bureau of Labor Statistics, *Employment and Earnings,* monthly.

than 60 percent of the first occupations of the sons of fathers who were lower manual workers or laborers were one category or more above their fathers; 18 percent of these sons entered white-collar occupations. Approximately 50 percent of the sons of farmers entered other occupations with nearly 11 percent entering white-collar occupations. The sons of fathers who were in higher level manual and white-collar occupations did not move up in as large a proportion, but more than 20 percent of the sons of sales and clerical fathers entered occupations in the profes-

TABLE 5–3
Mobility from Father's Occupation to Son's First Occupation for U.S. Males 25 to 64 Years Old (percentages)

	Son's First Occupation					
Father's Occupation	*Higher White Collar*	*Lower White Collar*	*Higher Manual*	*Mid Manual*	*Lower Manual*	*Farm*
Higher white-collar (professionals, managers, proprietors)	28.6	28.2	9.8	22.6	8.5	2.4
Lower white-collar (sales and clerical)	21.1	33.3	7.9	25.1	9.6	3.0
Higher manual (craftsmen and foremen)	7.4	20.5	17.4	36.0	14.0	4.6
Mid manual (operative and service workers)	6.6	17.3	9.6	47.5	14.8	4.1
Low manual (laborers)	4.6	13.6	6.8	37.2	30.3	7.6
Farm	4.1	6.7	5.8	21.0	12.0	50.3

The entry in each cell is the percentage of sons whose fathers were in the occupational category listed at left whose first job was in the category listed at the top. For instance, 28.2 percent of the sons whose fathers were in higher white-collar occupations were first employed in lower white-collar occupations.

Source: Adapted from Peter M. Blau and Otis Dudley Duncan, *The American Occupational Structure* (New York: John Wiley & Sons, 1967).

sional-managerial category. A significant portion of the sons of these white-collar fathers, more than 40 percent, started working in manual or farm positions. Since these were the first positions, however, it is possible that a significant proportion of these moved to higher status positions during their career. Recent studies of female intergenerational mobility indicates some similarity to patterns of male mobility, but the analysis is complicated by differences in occupational distribution among males and females.[38] The achievement of greater equality for women may modify the patterns of mobility.

The changing distribution of occupations in the United States accounts for a portion of this intergenerational mobility. Other factors including education have been considered as contributors to mobility. Jencks and his associates[39] have indicated that a significant amount of luck or chance is involved in the mobility patterns. Certainly the allocation system in American society does not channel all young people into the same stratum as their family of origin. If this were true, of course, there

[38] Peter Y. DeJong, Milton J. Brawer and Stanley Robin, "Patterns of Female Intergenerational Mobility: A Comparison with Male Patterns of Intergenerational Mobility," *American Sociological Review*, vol. 36, no. 6 (December 1971), pp. 1033–1042, and Andrea Tyree and Judity Treas, "The Occupational Mobility of Women," *American Sociological Review*, vol. 39, no. 3, pp. 393–402 (June 1974).

[39] Christopher Jencks, Marshal Smith, Henry Aeland, Mary Jo Bane, David Cohen, Herbert Gentis, Barbara Heyns, and Stephen Michelson, *Inequality: A Reassessment of the Effect of Family and Schooling in America* (New York: Basic Books, 1972).

would be little impact from nonfamily forces such as education. The exact proportion of mobility that is attributable to education has not been determined. It is apparent, however, that some forces operating in the educational system have some impact.

One of the factors is the attraction which positions that are defined as higher or better have for persons in lower-status occupations. This motivation to move up in the occupational hierarchy is almost universal in American society. The sources of this motivation may be quite varied. Many families, if not most, aspire for their sons and daughters to achieve a higher position than they have. Children learn early in life that this is not only desired, but is highly valued by their parents. Closely associated with this attraction to higher-status positions is the belief that education provides the means by which one can move up into the system. Although it may be difficult to separate the motivation acquired in the family from the education system, it is clear that the belief in education as a means of upward mobility is widespread and is reinforced in the educational system.

In addition to supporting and enhancing the motivation to achieve higher occupational statuses, it is likely that the educational system provides additional impact through several means. One of these, certainly, is teaching those patterns of behavior that are acceptable in higher-status jobs. Standard English as taught in the school is probably a significant aspect of the behavior which qualifies one for mobility from lower- to higher-status positions. In addition to the general socialization, the specific qualifications or certifications for many jobs are obtainable only in the formal educational system. Teaching, law, medicine, and numerous other professional occupations require previous occupational training in the school system before certification can be obtained. Many other occupational groups set educational requirements for entry even though the specific knowledge necessary for the occupation may be acquired in other ways.

As we noted in our discussion of the allocation system, the teacher's and counselor's advice make significant contributions to the student's expectations.[40] Certainly a part of the allocation process involves the selection of some students from lower-status family backgrounds for higher levels of education and to higher-status positions. This, of course, is dependent to some extent on the student's performance in the school both in academic areas and in other types of behavior.

Although the educational system serves to allocate people to different levels of occupations rather than provide equal opportunity for students to choose their level, it must not be assumed that education contributes nothing to the mobility of students from generation to generation.

[40] Rehberg and Hotchkiss, "Educational Decision-Makers."

Educational Change and Equality

The relation of education to social stratification is indeed a complex one. We have reviewed several aspects of this relationship to illustrate, if possible, some of these complexities. We cannot specify either the exact degree of relationship or the extent to which changes in the educational system might reduce or increase the inequalities in the social structure. The interactions with other social forces make precise formulas identifying the effect of education on social structure unfeasible at this time. "When people are ranked in a vertical arrangement [hierarchy] that differentiates them as superior or inferior, then we have social stratification. . . . What is ranked and who is ranked where in the social hierarchy are consequences of the value preferences existing in the total society and not just in the schools. Social stratification refers, in essence, to structured inequality."[41] To reduce inequality, then, is to reduce the stratification system. Few would contend that the schools are capable of creating a nonstratified society or, in fact, that such is within the power of any single agency.

It does not make sense from an open system's perspective to assert that the school alone can or will eliminate conditions of social inequality. For the school to change the social structure implies considerable change in the economic system, the political system, and every other system including help from the students and their families. But the same can be said for the other institutions. Changes in the economic system or the political system would require changes in the educational system. There is a constant reciprocal interaction and influence.

Many advocates of social change despair that a just social equality can be effected by changing our education system. Some argue that school reform is never likely to have any significant effect on the degree of inequality among adults and that the nature of certain norms and the concentration of power and prestige in the middle and upper social strata will prevent schools from affecting the distribution of power and prestige in any important way. Certainly, there is much in our tradition, as well as in the way things are currently done, which seemingly supports such a contention—at least the contention that education has not been much of a leader in reducing inequality based on sex, race, ethnicity, or economic status.[42]

Alan Pifer, in discussing how higher education has served black Americans, characterizes a tradition for black people which is similar to the histories of other minorities in many places and times.

[41] D. Stanley Eitzen, *Social Structure and Social Problems* (Boston: Allyn and Bacon, Inc., 1974), p. 73.

[42] Jencks et al., *Inequality*.

> In the more than 300 years of its history, American higher education, with the exception of the special colleges for Negroes, showed little evidence until recently for any sense of responsibility for the education of blacks. Our colleges and universities were, on the whole, no better than handmaidens of a system which first enslaved and then systematically oppressed black people. It would be hard to demonstrate that these institutions were ever demonstrably in advance of general public opinion in taking steps to right the great historical wrong done to blacks.
>
> Secondly, from the black point of view, it could hardly be claimed that higher education, for all it has done in recent years to make up for its earlier failures, has as yet achieved a state of real integration. Granted that such a goal may not be fully attainable without the assistance of many other agencies in society, higher education could, nonetheless, probably have gone much further on its own toward reaching the goal than it has."[43]

There are two implications of Pifer's statement which are of particular relevance for understanding educational reform. One is to be found in the phrase "granted such a goal may not be fully attainable without the assistance of many other agencies in society . . ." Too often, we academicians, as well as the public, in our concern for which is the most important—family, peers, schooling, economic, political or religious systems—tend to overlook the essential contribution made by each. The fact that there is only one part oxygen to two parts of hydrogen in water does not mean that oxygen is any less crucial. Whether education is contributing one part or 20 parts to inequalities should not be the first concern. The first concern is whether the educational system is crucial at all to inequality in society and in what ways. The answer is patently obvious that through educational segregation, differentiation, and allocation to different positions in the social hierarchy, women and many minority groups have been kept in a disadvantaged position by having their admission into various educational programs and occupations barred. The issue, then, is not really one of whether educational differentiation and stratification make a difference in social equality; rather, the issue involves the question of whether such differentiations are just.

A second question suggested by Pifer is whether the educational system can be changed or modified in a way that will reduce unjust group inequalities, and if so, in what way? Obviously, the answer to the first part of the question is more obvious. Yes, changes in the educational system have occurred with resultant reductions in various unjust inequalities of opportunity. For example, Pifer goes on to state:

> Granting, then, the essential validity of the black indictment of higher education, there are, nonetheless, some positive things one can say about

[43] Alan Pifer, "How Well Has Higher Education Served Black Americans?" *Change: The Magazine of Higher Education,* vol. 6, no. 3, April 1974, p. 8. Reprinted by permission of *Change* and Alan Pifer.

> what it has done for blacks in American life. There can, for example, be little doubt that it has been largely responsible for the development of a black elite that has provided leadership to the black community and is beginning to claim some share of the leadership of our national life generally. This elite is growing rapidly today and is starting to penetrate virtually every aspect of the society. It is true that we are probably a long way from seeing a black president of General Motors or of the Chase Manhattan Bank, but blacks now sit on the boards of directors of both of these corporations and on many other corporate boards. In some instances, the high position occupied by blacks is little more than tokenism, but many institutions have moved well beyond that. There is no reason to suppose that substance rather than show in the integration of the American leadership class will not grow.
>
> Secondly, it is clear now that higher education for blacks, especially in the Negro colleges, did play an important part in the civil rights movement. Not only were many civil rights leaders, such as Martin Luther King, graduates of these institutions, but in many cases it was students from them who courageously challenged injustices entrenched in the laws supporting segregation."[44]

Small changes identified as tokenism, regardless of how much it is despised by both those who want no change and those who are the victims of discrimination, should not be overlooked for its functions. Once token changes occur, the absolute normative barriers to educational or occupational entry may lose their powerful legitimizing force for preventing change. While it is probably true that many individuals and organizations have employed a few token women or minority persons into formerly restricted positions to reduce the "heat" or press for equality of opportunity, token employment tends to legitimatize their rights in the culture at large. Educational institutions have played a part in the initial change away from discriminatory practices by providing higher education for some minority members who in turn increased the pressures for change. Such a reservoir of credentialed persons, we believe, played a part in making possible the changes which have occurred.

Another way the schools may modify the bases of stratification is through their role in providing an arena in which dissident views may be presented. Of course, free speech is often more academic than real in an absolute sense, but nevertheless, in heterogenous cultures, minority views are often initially expressed in schools and colleges. Educational institutions have also tended to provide more freedom for controversial discussion than other institutions, and, thereby, they have provided training grounds for the development of the leadership necessary for social change.

The schools have also influenced discriminatory practices through

[44] Ibid., p. 9.

their legitimization function in society. Schools in a secular society come to take a role in determining what is right and appropriate that in sacred societies is more vested with religious institutions. In a society characterized by an empirical, pragmatic, and scientific value preference, schools are often arbitrators of moral issues. More and more, schools are the sources of valid sex information for children and youth. The schools have long had a political socialization function, and, with recent court decisions regarding equality, schools from elementary through higher education have provided the arena for debate, data gathering, tabulation, and pronouncements about what is equal and what is not. Religious leaders are no longer the major consultants to government on what should be the proper order in human relations, but educators often are. In nearly every court case concerning equality of opportunity, educators and social scientists employed in schools have been consulted frequently by both plaintiff and defendant.

Schools may also contribute to the enhancement or reduction of discrimination in many other subtle ways. They can, by merely selecting the spots where they will build their school buildings, affect human relations between groups. The types of curricula they offer, their choice of heroes to be honored, the values they propagate, and the resources they expend; all of their activities have the potential for affecting human relationships in society.

We therefore have reasonable bases to assert that some types of gross discrimination, inequities, and impositions of inferiority still occurring in education can be lessened with positive results for social equality. But certain of the school's contribution to inequality, like those of the family, peers, and community, are subtle and often go unrecognized. Identification of these contributions to inequality and other relations between school and social structure will, we believe, reduce the barrier to achieving democratic ideals in school and society. The analysis of segregation in school and society in the following chapter will, we trust, also contribute to this goal.

Suggested Readings

Samuel Bowles, "Getting Nowhere: Programmed Class Stagnation," *Society*, 9, no. 8 (June 1972).

Samuel Bowles, "Unequal Education and the Reproduction of the Social Division of Labor," in Martin Carnoy, ed., *Schooling in a Corporate Society* (New York: David McKay, 1972).

Aaron A. Cicourel and John Kitsuse, *The Educational Decision Makers* (Indianapolis: Bobbs Merrill Co., 1963).

David K. Cohen, "Immigrants and the Schools,'" *Review of Educational Research*, 40, no. 1 (February 1970) pp. 13–28.

James S. Coleman et al., *Equality of Educational Opportunity* (Washington, D.C.: U.S. Government Printing Office, 1966).

Fred Crossland, *Minority Access to College* (New York: Schocken Books, 1971).

John C. Garfield, Steven L. Weiss, and Ethan A. Pollack, "Effects of the Child's Social Class on School Counselor's Decision Making," *Journal of Counseling Psychology*, 20, no. 1 (March 1973), pp. 166–67.

Edmund Gordon, "Broadening the Concept of Career Education," *IRCD Bulletin*, ERIC Information Retrieval Center on the Disadvantaged, 9, no. 2 (March 1973), pp. 1–7.

Julius W. Hobson v. *Carl F. Hansen*, 269 F Supp. 401 (1967).

Christopher Jencks et al., *Inequality* (New York: Basic Books, 1972).

David C. McClelland, "Testing for Competence Rather than for 'Intelligence'," *American Psychologist*, 29, no. 1 (January 1973). Advocates a major change in the educational system to one of training to meet criterion of performance rather than relative standing.

William H. Sewell, "Inequality of Opportunity for Higher Education," *American Sociological Review*, 36, no. 5 (October 1971).

Walter Shaffer and Carol Olexa, *Tracking and Opportunity* (Scranton, Pa.: Chandler Publishing Co., 1971).

Edward Zigler, "Social Class and the Socialization Process," *Review of Educational Research*, 40, no. 1 (February 1970), pp. 87–110. An excellent review and critique of the literature up to 1969 on social class in relation to school.

6

Segregation, Education, and Social Solidarity

ALTHOUGH the concept segregation has been most frequently used to refer to the provision of separate schools for students from different racial groups in the United States, it has a much more comprehensive meaning. For our purposes any system of school organization which provides different schools or different programs for the children of different racial origin, income, religious affiliation, ethnic background, sex, areas of residence, or categories of the society will be identified as segregation. This contrasts with the provision of a common school program for all children. Any system of school organization which results in differential school programs for children from different strata of society or from other identifiable categories may be viewed as a type of segregation. Segregation may occur by operating separate schools for different groups of children or by providing separate programs within a particular school.

Types of Segregation

Patterns of segregation take many different forms. In Great Britain the students attend separate grammar schools, secondary modern schools, or technical schools after the basic primary education. Similar streams or branches are provided in Germany under the categories of *Gymnasium, Mittleschule,* and *Volkschule.* The separation of children into these differentiated educational programs is based upon some index of school achievement, but it is well established that the programs reflect differences in the socioeconomic status of the families from which the children come. Although we do not identify separate streams in the United States as markedly as in European societies, there are several bases upon which American students are segregated.

The Geographical Basis for Segregation

In a predominantly rural and small-town American society, the community or neighborhood school formerly provided the basis for a common education; when all the children in a prescribed and reasonably small geographic area attended a single school they were likely to receive a reasonably common education and interacted with each other in a single educational institution. Similar urban neighborhood areas now provide the basis for extensive differentiation and segregation of children from different strata of society. In his book *Slums and Suburbs,* James Conant dramatically illustrated the differences in educational programs among children in these identifiable neighborhood areas.[1] Within the boundaries of American cities similar differentiated programs can readily be identified, and different neighborhoods or attendance areas or even school districts frequently reflect differences in socioeconomic strata. As every American readily recognizes, many suburban areas are almost 100 percent middle or upper-middle class in contrast with the central cities, which are characterized by a high proportion of poor people. Other suburban areas are composed of lower socioeconomic levels, but these geographic areas are frequently clearly distinguished from middle-class suburbs and are relatively homogenous in social composition. Various neighborhoods within urban areas are also identified by racial or ethnic differences. Except for those areas in which racial segregation was formerly required, the geographic patterns of segregation are probably the most common basis for racial or socioeconomic segregation in American schools.

Information on the exact proportion of American students who attend schools identifiably segregated by race or social class on the basis of geographic area or space is not available. Although precise data are not available, there are many schools serving a particular geographic area that have a very high proportion of upper socioeconomic level children and others with a very high proportion of poor people. Similarly, racial and ethnic separation is frequently based on geographic areas. The neighborhood or community school which has long been advocated in America as a convenient and desirable method of organization has become a synonym for segregated education and a means of perpetuating a stratified society.

[1] James Conant, *Slums and Suburbs* (New York: McGraw-Hill Book Company, 1961).

Racial Segregation

Until 1954, segregation of black and white students was legally required in 17 states and permitted in several others. Patterns of residence in many metropolitan areas provide the basis for segregation on the basis of race as well as geography. The survey of a sample of American schools carried on in 1965 indicated that more than 65 percent of black children in the first grade were in schools that were 90 percent or more black.[2] More than half of the black twelfth-grade students represented in the same survey were similarly in predominantly black schools. Over 80 percent of the white children in this sample were in schools that were 90 percent or more white. The 1970 data on racial segregation shown in Table 6–1 indicate that over 60 percent of all Negro students

TABLE 6–1
Percent of Negro Students Attending School at Increasing Levels of Isolation in 21 States[1] by Geographical Region (Fall 1970)

	Percent Minority Schools				
Area	*50 to 100*	*80 to 100*	*90 to 100*	*95 to 100*	*100*
Continental United States	66.9	49.4	43.3	38.2	14.0
21 States and District of Columbia	68.3	50.5	44.5	41.8	14.8
8 Northern and Western States	75.2	60.4	54.0	47.5	13.0
2 Border States	72.1	58.0	55.2	51.0	27.5
11 Southern States	60.9	39.3	33.3	29.2	14.1

[1] Containing 94 percent of the nation's black students.
Source: *Select Committee on Equal Educational Opportunity*, United States Senate, page 105.

were enrolled in schools with 95 percent or more minority group enrollment. Minority in this instance includes American Indians, Orientals, and Spanish named Americans as well as Blacks. The vast majority of white elementary and secondary students in the United States attend schools that are either all white or predominantly so.

Although some racial segregation results from forces other than specific design, it serves to reflect and maintain the stratified nature of American society. While there has been a significant increase in the proportion of black students attending school with whites in the formerly segregated Southern states, the Northern and Western states have maintained a high proportion of racially segregated schools. (See Table 6–1). According to the federal government, in 1972, 46.3 percent of all black pupils in the South were attending majority white schools, compared

[2] James S. Coleman, et al., *Equality of Educational Opportunity* (Washington, D.C.: U.S. Government Printing Office, 1966).

to 36.3 percent nationwide and only 21.7 percent in Michigan, for example.[3]

Racial segregation occurs within schools as well as between schools. Segregationist school administrators have sometimes maintained separate classes for black and white students when they are mixed within the same school. In other cases, the same result occurs from grouping and tracking of students on presumably other bases. McPartland's analysis of a portion of the Equality of Educational Opportunity data indicates that a significant proportion of black students attending presumably desegregated schools remain in essentially racially segregated classes and curriculum tracks.[4] The effect of such segregation on the students may be similar to or in some cases even more undesirable than the attendance at racially segregated schools.

Segregation by Socioeconomic Status

The segregation of students from different socioeconomic-status backgrounds in different schools is largely de facto in nature. Such segregation in public schools results from the socioeconomic differences in residential areas. Some school attendance areas and school district boundaries are designed either openly or in an informal manner to maximize the segregation of lower- and upper-status children. We do not have data comparable to the racial segregation data to illustrate the proportion of students of a given socioeconomic level in schools composed predominantly of their own social class. Recent data obtained in a statewide assessment program in Michigan reveal a wide range in the mean score on a social and economic index of children in the fourth and seventh grades. Some schools have an index as low as 35, which indicates that a very large proportion of the students come from low socioeconomic levels. On the same index, other schools have a score of more than 60. A very high proportion of pupils in such schools come from families of higher socioeconomic status.

Nearly 100 percent of the pupils in most private nonsectarian schools in the United States come from higher socioeconomic-level families. Although some private schools provide some scholarship assistance to students from lower-income families, the cost of providing such education nearly eliminates students from lower-income families. Children of higher status, whose families do not wish or do not feel able to send them to private schools, will attend public schools with other children of the same social-class background.

---

[3] *Kalamazoo Gazette,* May 6, 1974, p. 9.

[4] James McPartland, *The Segregated Student in Desegregated Schools* (Baltimore: The John Hopkins University, Center for the Study of Social Organization of Schools, Report No. 21, 1968).

Similar patterns of socioeconomic segregation are found in other countries, although the patterns may result from somewhat different practices. A recent study of the eighth-grade students in Giessen, Germany, revealed that the mean socioeconomic statuses of eighth-grade students enrolled in *Gymnasium, Mittleschule,* and *Volkschule* were significantly different in each comparison. Although the students are allocated to these schools on the basis of primary school achievement, the social-class composition is clearly discernable by type of school attended.[5]

The socioeconomic differences are frequently also a basis for segregating within a school. The various "ability" groups, sections, and tracks within the school are highly related to the socioeconomic background of the students. Rist's review of research in this area clearly demonstrates that tracks reflect the socioeconomic classification of students.[6] This, of course, is most dramatically indicated in the composition of the classes for "educable" mentally retarded students in the school. Various types of organizational practices are therefore related to the process of social-class segregation in schools in various parts of the world.

Religious and Ethnic Segregation

Segregation by religious and ethnic origin is more characteristic of nonpublic than public schools and the two classifications sometimes overlap. In 1973, almost five million elementary and secondary school students in the United States were enrolled in church-related schools, with Roman Catholic school enrollment accounting for about 90 percent of parochial school enrollment. Although some pupils from non-Catholic and other religious groups not identified with a particular school attend the parochial schools, the vast majority of this enrollment reflects a voluntary segregation on the basis of religion. In many of the religious schools, there is a parallel pattern of segregation by ethnic origin. Members of many Roman Catholic parishes, for example, are predominantly of Mexican, Polish, Italian, or German origin.

Current trends in parochial school enrollment are mixed for various parts of the country. In the Southern United States and some urban areas, some parents send their children to parochial schools to avoid racial integration. Many new private schools have also been established to maintain segregation. Recent estimates indicate that nearly one-half million students, or just over four percent of the total enrollment in 11 Southern states, are in such private schools.[7] This tendency to enroll

[5] Michael Auer, "Self-Concept of Academic Ability of West German Eighth Grade Students" (Dissertation, Michigan State University, 1971).

[6] Ray C. Rist, *Restructuring American Education,* "Introduction" (New Brunswick, N.J.: Transaction Books, 1972).

[7] Southern Regional Council, *Lansing State Journal,* February 11, 1971.

students in parochial and private schools to avoid racial integration is counteracted by a trend resulting from economic forces and possible changes in public sentiment. The overall result indicates a decline in the elementary and secondary parochial school enrollments between 1964 and 1974. The enrollment in some 13,360 Catholic schools was over 5.5 million in 1964, but decreased to approximately 3.6 million in 10,350 schools by 1974 (National Conference of Catholic Bishops). The decline in parochial school enrollments in many communities has been associated with the employment of an increasing proportion of lay teachers at much higher salary levels than the religious order personnel receive. The increasing cost of parochial education has made it difficult for many parishes to finance parochial schools without heavy increases in tuition or fees. As a consequence, increasing proportions of the parochial school enrollments are likely to be greatly affected by legislation, court action, and constitutional amendments concerned with public support for parochial education. Resistance to public support for church-related colleges is less than that to elementary and secondary parochial schools. Some support for religion-related schools for various purposes is likely to continue because the collapse of such educational institutions would seemingly place a greater burden on public schools.

Historically, a clear case of imposed ethnic segregation has been the separate schools provided for native Americans. Although the policy of the federal government and various states with Indian populations has varied from time to time, there have been separate schools for American Indians in many areas for more than a century. These have been provided by the federal government under the Bureau of Indian Affairs rather than by state departments of education. Recent reports of the Bureau of Indian Affairs indicate that probably 30 percent or more of the American Indian children attend schools specifically organized for Indian students.

Although precise data are not available, we know that religious and ethnic segregation sometimes occurs within public school systems. In areas with high concentrations of Spanish-Americans like the Southwestern portions of the United States, where 17 percent of the total student body is Spanish-American, approximately 30 percent of these Spanish-speaking students are enrolled in schools with more than 80 percent Spanish-Americans. In Connecticut, Illinois, New Jersey, and New York, where only 5 percent of the students are Spanish-American, over 50 percent of these attend schools that are more than 80 percent students of Spanish origin. The total for the United States excluding Hawaii indicates that more than 31 percent of the Spanish-American students attend schools that are composed of more than 80 percent Spanish-American children. Spanish-speaking students in mixed public schools are more likely to be in the non-college-bound sections and tracks than are students who speak standard English. Although it is a small portion of the total population, the vast majority of children of the Amish religious sect attend schools that are almost 100 percent Amish.

The patterns of segregation in relation to language and national origin vary somewhat from society to society, but some form of the practice exists in most nations of the world. In Canada, the pervasive pattern of segregation is based upon religion, language, and national origin, where Protestant and Catholic schools are both supported by public funds. Educational differences in Canada clearly depend upon differences in the usage of the English and French languages, and, of course, the students' national origins.

British and Irish grammar schools are also clearly related to the religions of Protestantism and Catholicism and the language structures of the different social classes served through their different educational programs. The development of comprehensive schools to reduce the stratified and class-segregated schools in Britain has not progressed at a rapid pace.

Segregation within Schools

We have already referred to a variety of tracking and grouping programs which serve to segregate various types of students on the basis of interests or presumed ability. The students assigned to slower groups in elementary school or secondary school non-college-bound programs come, in a large proportion, from lower-status families. Since those in the college-bound programs or superior groups are more likely to have middle or upper class origins, the organization of such curricula or tracks in many school systems also provides for racial and class segregation.[8] Also, vocational or technical high schools which have become more popular are frequently located in separate buildings with larger proportions of minority and poor students than exist in the general populations of the communities served. Junior and community colleges also tend to provide separate vocational programs for the lower income students and advanced academic work for those of higher income levels. And, of course, similar distinctions can be seen within, as well as between, many private universities and colleges.

The U.S. Office of Education reports that over three million children attending public schools were enrolled in special programs for various

[8] Jim Jones, Edsel L. Erickson, and Ron Crowell, "Increasing the Gap Between Whites and Blacks: Tracking as a Contributory Source," *Education and Urban Society,* vol. 4 (1972), p. 339, and Roger Hugh Kariger, "The Relationship of Lane Grouping to Socio-Economic Status of Parents," doctoral dissertation, Michigan State University, 1962.

types of students.[9] In 1963, over 400,000 students were in special programs for the mentally retarded. By 1971 approximately twice as many students were in such programs. Similarly, more than twice as many students were in programs for the gifted in 1971 as in 1963. In 1971 nearly one-half million students were enrolled in gifted programs. These figures indicate the very significant increase in this type of segregated educational programs.

The trends in ability grouping or tracking of students in American schools are not easily established, but available data indicate that the majority of school systems continue the practice in some form. Data obtained from a sample of school systems in 1970 indicate that "better than 55 percent of the school districts from which replies were received do some grouping in more than one subject or grade on a district-wide basis and approximately 77 percent do grouping of some kind. The percentages are not significantly different from those reported by the N.E.A. Research Division in their 1962 summary."[10] A minority of the districts (13 percent) reporting in this study had started the practice between 1940 and 1954 but more than half had introduced the practice since 1955. Since people from minority group and lower-socioeconomic-status families are more likely to be placed in lower educational level groups or tracks, the extensive grouping practice is clearly related to the racial, ethnic, and socioeconomic stratification of the society.

On the basis of teachers' evaluations and tests, students are allocated to reading groups, special classes, or advanced sections for differentiated types of elementary school programs. This process of grouping and tracking generally starts early in most American schools.[11] By junior high school, they are classified into different groups according to some measure of ability and assigned to differentiated subject matter programs. "In the high schools the organization of psychometric data leads to the grouping and the career-linked curricula. By this time the flexibility is quite low and life decisions have largely been determined."[12] Community colleges with open admission may extend the tracking practice with terminal and transfer type programs.

"A wide range of data are used in the process of classification for tracks or other differentiated programs. These classifications are generally substantiated by various types of aptitude or achievement test data.

[9] U.S. Office of Education, "Special Education of Exceptional Children," reported in *Biennial Survey of Education* (1968), Table 35.

[10] Warren Finley and Miriam Bryan, *Ability Grouping 1970,* (Athens, Georgia: Center for Educational Improvement, University of Georgia, 1971), p. 7.

[11] Ray C. Rist, "Student Social Class and Teacher Expectations: The Self-Fulfilling Prophecy in Ghetto Schools," *Harvard Educational Review,* vol. 40, August 1970, pp. 411–450.

[12] Carl Weinberg, *Education and Social Problems,* (New York: The Free Press, 1971), p. 270.

It is clear, however, that the practice results in classification according to socioeconomic and racial status, albeit in the name of ability grouping . . . students attending lower income predominantly negro schools . . . typically are confined to the educational limits of the lower tracks."[13] There is also evidence that students are assigned to tracks or ability groups in part at least, on the basis of their social class identification quite apart from their achievement test scores.[14] Although some maintain that such classification is in the best interest of the students so that they may compensate for their disadvantages, the overpowering evidence indicates that once grouped in particular categories and labeled, there is little chance of moving into another category.[15]

Public Policy on School Integration

The relation of educational policy and practice to the integration of the society focuses attention on the public policy regarding school desegregation. The contemporary policy in the United States as in other societies can best be characterized as mixed. Although not always enforced, both federal legislation and court decisions have maintained that racially segregated schools in the United States are contrary to public policy. However directly or indirectly, some legislation and administrative actions contribute to segregation. For example in the United States, the vocational education legislation provides funds for the establishment of separate area vocational high schools which tend to segregate lower-status students and allocate them to lower-status careers. Significant proportions of both houses of the U.S. Congress are on record to reverse the desegregation policies and former President Nixon clearly stated his concurrence in this effort. While the U.S. Supreme Court has outlawed direct financial aid to parochial schools, both the federal government and many states have provided categorical assistance for various educational functions in parochial schools and have supported in numerous ways the programs of private and church-related colleges and universities.

Although the Federal District Court and the Circuit Court of Appeals in Washington held tracking unconstitutional in 1967,[16] the majority of American school systems practice some system of tracking. This con-

[13] Julius Hobson *vs.* Carl Hanson, 269 F Supp 401 (1967). Also *Congressional Record,* House, June 21, 1967.

[14] Kariger, "Relationship of Lane Groupings to Socio-Economic Status of Parents," and Walter E. Shaffer, Carol Olexa and Kenneth Polk, "Programmed for Social Class: Tracking in High School," *Transaction,* vol. 7, no. 12 (October 1970), p. 40.

[15] Hobson *vs.* Hanson, and Kariger, "Relationship of Lane Groupings to Socio-Economic Status of Parents."

[16] Hobson *vs.* Hanson.

fusion in American policy is not a new phenomenon in American history. At the turn of the century, when the Plessey-Ferguson decision established the pattern of segregated Negro schools and federal-government–operated separate Indian schools in the United States, it was the clearly established policy in all states that European immigrant children should acquire American culture and be taught in English. Some states now require some instruction in a native language other than English and other states require bilingual instruction.

These divergent and sometimes incompatible practices and policies derive from divergent and sometimes incompatible goals and values described earlier. The mixture of goals and public policy regarding school segregation and program differentiation makes it difficult to specify at any particular time either the general or the precise policy. Policies frequently vary in some degree from one state or court jurisdiction to another and they change with the passage of new laws and new court decisions. A brief review of public policy as expressed in current laws and court decisions regarding school segregation provides a basis for understanding the current relation of education and social integration.

Changing Policy on Racial Segregation

Public policy concerning the segregation of black and white students and teachers in public schools varied from state to state for several decades after the abolition of slavery. Several Northern states had legislation forbidding segregation, but the former slave states in the South generally developed segregated schools after a brief period of integration. The Plessey-Ferguson decision of the U.S. Supreme Court established the principle that separate but equal facilities met the constitutional requirement. For the next half-century 17 states required that blacks and whites be segregated in all schools and some other states permitted segregation of blacks and whites in public schools as well as in private institutions.

After several years of challenges to the separate but equal doctrine in the courts, the U.S. Supreme Court in *Brown* vs. *Topeka Board of Education* established the principle that separate schools for the races were inherently unequal. Chief Justice Warren, writing for a unanimous Court, stated the principle as follows:

> We come then to the question presented: Does segregation of children in public schools solely on the basis of race, even though the physical facilities and other "tangible" factors may be equal, deprive the children of minority group of equal educational opportunities? We believe that it does . . . The effect of this separation of educational opportunities was well stated by a finding in the Kansas case by a court which

> nevertheless felt compelled to rule against the Negro plaintiffs: Segregation of white and colored children in public schools has a detrimental effect upon the colored children. The impact is greater when it has the sanction of the law; for the policy of separating the races is usually interpreted as denoting the inferiority of the Negro group. A sense of inferiority affects the motivation of a child to learn. Segregation with the sanction of law, therefore, has a tendency to [retard] the educational and mental development of Negro children and to deprive them of some of the benefits they would receive in a racially integrated system.[17]

The belief in the different abilities and aptitudes of black and white students as well as the belief that parents and local groups should have a choice in the schools which their children attend caused much objection and delay in conforming to the 1954 decision and the subsequent orders issued by the Supreme Court in 1955.

The patterns of resistance to integration in the states where segregation had been required by law, de jure segregation, differed somewhat from the resistance in de facto segregation situations in which housing patterns, voluntary action by the school districts, or other factors produced segregated attendance areas. The variation in court decisions on de jure and de facto cases require somewhat separate discussion for an understanding of the current public policy.

The former de jure segregated states made vigorous efforts to evade the integration of schools by a variety of devices. Among these was the provision of state funds for tuition grants to private schools, the insistence on freedom of choice so that parents might send students to schools which they preferred, and subsequently, insistence that race should not be a consideration for assignment to schools. The latter occurred after other devices were outlawed and was designed to permit the local school district to assign on some other basis such as test scores or neighborhoods which would coincide with the racial classification. The various devices succeeded in maintaining essentially segregated schools through the South for more than a decade.

In 1968, the U.S. Supreme Court decided a case in which freedom of choice in school attendance was the major issue. The Court acknowledged that freedom of choice might be a valid remedial measure for segregation in some circumstances, but stated that it could not be used as a basis for continued segregation. At that time, the court specified that "the burden on a school board today is to come forward with a plan that promises realistically to work . . . *now* . . . until it is clear that state-imposed segregation has been completely removed."[18] They further held that school authorities are "clearly charged with the affirmative duty

[17] Brown *vs.* Topeka Board of Education, 347, U.S. 483 (1954).

[18] Green *vs.* County School Board, 391, U.S. 430 (1968) at pp. 437–438.

to take whatever steps might be necessary to convert to a unitary system in which racial discrimination would be eliminated root and branch."

Although the court decision in the Green case placed positive obligation on the school districts of the South to integrate forthwith, this did not eliminate segregation. The North Carolina legislature had forbidden the busing of students in order to achieve racial integration and forbade the assignment of students to schools on account of race for the purpose of achieving racial balance or integration in schools. In 1970 the Supreme Court struck down such state laws which served to prevent the development of unitary school systems in the South. The court declared, "if a state imposed limitation on school authorities' discretion operates to inhibit or obstruct the operation of a unitary school system, it must fall; state policy must give way when it operates to hinder vindication of federal constitutional guarantees."[19]

In the same decision, the court declared, "Just as the race of students must be considered in determining whether a constitutional violation has occurred, so also must race be considered in formulating a remedy. To forbid, at this stage, all assignments made on the basis of race would deprive school authorities of the one tool absolutely essential to fulfillment of their constitutional obligation to eliminate existing dual school systems."

In this decision, the court made clear that states could not perpetuate segregated schools contrary to the federal court decision by legislation which would prevent the use of busing or racial assignments designed to bring about a unitary school system.

At the same time in a companion decision the U.S. Supreme Court undertook to provide guidelines for the racial integration of schools in the states which were formerly segregated by law. The court delineated a series of problems associated with the general issue of student assignment to achieve racial integration. They identified the problems as follows:

> The central issue in this case is that of student assignment, and there are essentially four problem areas:
> (1) to what extent racial balance or racial quotas may be used as an implement in a remedial order to correct a previously segregated system;
> (2) whether every all-Negro and all-White school must be eliminated as an indispensible part of a remedial process of desegregation;
> (3) what are the limits, if any, on the rearrangement of school districts and attendance zones as a remedial measure; and
> (4) what are the limits, if any, on the use of transportation facilities to correct state-enforced racial school segregation.[20]

---

[19] North Carolina State Board of Education *vs.* Swann, 402, U.S. 43 (1971).

[20] Swann et al. *vs.* Charlotte-Mecklenburg Board of Education, U.S. 402, U.S. 1, (1971).

Although the court did not require the achievement of absolute racial balance in bringing about desegregation, an awareness of the racial composition of the whole school system was accepted as a useful starting point in remedying the previous unconstitutional segregation. The achievement of a reasonably equal proportion of black and white students in the schools of a district was accepted as an appropriate guideline. The criterion by which the court should judge the desegregation plan of a district was its effectiveness rather than some arbitrarily prescribed technique or procedure.

The court recognized that the elimination of all- or predominantly one-race schools in every district, particularly large city districts, might not reasonably be expected. The presence of such schools, however, must be examined carefully to determine that they are not a part of a state-enforced segregation system. School authorities and district judges are charged with responsibility to make every effort that one-race schools are eliminated. The presence of one-race schools in systems that have a history of segregation warrants a presumption against such schools.

The third problem on which the court focused in the Swann et al. *vs.* Charlotte Mecklenburg Board of Education decision was the neighborhood school attendance area. In many cities the boundaries of attendance zones around a particular school could be drawn to maintain racial segregation. Many districts that had previously had not done so became firm advocates of neighborhood as a desirable method of school organization. In this decision, the court made it quite clear that "the objective is to dismantle the dual school system." They further indicated that almost any reasonable system of school attendance pairing, clustering, grouping that cut across local neighborhood boundaries was an acceptable method of school organization. Such attendance zones may be administratively inconvenient and impose some burdens but the maintenance of neighborhood school attendance zones to perpetuate a dual school system is clearly outlawed.

This guideline of the court is, of course, directly related to the question of transportation. When students are assigned to schools some distance from their home, transportation generally must be provided. The court recognized that school transportation or busing has long been a common practice in all parts of the United States. Nearly two fifths of the nation's public school children were transported in the 1969–70 school year. In many instances, busing had been used to maintain segregated schools, and the court recognized that the use of bus transportation for desegregation was as reasonable as its use for other purposes. Objection could be raised to transportation of students only on the basis that the time or distance of travel was so great as to risk the health of the children or infringe significantly on the educational process. Busing was, therefore, approved as a means of achieving desegregation so long as it, like other methods, was reasonable, feasible, and effective in achieving desegregation *now*.

The guidelines laid down in the previous discussion were specifically to be applied to the previously de jure segregated schools. In 1965, in a U.S. district court, Judge Sweany held that de facto segregation or racial imbalance was unconstitutional and indicated the basis for his decision.

> The defendants argue, nevertheless, that there is no constitutional mandate to remedy racial imbalance . . . but that is not the question. The question is whether there is a constitutional duty to provide equal educational opportunity for all children within the system. While Brown answered the question affirmatively in the context of coerced segregation, the constitutional fact—the inadequacy of segregated education—is the same in this case, and I so find. It is neither just nor sensible to prescribe segregation having its base in affirmative state action while at the same time failing to provide a remedy for segregation which grows out of discrimination in housing, or other economic or social factors. Education is tax supported and compulsory, and public school educators, therefore, must deal with inadequacies within the educational system as they arise, and it matters not that the inadequacies are not of their making. This is not to imply that the neighborhood school policy per se is unconstitutional, but that it must be abandoned or modified when it results in segregation in fact.[21]

In this decision, the judge focused on the constitutional duty to provide equal educational opportunity for all children. If segregated schools are unequal as held in Brown *vs.* Topeka Board of Education, they are presumed to be unequal in any case regardless of the reasons for their existence. On this basis, there is an obligation on the board to provide reasonably equal educational programs and to take whatever action may be necessary to do so. Other courts have held that there is no obligation on the board to eliminate de facto segregation when the forces producing this were not of their making. Judge Keith in the Eastern Michigan Federal District Court, however, held that failure to correct segregation practices over a period of time had given the segregated patterns the force of law and thus they had become de jure segregation. On this basis, Judge Keith ordered the Pontiac, Michigan, School District to desegregate and authorized a rearrangement of attendance areas with extensive busing of students.[22] This decision was upheld by the U.S. Court of Appeals and the school district has complied with it.

[21] Barksdale *vs.* Springfield School Committee, 237 F. Supp 543 (D Mass 1965) at 546.

[22] Davis *vs.* School District of City of Pontiac, 309 F. Supp 734 (E. D. Michigan, 1970), 443 F 2nd 573 (6th Cir., 1971), Cert. denied, 404 U.S. 913 (1971).

The U.S. Supreme Court established the principle that intentional action by a state or a school district which leads to or permits the segregation of schools is a denial of equal protection and requires affirmative action to correct even where segregation has not been mandated by the state.[23] In this case, the Court also held that proof of intentional segregation in one part of a school district was evidence that such a policy applied to other parts unless the school district presented convincing evidence to the contrary. Justice Powell and Justice Douglass argued that the distinction between de jure and de facto should be disregarded in school segregation cases and that the existence of segregated schools in a district should be an unconstitutional denial of equal protection regardless of legal mandate or intent.

Judge Roth also held that de jure segregation existed in the Detroit School District because of long-standing policies of the state and federal government as well as the school district.[24] State school district boundary policies, school financing, and federal housing policies were all shown to contribute to the school segregation. To remedy the situation, Judge Roth ordered 53 surrounding suburban school districts combined with Detroit in a series of school clusters within a metropolitan district.

In a five to four decision, the U.S. Supreme Court reversed that portion of the Roth decision ordering a metropolitan remedy involving 53 other school districts.[25] The majority held that the Court could not impose a multidistrict remedy for a single district violation when there was no finding that the other districts had failed to operate unitary districts. This decision apparently ignored the fact that the school districts are created by the state and that the State of Michigan was found to have participated in a constitutional violation. By this decision, the state is absolved of the responsibility to provide effective desegregation remedies which cross district boundaries unless other districts have been found in violation of the Constitution.

Strong dissents by Justice White and Justice Marshall were both concurred in by four justices. The latter maintained that the Court was taking a "giant step backward" in the trend toward desegregation and equality of education. Since an adequate remedy could not be achieved within Detroit, the Court's decision guaranteed that "Negro children in Detroit will receive the same separate and inherently unequal educa-

[23] Keyes *vs.* Denver School District No. 1. 413, U.S. 189, (1973).

[24] Bradley et al. *vs.* Milliken et al., U.S. District Court 338 F. Supp. 582 (Sept. 27, 1971), held that Detroit school system was segregated; 345 F. Supp. 914 (June 14, 1972) disapproved "Detroit only" plan and directed preparation of a "metro" plan; upheld by Appeals Court 484 F 2nd 215 (6th Cir. 1973); S.C. cert. granted Nov. 19, 1973, 94 S. Ct. 538.

[25] Milliken et al., *vs.* Bradley et al., Supreme Court of U.S., No 73–434, 73–435 and 73–436 (July 25, 1974). Also Dissents by Justice White and Justice Marshall.

tion in the future as they have been unconstitutionally afforded in the past."[26]

The predominance of a black school population in Detroit as in Washington, D.C., and other cities makes it impossible to desegregate the schools within the district without creating all predominantly black schools. If the current white attitudes toward integration prevail, the requirement that desegregation must occur within the district is unlikely to halt or reduce white migration out of the city. The evidence from other cities, however, does not support the contention that city desegregation increases white flight to the suburbs.[27]

The recent district and appeals court decisions stimulated a strong anti-busing movement in federal and state legislation as well as public support for segregated schools. School boards have been recalled, constitutional amendments proposed, and legislation passed to prevent busing to achieve racial integration of schools. Although the Detroit decision seems to modify the Court policy supporting desegregation, the dissents and other forces give some promise of a continuing desegregation policy. School segregation is still a major subject of debate and controversy more than 20 years after the 1954 decision which presumably changed the national policy.

Although the policy regarding racial segregation is not clear, it has moved haltingly toward the elimination of racially segregated schools. It should be recognized, however, that these policies have thus far been applied primarily to black and white segregation. The patterns of segregated Indian schools, supported by the Federal Bureau of Indian Affairs, still exist in some sections of the United States. The policies expressed by federal legislation and the President have not always concurred with the Court. Former President Nixon and President Ford have publicly opposed busing as a means of achieving racial integration and the U.S. Congress outlawed busing past the second nearest school unless ordered by the Court to achieve racial desegregation of the schools in a district.

Ethnic and Religious Segregation

Public policy regarding the segregation of some ethnic group students has been determined by the policy concerning racial segregation. The large concentrations of Puerto Rican population in such cities as New York and the Mexican-American populations in Southwestern parts of the United States have been considered in the same manner as black students when dealing with public school attendance patterns. Many other ethnic groups and the Spanish-speaking ones to some extent have

[26] Ibid. Marshall Dissent p. 2.

[27] Jane R. Mercer and Terrence H. Scott, "The Relation between School Desegregation and Racial Composition of California School Districts, 1966–73," unpublished report, 1974, cited by permission of authors.

attended religious-sponsored schools, particularly Catholic schools. The public policy regarding parochial schools, therefore, is relevant to some ethnic groups, as well as religious groups.

Legislative action as well as court decisions has traditionally permitted religious bodies to sponsor schools which provide secular as well as religious education for children of families who wish to have this type of education for their children. This issue has revolved around the "freedom of religion" policy in the United States Constitution. The implications, however, of the dual parochial and public school system for the society generally is similar to segregation of schools on other bases. The current policy is best indicated by the 1971 Supreme Court decision in which Pennsylvania[28] and Rhode Island[29] laws were held unconstitutional. Both laws provided financial support for salaries of teachers of secular subjects in elementary and secondary schools. The Court held that these acts violated the establishment of religion clause by fostering "excessive entanglements." While total separation, as held in prior rulings, was not possible in such areas as welfare of students or the sharing of books, the court felt ". . . teachers had a substantially different ideological character than books." The beliefs of a teacher, the court felt, are more important than the subject being taught.

On the same day, the court found constitutional the Federal Higher Education Facilities Act of 1963 by which $240 million in federal funds paid for construction of academic buildings on campuses of private colleges including those which are church related. The majority held that college students are much less impressionable and susceptible to religious indoctrination than are elementary and secondary students. Therefore, since religious indoctrination is not a primary activity of the four-year colleges involved, there is less likelihood that religion will permeate secular education.

Unless the U.S. Constitution is amended, this opinion seems to bar, for a time at least, the provision of direct tax support for religious controlled elementary and secondary schools. A constitutional amendment permitting such public support of religious schools seems unlikely. The voters of Michigan overruled both the legislature and the governor who had proposed legislation providing state funds for the secular teaching provided by parochial schools. It would appear from these data that the American public is not likely to approve the direct support of parochial schools in the near future.

It should be recognized, however, that various types of federal and state support have been provided for institutions of higher education with church affiliation and that categorical assistance for such purposes

[28] Lemon *vs.* Kurtzman, 310 F Supp 35 (E.D. Penn 1969) and 403, U.S. 602 (1971).

[29] Robinson *vs.* DiCenso, 316 F. Supp 112 (D.C. R.I. 1970) Supreme Court. Same as Lemon and Kurtzman (1971).

as transportation, school lunches, and instructional materials has been available to students of parochial schools at all levels.

Freedom to operate private and parochial schools continues as established public policy. However, the decision preventing direct financial assistance makes it more difficult to finance parochial schools and is likely to further reduce their number.

Segregation of Socioeconomic Status Groups

The denial of equal educational opportunity to students because they come from poor social strata has long been condemned. The actual provision of unequal education, however, has not been universally condemned. Expenditures for education vary greatly from one school district to another. Most states use some system to reduce the inequalities in financial support allocated to local school districts, but local differences in the resources available and their unequal allocation to schools frequently provides less financial support for some schools than others. Although the amount of expenditures is not highly correlated with quality of output, discrepancies in expenditures may affect subjective evaluations of school quality. The organization of school districts in such a manner that some have decidedly superior resources and are composed of families from higher socioeconomic levels while other districts have lower resources and lower-status families provides a basis for the socioeconomic segregation of children. Evidence from standardized achievement test data and the assessment programs now available indicate that school districts as well as schools vary a great deal in achievement. On the whole, districts with high mean socioeconomic status are higher-achieving districts.

The barriers of district boundaries may, therefore, segregate the poor from the more affluent. There is no strong public sentiment to modify district boundaries to eliminate socioeconomic segregation. A few states have reorganized school districts into larger metropolitan or county units combining rural, suburban middle-class, and the central city areas. Most boundaries of districts, however, particularly the larger metropolitan ones, still define a degree of socioeconomic segregation. Many large districts encompassing wide ranges of social strata maintain socioeconomic segregation within the school district by attendance areas. Although such segregation and discrimination do not converge with our belief in equal educational opportunity, neither the courts nor legislatures have established a public policy to achieve equality of education among socioeconomic strata. Recent state court decisions which hold that differences in school financial support resulting from dependence on property tax is a denial of equal protection of the law may force greater equality in school expenditures even though the U.S. Supreme

Court has not required such action.[30] Equal expenditure does not reduce segregation between districts, or guarantee equality, but it may provide somewhat better resources in poorer districts. The failure of the Supreme Court to order district reorganization in metropolitan Detroit perpetuates a policy of socioeconomic as well as racial segregation maintained by district boundaries.

Tracking and Ability Grouping within Schools

In 1967, Judge Skelly Wright held that the tracking system in Washington, D.C., public schools was unconstitutional. His position is clearly stated in the following brief excerpt:

> Even in concept the track system is undemocratic and discriminatory. Its creator admits it is designed to prepare some children for white-collar, and other children for blue-collar jobs. Considering the tests used to determine which children should receive the blue-collar special and which the white, the danger of children completing their education wearing the wrong collar is far too great for this democracy to tolerate. Moreover, any system of ability grouping which through failure to include and implement the concept of compensatory education for the disadvantaged child or otherwise fails in fact to bring the great majority of children into mainstream of public education denies the children excluded equal educational opportunity and thus encounters the constitutional bar.[31]

This decision was upheld by the Circuit Court of Appeals in 1969.[32] A few other district courts have similarly held tracking programs as discriminatory, but the U.S. Supreme Court has not yet heard a tracking case. The highest court dismissed without comment the appeal of the Washington, D.C., case. Although some federal courts have held tracking and ability grouping as commonly practiced unconstitutional, public education authorities and the state legislators have encouraged tracking and ability grouping through a wide variety of legislation and state education policies. Increasing support for special classes for the presumably retarded and the presumably gifted as well as both federal and state funds for separate vocational tracks have encouraged the expansion of such differentiated and segregated educational programs for different groups in spite of the court decision outlawing tracking practices.

A recent U.S. Supreme Court decision[33] concerning a matter far re-

[30] Serrano *vs.* Priest, 5 California, 3d. 584, 487, P2nd 1241 (1971), and Van Dusartz *vs.* Hatfield, 324 F. Supp 870 (1971), and Rodiquez *vs.* San Antonio Independent School District, 337 F. Supp. 280 (W.D. Texas, 1971). San Antonio Independent School District *vs.* Rodiquez, 337 U.S. 1 (1973).

[31] Hobson *vs.* Hanson.

[32] Smuck *vs.* Hobson, 408 F 2nd 175 D.C. Circuit, 1969.

[33] Wisconsin *vs.* Constantineau, 39 U.S.L.W., 4128, January 19, 1971.

moved from the public schools may have significant implications for school tracking and special class placement. "The court ruled that a Wisconsin law requiring the posting of names of alleged problem drinkers in taverns and package stores for the purpose of preventing the sale of liquor to them constituted stigmatization serious enough to require due process."[34] The labeling or characterization of a person in a manner to stigmatize him without proper hearing was declared contrary to the due process provision of the constitution. Similar claims are being made with regard to the stigma resulting from classification as mentally retarded.[35] The negative perception of such labeling and possible harmful effects have long been recognized. If the stigma concept outlawed in the drinking case is applied to school class placement, a major shift in educational policy will occur. The major emphasis in public educational policy, however, still favors the expansion of differentiated and unequal educational programs.

Some court decisions and legislative enactments indicate that the courts have moved in the direction of desegregation and the elimination of some inequalities in educational opportunity. It is far from clear, however, that this is the probable outcome on this issue. The current division in society with regard to school segregation, recent elections, recent legislation, and the Detroit decision suggest the reverse direction. Opposition to busing to achieve racial balance and integrated educational programs may prevail.

The diverse efforts and the division of American policy on the questions of school segregation and differentiation reflect the ambivalence of Americans with regard to the basic values. We profess belief in equality of opportunity and an open society in a common culture. At the same time we struggle to maintain a segregated, stratified system of education supported by differences in expenditure and exemplified through a widely differentiated and stratified educational system. The differential levels of educational outcomes among the students from different strata in society will be discussed in a later chapter. Our concern at this point is the impact of this system on the social structure of the larger society.

Education and Cultural Solidarity

An analysis of the role of education in the segregation and stratification of the society requires some attention to the matter of maintaining

[34] *Inequality in Education*, no. 7 (Cambridge, Massachusetts: Center for Law and Education, Harvard University, 1971), p. 38.

[35] Stewart et al., *vs.* Phillips et al., Civil Action No. 70–1199 F. (D.C. Mass.) reported in *Inequality of Education*, no. 6, p. 20.

a common basis for social interaction. An underlying assumption of the discussion of school segregation holds that the segregation or integration of schools affects the social integration and solidarity of the larger society. The National Advisory Commission on Civil Disorders examined the integration of American society and concluded, "Our Nation is moving toward two societies, one black, one white—separate and unequal."[36] Although numerous factors affect the division of a society, the commission on Civil Disorders concluded that the organization of education contributed significantly to the division or integration of policy. They included in their recommendations the following: "We support integration as the priority education strategy; it is essential to the future of American society. . . . we have seen the consequences of racial isolation at all levels and of attitudes toward race, on both sides, produced by three centuries of myth, ignorance, and bias. It is indispensable that opportunities for interaction between the races be expanded."[37] The separation of Chicano and Anglo, native American and those with European origins, and Black and White students in separate schools or the separation of poor from the affluent not only fails to provide opportunity for achievement, interaction, and understanding, but creates barriers between segments in the society and impedes mobility. Recent conflicts in American society are indicative of the potential division in the social order. The recent pressure from both Blacks and Whites for separation of racial groups in urban schools and the decentralization of control in local communities reflect this division in our society. The failure to provide a common integrated educational program no doubt has contributed to this state of American society.

The authors would concur with the National Advisory Commission that the educational system may contribute either to division or solidarity. The extent to which it affects a society in one direction or the other may depend on the degree to which the schools provide to the many subcultural groups in the pluralistic society common socialization in a common culture. Many contemporary educators and other leaders have emphasized the importance of maintaining a multi-ethnic society. The demand for teaching Chicano culture or African culture in the public schools is symbolic of this movement. Preservation of these cultural traits is highly valued as a means of maintaining identity with one's cultural heritage. However, if this movement converges with the demands to completely segregate the various subcultures and social strata, it may facilitate the division of the society and produce even greater hostility against minorities rather than the integration, equality, and social solidarity of racial and ethnic groups in a pluralistic society.

---

[36] *Report of the National Advisory Commission on Civil Disorders* (New York: Bantam Books, N.Y. Times Company, 1968).

[37] Ibid., p. 25.

A minimum level of common values, language, modes of interaction, and other cultural phenomena is essential in maintaining a society. If educational segregation reinforced with separate ethnic curricula and group isolation prevails, the long-range impact is likely to be increased division and separateness with all of the inequalities which characterize such divisions. If multi-ethnic education, on the other hand, means that all groups should have a common appreciation of diverse cultural elements such as African music, soul food, Polish dances, tacos, and the migrant stream culture in order to provide some alternative culture patterns within a common culture, the long-range result may be cultural richness and mutual understanding. Different curricula based on such cultural variations in segregated and differentiated school programs similar to the current stratification system will not enhance mutual appreciation or enrich the common culture.

The educational system can serve to socialize the diverse groups in either way—separate and segregated cultures or joint integrated and common cultures. As the National Advisory Commission on Civil Disorders recognized, the society has nearly, if not already, reached the point where its common culture and integrated functioning are threatened. In a similar fashion, the potential division of Canada into English and French societies may be imminent. Although we cannot precisely identify the contribution of separate schools to this division, few would argue that the organization of schools was irrelevant in either the United States or Canada. It is therefore essential for those wishing to develop an open society for all regardless of race, ethnicity, religion, sex, or affluence to organize the schools in such a way that they provide a common base of skills, knowledge, and beliefs in equality and our common aspirations. Some educators have also emphasized the importance of a school curriculum in which students develop a commitment to an open society; a society in which individuals from diverse cultural, racial, and social class groups have an equal opportunity to participate.[38] Such a commitment is essential to maintain an open society, but it must be one with sufficient common culture to hold the varied ethnic and racial groups together, or the diverse cultures will exacerbate the differences and inequality. However, contemporary public policy does not seem directed toward the enhancement of a common culture. Although the courts and some legislation have maintained the concept of equality of opportunity, the current opposition to shared educational experience, the integration of schools, and other affirmative action reflects an ambivalence on these values. Mutual understanding and appreciation of multiracial and multi-ethnic origins and life styles is essential,

[38] James A. Banks, "Curriculum Models for an Open Society," in Delmo Della-Dora and James E. House (eds.), *Education for an Open Society*, (Washington, D.C.: Yearbook Association for Supervision and Curriculum Development, 1974), pp. 43–65.

but the perpetuation of these differences through segregation and diverse socialization is not likely to promote social solidarity or reduce the inequalities of our time.

Differentiation in Education and Structure of Society

Throughout this section we have been concerned with the relation of the educational system to the society in which it is functioning. We have noted the uncertain role of education in the process of social change. We at least entertain the hypothesis that the educational system may assist in the development of emerging societies. We recognize the significance of the system of educational control in the determination of educational policy and practices. The most salient question in American society involving the relationship of education to the structure of the larger society concerns the impact of school segregation and differentiation on the stratification system.

The contemporary concern with this pressing issue identifies the belief that the nature of our society is dependent at least in part on the way in which the educational system is organized and the way it performs its functions. Many advocates of social change through education despair that mobility and equality can be effected in any significant degree. The concentration of power and prestige in certain social strata may prevent the school from affecting significantly the distribution of power and prestige in the society. Evidence certainly can be supplied to support such a contention in American society. The ambivalence of American beliefs and the parallel emphasis on equality and differentiation may, however, create a situation with sufficient fluidity to entertain the possibility that education may affect the structure of the society. Certainly recent years have provided some evidence that some modification of the educational differentiation patterns might be achieved and through this a modification of the social structure.

The possibility of change in the social structure of society through education is dependent of course on the degree to which education is causally related to social status and other structural variables. Some contemporary scholars have maintained, after examining the evidence available, that education has little or no effect on the degree of inequality in adult society[39] and that "school reform is never likely to have any significant effect on the degree of inequality among adults."[40] Much

[39] Christopher Jencks, et al., *Inequality: A Reassessment of the Effect of Family and Schooling in America,* (New York: Basic Books, 1972).

[40] Mary Jo Bane and Christopher Jencks, "The Schools and Equal Opportunity," *Saturday Review of Education,* September 16, 1972, pp. 37–42.

of this argument is based upon findings that educational resources are not significantly related to the outcomes of schools and that the differences in cognitive achievement produced by reorganization of the schools have not been great. The data available at this time does not allow us to determine for sure whether an expansion of resources into schools is likely to reduce inequalities in either achievement or later status.

In contrast to the position of Jencks and his associates on the relation of education to social status is the widely held belief that the level of educational achievement affects the job which the individual is able to obtain and his position in the social structure. It takes no elaborate study to demonstrate that one does not become a doctor, lawyer, major business executive, teacher or member of many other occupations without the achievement of a specific level or type of education. This fact of course is clearly demonstrated by the high correlation between the level of education and the prestige or status level of occupations in American society. As we have noted earlier, the level of education of course is also highly correlated with the family background of students. This relationship is so pervasive and intertwined that it is impossible at this time to separate the effect of family background and school characteristics on the achievement of students in school.[41] There is ample evidence, however, that employers use educational level as a criterion for selection of employees,[42] and that some people from lower-status family backgrounds achieve high-status positions by means of the educational achievement channel.[43]

These conflicting conclusions concerning the relation of education to status or position in the social structure apparently result from the fact that education serves two functions. It processes many children and youths through the system with little modification of their chance of moving in the social structure. At the same time, the school apparently certifies and perhaps qualifies students for different levels of occupation. In this process the schools select some for mobility in the social system. The complex interaction of family background, educational programs, school achievement, and occupational allocation through differentiated curricula produces a result that can be analyzed in different fashions with different conclusions concerning the function of education in relation to the social structure.

Since the educational systems have been stratified and segregated in the past, it is difficult, if not impossible, to know what impact an

[41] James S. Coleman, et al., *Equality of Educational Opportunity* (Washington, D.C.: U.S. Government Printing Office, 1966).

[42] Randall Collins, "Functional and Conflict Theories of Educational Stratification," *American Sociological Review*, vol. 36, December 1971, pp. 1002–1019.

[43] Bruce K. Eckland, "Academic Ability, Higher Education and Occupational Mobility," *American Sociological Review*, vol. 30, October 1965, pp. 735–746.

integrated equality-oriented educational system would have on the structure of society. Certainly continued school segregation, differentiated educational programs and unequal outcomes are unlikely to enhance social equality and solidarity.

Suggested Readings

Readings suggested for Chapter 5 are also relevant for Chapter 6. Additional suggestions follow:

James Bosco and Stanley Robin, "White Flight from Court Ordered Busing," *Urban Education,* 9, no. 1 (April 1974), pp. 87–98.

Delmo Della-Dora and James E. House, eds., *Education for an Open Society,* yearbook (Washington, D.C.: Association for Supervision and Curriculum Development, 1974).

Edgar G. Epps, ed., *Cultural Pluralism* (Berkeley, Calif.: McCutchan Publishing Corp., 1974).

Edsel L. Erickson, Clifford E. Bryan, and Lewis Walker, "The Educability of Dominant Groups," *Phi Delta Kappan,* 53, no. 5 (January 1972).

O. Wayne Gordon ed., *Uses of the Sociology of Education, Section III, The Seventy-third Yearbook of the National Society for the Study of Education* (Chicago: Univ. of Chicago Press, 1974). This section contains several excellent articles analyzing school desegregation issues.

Andrew T. Kopan and Herbert J. Walberg, *Rethinking Educational Equality* (Berkeley, Calif.: McCutchan Publishing Corp., 1974).

Ray C. Rist, *Restructuring American Education* (New Brunswick, N.J.: E. P. Dutton and Co., 1972).

David Rogers, *New York City and the Politics of School Desegregation* (New York: Center for Urban Education, 1971).

David Rogers, *One Hundred and Ten Livingston Street* (New York: Vintage, 1969).

Lilian Rubin, *Busing and Backlash: White Against White in an Urban School District,* Berkeley, Calif.: University of California Press, 1972).

Harmon Ziegler and Michael Boss, "Racial Problems and Policy in American Public Schools," *Sociology of Education,* 47, no. 3 (Summer 1974), pp. 319–36.

part three

The School as a Social System

7

The Organization of Education

In one sense a school is an umbrella over many individuals, groups, and programs, each with unique as well as common purposes. While many of these persons and substructures cooperate in the attainment of general school objectives, they often operate at cross purposes. For instance, the English classes in a school may be conducted in a fashion that increases the pressure for certain students to drop out, while at the same time another program in the school is trying to keep these same students from leaving school. Before we carry this point further, however, we should consider the nature of school organization.

First of all, every school is organized in a myriad of ways, supposedly to achieve the varied purposes of each of its many groups and individuals as well as to achieve the broad goals of the school itself. We may view a school's organization from any one of several perspectives, depending on our purposes. For example, a school may be viewed with reference to the distribution of formal authority or informal power over various matters; the teaching of particular skills, knowledge, and attitudes; the maintenance of assumed cultural patterns, such as the separation of black from white subcultures or the promotion of selected religious values; or the provision of services to the community, such as basketball entertainment or a trained manpower pool with electronics skills. We may also examine educational organizations for their economic and political functions. In other words, when we speak of school organization, we need to clarify the purpose of our inquiry and the particular aspects of organization involved. Too often an organizational chart of formal authority which shows school boards, administrators, teachers, other staff, and students is used to describe the organization of the school as if it were the only way the school is organized. But the formal organizational chart may be only partially relevant even for questions of authority and power. Teachers, custodians, secretaries, and students, as well as administrators, often have power to manage school affairs even though they might not be so recognized on formal organizational charts. The informal relationships between members of the organization may materially affect decision making and other behavior within the organization.

This is not to say that the formal organization of a school makes no difference. On the contrary, different modes of organizing the educational system—into traditional graded or nongraded programs, open classroom, middle schools, tracks, neighborhood schools, centralized or decentralized administrations, etc.,—are crucial matters for those concerned with the processes or outcomes of schooling. What must be remembered, however, is that all programs are likely to have unintended outcomes which may go unrecognized. For example, a program that is set up to enhance the reading skills of students by placing them in special classrooms for concentrated attention by specially trained teachers may have the unintended consequence of creating an image of these students as "retards" or as innately inferior. This image of the student as retarded then may cause the teachers to teach them less and the result is a "self-fulfilling prophecy"—the students learn less. Or a tracking program may become an unintended vehicle for segregating black and white students, which in turn contributes to racial conflicts and school riots. While it is important to understand the objectives of any school organization, each must be examined in terms of its unintended results as well as its intended consequences.

Other points can be made concerning the manifest or intended goals people have for education. People are constantly trying to organize and reorganize their schools to achieve the kind of society and personal attainment they desire. Indeed, most of the cultural conflict over education—whether it is over compensatory education, busing of students, discrimination, decentralization, teacher associations, types of curriculum, means of financing, sex education, or equal opportunities—is often based on differing values relative to the kind of society individuals and groups wish to maintain or bring about. It is interesting to note, however, that much of the available knowledge about the nature and function of various school structures is not employed by those responsible for educational programs. Perhaps as a result, and regardless of their intentions, the managers of education often fail to bring about their stated aims. Similarly, educators and their publics often have contradictory and unclear notions about what exactly is going on in their educational programs. We believe that one of the sources of such confusion is a failure to understand their school's operations from a social systems perspective.

Just as an understanding of the human system requires a set of concepts and principles which relate the various components to one another and to the larger environment, so does an understanding of the school system. Any school is more than an aggregate of humans, buildings, and equipment. A school is also a set of patterned relationships or social structures with individuals and groups reacting to one another in particular ways. We will present a number of sociological concepts and perspectives for analyzing how people and groups within educational organizations are likely to act toward one another and why they react as they do.

In previous chapters we discussed the relationship of schools to other institutions. It will be important to keep in mind these relationships between schools and the rest of society as we examine the internal operations of education.[1] For example, we will discuss ways in which internal organizational patterns of counseling and teaching are sometimes influenced by economic pressures from outside the schools. We will also need to keep in mind that schools function, in large part, to satisfy felt needs of individuals and groups in society.

A basic dilemma emerges, however, as educational systems also develop their own needs to survive and these needs may not be in accord with societal needs. Schools develop their own boundaries and production goals and these are sometimes at cross purposes with governmental agencies, family aspirations, and economic interests. The same kinds of conflict also occur between the needs of various units within a school system and those of the total school operation. For example, the teaching staff and the counseling staff may each develop their own boundaries and objectives which may, on occasion, be both counter to one another and counter to the objectives of the school administration. This chapter and subsequent chapters in this part of the text will examine the boundaries and patterns of conduct of the three major groupings around which the schools are generally organized: the managers of education, the professional staff, and the clients of educators, their students. First, however, several sociological concepts and principles relevant to our understanding of school organization should be considered.

One of the more important of these general concepts involves the distinction between *systems properties* and *properties of individuals* making up the system.

---

[1] See for example Ralph W. Larkin, "Contextual Influences on Teacher Leadership Styles," *Sociology of Education,* Fall 1973, vol. 46, no. 4, pp. 471–499. In this study Larkin shows that both the demographic context and the internal organization of the school had strong effects on the leadership styles of teachers in their classrooms.

Systems Properties of Schools

One way of illustrating a *systems property* is to consider the case of an economically poor student who attends a school made up of predominantly upper-class children. The affluence level of the school may be determined by the affluence levels of the children in the school, but it is not the same thing. Sociologists of education have demonstrated that the *socioeconomic composition of a school* is often an important variable independent of any particular student's socioeconomic status, and that when a knowledge of the economic composition of the school is used alone, or in combination with a knowledge of the individual's economic status, our understanding of student performance is increased.[2] With knowledge not only of the individual's social class but also of the social class context in which he operates at school, our understanding of other school activities may benefit as well. For example, Herriott and St. John found that the principal's performance in school has varying influence on teachers, depending on the social class composition of the student body.[3] However, the socioeconomic composition of the school is but one way of characterizing a school. There are three types of properties used to characterize systems: analytical, global, and structural.[4]

Analytic Properties

Properties of systems which are based on information about members of that system we refer to as *analytical properties*. The socioeconomic composition of a school or school system is an analytical property. Racial composition is an analytical property of particular interest to sociologists of education in nations concerned with racial conflict within their schools. Note, however, that any simple association between an analytical property of a school, such as the school's socioeconomic status level, and a product or outcome of that school, such as student performance,

---

[2] Robert E. Herriott and Nancy St. John, *Social Class and the Urban School* (New York: John Wiley & Sons, Inc., 1966). See also Ruth VanKampen, "A Study of the Effect of School Socio-Economic Composition on Student Achievement" (Master's thesis, Western Michigan University, 1969); Neal Gross and Robert E. Herriott, *Staff Leadership in the Public Schools* (New York: John Wiley & Sons, 1950), p. 43; James Coleman et al., *Equality of Educational Opportunity* (Washington, D.C.: U.S. Department of Health, Education and Welfare, U.S. Government Printing Office, 1966), p. 22.

[3] Herriott and St. John, *Social Class and the Urban School*, p. 152.

[4] The concepts "analytical," "global," and "structural" are drawn from the work of Paul F. Lazarsfeld, "Evidence and Inference in Social Research," *Daedalus*, vol. 8, no. 4 (1958), pp. 99–130.

should not be viewed as necessarily a cause and effect relationship. The socioeconomic composition of a school may only be associated with student performance through its association with other conditions, such as stereotypes held by educators. Teachers, administrators, and the community may respond differently to clusters of poor or wealthy children and that may be one reason for the varying levels of statistical association between the economic compositions of schools and achievement in varying cultures. Some researchers and educators recognize, for example, that the association between racial composition of schools and student achievement in the United States is in part a result of inferior expectations held for black children and black schools by educators and lay persons, and that, with an enhancement of teacher expectations, the association between race and achievement would become less.[5] In other words, just because a school is made up of poor or black children is no reason that such children must, of necessity, learn less than others. This will be discussed and documented in greater detail in later chapters.

As one may readily infer, vast numbers of analytical properties may be used to describe schools. Some of the other analytical properties of relevance to sociologists of education concern secular-religious differences, ideological differences such as "conservative" and "liberal," and differences in occupational orientation, with some schools valuing universal higher education while others value earlier vocational entry for the poor.

Global Properties

There are other features of schools which are based on neither the characteristics of the members of a system nor on the nature of the members' relationships to one another. For example, we may be interested in whether certain schools possess certain programs (libraries, data-processing services, counselors, etc.). We might also be interested in differences among school systems in the extent to which each allocates its resources to teaching, research, administration, community service, etc. Schools may also differ and may be categorized on the basis of their goals as set by their communities, which are not always the same as the goals of the staff. For example, some schools may be established as college preparatory schools while the school's staff prefers a more vocational orientation. The goal orientations of schools when not made up of the objectives of the staff or students we would consider as global properties.

[5] See for example James McPartland, *The Segregated Student in Desegregated Schools* (Maryland: The Center for the Study of Social Organization of Schools, The Johns Hopkins University, 1968).

Structural Properties

The reader may have noticed that analytical and global properties of schools do not explicitly describe how the counselors, teachers, students, and others in a school relate to one another. As such, analytical and global properties do not describe education as a social system, which is defined in terms of how the parts of a system relate to one another in typical or patterned ways.

Sociologists, as well as others, are interested in how individuals or groups within education relate to one another. In one classroom, the teacher and students may interact as partners, while in another classroom the teacher and students may relate on an authoritarian basis with most of the power vested in the teacher. Such classroom patterns as "authoritarian," "democratic," and "laissez faire" are *structural properties,* and these terms have frequently been used to describe interaction patterns between teachers and students within classrooms. Structural properties of particular concern to sociologists of education include both formal and informal power and authority relationships, such as the bureaucratic structure, and the clique structures among counselors, social workers, physical education teachers, English teachers, and others.

Considerable attention has also been directed to the relationships between parents and students. Some might feel that parents should be left out of any analysis of structures within education. As we previously indicated, however, a social system does not have to have an existence within some grouping of walls and windows. As a matter of fact, in many schools parents are given certain formal teaching roles within the school system. Professional educators actually organize, instruct, and expect parents to teach certain skills and values which further the aims of the educational system. The point is that merely looking at the formal organizational roles of teachers, students, administrators, and school board members is a sure way to miss out on much that is important in an educational system. Many, for example, fail to see the powerful administrative and teaching roles that custodians sometimes play.

School Climate. Associated with the formal and informal patterns of relationships within the school organization are norms and expectations which are applied to the various members of the organization. The set normative definitions of behavior which characterizes a school social organization has been identified as school climate. At the larger society level the concept culture is essentially equated with climate. The climate or culture in one secondary school may include the norm and expectation that most students should and will go on to college. In another school the climate may be characterized by norm and expectation that most students should and will enter the work force at semiskilled or lower levels on completion of high school. In the first school the pattern of relationships will be quite different from that in the latter school. School climate as well as organization may significantly affect the nature and type of behavior learned in school. Two chapters in the last section of this text will be devoted to the consequences of climate and organization for student achievement. We view school climate as referring to normative relationships which characterize schools and not to such analytic properties as racial or socioeconomic composition. Composition variables, at best, provide only data for estimating or inferring how people are relating to one another—they are not direct measures of school climate.

The School as a Complex Organization

One perspective, of special relevance for understanding the internal power structures which operate in the control of educational systems, has been summarized by Ronald Corwin in his characterization of a complex organization.

> A complex organization consists of (1) stable patterns of interaction, (2) among coalitions of groups having a collective identity (e.g., a name and location[s]), (3) pursuing interests and accomplishing given tasks, and (4) coordinated by power and authority structures.
>
> Patterns of interaction among people are determined partly by their positions in their organizations. These positions, and the relationships among them, form the *power and authority structures* which are largely responsible for coordinating an organization's primary activities. Positions are comprised of work *roles,* consisting of related norms, which are maintained in part by common expectations and in part by sanctions imposed for conformity and deviation. Responsibility for performing the key processes (to be described) is allocated *via* these roles.
>
> Among the most vital relationships are those which define the system of *control* over work and of one member over another. The control system, in turn, includes three components. The first is the *official status system* by which the authority to issue commands is delegated to a hierarchy of positions. *Informal prestige and power* also accrue to each position in the official hierarchy. The *prestige* hierarchy, an expression of the value system, reflects the relative importance assigned to each position by organization members; the *power* hierarchy reflects the actual opportunity which positions provide to members for controlling others. The distribution of power and authority determines the degree of centralization and decentralization of the decision-making process.
>
> *Rules and Procedures* make up the second component of the control system. They provide guidelines for coordinating the organization's parts and for regulating the conduct of its members. The number, scope, specificity, and enforcement of rules and regulations establish the degree of standardization throughout the organization.

> The third component, the *division of labor,* is partially produced by and supplements the first two. Whereas the status system refers to hierarchies of power and authority, the division of labor is determined by assignments of responsibilities laterally to distinct units (positions) at the same level in the hierarchy. It establishes "who does what." In fixing responsibility, however, the division of labor also assigns prestige and power to positions, often on a basis somewhat different than dictated solely by the status hierarchy. For example, although English and shop teachers are peers in the official authority system, in fact English teachers usually have more prestige, and in some upper-middle-class communities they also have more influence because of the importance of their jobs for getting children into college.
>
> These characteristics are dynamically commingled. The division of labor produces specialization, or the process of breaking work down into spheres of responsibility, some of which are officially designated as *offices.* It sets in motion the counterprocess of coordination, which is accomplished through centralized positions of authority and standardized work procedures. Specialization and centralization present a picture of complex organization in a state of simultaneous expansion and contraction of responsibility, a repetitious process of delegation and recontrol.[6]

Although some small school systems may not demonstrate all of the characteristics of a complex organization, most educational systems are clearly identified by the characteristics which Corwin has described. Obviously, the expectations and the power or authority associated with different positions in a school organization are all a part of the process by which control is exercised.

The Exercise of Internal Control

Although the typical school organization is subject to external influences, there are forces within the organization which are also important in specifying authority and what is to be considered appropriate behavior for members. For example, the behavior of a school principal is clearly influenced by the expectations that other administrators, teachers, and students hold for principals, the prestige of the position within the organization, the existing rules and procedures for principals, and the division of labor that characterizes the other roles within the organization. Of course, each member of a school is also affected to some degree by the expectations held for him by persons outside the school. Nevertheless, even the pressures emanating from outside are often affected by the public information provided by the school organization and by the organization's rules and procedures for its members when they interact

[6] Ronald Corwin, "Education and the Sociology of Complex Organizations," in Donald A. Hansen and Joel E. Gerstl, *On Education—Sociological Perspectives* (New York: John Wiley & Sons, Inc., 1967), pp. 161–62. Reprinted by permission of John Wiley & Sons and Ronald Corwin.

with the community. In other words, the school has considerable influence over both the internal and external forces that control conduct within its boundaries.

In fact, the complex and sometimes bureaucratic nature of school systems often enables them to mute the impact of community expectations, if not actually to determine or shape them. Even when educational policies are formulated in the most powerful segments of the community, as when school legislation is passed or legal decisions are issued to force changes in the actions of educators, the bureaucratic and complex structures of large school systems are often capable of practical nullification. Unfortunately many people do not understand that the conditions necessary for the creation of educational policies are seldom the same conditions needed to implement the policies. David Rogers contends that it is almost impossible to bring about changes in education through the mere creation of law or even through changing the policies of school administrators.

> Policy statements are only the beginning of the process. Those who make the decisions, even if they were more eager foı reform, must negotiate with the professional staff to secure compliance with their directives. They must secure efficient coordination of the actions of all units carrying out the plans, and they must provide rewards and punishments that will ensure compliance, institute performance measures, and evaluate how the plans actually worked. Legal and bureaucratic constraints, however, limit the power of the superintendent and the board over the headquarters and field staff, and reforms mandated from above are seldom carried out as they were intended.[7]

What characteristic of school organizational structures interferes with the implementation of policies emanating from school and community authorities? One answer may lie in the previously noted distinction between power and authority. Power and authority often go together, but not so often as many mistakenly believe. Indeed, most administrators in schools, as well as administrators in government and business, eventually face the realization that their powers seldom equal their authority; they often have power without authority and authority without power.

Some understanding of impediments to policy implementation can be found by examining the administrative structure of large school organizations. David Rogers, studying the New York City public school system, identified eight impediments to policy implementation requiring basic changes in the system: (1) overcentralization; (2) vertical and horizontal fragmentation of suborganizations of the schools; (3) chauvinism of units; (4) strong, informal peer pressures for self-protection; (5) compulsive rule following; (6) rebellion of lower level supervisors

[7] David Rogers, *One Hundred and Ten Livingston Street* (New York: Vintage Press, 1969), pp. 266–67.

against directives, alternating with overconformity and sabotage; (7) insulation from clients, and internal politics accompanied by personal interests over-riding interests of clients; and (8) the tendency for decisions to be made in committees making it difficult to pinpoint responsibility and authority.[8]

Overcentralization. In large, complex school organizations there are likely to be so many levels in a chain of command that considerable time, sometimes a matter of years, is required just to get a policy initiated, not to mention the time needed to create the conditions necessary for enactment. For example, if the policy change is initiated at a lower level by a teacher or principal, the proposal may have to go through several committees where it may be tabled for long periods of time, modified, or delayed by fillibuster. Even after positive action by all necessary committees and administrators, the procedure may need to be repeated just to establish a basis for reasonable compliance. With power, particularly veto power, dispersed throughout a large, complex organization while authority is more or less centralized, desired policies are difficult to implement. Furthermore, the upward orientation of persons in the chain of command may result in inaccurate information's being processed. Administrators and school board personnel often receive very distorted information about exactly what is going on with reference to their policies.

In addition, in large, complex organizations authority and power often are not clearly fixed. In some cities, the principals and other administrators may have their own union or professional associations—as do the teachers, maintenance personnel, and other staff, each with some powers of veto and some authority. Furthermore, many policies require considerable cooperation and resources, the details of which cannot be specified in advance. The good will and skill of a mass of teachers needed to carry out a major policy regarding the way they teach reading cannot be attained by simple edict. A whole series of additional policies and actions may be necessary to produce cooperation, new skills and attitudes, modified plant and working conditions, a reallocation of finances, and a rechanneling of authority. Any supportive policy or action may also be subject to veto in many places throughout the system.

Vertical and Horizontal Fragmentation. As we stated in the beginning of this chapter, a school is often an umbrella covering or including many groups with competing purposes. For example, teachers may see the school social workers as having a different function than do the social workers themselves, or the counselors and social workers may compete for the same clients, funds, or responsibilities. Often teachers in one school program has little or no idea of what is going on in

[8] Ibid., p. 267.

other school programs around them even when those programs are relevant to their own efforts. Teachers, counselors, attendance officers, social workers, administrators, paraprofessional staff, librarians, janitors, media specialists, personnel data managers, coaches, and others sometimes get so involved in their own activities that they have little involvement with others outside of their units. In large school systems this is particularly true. In very large organizations teachers may not even know what other teachers of the same subjects at the same age levels are doing in their buildings. The fragmentation of effort and power that occurs in such a setting makes it quite difficult to coordinate activities across program boundaries. For example, a program to decrease the dropout rate, which probably would need implementation in all segments of the school in order to succeed, would be very difficult in a large, fragmented school organization.

Unit Chauvinism. One typical consequence of the division of labor by groups, the fragmentation of functions and work setting, and the separate training programs from which each tends to emerge (e.g., social workers from school of social work, psychologists from departments of psychology, teachers from colleges of education) is a tendency toward chauvinism by which each group tends to see undesirable features of education as attributable to the incompetence or motives of other groups. It is not uncommon to observe an exaggerated self-glory expressed by professors for their discipline, be they from the arts, sciences, or professions. Similarly exaggerated feelings of the worth of one's unit can also be observed among many of the staff in other educational organizations. The result is often a resentment of any explicit or implied criticism of their units of membership. Policies asserting a need for change in any unit of education almost inevitably conflict with the pride and felt needs for added rewards and power held by some. Chauvinism in a unit is also accompanied by attempts of the members to protect and expand their power and authority. Serious cooperation by all units to accomplish organizational goals is nearly always hampered to some extent by the chauvinistic needs of any single unit and its members.

Peer Pressures. Accompanying chauvinism, overcentralization of authority, dispersal of power, and fragmentation of programs are the peer pressures which develop to protect and expand the unit. In a university, sociologists, psychologists, educators, chemists, and all others affiliated with departments tend to exert pressures on each other to support, protect, and expand their departments. Sometimes the pressure is overt; sometimes very subtle. In any case, it is usually present. In elementary and secondary schools, and in college, the pressure exerted by counselors upon each other, by teachers upon each other, by departments upon each other, or by administrators upon each other, can also be very great. While such peer pressure may on occasion produce a desirable esprit de corps and generally support organizational goals, it may also hamper individuals who attempt to place larger organizational values first when conflict occurs. In a similar sense, organizational values are usually stressed by peers over community values. Thus, when political or economic values of teachers' organizations come into conflict with community values, peer pressure will operate to keep the educators on the side of organizational needs. Occasionally peer pressure has kept policies directed from the community through school boards and administrators from ever being enacted.

Compulsive Rule Following. "If I bend the rules for you, I'll have to do it for everyone else," is a common statement in a system where rules which were originally designed to help achieve various purposes or aims have become aims in themselves. In such cases, people are hired to ensure conformity to rules; enforcement rather than achieving the intended purpose of the rule becomes the prime concern. In large complex organizations there are many people whose only responsibility involves the enforcement of rules. When major rules become outdated or impede organizational goals, they may be changed; but such change is not easily achieved. The difficulty of reform is greatly increased by resistance of those whose economic and psychological interest lies in maintaining the status quo regardless of school or community needs.

Rules also proliferate in complex organizations until they become a maze which only a few people can comprehend. In large, bureaucratic school systems there are few people on the staff, let alone from outside the school, who know all the procedures and rules to be followed to bring about change. Important projects can be stalled or stopped simply because minor rules were not followed. For example, one of the authors was present when a lower-level administrator turned down and sent back to a school group a proposal for a school project because a local rule requiring a 200-word abstract was violated; the abstract had 210 words. As a result of the time required for reprocessing, the proposal was submitted one day late and over $200,000 was lost to the community and school system.

Another consequence of such rigidity is that some people become cynical about rules and those charged with the responsibility of enforcing them. Some who might otherwise be highly motivated to work toward bringing about changes within the school may feel the bother of learning and carrying out the rules is too great to warrant their effort, and the school system is, as a result, the loser. Others may simply ignore the formal procedures for bringing about change and operate outside the system.

Rebellion and Overconformity. Associated, at times, with any hierarchy of power is a kind of rebellion characterized by overconformity. The typist who knows the correct spelling but chooses to type a word as it was misspelled by his or her supervisor, or the person who carries out the directive of a superior without comment, knowing it will result in undesirable consequences for the "boss," may be engaging in a type of rebellion. Similarly, nearly every dominant position requires cooperation on the part of subordinates to provide feedback so that inappropriate directives can be minimized. Many supervisors recognize that the so-called yes-person who never disagrees is often a handicap to the supervisor as well as to the organization.

On the other hand, there may be more risk to the subordinate in not being a yes-person; often it is safer in large complex organizations to simply do as one is directed to do, even if the directive is wrong. "I only do what I am told," expresses the attitude of a considerable number of employees in many complex organizations, including educational institutions. Some administrators, primarily concerned with promotion, may well choose the safe way and simply do what they are told, even when the results may not benefit their supervisors or promote the goals of the system. Obviously, if one dislikes his or her supervisor, there is no safer way of rebelling than simply carrying out orders that are likely to have negative consequences for the supervisor.

Sabotage is another common form of rebellion. Industry and business have long recognized the costs and prevalence of sabotage. On occasion, mail carriers have been known to throw away or destroy sacks of mail, laborers on assembly lines have thrown loose nuts and bolts into car bodies, trucks have been damaged and goods stolen. In a similar sense, many educational programs have been sabotaged by educators. Money allocated for a compensatory program for the poor may be rechanneled by administrators to support other programs they personally prefer. There have been local communities and school systems in the United States which have sabotaged many federal and state programs for the disadvantaged in this manner. The scandal has been so widespread, in fact, that governmental actions have been initiated to demand the return of funds from certain local school systems.

Sabotage also occurs within school systems. Some administrators and teachers may attempt to prevent the success or the publication of success of various programs which they oppose. Conversely, they may promote success stories about their preferred programs which, in fact, have failed. Sabotage, like "white-collar crime," takes many forms and often goes unrecognized, but it can occur at all levels of school organization.

Insulation from Clients. Teachers and other educators are often insulated, in many ways, from scrutiny by the public they serve: parents of students, administrators, and even students. Similarly, administrators are often able to limit surveillance of their actions by others. As a consequence, the personal interests of educators do, on occasion, take precedence over clients' interests or organizational policies. The more complex and bureaucratic the school system, the easier it is for the staff members to insulate themselves and pursue their personal interests at the expense of the organization. We have known of educators' maintaining responsible full-time positions in major businesses while holding supposedly full-time positions in school systems. A few educators, particularly in higher education, may use school time to further their own political, economic, or social aims, alloting little or no time for class preparation. Some school systems have regulations against more than a limited amount of outside work, but such regulations are often difficult to enforce. In addition, regulations against outside work are meaningless for some kinds of activity, such as studying and playing the stock market. Furthermore, one can work for one's own interests, without regard for the interests of clients, totally within the organization. An example would be a teacher or professor who spends very little time preparing for class and uses the time saved to ingratiate himself or herself with superiors and colleagues. On the other hand, some schools actually reward and encourage personal advancement over institutional needs, particularly at the college level. In small school systems, the activities of the staff are easily known, but in large school systems there are many positions which are shielded from the view of clients, peers, and authorities.

We do not mean to imply that most educators in large systems are using school time for their own interests. Rather, we believe that most educators are conscientious and have the integrity commonly expected of public servants. But we also believe that in large complex organizations there is more opportunity and more actual pursuit of personal interests, at the expense of organizational values, than in small school systems.

Committee Structures. In large, bureaucratic organizations, committees perform important functions. One highly valued consequence of developing or approving policies in committees is that such a process often helps to assure greater compliance with the policies than would be elicited by a simple administrative edict. On the other hand, the tendency to make decisions in committees makes it very difficult to pinpoint responsibility or authority. Committee actions are sometimes unresponsive to the interests of students or the school to a degree that would be most unlikely were the individual members personally responsible for their decisions. In the anonymity of committees, weak, arrogant and pompous persons are sometimes able to assume positions and promote causes that would not be tolerated of them if they were personally accountable.

Commitee structures which are hidden from view are also excellent settings within which to pursue personal interests through political maneuvers, exchanging favors, and intimidation. And interestingly, one may be a poor instructor, incompetent in his field, an ineffective administrator, displeasing to many peers, and still be effective in committee structures. Fortunately, most educators are capable individuals with integrity. Those few who are not, however, are most able to assert themselves, often under a rhetorical smokescreen of clichés extolling themselves, their schools, and their work units, when their positions are in large bureaucratic and complex school organizations.

Each type of organizational pattern mentioned above, from overcentralization of authority to insulated committee structures, as Rogers points out, ". . . may not be bad if not carried too far. In [some] school systems, however, they are carried to the point where they (often) paralyze the system in the face of rapid social changes that demand new administrative arrangements."[9] It must be recognized that schools do continue to exist and carry out their functions reasonably well in spite of all the difficulties which may interfere from time to time.

Structural Processes

Implied in our preceding discussion of educational organizations are processes governing the integration, cohesion, or strain occurring among the various individuals and groups within the system. There are, according to Katz and Kahn, three interrelated forces or processes by which organizations are held together: roles, norms and values. "(1) People (and suborganizations) are tied together because of the functional interdependence of the roles they play: . . . (2) the normative requirements for these roles add an additional cohesive element; . . . and (3) the values centering about the objectives of the system furnish another source for integration."[10] Elaborating on the work of Katz and Kahn, Max G. Abbott observes that "standardized behavior, which grows out of interdependent or complementary social relationships, is termed role behavior and the network of standardized role behaviors constitutes the formal structure of the organization."[11] In other words, the standardized behaviors of superintendents, teachers and other members of a school system constitute, by definition, the formal organization of the school. Nevertheless much behavior in an organization is not standardized or spelled out. Furthermore, ". . . a formal structure tends to run counter to individual differences among workers, . . . and since individ-

[9] Ibid., p. 268.

[10] Daniel Katz and Robert L. Kahn, *The Social Psychology of Organizations* (New York: John Wiley & Sons, Inc., 1965), p. 38. For a discussion of the application of these concepts to educational organizations see Max G. Abbott, "The Social Psychology of Organizations," *Educational Administration Quarterly*, vol. 20, January 1967, pp. 100–109.

[11] Abbott, "Social Psychology of Organizations."

ual needs rarely coincide with organizational imperatives, there does develop within the formal organization an informal structure."[12] There are many informal codes of behavior by which individuals and groups relate to one another, cooperatively or competitively, which may allow them to satisfy their own needs; and their own needs may be counter to those of the organization.

Certain of the informal social psychological processes by which individuals relate to one another in hierarchial organizations may be understood in relation to three sets of concepts. The first involves an elaboration of the concepts of social position, status, and role. The second concerns the bases or sources of power available to role occupants and programs. The third involves the informal kinship of clique systems which emerge in every organization and become very potent vehicles for social control.

Social Position, Status, and Role[13]

Every teacher, administrator, student, and citizen has some degree of understanding about the social structure of any school with which he or she has been involved. Each of us can describe, or at least has an image of, some of the relationships that exist between various individuals in schools with which we are familiar. For most people these images are highly personal and usually involve particular relationships between particular individuals. We are not so much concerned here with such relationships between individuals as with those relationships that commonly exist between positions such as administrator, teacher, counselor, and student.

The school, like other organizations, can be examined by description of the positions which various people in the group occupy. Although different persons behave somewhat differently in each position, each position calls for certain kinds of behavior. By a position in the social group we mean the images people have of the behavior of persons who occupy this place and the expected set of relationships with others

[12] Ibid.

[13] The concepts of status and role have been used in many different ways by different social scientists. The variation in usage results, in part, from the different perspectives of the several social-science disciplines. Status and role, particularly the latter, have been used extensively in anthropology, sociology, and social psychology, and though the meaning varies among them, role theory provides a common link between the disciplines. See Neal Gross, Ward Mason, and Alexander McEachern, *Explorations in Role Analysis* (New York: John Wiley and Sons, Inc., 1958), pp. 11–20; Lionel J. Neiman and James W. Hughes, "The Problem of the Concept of Role—A Re-Survey of the Literature," *Social Forces,* vol. 30 (1951), pp. 141–49; and Theodore R. Sarbin, "Role Theory," in Gardner Lindzey (ed.), *Handbook of Social Psychology* (Cambridge: Addison-Wesley, 1954), vol. 1, pp. 223–258, for analysis of the different approaches to status and role usage.

in the group. For example, most persons recognize that there is a position in our schools called "teacher" and that the position implies certain types of behavior. When we refer to the father in the family, it is not necessary to identify any one person occupying this position for us to know something about the behavior of people having this status. In the same manner, the positions of teacher, administrator, or student are identifiable without reference to particular persons. Elementary-school teacher, football coach, dean, principal—each calls to mind relationships to students and others which are commonly understood. Naturally, the depth and sophistication of our understanding of role relationships will be determined in part by our own experiences and general knowledge of the workings of educational institutions.

Of course, every person who occupies a position in the family or the school has some idiosyncratic or unique way of acting. But there are expected behavior patterns that are generally recognized as indispensable to a particular position. These expected patterns provide the basis for our analysis. Finally, it must be underscored that we are discussing types or constructs both of positions and of relationships, and not specific case histories. No one person would behave in exactly the way positions are described here. We will generalize and abstract from the common behavior patterns the significant characteristics of various positions in the school system.

In broad terms, there are two levels of social structure in our schools, one involving the *employees* of the system; the other, consisting of the *clients*. Robert Dreeben writes:

> The crucial fact about schools is that they include two distinct categories of members who are affiliated with the organization in radically different ways. Principals, their administrative subordinates, and teachers all represent extensions of a bureaucratic hierarchy since all are employees of the system and obligated through employment contracts to carry out system-wide policy. Pupils, in contrast, are something akin to clients of the school or conscripted beneficiaries, to be more exact. They are consumers of an educational service, not functionaries obligated to effect policy."[14]

Insofar as elementary and secondary schools are concerned, we can also make a distinction between the two levels by calling the first an *adult* social structure; the latter, a *youth* social structure. In institutions of higher learning we find a gradual decrease in age difference between teachers and students as we move from the college to the professional or graduate school level. However, in many respects even older graduate students are treated as if they were young adults or children.

Since the students of several age groups in widely varying activities

[14] Dreeben, *The Nature of Teaching* (Glenview, Ill.: Scott Foresman and Company, 1970), p. 46.

greatly outnumber the adults, there is a greater variety of statuses in this system than in the adult structure. In order to understand the nature of both social structures, it is necessary to recognize the relationships between the two groups. As we shall see in the next chapter, there are instances when clients and employees tend to constitute a single or at least overlapping system and other times when the two are quite distinct and separate. Recognizing that there are few comprehensive, empirical studies of the social structure of schools, we shall indicate some of the more salient characteristics of these two parts of the school social structure.

Status and Role. The concepts of status and role have particular value in analyzing the nature of the positions in the school system. In actual behavior, however, status and role are inseparable social phenomena. For this reason, they are sometimes combined in a single concept: *status-role.* This coupling of the two means that the complex of expectations which apply to a particular position in a social system also apply to the individual occupying that position. Status and role may be distinguished from the concept "position" in the following manner. *Position* may be defined simply as location in a social group or social system. This is the common use of the term as we apply it to the teacher, the principal, the administrator, or the student. Status may be defined as the expectations which various persons or groups interacting with a particular position hold for any occupant of that position. Thus, the status of teaching includes the expectations that all relevant persons and groups hold for any person occupying a teaching position.

The expectations which various persons and groups hold for the occupants of a more narrowly prescribed status may vary somewhat from the general status expectations. For example, the expectations which parents, students, or other school personnel hold for English teachers or for first-grade teachers in an "old part of town" school may be somewhat different from the expectations for teachers in general. This type of expectation for a particular status in a given particular social situation is identified as an *office.*

The expectations held for a specific person occupying a position may be different in some respects from those held for another occupant of the same position. Thus parents, students, or administrators may expect Mr. Jones' behavior as an English teacher to vary from Mrs. Smith's behavior in the same situation. These specific expectations we term *role.* We distinguish role from status and office by identifying it as the expectations which persons or groups hold for a particular occupant or actor in a status.[15]

[15] A more detailed explanation of these and related concepts is given in W. B. Brookover, "Research on Teacher and Administrator Roles," *The Journal of Educational Sociology,* vol. 29 (1955), pp. 2–13.

The influence of role expectations on the behavior of a specific actor in a particular role is affected by the degree of his involvement in the group whose expectations are being considered. The individual actor may have little self-involvement in or self-orientation to the expectations of a particular group. For example, a teacher may be indifferent to the expectations of parents, but the same teacher as actor may be highly concerned with the school administrators' expectations. The latters' expectations will greatly affect this teacher's behavior.

The impact of any person or group's role expectations on the behavior of a particular person occupying the role depends on his perception of those expectations. The similarity between Mr. Jones' perception of what the students or any other group expect and the others' actual expectations of him depends on the clarity of communication between Mr. Jones and the students. In some instances, he may have a distorted understanding of what others expect and behave differently as a result of his inaccurate perception. Mr. Jones' perception of others' expectations also may be affected by his self-involvement in the group whose expectations are being communicated. If he has little interest in or concern with the students' expectations, his understanding of them may be erroneous.

Figure 7–1 is designed to show the relationship between status, office, role, actor, role perception, self-involvement, and related concepts that have been used in what is broadly known as role theory.

FIGURE 7–1
Paradigm of Status-Role Concepts

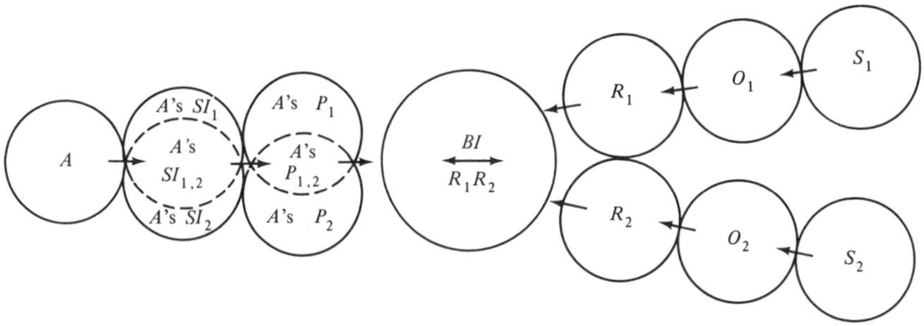

A = Actor's personality brought to situation (previous experience, needs, and so on)
SI = Self-involvement–actor's image of the ends anticipated from participation in the status. A projection of his self-image into the role
P = Actor's perception of what he thinks others expect of him in a particular role
BI = Behavior in interaction with others in which P and R are continually redefined
R = Role–Other's expectations of actor, "A", the incumbent in specific position
O = Office–(Others' expectations of any actor in particular situation) that is, history teacher in X school
S = Other's expectation of any actor in broadly defined position–that is, teachers

Source: Adapted from W. B. Brookover, "Research on Teacher and Administrator Roles," *Journal of Educational Sociology*, vol. 29 (1955), pp. 2–13.

The central circle in the paradigm labeled *BI* represents the actor's *behavior in interaction* with members of the particular group involved in the role-defining situation. This is the behavior of the actor as he takes the role within the group. The actor's personality is his behavior as seen by others and himself in such interactional situations. One of the significant characteristics of behavior in interaction is that it is always in process. It is not fixed or static. It may involve continuous redefinition of both the role expectations and the actors' perception of them as interaction between the actor and others occurs. Furthermore, there are differing kinds of expectations.

Types of Expectations. Three categories of expectations are held for each of the status-roles of educators in a school system which have been referred to as: (1) primary expectations, (2) peripheral expectations, and (3) secondary expectations.

Primary expectations refer to behaviors expected of individuals in given roles which are assumed to contribute to the accomplishment of major organizational goals. For example, a school superintendent may be expected to supervise the budget and establish hiring and curriculum policies which will result in the students' being eligible to go on to selected colleges; in a vocational school setting, teachers may be expected to train students in salable work skills, report students' progress and carry out administrative assignments relevant to the promotion of career education. These expectations are standards, in effect, for educators to facilitate their achievement of major organizational goals.

Peripheral expectations are those expectations or standards of conduct held for role incumbents relevant to the attainment of minor goals of the school system. For example, educators may be expected to belong to local social, church, and service clubs to facilitate good school-community relations and to attend professional meetings to develop skills and contribute to positive public images.

Secondary expectations stipulate the behaviors and attributes expected of persons in given roles that are not necessary for the accomplishment of organizational goals. The expectation that only females teach kindergarten, or that teachers be black or white, Christian, Jewish or Moslem, or be liberal or conservative are examples of secondary expectations. Contrary to literal meanings, our so-called secondary expectations often have a greater bearing on who is selected for various administrative and staff roles than those expectations most likely to contribute to organizational goals.

Role Conflict and Consensus

Sociologists as well as educational practitioners have long recognized the importance that *consensus* has in binding schools as well as other organizations or systems together. Individuals and suborganizations of a school must hold some consensus for the unity of that school to be recognized. However, total consensus is almost never possible in any situation where people enter from diverse backgrounds and with differing aspirations, competencies, and reference groups; and yet, as Preiss and Ehrlich state:

> With respect to the articulation of roles in a system of interaction, the problem of consensus exists at two levels. First, there is the problem of consensus with respect to the ends and objectives of the system. Second, there is the problem of consensus with respect to specific roles and specific role expectations. Clearly, there is some requisite consensus, that is, some set of basic agreements minimally necessary for a social system to operate. Beyond that there must be some further range on consensus for the system to operate efficiently, if not for the system to maintain itself in some adaptive or innovative manner.[16]

How is it done, what is the process by which school systems attain minimally necessary consensus and resolve conflict so as to integrate their various diverse programs and attain some semblance of unity? How is it that large numbers of actors of rather diverse perspectives accept jointly a set of rules regarding procedures and goals? To begin with, we may note that there are several types of conflict.

Types of Role Conflict. Robin and Ivey,[17] elaborating on the work of Gross, Mason and MacEachern and others,[18] summarize four types of role conflict which may occur.

(1) Role conflict stemming from role definers: There are situations in which legitimate role definers disagree about the normative content of a role.

(2) Role conflict internal to the role: The definers of a role may be in agreement and their role specifications congruent, yet the various expectations confronting the role taker are such that the individual cannot fulfill all of the obligations in the role.

(3) Role conflict stemming from the role in interaction with the social system: (a) A type of "functional" role conflict occurs when the normative prescriptions of a role are not sufficient to allow the role taker to perform the functions expected of his role in the larger

[16] Jack J. Preiss and Howard J. Ehrlich, *An Examination of Role Theory: The Case of the State Police* (Lincoln, Nebraska: University of Nebraska, 1966), p. 174.

[17] Stanley S. Robin and Allen E. Ivey, "Role Theory, Role Conflict and Counseling: A Conceptual Framework," *Journal of Counseling Psychology*, vol. 13, no. 1 (1966), pp. 29–37.

[18] Neal Gross, Ward Mason, and Alexander W. MacEachern, *Exploration in Role Analyses: Studies in the School Superintendency Role* (New York: John Wiley & Sons, Inc., 1958).

social system in which it is situated. (b) Role conflict also arises because of the multiplicity of roles an individual assumes.

(4) Role conflict stemming from the interaction of the individual and his role: This is the situation where the role definers' demands exceed the limits of the role taker's capacity.[19]

The Resolution of Role Conflict. Several factors are involved in the determination of how a particular actor may resolve the perceived conflict in any particular situation. First of all, the actor may be relatively uninvolved in his relationships with one or more "groups" that hold expectations for him. For example, teachers may be unconcerned about what the P.T.A. members expect and many orient their behavior to the expectations of the administration and other teachers. In this case, teachers, though perceiving the differential expectations, are not concerned with the incompatibility because one set of expectations is irrelevant to them.

A second and slightly different approach assisting the resolution of incompatibility may be identified as the actor's definition of the legitimacy of the expectations. If, for example, a woman teacher feels that parents have no right to expect her to refrain from smoking, she may disregard these expectations, even though she is fully aware of, and perceives, the parents' expectations.

A third factor which often is very important in the solution of role conflict is the relative influence or power of the persons holding expectations and sanctioning. This is illustrated by school board members' expecting teachers to live in the school district and buy their groceries and other merchandise in the school's community. However, it is increasingly evident that many teachers do not live in the communities where they teach. This is in sharp contrast with the past, when teachers who did not live in the community frequently were dismissed. Current efforts toward decentralization and greater community control may result in again applying such sanctions in accordance with expectations that teachers live in the community.

Force or sanctions are not equally relevant to all role occupants. The manner in which a person resolves a role conflict may vary with his self-involvement in the position and his relation to the relevant reference groups. Some, concerned primarily with remaining in the position, may behave in a way which they feel will avoid dismissal. Others may be more concerned with fulfilling the expectations of a particular group and, therefore, disregard the expectations of others, regardless of their power. Thus a teacher primarily concerned with keeping a job for a lifetime will behave so as to retain the teaching position, even though he or she may consider others' expectations as improper or inappropriate. Our interpretation of the legitimacy of others' expectations and their

[19] Robin and Ivey, "Role Theory, Role Conflict, and Counseling," pp. 30–31.

sanctions is also modified by our involvement in the situation and by our orientation to the various groups which hold expectation for us.

The particular behavior each educator follows will depend on varying combinations of accommodation to these factors, as perceived by the actor. In many instances, the educator may conform to the expectations of one or more groups; in others, he or she may avoid the conflict by not conforming to any of the expectations; or he may work out some compromise between incompatible expectations. The success of a person in any school position may depend in large measure on the skill with which that person is able to resolve the role conflicts with which he is faced.

Bases of Role Power

One of the most important features of any educator's role or educational program is the extent to which that role or program has autonomy—is not controlled by others. Just as every educator or program is to some extent controlled by its environment, no person or organization is totally without some spheres of self-government. Understanding the extent and nature of that freedom from external control which may be exercised by various segments of the school community is of crucial importance if we are to understand the process of education. The educator, whatever his or her part in the educational system, has some degree of freedom to make certain decisions. The teacher, for example, has autonomy in a number of facets of the teaching role, but many aspects of the role allow little or no autonomy, such as not being able to dictate working hours, allowable number of sick days, number of students, or choice of textbooks. In what areas should the teacher, student, and administrator have autonomy if the educational system is to achieve its aims? In what ways are the aims of education and other societal concerns impeded by granting certain autonomies to faculty or students? What are the organizational bases of support? These questions and similar ones are of major importance to sociologists of education.

Functional Autonomy. Fred E. Katz[20] advances two bases for a person in a role to achieve functional autonomy, whether authorized or not: (*a*) "autonomy structure related to specialization," and (*b*) autonomy structure related to the social affiliations of members of the organization. Autonomy based on specialization refers to the fact that persons occupying roles of teachers, custodians, principals, superintendents, or any other role in the system are granted certain protections to exercise their specialized judgments from their superiors, fellow spe-

[20] Fred E. Katz, "The School as a Complex Social Organization," *Harvard Educational Review,* vol. 34 (1964), p. 434.

cialists, and clients. Autonomy based on affiliation refers to the fact that individuals within a system are also likely to be members of many different social groups and these memberships may confer autonomy. The teacher who is a personal friend of the superintendent or mayor may have autonomy in his or her teaching role not because of being a teacher but because of his or her social alignments.

An important corollary of this is that individuals do not necessarily have a major commitment to any given role.[21] It is quite possible for a professor or elementary teacher to be little committed to the role of teacher and more to his other roles.

Katz explains the bases for autonomy, showing the source of autonomy and where in a social organization the autonomy is enacted:[22]

I. Autonomy is internal to organizational roles and is
   a. enacted *in* the organization
   b. enacted *outside* the organization

II. Autonomy is external to organizational roles and is
   a. enacted *in* the organization
   b. enacted *outside* the organization

Autonomy which is internal to one's role refers to "that sphere of autonomy which is regarded as an intrinsic part of the role occupant's contribution to the organization."[23] The principal, for example, may exercise certain autonomy in school and in certain of his social relationships outside of the school by virtue of his being a principal. Similarly, that same principal may exercise autonomy in his role as principal as a function of his roles outside the school; he may, for example, be Chamber of Commerce president and thus experience fewer restrictions outside of school than other principals simply because of his power roles in the community.

Cosmopolitan and Local. When a person is able to bring power to a role because of alignments with others external to the role's organizational setting, that person is referred to as a *cosmopolitan.* To the extent that a person develops power from others within his work setting, that person is referred to as a *local.*

In university settings it is easily seen how local and cosmopolitan persons function.[24] For example, in most university departments there are those members of the faculty who have developed what influence they have by doing things for and developing positive relationships with colleagues and administrators. They often do much of the "house-

---

[21] Ibid., p. 443.

[22] Ibid., p. 443.

[23] Ibid., p. 434.

[24] See for example Cornelis J. Lemmers, "Localism, Cosmopolitanism, and Faculty Response," *Sociology of Education,* Winter 1974, vol. 47, no. 1, pp. 129–158.

keeping" work for their departments in committee assignments. Such persons often find an important part of their self-identities in being members of their department and university. On the other hand, there are those faculty members who gain their influence in their school setting by doing research and writing or carrying out activities outside of school, all of which may establish alignments outside of their organizational settings. Some educators, for example, are able to bring large grants of money to their departments which support other faculty and students and which may be viewed as helping the image of their schools. Such people are likely to be retained, regardless of their effectiveness with students or colleagues, because of their external connections and power.

Conflict between locals and cosmopolitans seems almost inevitable. In fact, there are many conflicts in schools that can be seen as resting in part on local versus cosmopolitan pressures, even though not recognized as such by the participants. The conflict is understandable, since cosmopolitans and locals are likely to have different reference groups; each is immediately concerned with a different audience and with a different value system. For example, those professors who are busy trying to enhance their reputations and their schools' reputations by contributing to knowledge are not so likely to grant much respect to those of their colleagues who spend all of their time on committees and teaching, and vice versa. No matter how important and fundamental the issues in the commonly found controversy over teaching versus research, and the issues are fundamental, part of the controversy rests with cosmopolitan versus local orientations. Cosmopolitans, usually fewer in proportion to locals, sometimes irritate locals and locals are sometimes merely tolerated by cosmopolitans.

It should be noted that some are able to build strong bases of support in both local and cosmopolitan roles. There are many internationally recognized scholars who have developed very positive and strong relationships with their peers within the organization. Even so, conflicts between local- and cosmopolitan-oriented staff are not unusual, particularly in expanding universities. Each, however, is usually dependent on the other. The serious researcher who desires to spend most of his time on scholarship often depends on his colleagues to spend countless hours on committees setting up teaching schedules, planning numerous activities, counseling others, and carrying out numerous other facilitating activities. The local, in turn, often needs the cosmopolitan to legitimate his organizational setting to outside groups. For example, legislators are more likely to fund those medical colleges whose faculties include doctors who create positive public images for their schools. Some of the so-called great universities have taken an even more direct approach by seeking to employ people on their staffs who have important alignments. Famous military and political persons with little experience in education or scholarship are often made presidents of major universities. Such cases suggest that we can also speak, quite appropriately, of cosmopolitan and local schools. There are universities which are widely anchored in their alignments to the economic, political, religious, and social powers of societies. There are other colleges which are so local as to be almost ignored by local politicians. Clearly, whether a school is likely to emphasize more cosmopolitan or local orientations depends on many conditions. For example, if students come from upper-class families throughout the country and go on to occupy leadership positions in banking, industry, art, and so on, across the land, the possibility and the need for powerful alignments are greater than when a limited segment of society is served. Endowments, who serves on the board, ability to confer prestige, and the cosmopolitan status of the staff are all important in determining the cosmopolitan status of the university.

The point of this discussion is that as we examine a school we should recognize that the nature of any segment of the organization or the social structure is not likely to be discerned by merely examining the formal school organization requirements and expectations. We must examine the relevant relationships among educators, students, and organizational units both within and outside of the school if we are to understand how school organizations function. Obviously, generalizations about various roles and subsystems that apply to all levels of education from early childhood to professional school in all societies are impossible. Therefore, in characterizing the social structure of the school, we have limited ourselves to a few prototypes of elementary, secondary, and higher public education in western culture.

Suggested Readings

J. Victor Baldridge, *Power and Conflict in the University* (New York: Wiley-Interscience, 1971). Presents a point of view that decision-making activities should be seen as a political process and not simply as a bureaucratic outcome.

Charles E. Bidwell, "The School as a Formal Organization," in J. G. March (ed.), *Handbook of Organization* (Chicago: Rand McNally, 1965).

C. Brooklyn Derr, "Organization Development in One Large Urban School System," *Education and Urban Society*, vol. 2, no. 4 (August 1970).

Neal Gross, J. B. Giacquinta, and M. Bernstein, *Implementing Organizational Innovations* (New York: Basic Books, 1971).

Richard H. Hall (ed.), *The Formal Organization* (New York: Basic Books, 1972). A wide range of readings on the characterization of complex organizations.

John Kasarda, "The Structural Implication of Social System Size," *American Sociological Review*, February 1974, vol. 39, no. 1, pp. 19–28. This article presents a good review of the literature and research evidence that size of the organization affects internal organization; a subject not treated due to space limitations in this chapter.

Cyril Lofer, *Organization in Theory and Practice* (New York: Basic Books, 1972). Original British and American contributions to how organizations deal with problems of leadership, change, and conflict.

Nicos P. Mongelis, *Organization and Bureaucracy,* (Chicago: Aldine Publishing Company).

David Rogers, *New York City and the Politics of School Desegregation* (New York: Center for Urban Education, 1971). An abridgment of *One Hundred and Ten Livingston Street* by David Rogers, discussed in this chapter.

Rolf E. Rogers, *The Political Process in Modern Organization* (New York: Exposition Press, 1971).

Thomas A. Shaheen, "A Choice: Bureaucracy or Curricular Renaissance?" *Educational Leadership,* March 1974, vol. 31, no. 6, pp. 492–96. Provides a summary outline for the beginning student of some of the positive functions of school bureaucracy and implications for change.

8

The Managers of Education

Many people assume that those solely responsible for establishing and implementing educational policies are school boards and their delegated school administrators. The actual decision makers, however, are far more numerous and diverse than can be seen from examining board member and administrator roles alone. As we have emphasized, often there are powerful community forces that dictate policies. In addition, teachers, teacher aides, librarians, coaches, financial aid officers, curriculum consultants, speech pathologists, secretaries, custodians, plant development specialists, school public relations personnel, grant writers, school attorneys, educational researchers—and even students—often have a hand in creating and implementing policies. Various members of these diverse positions often decide informally how funds are to be obtained and spent, what curriculum materials are actually used, who gets taught what, and who gets what jobs.

Furthermore, when board members and school administrators do manage, they too often manage outside their formal roles, using authority, power, and influence not due them because of their school offices. Informal cliques, made up of persons drawn from both inside and outside the formal administrative structure, manage many of the affairs of education. Later in this chapter we will discuss how clique systems affect the exercise of power and authority. Before that, we will examine the formal and traditionally recognized management roles in our schools, paying particular attention to the distribution of authority and power.

School Boards

That group of persons selected to be legally responsible for the operation of a school may be known variously as a board of regents, a board of education, a board of trustees, a board of directors, or a school board. Whatever the label, nearly every school at every level, public or private, has its board. In urban and large rural districts, however, only rarely do these boards exercise close control over administrative and teaching matters. Generally, the board is rather remote and only sets broad policies, which may or may not be carried out depending on conditions. Sometimes the board may be merely a group of figureheads with little or no real authority. The fact that most boards meet rarely and are often a considerable distance from the classrooms and students for whom they are responsible makes it easy for school people to ignore them, to control the kind of information school board members receive, and to proceed with the real management of education.

Of course school boards often make decisions which have considerable impact. The point here is simply that school boards, in spite of legal traditions and the "lip service" to formal authority, are but one input into the management process. Their actual power is often exaggerated, particularly in the heat of publicity.

School boards are employers of labor, partially control huge budgets, and often make important decisions for their school organizations and communities. They also have the authority to officially sanction the decisions and actions of others, although other persons in the community or school are frequently the actual decision makers. Most school board members are amateurs in the area of education and frequently, therefore, defer to the assumed expertise of the superintendent and his staff on matters of policy or administration. As can be seen in Table 8–1, only a very small proportion of school board members are likely to have formal training or experience in educational management. The women members on a typical school board are likely to be housewives from upper-middle and upper income families. What this says about the political nature of school boards, however, is difficult to ascertain.

In 1966, DeBeer found that the largest proportion of suburban school board members, 46 percent, were in professional or technical occupations.[1] Although DeBeer's data do not give us precise indication of the status of the board members in their communities, his data along with the findings reported in Table 8–1 suggest a range of education and income largely within the upper-middle class. It is not likely that any

[1] Wayne DeBeer, "Certain Characteristics and Attitudes of School Board Members in Suburbia" (doctoral dissertation, St. Louis University, 1966).

TABLE 8–1
Occupations of School Board Members

Occupation	Percent
Housewives	14.2%
Lawyers	12.1
Educators	6.9
Medical Doctors	4.6
Government Employees	3.8
Insurance	3.7
Retiree	3.4
Scientist/Engineer	3.1
Clergyman	3.0
Real Estate	2.6
Dentist	2.1
Banker	1.9
Contractor	1.7
Accountant/CPA	1.5
Skilled and Lower	35.4
	100.0%

Source: Wayne DeBeer, "Certain Characteristics and Attitudes of School Board Members in Suburbia" (doctoral dissertation, St. Louis University, 1966).

significant numbers of board members come from the lowest strata of society.

There has been a widely held belief that the class status of school board members has a conservative impact on the schools. A recent study by Thomas Morris of the attitudes of school board members in the United States toward foreign affairs and public finance supports this general conclusion.[2] Morris studied 20 large and 20 small school districts and observed that:

(1) The school boards from large districts were more conservative in areas of foreign affairs and public finance than their superintendents, who were moderately conservative to mildly liberal.
(2) The school boards from large districts were, on the other hand, less conservative in areas of public finance and foreign affairs than school boards of small districts, who were equally as conservative as their superintendents.[3]

Other findings, however, suggest that conservative attitudes toward public finance and foreign affairs may mask more liberal attitudes of board members toward education. DeBeer found in 1966 that board members tended to favor professional negotiations, centralization of districts, and special aid for underprivileged groups.[4] In 1966, these

[2] Thomas J. Morris, "A Comparison of Liberal and Conservative Socio-Economic Values of School Boards and Their Superintendents" (doctoral dissertation, University of Virginia, 1966).

[3] Ibid., p. 60.

[4] DeBeer, "Attitudes of School Board Members in Suburbia."

views could well be classed as more liberal than conservative. Larson found that school board members from the upper income levels were more open-minded to innovations than were board members from the lower income levels.[5] Indeed, there is some support for the view that, on school matters, school board members are somewhat more liberal than most of the citizens they represent. Carver found that board members were more open to change than most citizens with respect to school programs and staff personnel matters, and that they tended to be similar in orientation to citizens who had higher incomes and education levels.[6] On the other hand, Polk found that the goals that school board members held for their communities were not related to their educational levels, incomes, or political affiliations.[7]

Perhaps the occupation of the board member is less important than his intended audience. If it is true that many board members use their board positions to run for other political offices, to gain economic advantages, or achieve prestige with a group, this situation would partially explain the irrelevance of occupation to political orientation.

The backgrounds of board members do, however, suggest the areas in which they are most likely to have expertise applicable to their board member roles. If school board members possess special knowledge or skills for the management of their schools, they are likely to involve (*a*) ability and sensitivity in public relations matters, (*b*) knowledge of community resources, (*c*) more than average ability to manipulate community powers, and (*d*) an understanding of budgets. Experience in the role of employer might also be added to this list, although experience as an employer of nonprofessionals is not entirely applicable to relationships with teachers today. Although a major *formal* function of a school board is that of employer of teachers and other staff, the practicality of fully performing the employer role in large school districts is minimal. Even in smaller schools, the boards, because of lack of time and expertise, often delegate employer responsibilities to their chief executive or other administrators. Of course, boards can and do exercise considerable power as an employer on occasion. A Pennsylvania board member of a small district reported an incident in which he disagreed with the superintendent's recommendation on a particular teaching position. When asked how he justified the board's refusal to employ the

[5] Raymond O. Larson, "School Board Members' Values, Belief Systems, and Satisfaction with the School Board Role" (doctoral dissertation, The University of Wisconsin, 1966).

[6] Fred D. Carver, "Relationships between Education Level, Family Income and Expectations of Citizens for the Role of School Board" (doctoral dissertation, The University of Wisconsin, 1967).

[7] Charles M. Polk, "An Analysis of the Community-Oriented and Self-Oriented Board Member" (doctoral dissertation, University of Pittsburgh, 1965).

recommended teacher, he said, "We're the boss. We're supposed to run the school."

In their authorized role as employer, many school board members probably regard teachers as hired labor with limited professional status. Describing the situation of college teachers up until a decade or two ago, Robert Nisbet writes:

> . . . there was the deep-seated conviction in this country, largely as the result of the American system of lay boards of trustees, that the professor was an employee, literally a hireling and hence as subject to the wishes of his employers as anyone who worked for a railroad or department store. It is not easy today to summon up an accurate vision of how powerful trustees, individually and generally, once were in the minute decisions of colleges and universities—or how fundamentally indifferent they were to those values of teaching and scholarship that had come to this country at the end of the 19th century from Europe.[8]

The typical school board member probably grants teachers more prestige than custodians, bus drivers, or repairmen, but not enough to willingly grant them professional autonomy. In a few extreme cases in private education or upper-class communities, the school board may even see its relationship to teachers as master to servant. Upper-class or wealthy people who employ tutors or send their children to private schools often look on their relationship with teachers as similar to that with a gardener or housekeeper. In their minds the teacher is employed to do a particular task for which the parents are responsible but choose not to do.

Recently, however, teachers, administrators, teacher aides, custodians and others, with the aid of legislation, court opinions, public opinion, and collective power, have been changing their traditional relationship to school boards. Teachers have sought a professional, self-jurisdictional status, and they have made considerable headway. It is no longer uncommon for teachers to negotiate directly with their school boards, often with the services of highly trained professional negotiators. The result is that more and more personal employer-employee relationships are ending and once dominant employer powers of school boards, though still legally authorized, are being muted. The licensing of most nonteaching staff, tenure laws, strong state and national associations, the concomitants of large school and government bureaucracies, and the increasing mobility of all citizens, including educators, has reduced the power of many boards to exercise their legal authority.

A significant analysis of the controlling influences on decision making at the local community level, conducted about two decades ago,

[8] Robert A. Nisbet, "The Permanent Professors: A Modest Proposal," in Charles H. Anderson and John D. Murray (eds.), *The Professors* (Cambridge, Mass.: Schenkman Publishing Company, Inc., 1971), pp. 111–12.

offers some insights into an emergent condition of school boards involving their relationship with citizen groups.[9] In studying the major school districts in Massachusetts in the 1950s, Gross and his associates found that increasing pressures were being applied to school superintendents and school board members by citizen groups. In the last few years these community pressures seem to be gaining in momentum through movements for decentralization, "accountability," parent participation, and so forth. It would appear that many adults in the community, lower class as well as middle class, see the schools as a means for social and economic mobility for their children and wish to play a more active part in school-community decisions. Whatever the cause, one thing is clear. The trend has been and continues to be one of transferring powers formerly held by school boards to community and school groups.

Administrators

The authority of school administrators varies according to the level of administration involved, the size of the system, the bureaucratic structure, the status of the clients, and a host of other conditions. Traditionally, the administrator has been viewed as occupying a "middle-person" position between teaching staff and school board. This was especially the case where teachers' organizations were not strong and the schools were small. In many large school districts in Canada and the United States, the teachers collectively deal directly with their boards and ignore their administrators on major decisions. Even so, on many matters the position of the school administrator is still that of a middle-person. At the very least, much of the communication between board and staff is filtered through administrative persons.

In the formal middle-person position, the administrator functions as a line official. The administrator supposedly interprets the policies and transmits the school board's orders to the teachers. In reverse, he is supposed to be the channel of communication from the teachers to the board. He is theoretically expected to transmit teachers' requests for equipment, salary adjustments, and other information which teachers and the administrators consider essential for board action.

In most school systems, certain administrative officials possess delegated decision-making responsibility considerably beyond that of middle-person in a bureaucratic structure. They often hire and dismiss teachers and other administrators, requiring board support only in matters of

[9] Neal Gross, *Who Runs Our Schools?* (New York: John Wiley & Sons, Inc., 1958); see also Neal Gross, Ward S. Mason, and Alexander W. MacEachern, *Explorations in Role Analysis: Studies of the School Superintendency Role* (New York: John Wiley & Sons, Inc., 1958).

public controversy. Often there is only the implicit support of the board for the administration's personnel actions. In addition, administrators are usually allowed or instructed, without specific board action, to make decisions about curricula and many other policies as long as such matters are not sensitive community issues. If the organization of the school is strictly a line one, the teachers will communicate with the administrative group, and only the administrators will communicate with the board. This is a rarity. Even in most small school systems, there are informal social networks which provide some teachers with direct contact with board members. Even so, the chief administrator is, in many ways, the most powerful managing force in education.

The administrator also performs a consultant function to both board and staff personnel. Here the administrator sometimes plays a more professional role, since he is expected by the public to have superior professional knowledge and skill. As consultant to the board, administrators are also expected to be politically sensitive and agile in helping them to formulate policies and verbalize the philosophy of the school. In this role, administrators make recommendations to the board for its approval or disapproval. This professional, quasi-political characteristic of higher level administrative positions is particularly important in relation to those activities which involve the board members in public controversy. Most school administrators seek to develop these aspects of their role. If the board respects the particular administrator's ability, qualifications, and political sensibilities, it may accept his recommendations in most matters of policy. If not, the board may rarely consult him and may disregard or be hostile to his recommendations when given. This aspect of the administrative role contains considerable potential for conflict. Robert Dreeben analyzes the basis for such conflict:

> Although the superintendent is legally the subordinate of the board because the board can hire and dispose of him, he is the superior of the board in expertise; and out of these two distinct bases of authority—legal status and expertness—a variety of political balances of power develop, some peaceful, some turbulent. Symptomatically, these power struggles often take the form of accusations of encroachment between board and superintendent (depending on whose ox is being gored). Rhetorically, the distinction between policy and administration is at stake, a distinction that totally misses the real point: the contrasting principles of authority.[10]

The other side of this role as consultant involves the relationship between the classroom teacher and the administrator. In large systems, teachers generally turn to special curriculum consultants, division heads, informal peer leadership and subordinate building administrators for

[10] Robert Dreeben, *The Nature of Teaching* (Glenview, Ill.: Scott, Foresman and Company, 1970), p. 45.

assistance. In large systems, central administration is a long way from the classroom. In some large systems principals and other administrators have their own unions or professional associations to negotiate with higher level administrators or directly with the board. In small systems, the several levels of administrative positions tend to function in unity under central direction. In large systems, administration is dispersed, often uncoordinated and competitive; its "unity" is found only on organizational charts.

The teacher in the small system typically learns to achieve some protection by using administrators as buffers between themselves and other administrators, board members, students, and parents. Asking administrators to give advice is but one of the ways in which teacher transfers responsibility to an administrator. By carrying out the advice of administrators, the teacher transfers responsibility to the administrators for any undesired consequences of the teacher's action. Typically, for example, the building administrator thus becomes a safeguard as well as a supervisor or advisor of teachers. In this sense, administrators become managers of conflict in their schools.

Quite different facets of many administrative positions are what we may call the "office boy" and "bookkeeper" roles. In large systems a considerable amount of clerical work is assigned to junior staff, but even in large school systems the preparation of reports and the maintenance of lower level school records frequently rest with a highly paid administrator. In many schools administrators are often the only persons free from classroom responsibilities and, therefore, the only ones who can run errands for other administrators, teachers, and board members. In some very small school systems where a school trustee functions as policy maker, this is the primary characteristic of the administrator's position. In both large and small school systems, one can often find administrators who are merely "flunkeys" for other administrators. Of course, most administrators do, in fact, manage much of what goes on in schools, particularly events occurring outside of the classrooms.

Administrators, like others, frequently strive to redefine their roles. Apparently, many of them are being taught to provide lip service, at least, to a function as democratic leaders instead of operating as line officials in the communication of the board's policy decision to the teachers. Such democratic administrators expect to act in a chairperson's position, with teachers participating in the formulation of school policy. Nevertheless, as we will discuss in the next chapter, teachers expect their administrators to set policy and to direct teacher activities. On the other hand, there are many who want to be able to ignore their administrators, feeling, perhaps, that the less they hear from them the better. The result, of course, is a dilemma for the democratically inclined administrator.

Administrators caught up in the democratic spirit also find themselves in conflict with others of their publics. There are many members of the community who want authoritarian leadership from their school administration. Furthermore, the administrator of democratic preferences can seldom escape authoritarian features which are common to many administrative roles such as being a chairperson and organizer of policy-making groups. In addition, the administrator continues to be in many situations the only channel of communication between the board, citizens, and teachers, which also tends to increase his or her authority. No doubt many administrators who attempt to function democratically behave, of necessity, in accordance with more authoritarian definitions of the position on certain occasions. Not all decisions and policies can be formulated by democratic processes involving the teachers, the board, and the community. At times the chief school administrator, as well as lower level administrators, is forced to make decisions without waiting for democratic action. The same can be said for teachers and other members of the school. Teachers and students often establish practices, such as teaching sex education, long in advance of their acceptance by boards of education and administrators. In large bureaucratic organizations, to wait for the wheels of administration may mean a long wait indeed. Teachers and others learn to rely on their own initiative and not on administrative processes for much that they do in their classrooms.

Teachers as School Managers

The position of teacher in relation to administration may also be characterized by formalized duties and privileges and by informally achieved powers. We have already defined the position of the teacher in some respects by our analysis of the school board members and administrators. The teacher's official status is subordinate in formal authority both to the administrator and to the school board. In practice, however, few can tell a teacher how or what to teach. A teacher's social behavior outside the classroom is more easily controlled than what is done behind classroom doors. In the classroom the teacher is the real manager of essential activities. Thus, in the teaching of mathematics, for example, the teacher usually claims an expertise and an accompanying immunity from the authority of those regarded as less expert, regardless of public sentiment or legal sanction. Unless one submits willingly to authority, authority loses much of its meaning; and teachers are less and less willing to submit themselves to the "nonexpert" authority of administrators. Like professors, elementary and secondary teachers are more and more assuming management prerogatives.

Teachers, we contend, play important administrative or management functions in nearly every school. Teachers carry out obvious management assignments such as setting up and directing such programs as physical education, foreign languages, or student government; they also participate on formally constituted school and community committees with various administrative tasks, such as granting promotion or tenure, or choosing textbooks, or setting salary scales or hiring procedures. And teachers play one of the most important organizational roles through their contribution to organizational goals or policies. The setting of both broad goals and subgoals is an important managerial function of a teacher's role. Unique expertise is usually acquired by those who must in the end carry out programs, and the power to implement or to implicitly veto programs often rests with such persons, regardless of formal authority. For these reasons, teachers must be involved in managerial matters, if their cooperation is to be acquired.

The goals of a school, as pointed out by Rabow and Robischon, are important for three reasons.[11] First, goals are guidelines for organizational activity and help focus the energies of members by defining particular actions as relevant. Second, goal attainment requires technological processes which depend on social acceptance. Goals influence choices of means in achieving goals. For example, the use of teaching machines may be rejected by some regardless of their efficiency in teaching a valued skill to students because teaching machines are viewed as conflicting with other personal or organizational values. Third, the goals of a school system may legitimate the organization's activities. As a consequence, goals influence basic social processes, communication patterns, authority structures, and division of labor.[12]

Rabow and Robischon provide some evidence that goals of schools are modified by the personal experiences of the teachers in their schools.[13] In other words, the managerial function of helping to establish and organize for goal attainment is actually an important feature of the behavior of many teachers.

There are other instances when a teacher's position in the community may involve managerial powers greater than that of the board or administration. This is illustrated by the following case:

> After some years as a teacher, "A" became a businessman in the community in which he taught. He also was active in the councils of the leading political party. Later he again held a series of teaching positions in the school. After several years, a school trusteeship became

---

[11] Jerome Rabow and Thomas Robischon, "The Public School: Organizational and Teacher Goals," *Education and Urban Society*, vol. 4, no. 4 (1972), p. 468.

[12] Ibid.

[13] Ibid., p. 485.

> vacant and "A" used his influence to get the widow of one of the leading politicians elected to this position. She soon decided, on the advice of others, that "A" should not be reemployed in the school. He was asked to resign and did so. Immediately, a large number of patrons of the school expressed concern about his resignation. When pressed, he informed them that he did not resign voluntarily. Petitions were circulated and a mass meeting was arranged to demand the reinstatement of "A" or the resignation of the school trustee. The political leaders of the community, as well as the patrons, were mobilized. The person who had requested the resignation of "A" resigned her position in the face of strong demands of both the patrons and politicians. "A" was reinstated and "B" replaced as school trustee. "B" was the choice of the political leaders, but he was selected only after consultation with "A."

This case is not unusual. In every school there are teachers who have the ability to organize outside pressures, and, collectively, teachers' associations are very capable indeed of bringing community pressures to bear on administrators and board members. In the past, teachers who were asked to resign generally did so quietly. Today, a court suit or public controversy is a typical outcome, particularly in matters held by teachers to be teachers' prerogatives.

As an employee, the teacher is, of course, vulnerable to the power of either the board or the administrator, and may become a scapegoat for board or administrative personnel. Those in authority may make it impossible for the teacher to carry out an assignment successfully, and they seldom take responsibility for a teacher's failure. The teacher is also frequently assigned unpleasant or impossible tasks because of the administrator's unwillingness to tackle the work. This is illustrated by the case of a school administrator who for many years had also been an athletic coach. When he realized that a bad season was coming up, he turned the coaching responsibilities over to one of the teachers. During the ensuing season, the administrator frequently criticized the new coach and discussed his failure with the patrons. At the end of the season the decision concerning the coach's reemployment was referred to the school board without recommendation. In this way, the administrator was able to protect his own position at the expense of another.

Even so, the teacher does have considerable autonomy in various facets of his or her role, many of which involve educational policy. Many of the day-to-day decisions in the educational process are made by teachers. Within the range of accepted activities, the teacher is not only permitted but also expected to exert authority over the conduct of the children. When teachers are faced with decisions for which there are no clearly understood norms, consultation with a lower level administrator and peer authority is a common practice. Such consultation is frequently a means of transferring a share of the responsibility for making the decision to the administrator or a group. This protects the teacher from the criticism of those who have the power to force compliance with their wishes. The process, it should be noted, involves the teacher in what we commonly consider as part of the management process. Teachers, in reality, manage much of the educational enterprise.

Of course, our analysis is only a general statement and does not take into account the numerous formally and informally recognized differences in teacher positions. Usually teacher management duties vary from one school to another. There are sharp differences between college, secondary, elementary, and primary grade teachers in the same community. The secondary school teacher generally has higher status and more administrative responsibilities than the elementary school teacher. Within the secondary school, teachers of some subjects often enjoy a higher status and are granted authority based on their unique expertise. Usually, teachers of academic subjects, such as English, mathematics, or social studies have somewhat higher status in the system than teachers of the vocational subjects. Vocational education teachers, however, probably are presumed to be more expert in their field than are the social studies teachers. In the past, in farming districts, the agricultural or shop teacher may have had higher status than academic teachers, but this is not typical today. On the other hand, while trade or industrial arts teachers generally have lower status, they hold other community roles not available to teachers of the more academic subjects, which in turn gives them more influence over various school practices and policies.

Of course, no role is static or unchanging. Certainly this must be said for the role of teacher in Western culture. While the basic role is relatively stable and resistant to change, certain events are occurring to modify the tasks of teachers. One recently emerging managerial function for teachers is the management or administration of teacher aides, a growing phenomenon that can be expected to have several manifest as well as latent effects.[14] Teacher aides are supposed to assist teachers in accomplishing the major goals of the institution, one prime aspect of which is to control students. According to John Natzki's research, both the typical social attributes and the subordinate position of teacher aides make it difficult for them to act effectively in management roles.[15]

Teachers who are able to maintain efficient and "proper" social control over the child are often ranked higher in social status in their institutions

---

[14] William S. Bennett, *New Careers and Urban School* (New York: Holt, Rinehart and Winston, Inc., 1970), pp. 3–17.

[15] John Natzki, "Toward the Development of a Substantive, Sociological Theory of Teacher, Teacher-Aide Relationships" (doctoral dissertation, Western Michigan University, 1972), pp. 5–26.

than those who are not able to do so. Similarly, the same standard is often held by the teacher for the aide. The teacher expects the aide to control children. However, to account for how aides are viewed by teachers, one must first understand the interactional context in which the activity occurs. That is, it is not just a question of whether aides can control but whether they can do so in a way that is compatible with what is expected by the teacher.

Teachers aides in the United States tend to be somewhat older than the teachers. Also, they tend to be predominantly from lower income groups. This is because many of the teacher-aide programs were begun in predominantly low income areas and the funding agencies required that the aides be from the school community. Aides are also more likely to be married and have larger families than the teachers. Finally, teacher aides tend to reside close to and know the children with whom they work. As reported by Natzki, they are, by virtue of their personal and social characteristics and life experiences, often as well prepared as teachers to control and discipline the children.

In fact, for aides the problem of controlling the chidren is often secondary to the problems of discovering whether, when, and how teachers expect them to manage the affairs of the children. Aides are judged by teachers according to their "sensitivity to the teacher's authority"—the degree to which they are properly submissive to and respectful of the teacher as a figure of authority in the school.[16] Aides who are not fully aware of, or who do not fully appreciate, the assertions and claims made by teachers as to what is due them, by virtue of their position as teacher, usually come to be defined as "unsupportive" of the authority of the teacher. Thus, aides are ranked according to their ability to direct at themselves the social definitions of authority which teachers consider appropriate. In the following comments by teachers quoted in Natzki's study, we see the emphasis placed on the aide playing a "supportive" role with regard to the teacher.

> (*Teacher Quote 1*)
> . . . If I ever felt that I was being challenged by an aide, I think I would probably get rid of her [the teacher aide] whether she was doing a good job or not, because my position as a teacher is one which I do not want to feel threatened in. But, if the aide would be doing things for me, jeepers, the next thing you know the aide would have my job! That is self-protection.
>
> (*Teacher Quote 2*)
> She [the teacher aide] is a poised and animated person, sensitive yet practical, supportive but reserved. A more excellent person could not have been assigned to this position. She is scrupulous about retaining

[16] Ibid.

her supportive role as an aide and always refers children and parents to the teacher as the policy-maker and person with authority.

(*Teacher Quote* 3)

She [the teacher aide] seems to be quite flexible, adapting to the teacher she is working with. She keeps the teacher as the authority figure in the eyes of the children.[17]

Teachers' definitions of what constitutes proper respect for their authority vary greatly. To be regarded as sensitive to teacher authority, then, aides must discover what these definitions of authority are, and guide themselves, and their activities by these definitions. Aides who are successful in doing so—even aides who are not particularly well-educated, are not skillful, and lack experience in aide work—will be ranked higher in social status than aides who have better technical qualifications when the poorly trained aides respect the teacher's authority.

According to Natzki, the role boundaries between teachers and their aides are, from an organizational standpoint, fluid and undefined. The role boundaries for teachers and aides are as yet mostly the outcomes of personal characteristics in the relationship between teacher and aide. Particularly from the aide's standpoint, the problem involves discovering what the role boundaries are and what constitutes a violation of them. There is no clear consensus on definitions at this time.

The point of this discussion is that teachers do have important managerial functions—some are emerging and others are being created by superiors, such as responsibilities for supervising playgrounds or athletic events during lunch hours or after school. With the advent of strong teacher organizations, teachers can be expected more and more to move toward the major managerial functions now being carried out by teachers at many leading universities. Some university faculties have developed such managerial functions that their administrators are looked on as merely facilitating or impeding functionaries. In many universities, the faculty elects department chairpersons; many of the more prestigious and powerful faculties disdain administrative appointments.

Students as School Managers

Like administrators and teachers, students can and do manage their school in subtle and informal ways. Like the custodian in a small school, college students are sometimes able to have influence over who gets hired and promoted. In the authors' experience, some graduate and undergraduate students often develop direct and mutually supportive re-

---

[17] Ibid.

lationships with deans and senior faculty. In this way, they sometimes exert considerably more influence than young faculty members on matters of school policy. Recently the authors observed the skill of a number of students in creating a new college in a large university over the objections of many of the faculty. At the lower educational levels, the power of the student is largely dependent on that accorded him by the school authorities. Nevertheless, some students are able to manage the power of their families to effect changes at school.

As we have seen in our discussion of the board and staff social structure, there is more than one network of power relationships within the school system. From this discussion it should be apparent that, while it is possible to chart certain formal aspects of the authority structure in a school, it is quite difficult to account for the various informal power structures that inevitably arise when people interact. The business of plotting out the authoritative roles of students is all the more difficult because there are relatively few established management roles occupied by members of this group below the college level. The positions of the school board, administrators, teachers, and supportive personnel are permanent and quite stable occupational designations. The role expectations in these posts are well known and are integrated into the social systems of both the school and the community.

In the student society, the various positions and the interrelations that exist are not to the same extent a part of the basic community structure. There are, of course, some recognized and formally defined positions in the student society, but few of these are fully known to or recognized by the adult community. In fact, it seems fair to say that, with the exception of certain traditional student positions, most school-oriented positions lose their meaning once they are taken beyond the school door. Within the student body itself we can see that particular positions and roles have different connotations for different segments of the student body. In some schools students who participate in student government are rejected by their peers, since they are perceived as "sell-outs," who have abandoned their fellow students for the benefits which come from participation in officially sanctioned activities. We know of several instances both at the secondary and at the college level in which students who show an interest in governmental roles in the school have faced the ridicule of their peers. The old jargon "square" and "fink," applied to students who take on offices in the school society, reflect to some extent how these positions and their incumbents are viewed by others.

On the other hand, outside of the student government role, students are increasingly demanding a greater voice in administration, and it should be recognized that students do have power. Students may not always have formal authority to administer various facets of their schools, but even so they can often exercise control or influence; they have often "managed" to exercise their will in school matters. Of course, the role of students in administering their schools depends on age and educational level, the society within which a school is embedded, the actions of other individuals and groups in the system, and a number of other conditions.

In schools organized according to the philosophy of the famous Summerhill school in England, the students have considerable authority over what they will and will not study and how they will approach their courses. In the United States, many universities and colleges now place students on committees with considerable administrative power, even committees having to do with hiring, firing, and promoting professors and administrators. In many universities students deal directly with presidents and trustees on matters of curriculum and school policy. Students are also able to exert power through collective action in the community, which in turn shapes their schools.

In some countries the political process is very definitely a partial function of student efforts. In the United States students have recently begun to get themselves elected to city governments on the basis of organizing student voters. With the lowering of the voting age in the United States, perhaps greater political power will be accorded students to manage school affairs. It should be noted, however, that while we emphasize that students can exert political power under certain conditions, the facts are that for a variety of reasons they seldom do.

In any case, it appears that administrators and faculty are more and more willing to accord to students participant decision-making responsibilities over school matters. Where this occurs we can expect conflict to occur. There are many who will not relinquish power or authority without a struggle. It should be also noted that we are not considering the merits of various forms of student influence. Our only contention is that for the foreseeable future the student in Western culture will gain greater influence, both formally and informally, over educational-policy–making and that the changes will be accompanied by short-term conflict.

Supportive Staff

Managerial functions are shared occasionally also with the so-called supportive staff such as teacher aides, librarians, secretaries, consultants, media specialists, coaches, and custodians. While not given managerial authority by their positions in the school's bureaucratic structure, supportive staff often are able to manage educational processes and outcomes—by virtue of charisma, expertise, or access to power. Even in a small school, the custodian for example, may come to have considerable influence.

> At "H" school, Dick, the school custodian, occupied a strategic position in the school policy-making process. Dick was custodian from the beginning of this consolidated school till his death, approximately 20 years later. He knew all the patrons in the small community and had been active in local political affairs. More important, perhaps, was his own concept of the importance and significance of his activity in the school. As in many schools, the boiler room, the place he lived during the winter months as well as where he did his work, became a hangout for teachers, bus drivers, and others who wished to take a smoke or otherwise get out of the public view during the school day. Dick was particularly helpful to the teachers, and made special effort to make their work easier. He had all the teachers heavily obligated to him. Early in the history of this school, the school administrator realized that Dick had given him sound advice on the organization of the school. In order to fulfill the advisor role, which he rapidly achieved, Dick sought to learn as much as he could about the work of each teacher. Through these informal relationships, Dick came to occupy a position in which he could actually decide which teachers were to be reemployed and which dismissed. Each administrator in turn depended on Dick for information from the community, as well as for observations about the school. No major decision concerning teachers or policy concerning the school was made or adopted without Dick's advice.

Although it is not typical, this case from one of the author's files is cited because it illustrates the possible position that a custodian may acquire through informal relationships.

In another school, the clerk acquired similar influence. Through long service to a superintendent who gradually delegated more and more work to her, she came to occupy a position very close to that of the superintendent. When the superintendent retired, the clerk was transferred to another position in the school. The new superintendent discovered that many of his official duties and functions followed the old clerk. The informal system of relationships between the clerk and teachers, other administrators, and the board was such that the duties she had performed were still expected of her as a person and not as an adjunct of the superintendent.

One might question whether the case of the custodian's power to manage described above is illustrative of large school systems. According to recent research by Rafkey, it appears that custodians have gained a number of management functions.[18] In some states their legal responsibility for the school plant links them to an authority system of which the building's academic administration is not a part. Rafkey reports

[18] M. Rafkey, "Blue Collar Power: The Social Impact of Urban School Custodians," *Urban Education,* vol. 6, no. 4 (1972), p. 322.

on a common arrangement by which the custodial staff reports directly to the office of plant management, is hired by the office of plant management, is promoted by the office of plant management, and yet on many matters such as where to clean, is supposed to submit to the authority of the building principal. In one case, the custodian, in accord with his position and authority in the safety and security division of his school system, closed his school because of fire hazards. The principal ordered the school open but the custodian's authority in this matter was greater.

Similar relationships between bus drivers and patrons, on the one hand, and school board, on the other, may provide a channel of communication from the school both to patrons and to the board that completely circumvents the superintendent's office. Bus drivers have been in a position to dismiss both administrators and teachers, even though their position is officially subordinate to both.

The informal relations among these adults and other community members as well as teachers are affected by the other positions they occupy in the community. Bus drivers, clerks, and custodians are much more likely to be initimately and completely involved in the social relations of the community than are many teachers. For this reason, communication flows more freely between such persons and other community members than it does between teachers and community members. It is difficult for teachers who have not lived in a community prior to their employment to acquire such diffuse and total community positions. The "home" teacher who has previously established community positions may have extensive and intimate communications with other community members.

Although administrators and teachers also function in a set of informal relationships, the barriers between them and the community limit the communication that may occur. Administrators and teachers have been trained to accept norms that reinforce the sanctity of their groups. This commitment is not likely to characterize the behavior of the school's nonprofessional employees. Some administrators attempt to hold the nonprofessionals to a similar loyalty, but this claim is seldom accepted by all employees as an essential aspect of school organization. Teachers frequently criticize members of these groups for using informal nonprofessional means in achieving some end. However, the same criticism is in turn leveled at teachers who also on occasion reject administrative edicts and policies to chart their own courses of action.

At upper levels of the status hierarchy of supportive staff one expects informal influence to accrue. The secretaries of the department chairman, or of the college dean, or of the university president, generally acquire influence over and above the formal authority of their position. Depending on the reciprocal dependence of the administrator and his supportive staff, the authority vested with the administrator becomes informally extended to a greater or lesser degree to his supportive staff. In addition, the supportive staff sometimes accumulates power through their own clique structure. A teacher or administrator who treats his own secretary poorly may unknowingly become subject to negative treatment by other secretaries. The authors have known executive secretaries who have been able informally and subtly to influence promotion decisions.

The Influence of Informal Groups

Thus far, we have emphasized the position of the administrator as it is formally or officially recognized in the adult structure of the school. We have also noted that this position is frequently circumvented by the informal or unofficial system of relationships: for example, individual teachers may have direct communication with members of the board so that decisions are made between the teacher and the board member without the administrator's knowledge. A case in point is that of a teacher in a small school system who had on several occasions requested that the superintendent purchase some playground equipment. The request was never granted, and the teacher continued to carry on his work without the equipment. After several years, a friend of this teacher became a member of the board of trustees. Shortly after the election, the teacher mentioned that he had been trying for some time to get playground equipment. The equipment was soon delivered, and the superintendent knew nothing about the decision of the board to provide it. The teacher and school board member were members of the same clique. They were in one sense very much like members of a family, and the "kinship" between them had an important managerial function.

Kinship or Clique Patterns

At first glance, it may seem absurd to view the school as composed of a series of families. One famous scholar of the family, Radcliffe-Brown, defined kinship thus: "A kinship system is . . . a network of social relations which constitute part of that total network of social relations which is the social structure. The rights and duties of relatives to one another are part of the system and so are the terms used in addressing or referring to relatives."[19]

In elaborating on rules for becoming a member of kinship structures, another famous anthropologist and student of the family, Murdock, stated that there are three fundamental rules, any one of which is appro-

[19] A. R. Radcliffe-Brown, "Introduction," in A. R. Radcliffe-Brown and Daryll Forde (eds.), *African Systems of Kinship and Marriage* (New York: Oxford University Press, Inc., 1950), p. 1.

priate for entering a kinship system. Two are by genealogical descent and one is by "bilateral descent," which associates an individual with a group of very close relatives irrespective of their genealogical connection.[20]

Close examination of most school systems will reveal that there are, in one sense, families of educators and students which seem to have certain duties, loyalties, and rights with one another that are not shared with others in the school. Sometimes these "families" are organized around an academic discipline (this is particularly true in many colleges and universities); sometimes around an occupational function (e.g., counseling, teaching); sometimes around religious, ethnic, or racial identification or political ideologies; and sometimes around a time or place such as the first persons hired in a department or school, or proximity features in taking lunch or common avocational pursuits. Admittance to these families binds one to special loyalties and duties. While such families may not be formalized in any brochure and their existence may even be denied, they are maintained by reward, sanctions, and sentiments, and often play very important roles in school conduct. It is interesting to note that sometimes members of such families may even use the term "brother" and "sister" to refer to one another.

It should also be recognized here that many anthropologists no longer define the family in terms of the natural family of parents and children. Rather, they define the family as an institution, a unit of cooperation and a vehicle for the transmission of cultures.[21] We do not propose to push this idea too far, but we do contend that many such "school families," or "clique structures," or informal relationships can be discerned in most educational settings. We further contend that the functioning of the school is often impeded or facilitated by the conduct of these cliques or families; and that considerable conflict between professionals can be traced to competing "kinship" patterns within our schools. Interestingly, many of these clique patterns have a life beyond that of the individual members; they cooperate, they transmit their subculture, and they enforce their subculture. They often engage in activities to protect their spheres of influence, to maintain their traditions, to adapt to pressures from others, and to produce status and satisfaction for their group.

Certainly in our attempts to understand conflict and how schools are managed we will want to look for the possibility of subgroup conflicts. We will especially want to examine rather closely informal clique

[20] George P. Murdock, *Social Structure* (New Haven: Yale University Press, 1949), p. 145.

[21] Felix M. Berardo, "The Anthropological Approach to the Study of the Family," in F. Ivan Nye and Felix M. Berardo (eds.), *Emerging Conceptual Frameworks in Family Analysis* (New York: The Macmillan Company, 1966).

patterns among and between administrators, teachers, and students and their implications for the resolution of educational issues and the development of power.

Clique Formations

While differences in age and experience play some part in the kinds of relationships which develop among teachers, other factors are also involved.

The following analysis of the elementary and high school faculties occupying different buildings gives some idea of clique groupings.

The following legend is used to facilitate interpreting the cliques:

(Elementary School)

A–Kindergarten teacher	*G*–Fifth-grade teacher
B–First-grade teacher	*H*–Sixth-grade teacher
C–First- and second-grade teacher	*J*–Seventh-grade teacher
D–Second- and third-grade teacher	*K*–Fifth- and seventh-grade teacher
E–Third- and fourth-grade teacher	*L*–Kindergarten and third-grade teacher
F–Fourth-grade teacher	*M*–Fourth- and sixth-grade teacher

(High School)

N–Music teacher	*U*–Coach
P–Home economics teacher	*V*–Assistant coach
Q–Commercial teacher	*W*–Principal
R–Agricultural teacher	*X*–Literature and social science teacher
S–Industrial arts teacher	*Y*–Librarian and language and arts teacher
T–Superintendent	*Z*–Science and mathematics teacher

Five distinguishable cliques apparently were the result of common location, common levels of teaching, common problems, and common self-appraisal of ability. But further examination of the clique structure revealed a more divergent pattern. Here it was found that both in-school and out-of-school interests and activities were involved in determining the clique.

Clique 6, the sport group consisted of *T* and *W*, who were ex-coaches; *U* and *V*; and *N*, *P*, *Q*, *K*, and *M*, all of whom were actively interested in sports or married to men who were. This clique met regularly after all sporting events of the school for refreshments at the home of one of its members. Almost all the members were married and lived in places with sufficient facilities for entertaining the entire group. One unmarried member of the faculty, who always went with this group to all athletic events, would excuse herself from the after-game affairs. Age may have been a factor in this group. The range was from about 26 to 40 years.

Clique 7, the younger set, consisted of teachers *K*, *M*, *P*, *Q*, and *N*, and *N*'s wife. Members of this clique came to this school the same year, were between the ages of 25 and 30, and were characterized by many secondary likenesses. Teachers *K*, *M*, and *N* had attended the same school as undergraduates. *N*, *P*, and *Q* were interested in music. All were golf enthusiasts and all were frequently invited to non-school functions by townspeople.

Cliques 6 and 7 functioned outside the school but involved only the faculty of the school. The common factor involved was the use of leisure time.

Clique 8, an in-school clique, was a subdivision of the high-school clique. It had teachers *Y* and *X* as a nucleus and sometimes included *Z*. Teachers *X* and *Y* agreed on what was of prime importance in the high-school curriculum. They held seniority over the other teachers and believed discipline the secret to education. *Z* was interested in religious education and became connected with this clique because of a common regard for religious teaching. They were the final critics for innovations of teaching techniques.

Clique 9 might be called the boiler-room frequenters. It consisted of all the teachers who went to the boiler room to smoke. Among these were teachers *J, K, N, P, Q, R, S, U,* and *V*. The superintendent, *T*, was a semiactive member.

Clique 10 consisted of *U, V, T, W,* and *K*. This group governed the athletic setup of the school. It collaborated on matters pertinent to successful athletic programs, such as keeping the proper participants eligible and out of trouble. In this clique, *U* and *V* were the coaches; *T* and *W* were ex-coaches now in charge of administration and *K* was the coach of the junior-high teams.

In this school system the clique structure seemed to be based on common interests. If only one factor were the basis for the clique, it was usually not a closely knit organization. Many common interests seemed to result in more closely knit groups. Some of the factors apparently were age, ideals, interests, and location. The number of members in any given clique seemed to have little consistent effect on its rigidity.[22]

To some extent the formal positions in the faculty structure define the informal clique positions. We noted that the elementary- and high-school teachers have different status and are expected to behave somewhat differently. These status differentials are also factors in the informal clique relationships, although some cliques cut across the elementary-secondary barrier. The subjects taught also affect clique formation, as do ecological factors such as the location of schools and place of residence.

Length of service in the particular school is frequently a basis for differentials in position and power. In most schools a new teacher occupies a subordinate position to the older teachers. Some experienced teachers become disturbed by a new teacher's failure to recognize this differential. The new teacher is expected to show some deference. The following description of a small group of new teachers by a woman who had taught in the system for many years indicates something of

[22] The authors are indebted to a graduate student (who wished to remain anonymous) for this analysis.

her resentment of the newcomers and her pleasure at these teachers' failures.

> This group was composed of six women teachers who were all new to our system. They ate lunch, rode to work, attended professional meetings together, and spent most of their leisure time in one another's company. They came only to those school functions that were absolutely necessary. They always arrived at school and left at the same time as the pupils. At faculty meetings they worked hard to push through those ideas that would make their work easier or bring them more money. The other teachers in the system tried for some time to help or to become friendly with them, but they were politely but definitely rebuffed. Only two of these girls are returning next year.[23]

The failure of this group of young teachers to show proper deference to the older teachers was definitely contrary to the expectations of the veteran teacher.

Another factor which may play some part in the relationships that develop between the novice and the veteran is emphasis on teaching innovations. Typically, the new teacher enters the school system with a body of knowledge that includes information about the latest teaching-learning devices. The veteran teacher, being more or less removed from the current stream of educational innovations, may see in the new teacher a threat to her own status within the school. For the new teacher, on the other hand, knowledge of the latest technical apparatus may be the vehicle for successful and efficient integration into the school system. Older teachers and professors sometimes resent the promotion of new teaching-learning devices by younger members of the school staff. In this case, acceptance or rejection of some innovation may act as another barrier between the new and experienced teacher.

In addition to the factor of length of service, these analyses illustrate the significance of other factors in the development of informal clique relationships. Among these are the age and sex of teachers. For certain types of activities, men and women operate in separate, informal systems. Cliques, however, sometimes cut across the sex barrier. This is particularly true among married teachers. The clique involving married women sometimes included the husbands and other men teachers, as well as the wives of male teachers. The illustrations also suggest that habits of the teachers, such as drinking, fishing, and card playing are associated with clique relations.

It is impossible at this point to give an exhaustive analysis of the many factors that affect clique structure or to evaluate the relative importance of any particular one. Our purpose is only to examine the range of factors associated with these informal structures. Such relationships

[23] The authors are indebted to a graduate student (who wished to remain anonymous) for the report from which this case was taken.

frequently have a role in the management of schools and influence the behavior of the faculty of any school.

For practical purposes, knowledge of the clique structure and of the possible cleavages between the cliques is extremely important in faculty action. Studies of clique structure and opinion leadership in other social systems have shown the importance of informal group relations. Teachers are more likely to participate in school activities with enthusiasm and to attain desired results if they can function within such friendship groups.

It is also important, however, to recognize the possibilities of cleavages and struggles for power and rewards among informal cliques. Often cliques vie for favors of the school board, the administration, the students, or the patrons. Such competition may be the motivation for superior achievement, but it may also arouse destructive conflict. In connection with analysis of the clique structure of one school, an observer made the following comment:

> There were no outward signs of conflict among these cliques, but they definitely vied for the power position. Clique 1 was the most powerful group. Clique 3 and 4 combined forces in the name of youth and presented a threat to Clique 1. Clique 2 had long ago accepted a passive but stubborn role in the school because one or more of this group were friends with someone from another group. It was impossible for any one of the cliques to cloak itself in secrecy. This is indicated by an informal network which acted as a communications center in relating information about the administration's doings.[24]

In this case the struggle for power tended to be vitiated because of the interlocking system of relationships among the cliques. Communication about the administration traveled from one to the other, and this apparently defeated attempts of any one grouping to achieve greater power. Two cliques were reported to cooperate, particularly in their struggle with the most dominant or powerful of the school cliques. Many other cases demonstrate the extensive interaction among cliques and the frequent shifting of personnel from one to another in accordance with the immediate point of interest.

Suggested Readings

Richard O. Carlson, *School Superintendents: Career and Performance* (Columbus: Charles E. Merrill Publishing Company, 1971).

Roy G. Francis, *Crumbling Walls* (Cambridge, Massachusetts: Schenkman Publishing Company, 1970).

[24] The authors are indebted to a graduate student (who wished to remain anonymous) for this report.

James W. Guthrie, and Paula H. Skene, "The Escalation of Pedagogical Politics," *Phi Delta Kappen,* vol. 54, no. 6 (February 1973).

William J. Haga, George Groen, and Fred Dansereau, Jr., "Professionalism and Role Making in a Service Organization," *American Sociological Review,* February 1974, vol. 39, no. 1, pp. 122–133. An advanced treatment on what it means to become a professional manager in a bureaucratic organization; in this case a regional college.

Paul W. Hamelman, *Managing the University: A Systems Approach* (New York: Praeger, 1972). A general discussion of the methods for developing or discovering institutional goals, assessing their attainment, and having alternative means available from a systems perspective. This book seems to be illustrative of one trend in thought among school administrators.

Alfred Kuhn (ed.), *The Logic of Social Systems* (San Francisco: Jossey-Ross, Inc., Publishers, 1973). Fourteen behavioral scientists discuss basic problems of a cross-cultural management research. For the advanced student, this work may be a source of many insights for understanding the problems of managing education.

Willard R. Lane, Ronald G. Corwin, and William G. Monahan, *Educational Administration* (New York: MacMillan Company, 1967). A text for school administrators that applies many principles from the sociology of education.

Donald McCarty, and Charles E. Ramsey, *The School Managers* (Westport, Connecticut: Glenwood Publishing Corporation, 1971). School managers—board members and superintendents—are viewed in terms of their relationships to community power structures and to each other. A very readable and scholarly presentation of a major research study.

Sam D. Sieber, *Reforming the University: The Role of the Social Research Center* (New York: Praeger Publishers, 1972).

9

Teachers and Teaching

In recent years, important changes have occurred in the teaching profession outside of the classroom. The initial emphasis in this chapter is on changes in the collective power of teachers and professors. We will then consider some of the major social conditions associated with entering and leaving the teaching profession. Finally, we will discuss the types of expectations which affect the nature of the profession and will examine the powerful influence of tradition.

Teacher Organizations: Their Increasing Power

In the United States, according to the National Education Association, teacher strikes rose from only three during the 1960–61 school year to 180 during the 1970–71 school year.[1] For the ten-year period from 1960 to 1970 there were more than 500 strikes involving more than 500,000 teachers and 5 million man-days of instruction lost. During this period strikes occurred in 33 states and the District of Columbia. The vast majority of teacher strikes in the United States were conducted by organized teacher groups: two-thirds ($N = 331$) were by locals affiliated with the National Education Association; one-fourth (135) were by affiliates of the American Federation of Teachers; nine were by joint NEA-AFT groups; eight were by independent teacher organizations and 18 were wildcat strikes not sanctioned by official organizations.[2] During

[1] "Teacher Strikes, 1960–61 to 1970–71," *National Education Association Research Bulletin,* vol. 48, no. 1 (October 1970), pp. 60–72. Strike is used to include work stoppages, "professional days," and withholding services.

[2] Ibid.

the 1973–74 school year, there were 142 different teacher strikes in the United States.[3]

According to Ladd and Lipset, by the Spring of 1973, 304 schools of higher education were bargaining collectively and the number of college professors included was 55,000, approximately one-sixth of the nation's faculty in the United States.[4]

Given what we know about social organization and shared values necessary to produce a strike, we may conclude that teachers are "getting themselves together." No matter whether one supports or opposes teacher strikes, the facts are that teachers are becoming an increasingly powerful unified economic, political, and social force in North America.

For increasing numbers of teachers, at all levels, from elementary schools through higher education, such collective pressure tactics as strikes are no longer considered too "unprofessional" to undertake. Many teachers have affiliated with "blue collar" unions. Their associations, such as the American Association of University Professors, the Californian Junior College Teachers Association, and the National Education Association, have adopted bargaining and sanction processes formerly employed only by unions. These developments suggest that teachers have drastically changed their social and economic orientations. Of course, the 500,000 teachers involved in strikes during the 1960s and 1970s represents only one-fourth of over two and one-half million public school teachers in the United States. Are they alone in their views? Between 1965 and 1970, several surveys of teachers' attitudes toward school strikes were taken.[5] As shown in Table 9–11, by 1970, 73 percent of the teachers supported the use of strikes, an increase of 20 percent over a five-year period. As we approach 1980, the trend toward strong and relatively militant teacher organization continues. During the 1980s, we expect that even more teachers will have become organized and potent politically.

This increasing collective strength will have considerable impact on the conduct of teachers outside of their classrooms and on the nature of the profession. In addition, as the positions of professors and teachers change, so must the roles of others in the system and in the society as a whole. The traditional roles of instructors with respect to the conduct of teacher preparation and recruitment, working conditions, professional autonomy, income, and classroom activities are being altered every day.

---

[3] Michael H. Walizer, John Wallace, and Charles Keely, "Teacher Training Institutions and the Formation of Militancy Attitudes." Presented before Southwestern Sociological Association, Dallas, Texas, 1974, p. 1.

[4] Everett C. Ladd, Jr., and Seymour M. Lipset, *Professors, Unions and American Higher Education* (Berkeley, California: The Carnegie Foundation for the Advancement of Teaching, 1973), pp. 1–2.

[5] "Teacher Strikes."

TABLE 9–1
Teacher Responses to Question: Do You Believe Public School Teachers Should Ever Strike?

	Percent				
	1965	*1967*	*1968*	*1969*	*1970*
Yes, teachers should strike the same as employees in other occupations.	3	4	9	6	10
Yes, but only under extreme conditions and after all other means have failed	50	54	59	56	64
No, teachers should never strike.	38	34	23	30	21
Undecided	9	8	9	8	6

Source: "Teacher Strikes, 1960–61 to 1970–71" *National Education Association Research Bulletin,* vol. 48, no. 1 (October 1970), p. 70.

What are the reasons behind this new militancy on the part of teachers at all levels, kindergarten through university? John S. Chaney offers the following model (Figure 9–1) based on his study of teacher strikes.[6]

FIGURE 9–1
Public School Teacher Strikes

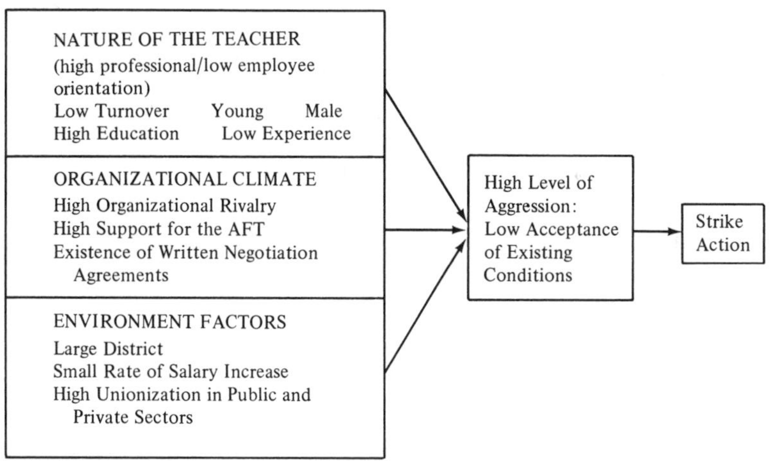

The model offered by Chaney, while certainly incomplete, is more inclusive than many other explanations and recognizes that at least three general conditions are relevant from an open system perspective: the teachers themselves, the schools, and the community context. Rosenthal,[7]

[6] John S. Chaney, "An Analysis of Public School Teacher Strikes in the United States, 1966–68."

[7] Alan Rosenthal, "The Strength of Teacher Organizations: Factors Influencing Membership in Two Large Cities," *Sociology of Education,* vol. 39 (Fall 1966), pp. 359–380.

Corwin,[8] Cole[9], Dreeban[10], and Keely et al.[11] are only a few of the sociologists who have shown the significance of trends toward teacher orientations of professionalism and vocational autonomy as a condition affecting their militancy. Studies also confirm Chaney's conclusions as to the importance of age,[12] sex,[13] school size,[14] and community.[15] Interestingly, even the teacher-training institutions have been concluded to make a contribution to teacher militancy.[16] Ethnicity and race do not appear to have any relationship to teacher militancy.[17] Whatever our eventual understanding of the complexities of the causes, teachers have found new power.

What does this new collective power of teachers mean for the individual teacher? Obviously, to answer this question requires a considerable amount of speculation at this time. However, a number of events might be expected to occur.

Control Shifts from the Local Level

To begin with, as teachers continue to organize and conduct collective action on province, state, and national levels, the traditional authority over education will shift from local to national levels. In the United States, state taxation will more and more replace local funds, and national funding will more and more replace state funding. As teachers set salary demands based on regional and finally on national conditions, the local districts and provinces and states must increasingly look to national revenues. While it is possible to retain a degree of authority over education at the local level when the funds are provided by state, province, regional, or national governments, some authority and power must necessarily go to the governmental levels providing funds.

---

[8] Ronald G. Corwin, *Militant Professionalism: A Study of Organizational Conflict in High Schools* (New York: Appleton-Century-Crofts, 1970).

[9] Stephen Cole, *The Unionization of Teachers: A Case Study of the UFT* (New York: Praeger Publishers, 1969).

[10] Robert Dreeben, "Review Essay: Reflections on Teacher Militancy and Unionization," *Sociology of Education*, vol. 45 (Summer 1972), pp. 326–337.

[11] Charles B. Keely, R. Greg Emerton, and Diane L. Keely, "Teacher Characteristics and Collective Bargaining Militancy." Paper presented to American Education Research Association, New Orleans, 1973.

[12] James A. Belasco, Joseph A. Aluto, and Lawrence A. Herbiniak, "Commitment and Attitudes," (Educational Resources Information Center: ED 037 416, 1970).

[13] Joseph A. Aluto and James A. Belasco, "Determinants of Attitudinal Militancy among Nurses and Teachers," (Educational Resources Information Center: ED 063 635, 1972).

[14] Sentelle, "Causes of Militancy," (Educational Resources Information Center ED 034 084, 1971).

[15] Ibid.

[16] Walizer et al., "Teacher Training Institutions."

[17] Keely et al., "Teacher Characteristics and Collective Bargaining."

With the transfer of funding from local to national levels, the teacher organizations also shift their attentions. Teacher organizations tend to increase their involvements with their legislators and exert less direct pressure on their local school boards. Increasingly, decisions relative to the schools will be made on the basis of national and regional needs rather than on the basis of local interests. For example, busing that is paid for by state or province funds means that requirements concerning types of buses, qualifications of bus drivers, who can ride the buses, and a host of other requirements are set by the state or province. Such extralocal requirements characterize recent educational programs that are supported and sponsored by national, state, and provincial governments.

The central question is not whether or not the local school district loses some control as funding sources are shifted to higher governmental levels; the primary issue concerns which controls can and should be retained at community levels and under what conditions. Simply to shift funding does not mean that all educational control must or will be transferred. Whatever the case, it should be clear that teachers, through collective action, are attempting to deal with local conditions through regional and national political and economic forces.

Teacher Autonomy

One further concomitant of collective action on state and national levels is that teachers are attaining greater autonomy from local school administrators and school boards. For example, recent court decisions have eroded traditional restrictions on the behavior of teachers outside of their classrooms. In the past, teachers could readily be fired for political activities. Within the last few years, however, a principle has been established that "the interest of the school administration in limiting the teacher's opportunity to contribute to public debate is not significantly greater than its interest in limiting a similar contribution by any member of the general public."[18]

> In the Pickering case, the Supreme Court of the United States reversed the decision of the Illinois Supreme Court which had upheld the dismissal of a high school teacher. The teacher had written to a local newspaper a partially erroneous letter critical of the school board's handling of a bond proposal and the subsequent allocation of funds between the athletic and educational programs. The Supreme Court noted that teachers are the members of a community most likely to have informed and definite opinions as to how funds allotted to a school system should be spent. Accordingly, it is essential that they be allowed

[18] Pickering *vs.* Board of Education of Township High School District 205, Will County, Illinois, 885 ct. 1781 (1968).

> to speak out freely on such questions without fear of retaliatory dismissal. The court said that the false statements in the letter were not knowingly or recklessly made, and that absent of such proof that they were, the exercise of the right of the teacher to speak out on such issues could not furnish the basis for his discharge.[19]

The courts have also restricted school boards and administrators from dismissing teachers without due process and for reasons that deny constitutional rights, even when tenure is not present. The following described a case involving a probationary teacher whose contract was not renewed.

> The teacher had requested a statement of charges and a hearing upon non-reemployment but the school board maintained that this applied only to tenure teachers dismissed during the school year but not to probationary teachers who were not offered another contract.
>
> The commissioner disagreed, saying that the only difference between the situations was the point in time and that nonrenewal was a dismissal. The commissioner held that the due process clause of the Fourteenth Amendment required notice and hearing. "The provision in (the state statute) . . . which states that a teacher who has acquired tenure shall not be dismissed without good and just cause should not be construed to imply that a teacher who has not acquired tenure may be dismissed without cause." But the commissioner did believe that the cause for dismissal of a nontenured teacher could be less than that required to dismiss a tenured teacher. In conclusion the commissioner said that "simple justice as provided not only by the laws of this state but by the Constitution of the United States demands that he know the cause for dismissal or nonrenewal of contract and have an opportunity to be heard on it."[20]

Given these recent court decisions, principals, superintendents, and other administrators no longer have the same formal authority to discipline or fire teachers. As we examine this increasing autonomy of teachers we should note the role of teacher organizations. All of the teacher organizations, in addition to maintaining lobbying groups to influence legislation, are developing strong legal arms to extend legal services to affiliate groups and individual members. The ability to take opponents to court, involving both the funds to meet costs and the ability to secure competent legal counsel, has made it possible for teachers to further extend their autonomy.

In the past teachers as a group have generally been viewed as socially and politically passive and dominated. This may have been true, but

---

[19] "The Teacher and the First Amendment," *National Education Association Research Bulletin,* vol. 48 (October 1970), no. 1, pp. 86–87.

[20] "The Teacher and Due Process," *National Education Association Research Bulletin,* vol. 48 (October 1968), no. 4, pp. 90–91.

today it is no longer the case, at least when compared with the general population. As we pointed out, teachers' organizations are becoming increasingly active politically. Furthermore, in 1970, according to a national survey, 22 to 31 percent of the teachers in the United States were involved as active members of political parties, nine percent as regular party workers, and three percent as candidates.[21] Interestingly, the political participation of the general public is less than half that of teachers.[22] On the other hand, a recent national survey indicates a marked decrease in political party membership for teachers occurring sometime between 1961 and 1971.[23] Whether this merely reflects alienation from political parties in a given election or represents a trend is impossible to discern at this time.

Aside from their political participation, teachers are tending to participate less than formerly in local community social organizations. For example, research shows a decrease in teacher participation in fraternal or auxiliary groups, church memberships, and youth groups.[24] Perhaps this finding is related to the fact that professors and teachers, as well as other workers, often live in communities other than those in which they work and play. Perhaps, as we suggested earlier, the teachers are transferring their interests away from local matters to regional and national concerns. Also, since teachers are more mobile and change jobs more often than in past years, they may tend to lean away from strong local community ties and loyalties. In any case, teachers are becoming increasingly active in state, province and national concerns through membership in teacher organizations and thereby more autonomous from local pressures.

These changes do not mean that teachers are totally or even largely autonomous from local school and community pressures. Teachers "are clearly not expected to espouse radical causes or belong to unusual religious sects."[25] Many teachers have lost their jobs for being vocally opposed to community-supported war, advocating certain freedoms for youth, or expressing other values contrary to the local norms. But we have pointed out, recent court decisions, stronger teacher organizations, and changing public attitudes are giving more political latitude to teachers then they previously enjoyed.

There are other reasons for recognizing the present and potential influence of teachers. More than one out of every 50 persons in North

---

[21] "The Teacher and the First Amendment."

[22] William S. Bennett and Edsel L. Erickson, "Teacher Profile," *Encyclopedia of Education* (New York: The Macmillan Company and The Free Press, 1971), vol. 9, pp. 43–49.

[23] *National Education Research Bulletin,* vol. 50, no. 1 (1972), p. 7.

[24] Ibid.

[25] Bennett and Erickson, "Teacher Profile," p. 45.

America earns his living in education. There are over two and one-half million elementary and secondary public school teachers alone in the United States, plus private school teachers, university and college teachers, and numerous communities which view education as essential to their existence. There are probably few other groups in society which, should it develop strong organizational structure, would have its unique combination of advantages. Teachers are usually articulate, they write to their legislators, they participate in community affairs, they are large in number, and they are often married to middle-income business and professional persons.

A Profile of Teaching[26]

Before further characterizing teachers as a group, however, it is essential that we take note of several cautions. To begin with, there have been few studies, validly conducted, which describe the public or private school teacher at any level in any nation. Furthermore, most studies of teacher characteristics done a few years ago have little relevance to today's world. Most investigations of teachers have been conducted in small homogeneous, semirural communities with conditions not comparable to those prevailing in large metropolitan areas. In addition, these studies have generally been limited to public school elementary and secondary teachers.

These limitations take on added importance given the rapidity with which Western societies have changed from rural to highly complex industrial societies with their increasing demands for highly trained teachers. The difficulty in accurately depicting teachers is further compounded by the fact that studies only a few years or a few months old have been followed by major events which may have modified the character of teaching in nearly every land. Attempts to educate teachers to adopt new perspectives toward children from poor families, attempts to extend successful teaching to the entire spectrum of social classes, changes in civil rights laws and fair employment practices, pressures to recruit a larger portion of minority people in teaching and educational administration, the emerging militancy of teachers to determine procedures for their recruitment, classroom conduct, dismissal, and reimbursement, waves of new students who have been in the military and are now entering education, and perhaps numbers of individuals who entered teaching to avoid military service, are but a few examples of the events and trends which have made a dramatic impact upon the character of teaching today.

[26] This section is based upon, and is an elaboration of, earlier work by William S. Bennett and Edsel L. Erickson, "Teacher Profile."

The Social Class Background

One has only to scan textbooks dealing with teachers and social class to realize the lack of general agreement among scholars regarding the socioeconomic background of those who enter the teaching profession. However, it is clear that, as our society has changed, so have the backgrounds of our teachers.

A quarter of a century ago, Carlson, in an article entitled, "Variation and Myth in the Social Status of Teachers," took exceptions to what he regarded as a myth about the social class background of American teachers. Rejecting the findings presented by those who emphasized the middle-class background and orientation of teachers, Carlson demonstrated that variation rather than uniformity characterizes the social class background of teachers. He reported that:

1. Teachers have origins from all levels of the social class continuum.
2. Teachers over-represent the top half and under-represent the bottom half of the social class continuum.
3. Approximately 36 percent of the teachers in the sample do not have origins in the middle class.
4. Various categories of teachers differ in their social class composition. As a category, male secondary teachers are lowest in social class origin, with about 48 percent originating in the lower classes. Female elementary teachers are highest in social origin, with about 23 percent originating in the lower class, about 74 percent in the middle class, and about 4 percent in the upper class.[27]

The recent data in Table 9–2, obtained 15 and 25 years after Carlson's study, indicate that a large proportion of teachers continue to be from lower socioeconomic backgrounds.

TABLE 9–2
Occupations of Teachers' Family of Origin (social class background)

	Percent	
Head of Household	*1961*	*1971*
Farmer	26.5	19.3
Unskilled	6.5	8.4
Skilled–Semi-skilled	23.4	25.7
Clerical or Sales	7.1	5.5
Managerial–Self-Employed	22.0	22.1
Professional–Semi-Professional	14.5	18.9
	100.0	99.9

Source: *National Education Association Research Bulletin*, vol. 50, no. 1 (1972), p. 6.

[27] Richard O. Carlson, "Variations and the Myth in the Social Status of Teachers," *The Journal of Educational Sociology*, vol. 35 (November 1951), pp. 104–118.

Another recent national study further confirms and extends the findings of Carlson. In this study it was found that the educational level of parents of both white and black teachers is low.[28]

Another important question concerning the teacher and social class is not his or her background but how the educator views and behaves toward students. Is there a particular social class orientation of teachers? Perhaps it is true that teachers, regardless of background, have subscribed to a white middle-class ethic. Many have so charged. Teachers as a group, when asked to indicate their liberalness or conservatism, report themselves to be slightly more conservative than liberals. As indicated in Table 9–3, only about four of every ten teachers indicate that they tend to be liberal or are liberal.

TABLE 9–3
Responses of Teachers to Questions of Political Philosophy

Political Philosophy of Teachers	*Percent*
Conservative	16.9
Tend to be conservative	43.6
Tend to be liberal	27.8
Liberal	11.7
	100.0

Source: *National Education Association Bulletin*, vol. 50, no. 1 (1972), p. 7.

On the other hand, several conditions have developed which may indicate a trend away from conservative orientations. In any case, it is clear that what constitutes conservatism and liberalism or middle class and lower class are more matters of confused political rhetoric than accurate discriptions of people's views and behavior.

Many universities have developed strong programs for teaching which attempt to minimize white middle-class biases. College students appear on national polls to be more oriented than their elders toward responsibilities to accept and assist minority and lower-class children. Teachers' organizations, with some exceptions, have begun to take stronger stands against unequal educational opportunities. Each of these pressures influences the views that teachers hold and act out.

Further evidence to support the view that a significant number of teachers are representing the "lower classes" is evident from an increase in the number of minority persons entering the teaching field. Changes in the population composition of major geographical regions and shifts in political power also appear to be associated with the increased hiring of minority teachers. The increased rate of black students entering and

[28] Data obtained from *Coleman Report,* analyzed and reported by William S. Bennett and Edsel Erickson, *Teacher Profile.*

staying in school and the concentration of black students in certain schools along with community demands have also brought about the addition of many black teachers. However, few Northern communities in the United States have openly admitted their placement policies for teachers. Even so, there is apparently a tendency for minority teachers to be placed in schools where there are heavy concentrations of minority youth. Recent court decisions and community pressures, however, may change this.

It should be apparent from this that the matter of social class in North America cannot be separated from ethnic and racial concerns. Bennett and Erickson note that, on a national level, teaching is probably the most racially mixed professional occupation.[29] In 1964, 88 percent of the teachers were white, 11 percent were black, and one percent were other nonwhite persons. These percentages fit rather closely the national census figures. As Bennett and Erickson point out, however, these figures obscure more than they reveal. In the North, the teacher is likely to be white regardless of his students' race, and in the South the teacher is likely to be the same race as his students. Uneven racial distribution in metropolitan areas is also shown by the fact that in the urban Northeast 11 percent of the teachers were nonwhite, while the comparable figure in the Midwest was only three percent but it was a huge 28 percent in the Southwest. While changes are occurring, it is unlikely that in the years prior to 1980 this uneven racial distribution will be overcome.

The teaching and learning implications of having teachers and students of the same or differing class or racial status will be discussed later. The racial and ethnic composition of the teaching profession has implications which go beyond learning effects. The social composition of the teaching profession has been an issue in a number of teacher strikes, in several court battles, and is at the heart of much of the effort to decentralize large metropolitan districts and grant greater control over teaching to local communities.

Becoming a Teacher

The behavior of teachers at every level is affected by their experience and background. An indication of why individuals become teachers is, therefore, relevant.

Of course, there are many reasons why people choose teaching as an occupation. Sometimes it is simply a matter of social inheritance—one takes on the work left by parents. Sometimes the entry into teaching is the new product of years of planning and preparation. Sometimes it is the result of social or economic pressures which are at work in

[29] Bennett and Erickson, "Teacher Profile."

a particular society. For some, the choice is based on a desire for community recognition and prestige. For others, a primary element is a desire to be of service to others, and for still others, particularly women and other minorities, the choice of being a teacher may result from a lack of alternative professional options.

In dealing with the problem of occupational choice, most investigators agree that no single factor determines what job is finally taken by the individual. The most comprehensive studies of occupational choice from a theoretical point of view were made over two decades ago by Ginzberg and his associates.[30] Their work is still relevant. Basing his study on a sample of students from junior high schools, senior high schools, and the college and graduate school of Columbia University, Ginzberg formulated an outline for the study of occupational choice.

Materials from the interviews were analyzed in three major categories: (1) "the self," which included questions about capacities, interests, and personal values; (2) "reality," which dealt with the influence of the individual's perception of the real world on his choice of occupation; and (3) "key persons," the investigation of the influence of parents, teachers, or friends.

The authors found that college freshmen have not quite arrived at the "brass tacks" stage of occupational choice and so they refer to this as the "exploration stage."

> Despite the marked shift toward realism which distinguishes the entire period of decision making in college and graduate school, these freshmen are still subjectively oriented, although their subjectivity has a different quality from that of the high school group . . . It is worth noting that the subject of occupational choice is seldom discussed even among close friends and almost never in a group.[31]
>
> By the time a student has become a college senior he or she has ordinarily entered the sub-stage of "crystallization." Crystallization is the process whereby the individual is finally able to synthesize the many forces, internal and external, that have relevance for his decision. The actual process cannot be observed save in retrospect; this is true not only for the observer, but for the individual. It is a commitment, and the individual recognizes that by his willingness to bring his explorations to a close and by his ability to make definite plans for the future, subject to change in details.[32]

The graduate student has entered the last stage of the realistic period of occupational choice—that is, the stage of specification. There are, however, many factors beyond the social-psychological conditions de-

[30] Eli Ginzberg et al., *Occupational Choice: An Approach to a General Theory* (New York: Columbia University Press, 1951).

[31] Ibid., p. 103.

[32] Ibid., p. 107.

scribed by Ginzberg that determine who becomes a teacher. Economic factors are important. As we pointed out, for many the teaching profession is a step up from their parents' socioeconomic status. For others, teaching has been a vehicle for avoiding other conditions. There are probably a number who got into teaching simply to avoid being drafted into the military. Opportunities and constraints associated with sex roles also are important.

Sex Biases. Most public school teachers during the mid-19th century were women. In fact, many normal schools, forerunners of our teachers' colleges, were initially for women only. On the other hand, college and university positions in most areas have traditionally been restricted to men. One consequence of these beginnings is that today the majority of university teachers in Western culture are men while the majority of elementary school teachers are women.

Another consequence has been that elementary teaching has been associated with the "motherhood role," with the training and socialization of the young, and with the protection of the needy. So firmly entrenched is this popular "sexist" image in our society that it becomes difficult for a man who wants to enter and remain as a teacher in the early education field to withstand the social pressures against doing so. The authors have talked with numerous college girls who are majoring in elementary education and find that only a few of them would be willing to consider as a husband a man who makes early elementary teaching his life's work. Some are willing to accept it as a transitory job—something to be used while their husbands look for a better position or train to become a principal, but few perceive it as serious work for a man. The sexual interpretation is not one-sided, since there are few college men who would seriously consider elementary school teaching as a career. There are men who would take an administrative position in an elementary school or perhaps a job as the physical education teacher (this is obviously perceived to be a more masculine role and one that need not embarrass the male), but relatively few would accept the role of first- or second-grade teacher.

This concentration of females in the early elementary-teaching role has probably had considerable impact on the development of curriculum and educational philosophy. In Canada and the United States, elementary education is generally different from secondary education in that one has traditionally been more "subject-centered" as preparatory for college, while the other has been more "child-centered." Education courses for the training of elementary teachers have given considerable emphasis to "tender loving care" and very little to skills and strategies for teaching subject areas. For example, there are few teacher-training programs to this day that require more than three semester hours of work in the teaching of reading—a task which is now considered a national problem. This is not to argue for or against a focus on the development of specific teaching skills for elementary teachers. The interpretation we offer is that sex roles have played an important part in shaping educational philosophy.

There does, however, seem to be some shift in this model. Recent societal pressures are causing some changes in instructional methodology and curriculum objectives. This press takes the form of evaluation and accountability programs and monies being made available for remediation programs in science and language as well as the demands of both minority and lower-class groups that their children be brought to higher achievement levels in the three "R's." Perhaps the changing sex role differentiation which is occurring as a consequence of recent court actions and through the efforts of various women's groups will further change the pattern.

There is one outcome of this pressure for change in early education which is certain. There will be competition and conflict. Teachers will be encouraged to be on one side or the other, and the other side will often be viewed as the work of either the "devil" or the ignorant. Teaching orientations are serious and moral matters to many teachers (as perhaps they should be) and to ask them to teach contrary to their values is bound to bring resistance. It should also be noted that any relatively quick and successful change in associating sex with various elementary and secondary teaching roles must be accompanied by changes in socialization in the family, schools, courts, and other institutions which will affect attitudes about what is male and female. The same is true in bringing about greater female participation in the upper academic arenas.

Whatever the conditions for becoming a teacher, they are probably not the same for leaving teaching. What are teachers like who leave teaching? Why do some drop out of education? Why do others change their sites of employment as often as they do?

Teacher Dropout and Mobility

Teaching as a profession has one of the highest turnover rates of any profession. Within only one year, six to ten out of every 100 teachers will probably leave teaching as a profession.[33] In spite of the recent shift toward a much greater supply of teachers than public school teaching positions, there continues to be a very high separation of teachers from the education field. Approximately 14 percent separate from teaching each year, and of these over 80 percent are by resignation.[34] In

[33] "Teacher Mobility and Loss," *National Education Association Research Bulletin* (December 1968), p. 119.

[34] *National Education Research Bulletin,* vol. 49, no. 4 (1971), p. 100.

specialized areas, such as teachers of the deaf and blind, the average length is often much shorter. It has been our experience that teachers of the deaf and blind last in their careers for only about three years. If lawyers and physicians were to leave in such large proportions, a national crisis might follow. In spite of the fact that most educators believe that it takes several years to become a maximally effective teacher and in spite of the general need for experienced teachers, the increasing salaries, and of recent years fewer teaching opportunities, teaching has been plagued with high turnover. What are the reasons? Is it due to economic considerations, to the manner in which schools are organized, to social system conditions? What is it that produces such high turnover among teachers? Bruce, in speaking of the community problem, said that ". . . of all the problems which boards of education have to contend with, the turnover of teachers is perhaps the most troublesome and confusing."[35]

Traditional Explanations. The difficulty school boards face in understanding teacher turnover also extends to educators and social scientists. Our knowledge about career change consists primarily of long lists of disparate reasons given by people after they have in fact changed jobs. Literally hundreds of after-the-fact surveys of teachers' reasons for leaving their positions have been conducted. It is commonly stated by teachers and investigators utilizing data gathered after the fact that teachers leave teaching to enter other occupations because of low salary, dissatisfaction with administrators, excessive teaching load, extra work beyond teaching duty, and similar reasons.[36]

The three major criticisms which can be applied to most of these studies are: (1) failure to distinguish type of teacher turnover, such as those leaving for another school district and those leaving education; (2) the post hoc nature of these studies; and (3) the lack of any theoretical structure concerning the dynamics of career change. Among most studies of teacher turnover, teacher mobility (a change in district of employment) is not distinguished from teacher dropout (teachers leaving education for other careers). A different set of factors may be more appropriate for explaining teacher dropout than would be appropriate for explaining teacher mobility.

Usually, however, implied economic notions (concerning salary) or

[35] William C. Bruce, "Teacher Turnover," *American School Board Journal,* vol. 149 (November 1964), p. 29.

[36] See for example John W. Blaser, *Factors Contributing to the Problem of Men Graduates Leaving the Teaching Profession* (doctoral dissertation, University of Idaho, 1965); Clifford D. Foster, "Teacher Supply and Demand," *Review of Educational Research,* vol. 27 (June 1967), pp. 260–71; and Earl C. Metz, *A Study of Factors Influencing the Withdrawal of Four Thousand Teachers From the Ohio Public Schools* (doctoral dissertation, The Ohio State University, 1962).

unstated beliefs about the function of "motivations" and "frustrations" are given. Without challenging the rigor of such explanations, it can be said that currently there is no commonly accepted set of propositions or scientific body of knowledge stating why career change occurs. The closest approximation is in the area of career development. There is the possibility, however, that factors which may explain the development of one's teaching career (e.g., economic security) are not the same as those which best explain why one leaves education. Furthermore, characteristics of the teachers' relationships with friends and spouse may be as relevant as psychological traits or economic factors. It is fair, at least to say that the burden of verification is still on anyone who states why career change occurs.

Gordon in 1963[37] and Foster in 1967[38] reviewed the research to that time and cited several descriptive studies of teacher employment conditions. Such conditions as low teacher status and low morale are often cited as the major causes of teachers' leaving education. Nelson and Thompson reported that teachers leave because of low salary, excessive teaching load, assignments beyond teaching duty, inadequate supervision, poor assignments for first-year teachers, discipline problems given to beginning teachers, pressure groups and control, poor mental hygiene which is intensified by teaching conditions, marriage, inadequate preparation or knowledge of subject, inability to handle classes, unfair teacher evaluation, inadequate facilities, poor faculty relationships, routine clerical duties, competition between school and industry for trained personnel, and poor school boards.[39] Snow reported that another factor may be that teachers can see very little clear-cut proof of their effectiveness. They have little feedback in order to appraise their own work.[40]

Taking an economic view of teacher turnover, many writers have stated, without solid evidence, since as early as the 1930s, that teachers would not leave teaching if they felt more secure professionally and socially and that their self-respect, morale, and professional interest would increase if their salaries were higher. Also, members of the community would attribute greater prestige to teachers.[41] However, higher salaries have not solved the teacher turnover problem. Salary alone is

---

[37] Garford G. Gordon, "Conditions of Employment and Service in Elementary and Secondary Schools," *Review of Educational Research*, vol. 33 (October 1963), pp. 381–90.

[38] Foster, "Teacher Supply and Demand."

[39] Robert H. Nelson and Michael L. Thompson, "Why Teachers Quit," *The Clearing House*, vol. 37 (April 1963), pp. 467–72.

[40] Robert H. Snow, "Anxieties and Discontents in Teaching," *Phi Delta Kappa*, vol. 54 (April 1963), pp. 318–21.

[41] See for example the early work of Verne Wright and Manuel C. Elmer, *General Sociology* (New York: Farrer and Rinehart, Inc., 1939), Chapter 12, pp. 217–35.

hardly an adequate explanation, when other factors are considered. While we accept financial rewards as a factor, we believe that the image of teachers expressed in the "teacher stereotype" is a much more important factor, and especially so when that image is held by the teacher's primary groups. Browning (1963) reported two studies in Montgomery County, Maryland, in which 241 former teachers responded that excessive pressure and overload and dislike for administrative and supervisory practices were the major reasons for turnover. Salary was mentioned infrequently, and then only by men (four out of 32).[42] Steiner reported in a California survey of 17,000 persons who left teaching between 1950 and 1959 that: (1) marriage, maternity, and moving out of state accounted for about 57 percent of those who resigned; (2) dissatisfaction on the job accounted for about ten percent; and (3) inadequate salaries accounted for about seven percent.[43]

In summarizing his impression of the many studies conducted over the past several years, Gordon stated, "When one looks for research going beyond the collection and rough classification of quantifiable facts about current conditions, the picture is rather bleak."[44] It appears that, despite the large number of studies, there are no clear conceptions of what is involved in conditions of employment or types of career change. Generally, these studies do little more than replicate previous surveys, as Gordon states, of "opinions, panaceas and . . . uncritical and highly biased descriptions."[45] Our own review of the recent literature on teacher turnover indicates more of the same. However, limited work in social science in the last two decades may offer new sociological insights into why teachers leave education.[46]

A Sociological Explanation. The fields of sociology and social psychology provide a common body of literature under the rubric of role analysis and reference group theories which, though not articulated into formal theories, are pertinent to teacher turnover. These orientations emphasize approval of others in role decisions. From this perspective a teacher would be guided in his occupational decisions by the expectations and approval of others.

Reference groups are not necessarily membership groups. A member-

[42] Rufus C. Browning, "How to Tackle the Problem of Teacher Turnover," *School Management,* vol. 7 (June 1963), pp. 80–82.

[43] George J. Steiner, "Report on Why Teachers Quit Teaching," *Chicago Schools Journal,* vol. 45 (October 1963), p. 35.

[44] Gordon, "Conditions of Employment and Service."

[45] Ibid.

[46] For example, in the 1950s Mason and Bain conducted a study discriminating between teachers who left teaching as a career and teachers who merely changed sites of occupation. Ward S. Mason and Robert K. Bain, *Teacher Turnover in the Public Schools 1957–58,* (Washington, D.C.: U.S. Department of Health, Education and Welfare, Government Printing Office, 1959).

ship group is one which requires a person to be a member or one in which a person is recognized by others as belonging. A reference group is one in which a person's attitudes and behavior are said to be influenced by a set of norms which he assumes he shares with others, even though he may or may not be perceived by the individuals of the reference group as being a member. The group thus serves as a frame of reference. When a person's membership group is also his reference group, the group is assumed to have the greatest influence on his behavior. With a similar focus, Bredemeier and Toby present a view, drawn from George Herbert Mead, that the individual adopts the group's standards of adequacy, worthiness, gratification, and security.[47] In this way, the teacher comes to value the group and tries to attain its expectations; he senses certain role obligations.

From this sociological perspective it is believed that to understand a teacher's behavior and decisions in a given role one must also take into account certain relationships which impinge on the teacher. We contend that the obligations a teacher has to family and friends often provide the most important norms. For a teacher to violate what he or she perceives to be the spouse's expectations concerning his or her career is also to jeopardize many other role relationships with that spouse; i.e., husband, companion, and so forth. In accord with this view, we believe that a teacher's perceptions of the career expectations held for him or her by his family and friends, and not necessarily the friends' and family's actual expectations, are the major factors in the teacher's decision to leave or remain in teaching.

One of the authors recently conducted a study employing this view of the family's and friends' influence on career decisions.[48] In this study, data were collected in the spring on whether or not first and second year male teachers viewed their families and friends as desiring that they remain in their school systems, leave to work in another school system, or leave teaching for another career. From such data predictions were made as to which teachers would return the following fall or leave teaching as a career.

Data were also collected on the teachers' career and job satisfaction, their morale, background conditions concerning previous mobility, teaching experience, the socioeconomic status of the family of their origin, their aspirations and vocational plans, their perceptions of disciplinary and academic characteristics of their students, and the support for teaching received from their students' parents.

---

[47] Harry C. Bredemeier and Jackson Toby, *Social Problems in America: Costs and Casualties in an Acquisitive Society* (New York: John Wiley & Sons, Inc., 1960), Chapter 1, pp. 3–11.

[48] Edsel Erickson et al., *Teacher Mobility, Teacher Dropout and the Expectations of Family and Friends, Final Report.* U.S. Office of Education Cooperative Project No. 68968, 1968.

Just as we anticipated, the most useful data for predicting whether a teacher would leave teaching were what that teacher believed his or her spouse or family desired. The second most useful data for predicting the career actions of teachers were information on the desires of friends with whom the teacher interacted frequently.

No substantive support was found for the following background factors as being useful predictors of which male first and second year teachers in a system would leave education as a career, move to another school system, or remain in their school systems: (1) total of previous teaching experience; (2) number of schools taught in; (3) parents' education levels; (4) socioeconomic status level of father in terms of social prestige; (5) best friend's SES level; (6) teachers' perceptions of their students' academic skills; (7) teachers' perceptions of their students' parents' cooperativeness and concern for their children; (8) teacher satisfaction with the job requirements; (9) teacher satisfaction with the career of teaching; (10) teacher satisfaction with others in school setting; (11) teacher occupational aspirations and plans in terms of social prestige levels; and (12) teacher orientations to move to higher status positions within education.

In summary, substantial inferential and empirical support for the utility of reference group theory was demonstrated in this study. The research provided evidence, from data about teachers' perceptions of the career expectations held for them by their spouses and friends, that it is possible to predict, far beyond chance, whether teachers will leave education as a career or move to other school systems. In addition, this study provided evidence of the way in which social groups, through the medium of the individual actor, contribute to the maintenance of large formal social structures and societal institutions.

In other words, such usual explanations as satisfaction with teaching per se, aspirations for social prestige and problems faced in the classroom were not found to be important variables in determining the career decisions of teachers. If these, and the other findings of the study, are further supported in other research, then it appears that efforts to reduce turnover among teachers should focus upon activities which will elicit the support of teachers' reference groups, particularly their friends and family.

Recognizing the influence of family and friends on the role of a teacher is also a reasonable position from a systems perspective. Too often we think we can understand what goes on in education by looking only at events occurring within a school setting. From a systems perspective, parents, friends, and others outside the formal school may have a very important role in affecting decisions within education. We have learned that the educational system is likely to extend beyond the formal school organization. This sort of perspective is also of value as we turn our attention to understanding student learning in the last section of this book.

Expectations for Teachers

A wide range of significant or relevant groups hold expectations for teachers. The expectations held by one group, of course, may well differ from those held by another. Although administrators, board members, and citizens frequently agree with teachers about the proper role of teachers, there often occur disparities in beliefs between and among these groups. The nature of the divergencies and similarities of beliefs about teaching, of course, seriously affects teachers in their assignments.

Areas of Divergence and Similarity

Obviously, we may examine the agreements and disagreements of teachers, administrators, and others from a number of perspectives. One way of examining expectations for teachers is to determine whether or not there are clear tendencies for educators and others to display differences related to their different roles in society. For example, educators are about twice as likely to approve of tenure for teachers as are parents of school children.[49] Educators and parents of school age children and other adult citizens are about equally favorable in their attitudes about their school board's efforts to improve the quality of education.[50] It should be apparent that such statements of difference or similarity mask a great deal. As to the above statements, it is true that about twice as many teachers (53 percent) as parents (27 percent) favor tenure; even so, nearly as many educators (47 percent) do not favor tenure as favor tenure. In addition, nearly three-fourths of the parents were opposed to tenure.[51]

A second type of variation in expectations, that variation occurring within a given group, needs to be examined as well if we are to maximize our understanding of inputs into the teaching role. This type of variation is illustrated by the expectations that a sample of citizens of a Midwestern city held regarding male secondary-school teachers' "giving special attention to poor students' work during class time, even though it slows down class progress." The responses are shown in Figure 9–2. Almost one-fourth thought the teachers absolutely must or probably should give such attention, while slightly more than

---

[49] George H. Gallup, "Fourth Annual Gallup Poll of Public Attitudes Toward Education," *Phi Delta Kappan*, vol. 54, no. 1 (1972), p. 37.

[50] Ibid., p. 39.

[51] Ibid., p. 37.

FIGURE 9–2
General Status-Role Expectations Held by Neighbors of Male Secondary-School Teachers in a Midwestern City as Indicated by Selected Items

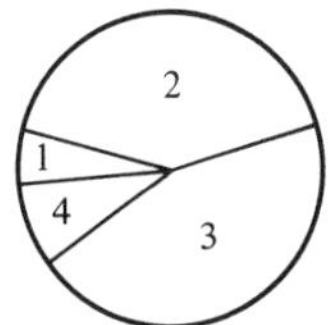

Assign Considerable Homework

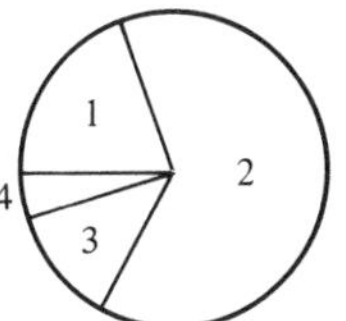

Be a Firm Disciplinarian

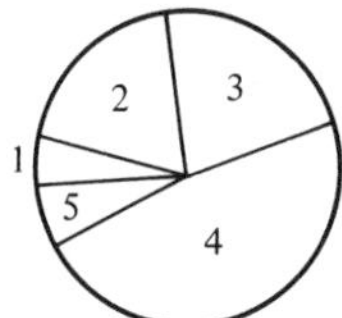

Give Special Attention to Poor Students' Work during Class Time, even though It Slows Down Class Progress

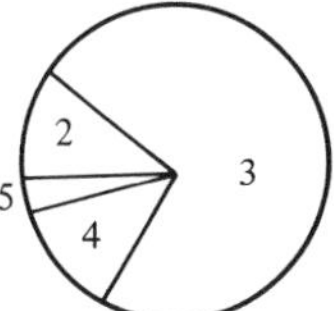

Belong to a Union such as the American Federation of Teachers

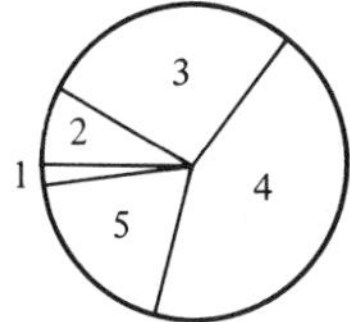

Strike for Higher Salaries

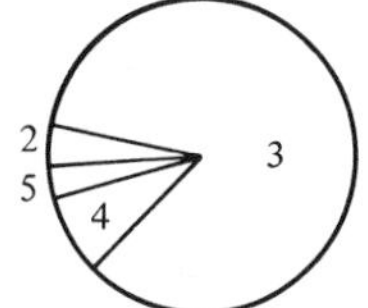

Take an Active Part in Social Fraternal Organizations such as the Elks, Moose, Eagles

1. Absolutely must 2. Probably should 3. May or may not
4. Probably should not 5. Absolutely must not

Source: Clinton Snyder, "General and Specific Expectations for Teachers" (doctoral dissertation, Michigan State University, 1955).

half thought they probably should not or absolutely must not. The mean of this distribution of responses would be between "may or may not" and "probably should not." However, the expectations vary from the four people who feel that teachers absolutely must give such attention to the six who said they absolutely must not do this. Only 17 of the 79 citizens held the noncommittal "may or may not" expectation.

This same group held homogeneous expectations with regard to other aspects of teacher behavior. Over 80 percent indicated the "may or may not" response to the item, "take an active part in fraternal organizations . . ." One should not, however, assume such consensus within a group on all aspects of teacher behavior.

A third type of difference in status-role expectation is between the general status expectations held for all teachers and those held for the specific person occupying the given role. Although we have hypothesized that such differences occur, there is little evidence to support it. Snyder found only a few more differences than might be expected by chance in the expectations which 80 citizens held for male secondary-school teachers in general as compared to their expectations of such a teacher who lived near them.[52]

Although definitive data are not available, some indication of the different expectations held for teachers by several groups can be derived from limited studies.

Doyle examined the convergence-divergence of expectations held for elementary teachers among administrators, school board members, and a sample of parents.[53] It will be noted from Figure 9–3 that the teacher's own beliefs or self-expectations are quite similar to her perception of administrator expectations and to what the administrators actually expected. The proportion of convergence with the teacher's perception of the school-board expectations and the school-board members' actual expectations is considerably lower, however. Parents' expectations and the teacher's perception of the parents' expectations indicate decided differences between each other and between the teacher's own beliefs about what she should do.

The data from Doyle's study of three different communities in northwestern Michigan concerning expectations held for elementary teachers in the actual classroom and school system indicate much greater agreement among expectations held by those who operate within the system than between the teachers and the parents who are outside the primary social system. This suggests that the teacher's own internalized beliefs about appropriate classroom-teacher behavior are affected more by direct interaction with superiors in the system than they are by contract with lay board members or parents. The least convergence found in Doyle's study is between the teacher's own beliefs and what are perceived to be parents' expectations. The parents' actual expectations are somewhat closer to the teacher's own beliefs than are teacher's perceptions of parental expectations.

Stability of Expectations and Teaching Roles

We mentioned that parents and teachers tend to differ in matters of opinion about tenure and agree on their positive attitudes toward

[52] Clinton Snyder, "General and Specific Expectations for Teachers" (doctoral dissertation, Michigan State University, 1955).

[53] L. A. Doyle, "Convergence and Divergence in the Role Expectations of Elementary Teachers," *College of Education Quarterly*, Michigan State University (Winter 1958), pp. 3–9; also Ed.D. dissertation.

FIGURE 9–3
The Convergence-Divergence Among the Role Definitions and Expectations of Elementary Teachers, School-Board Members, and Parents in Three Michigan Communities

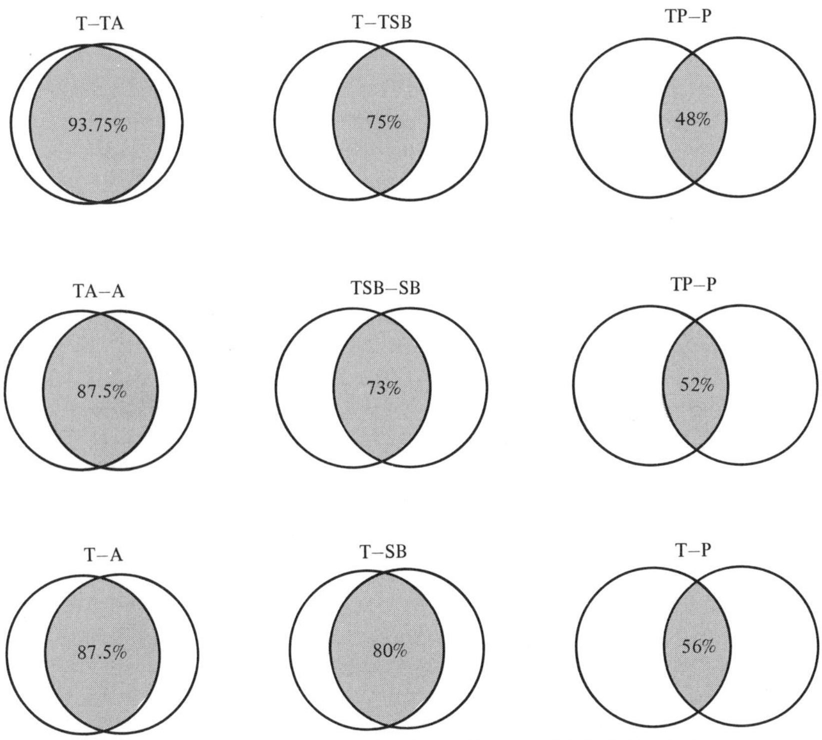

T–Teacher's own belief.
A–Administrator expectation.
SB–School board's expectation.
P–Parent Expectation.
TA–Teacher definition of Administrator's expectation.
TSB–Teacher definition of school board's expectation.
TP–Teacher definition of Parents' expectation.

Source: L. A. Doyle, "Convergence and Divergence in the Role Expectations of Elementary Teachers," *College of Education Quarterly*, Michigan State University (Winter 1958).

school boards. We might also point out that, by and large and in spite of the public controversy surrounding education and the scrutiny of our schools in the mass media, the overwhelming majority of adult citizens as well as parents with school age children do not place the blame for student failures in school, on the school work, on the school as a whole or on teachers in particular. Only six percent, seven percent, and nine percent of adult citizens, parents, and educators respectively place the blame for poor school work on schools; and only 12 percent, 13 percent, and seven percent, respectively, place the blame on the teachers.[54] Most (71 percent of adult citizens, 73 percent of educators)

[54] Gallup, "Public Attitudes Toward Education," p. 37.

place the blame for poor school work on either the children's parents or on the children themselves. Gordon De Blaey in his studies also found essentially the same community expectations for parochial teachers.[55] With such wide support for public and parochial schools and educators and such wide agreement that the failing student or his family is to blame, it is unlikely that there will be very much social pressure for drastic changes in the way teachers carry out their roles.

Given this condition, if the teacher's role is to be changed in any major fashion, it is likely to occur over a relatively long period of time as the result of unique expressions for change occurring in only a few communities and then spreading, as the latent (or a largely unintended) effect of innovations in school organization such as the introduction on a large scale of teaching aides. The fact that technological advances and knowledge are available to bring about major changes in teaching roles in accord with societal objectives is not sufficient to overcome the tradition and continued acceptance of that tradition by most people, including educators. People expect their children to be lectured to and educators expect to lecture. The most pressing concerns of educators and lay persons alike are with matters of discipline, segregation by class, race, or ethnicity, and finances, and not with teaching methods, school facilities, or curriculum.[56] The formal teaching process at every level, from pre-school to university, will not be easily changed given this general lack of concern.

The changes occurring for teachers are more likely to be with peripheral or secondary attributes commonly expected of teachers than with primary expectations. Teachers will probably be allowed more latitude in their social behaviors outside of classrooms, they will be allowed to express their own tastes in clothing and hair styles, a larger proportion of university teachers will be females, teachers will be given time off for lunch, and so forth. For all practical purposes, we see no signs that the way most teachers teach and the ability of teachers to determine how they will teach will be changed in any significant way in the next several years. For some, including the authors, this is a very pessimistic view, but we believe it to be correct.

If there is one important shift in the daily business of teaching, it will probably be with regard to relationships between teachers and administrators. But even here, what change will come is likely to involve the right to change and not change itself and will be facilitated by teacher organizations, court opinions, and other community powers. The teacher's attitude toward administration and the teacher's expectations for

---

[55] Gordon DeBlaey, *Public and Parochial Elementary Teachers Examine Role Conflict Between Parents and Teachers* (Grand Rapids, Michigan: Center for Educational Studies, 1971).

[56] Gallup, "Public Attitudes Toward Education," p. 40.

administrators will still retain their traditional nature. Why do we take this position? Perhaps the answers to a few questions will support our view.

How do teachers view the administrative structure with which they have to deal? For instance, do they see their principal as a head teacher, a first among equals? Or do they view him as more of a supervisor or administrator? Teacher attitudes relevant to these questions were recently collected in a national Teacher Opinion Poll.[57] One question to which teachers responded was: "What do you believe is the best way for school principalships to be filled?" Interestingly, three out of four teachers said that principals should be appointed by the superintendent or school board, about one in eight favored election by teachers, and less than one percent favored appointment by representatives of parents.

These same teachers responded to the question: "Do you agree or disagree that the salary of the school principal should always be higher than that of any other teacher on the school faculty?" Sixty-four percent of the teachers agreed that principals should receive higher pay. In addition, both men and women teachers tended to hold the same views.

In accord with the teacher's tendency to grant greater authority and status to their principals, the principals are viewed as having power. Only 11 percent of the teachers in another national poll[58] indicated that their principal had *little* autonomy and initiative. Over 95 percent of the teachers indicated that their principal had *considerable* (42.8 percent) or *some* (45.7 percent) autonomy and initiative. Seemingly, the typical teacher not only values an economic and authoritative position subordinate to his principal, but sees that as the case in fact.

One good measure of the public's attitude toward teaching as a profession can be found in whether parents would like to have their children become teachers. In a national study, parents were asked whether they would like to have a child of theirs take up teaching in the public schools as a career. Seventy-one percent of the parents of public school children said they would like their child to become a teacher, and less than 21 percent said no.[59] Apparently, then, teaching is held in relatively high esteem by a large segment of the public.

On the basis of these limited data it seems teachers, in spite of the public controversy surrounding their organizational efforts to enhance their power, still tend to see and value their principals' having authority and prestige over themselves personally. Teachers value the traditional hierarchy of positions in the school, with leadership,

[57] Teacher Opinion Poll, *Today's Education* (March 1970), p. 18.

[58] "The Teachers' View of the Authority Given Principals," *National Education Association Research Bulletin*, vol. 48 (December 1970), p. 125.

[59] Gallup, "Public Attitudes Toward Education," p. 44.

power, and a greater affluence granted to administrators. Teachers also value being teachers, and the public too holds teaching in high regard. Whether these views will change over the next several years is questionable. In spite of a long history of educators' advancing a philosophy of professional autonomy for themselves, they still tend to value, for their own schools, the traditional discriminations in authority structure which are imposed from without rather than from within their profession. This is also the position of their clients, the public, and their administrators. The result will probably involve little change in the practices of teaching, and yet there will be greater veto power over both the preferences of administrators and community persons.

Suggested Readings

AAUP/AAC Commission on Academic Tenure, *Faculty Tenure* (San Francisco: Jossey-Bass, 1973).

William S. Bennett, *New Careers and Urban School* (New York: Holt, Rinehart and Winston, 1970).

Stephen Cole, *The Unionization of Teachers: A Case Study of the UFT* (New York: Praeger Publishers, 1969).

Ronald Corwin, *Militant Professionalism: A Study of Organizational Conflict in High Schools* (New York: Appleton-Century-Crofts, 1970).

Robert Dreeben, "Review Essay: Reflections on Teacher Militancy and Unionization," *Sociology of Education,* 45 (Summer 1972) pp. 326–37.

———, *The Nature of Teaching: Schools and the Work of Teachers* (Glenview, Ill.: Scott Foresman and Co., 1970).

E. D. Duryea, Robert S. Fish and associates, eds., *Faculty Unions and Collective Bargaining* (San Francisco: Jossey-Bass, 1973).

Gerald R. Grace, *Role Conflict and the Teacher* (Boston: Routledge and Kegan Paul, 1972).

Ruth S. Jones, "Teachers: Socialized While Socializing," *Urban Education,* 9, no. 1 (April 1974), pp. 71–81.

Barbara H. Long and Edmund Henderson, "Certain Determinants of Academic Expectancies Among Southern and Non-Southern Teachers," *The American Educational Research Journal,* 11, no. 2 (Spring 1974), pp. 149–69.

Gertrude McPherson, *Small Town Teacher* (Cambridge, Mass.: Harvard University Press, 1971).

Donald Myers, *Teacher Power: Professionalism and Collective Bargaining* (Lexington, Mass.: D. C. Heath, 1973).

Bardwell L. Smith and associates, *Tenure Debate* (San Francisco: Jossey-Bass, 1973).

10

Student Social Structure

Beyond the general role of student, which is more or less standardized for each age-grade level, there are few formal organizational roles for students. These few official roles, such as student government president or secretary, involve relatively few students and are sometimes initiated, supervised, and controlled by the faculty and administration. On the other hand, there is an elaborate informal division of labor (specialization of roles) among students which has a substantial impact on the students themselves and on the life of the school or college. Therefore, analysis of student social structure must be carried out primarily at the level of the informal or interpersonal clique organization. In many elementary and secondary schools, and to a lesser degree in college, the activities that give a student prestige with his peers are those which lie beyond the classroom. In other words, students frequently gain or lose status and prestige with other students on the basis of their participation in extracurricular activities and the possession of social and personal characteristics considered desirable by their peers.

If we were to plot the sources of student prestige among peers, moving from elementary school through professional or graduate school, we would find a relationship such as that illustrated in Figure 10–1. The curve indicates that the maximum points on the academic dimension are reached in the earliest and the latest stages of formal educational training. The incoming school child sees the school as a place where learning is to take place. Parents, in anticipation of the first day of school, encourage their children to be good and "listen to the teacher." As the child moves along from one grade to the next, the student culture takes hold and personal and social nonschool factors attain their maximum point at the high-school level; at this stage of development the

FIGURE 10–1
Grade Status and Prestige-Giving Factors

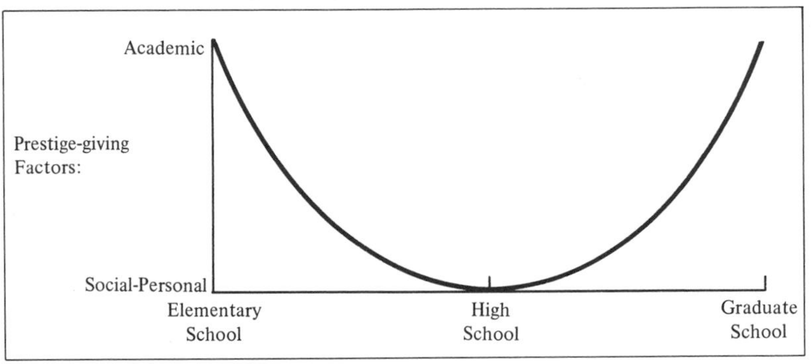

adolescent is between age grade stages and is most dependent on his peers.

As the transition from high school to college takes place, the importance of the social-personal factors undergoes a gradual decline, and the academic factor become most important again at the graduate-school or adult level. Part of the decline in personal-social factors as the passage through college and graduate school takes place may be attributed, of course, to student selectivity. In other words, the more education a person undertakes beyond high school, the more serious he will be about his academic training and activities. While we have not tested the above proposition empirically, we feel there is evidence to support its validity. Parsons, in a discussion of the classroom as a social system, notes that the elementary-school phase is concerned with the child's internalization of motivation to achieve and that the focus is on the level of capacity. The secondary school, because of its abundance of activities and variety of subject matter, exposes the student to a wider range of statuses, peers, and adults, forces him to choose among alternatives within the framework of the system.[1]

Several investigations have emphasized the saliency of personal and social factors as status determinants a the high-school level. In a classic, but still relevant study, Gordon noted the importance of semiformal organizations (extracurricular activities) and the informal organizations of students as agencies through which students gain or lose personal prestige. Although it is difficult from his analysis to determine the total impact of each of his organizational components, it is clear that knowl-

[1] Talcott Parsons, "The School Class as a Social System: Some of Its Functions in American Society," *Harvard Educational Review,* Special Issue, Sociology and Education, vol. 29, no. 4, p. 299.

edge and concern with intellectual pursuits may do little to enhance many a high school student's standing with his or her peers.[2]

Coleman, reporting the results of an investigation of ten mid-Western high schools, points out some of the consequences of the student culture. His research indicates that a possible effect of the student value system on education is removal of the highly intelligent students from an academic-achievement orientation to one that holds greater prestige among peers. Coleman contends that academic achievement as a status-giving item is of such little importance to students that some of the potentially excellent students move away from academic achievement and concentrate on participation in extracurricular activities.[3]

On the college level we get a similar picture from some researchers. They conclude that institutions of higher education do little to alter the value systems of their students, contending that changes in college-student values are not so much a product of faculty or curricular influences as they are of peer-group pressures. According to Jacob, the student shows a greater concern with what he sees as being important to the faculty or in accordance with the expressed values of the institution.[4] We contend, however, that the faculty of schools and colleges are influential and that past emphasis on peers had led many to mistakenly underestimate the influence of faculty. In Chapter 12, we treat and document this view in more detail.

At the graduate-school level, while the personal factor still is of importance, there is a clear shift to identification with academic criteria as a basis for attaining prestige with one's peers. In Table 10–1, we can see how a national sample of some 3,000 students and faculty in graduate schools in the United States responded to the following statement, "In every graduate department that we know of, some students seem to have a very high standing in the department, and some seem to have a low standing. But the reasons seem different in different departments. Listed below are some factors which might lead to high prestige."[5] It appears that the further along a student is in his or her graduate training, the more likely he or she is to deemphasize the personality factor. This change in pattern may be attributed in part to the socialization which takes place in our educational institutions.

[2] C. Wayne Gordon, *The Social System of the High School* (Glencoe, Ill.: The Free Press, 1957), p. 106.

[3] James S. Coleman, "Academic Achievement and the Structure of Competition," *Harvard Educational Review,* vol. 29 (Fall 1969), pp. 330–351.

[4] Philip E. Jacob, *Changing Values in College: An Exploratory Study of the Impact of College* (New York: Harper, 1957).

[5] William Erbe, "Informal Group Membership and Its Consequences for American Graduate Students." Paper read at the Institute of the Society for Social Research, University of Chicago, May 21, 1960.

TABLE 10–1
Frequency of Agreement that Eight Selected Factors Give Prestige among Graduate Students and with Faculty in Respondent's Department

	Among Students		*With Faculty*	
	Freq. Rank	*% Agree*	*Freq. Rank*	*% Agree*
Having a pleasing personality	1	80	4	42
Being original and creative	2	59	1	76
Keeping up with things outside the discipline	3	53	5	22
Demonstrating research and scholarly capacity	4	38	7	18
Not being too critical	5	38	7	18
Teaching ability	6	27	3	47
Being concerned about application of the discipline to nonacademic world	7	27	6	21
Dedication to the field	8	23	2	74

Source: William Erbe, "Informal Group Membership and Its Consequences for American Graduate Students." Paper read at the Institute of the Society for Social Research, University of Chicago, May 21, 1960.

From this brief overview of research dealing with student values, it appears that the model outlined in Figure 10–1 does reflect, at least in part, student groups as observed in various educational institutions. Again, however, it is important to point out that differences in student values and behavior will be found among schools and among students in the same schools.

Given the importance of the informal network of roles and statuses, it is best that we view the student social structure as a system of interrelations between formal and informal configurations. The team captain and the class president may occupy their formal positions because of their informal positions in a system of relations within the class or team. In the student society, the formally defined positions and the informal interpersonal relationships are closely interwoven, and the formal position often is not clearly defined. The two are, therefore, discussed together.

Student Cliques and Relationships

In contrast to the scarcity of studies of staff structure in schools and colleges, there have been many analyses of informal structures of student society. Most of these were made by the techniques of sociometric choice or other similar choice-and-rejection devices.[6] Briefly, the sociometric

[6] The current use of sociometric and related techniques for analysis of interpersonal relations stems to a major degree from the work of J. L. Moreno. Many others have used his methods and still others have used modified versions of the sociometric methods. We are using the term here to refer to both the sociometric and other closely related methods.

method is the procedure of asking individuals to indicate the persons whom they would like to take home for a visit, or with whom they would like to work, attend a movie, or carry on some other activity. Sociometric rejection is the indication of persons with whom the individual would not want to work, go to a movie, or share some other activity. The sociometric method permits us to diagram the interpersonal attractions and repulsions that exist between various members of a social group. Similar questions, such as "What persons are friendly to you? Which are unfriendly?" have also been used in this manner. These items, though the situational referent is not specific, sometimes produce a similar picture of the situation.

Also used to analyze the structures of schools and colleges and student groups is the participant-observer method.[7] In this approach the observer spends extended periods of time with the groups to be analyzed. Through such participation, he is able to record the system of relationships and the images members of the group have of each position in it. Some of the more clearly defined relationships can be explained by members of a student group. The staff in close and frequent contact with such student groups can do the same, but an untrained observer or participant may be unable to describe the numerous other interpersonal relations. The participant-observer method is essentially the objective analysis of a social group by a participant in the group. The data on which the discussion in this section are based have been gathered primarily by these two methods. To date, these methods have been most fruitful in the analysis of informal student groups.[8]

Age-Grade Positions and Their Interrelations

Perhaps the most obvious aspect of student social structures is the age-grade differences in position. We have already noted some of the cultural patterns associated with the system of grades and promotions. Here we want to call attention to the structural aspect of this system of age-grade relationships.[9] The major facet of the differential age-grade position is the subordinate-superordinate nature of the relationship. Older students in the upper grades of the school expect and receive deference from younger students. High-school students are admired by and dominate those in elementary grades. If the school has only ele-

[7] William F. Whyte in *Street Corner Society* (Chicago: University of Chicago Press, 1943) and A. B. Hollingshead in *Elmtown's Youth* (New York: Wiley, 1949).

[8] For a more total view of small group research and the classic operation of sociometric techniques, see A. Paul Hare, Edgar F. Borgetta, and Robert Bales (eds.), *Small Groups: Studies in Social Interaction* (New York: Knopf, 1955). Another classic analysis of high-school systems also can be found in James S. Coleman's *The Adolescent Society* (New York: The Free Press, 1961).

[9] See Gordon, *The Social System of the High School*, p. 54.

mentary classes, the upper age-grade students expect deference from those in the lower elementary grades. This superordinate-subordinate relationship gives the older students much power and control over the activities of younger students. The students in each age grade are expected to limit much of their association to their own or a near age-grade group.

The superordinate position and related authority of the higher grades are reinforced by many special positions reserved for these youth. The captaincy of the football or basketball team is generally held by a senior student. The student government presidency is generally reserved for a senior. At the elementary-school level, safety patrols, monitors, and other prestige positions are commonly reserved for those in the older grade levels. Frequently many roles have an apprenticeship program through which lower age-grade members may achieve the coveted office when they reach a particular upper-grade level. This procedure may apply to cheer leaders, student managers of athletics, major positions on the school paper, and various other positions. In each of these, advancement from one level to another depends on movement from one age-grade to another. In each, the person in the highest age-group is expected to be the leader or superordinate director of the group. This age-based hierarchy of power seems to continue right on through college.

Within each of these age-grade fragments of the school society there may be one or more formal organizations. At the high-school and college level it is common for each class—senior, junior, sophomore, freshman—to be organized, with a president, secretary, and various other officials and committees. One of the functions of such official organizations is to guarantee the identity of the group to prevent invasion from other age-grade groups. At the elementary levels there may be several teachers of each grade level in the school; hence formal organization is more likely to be based on particular classroom units. Many teachers encourage the development of a system of formal offices within their elementary school groups. These may have few official duties, but still the offices have meaning for the pupils. The selection of persons for offices in each class or grade often means the formalization of positions in the informal system of relationships.

While associations are usually limited to the student's own age grade or those near the same age, there are some situations in which this is not the case. In some school activities, members of different age-grade groups associate. This may be seen at the high-school level in bands, orchestras, or other musical organizations, as well as in athletics. In junior high school and the early high-school years, the differential rate of maturation between boys and girls results in some cross-age dating or predating relationships. Girls at this period sometimes reject boys of their own age grade in favor of older boys. The older high-school fellows may be "razzed" and otherwise sanctioned by their peers for dating younger girls, but in some situations such dating does occur.

In elementary schools there is a more subtle differentiation in the positions of boys and girls. It is common for each sex to play together, and while formally each sex may participate in common activities, it is not uncommon to have teachers and peers confer expectations for performance in subject and other areas on the basis of sex. Thus, while there may be no formal differences in the curriculum for males and females at the elementary level, there are often important informal differences. At the early adolescent level, even more informal as well as some formal differentiation in curricula is made for boys and girls. Girls are often barred from many athletic activities, especially high status varsity sports, even when more than capable. Recent congressional and court actions may bring about some changes here.

At the secondary level, the emphasis on varsity athletics for boys to the exclusion of girls and the heavy interscholastic schedules which most high schools carry result in many different activities for each sex. Ability is often cited as the reason, but equally important are the cultural values. There are comparable positions, such as that of drum majorette, open only to girls. Such differentiation is associated with prevailing definitions of male and female roles in the society. The traditional exclusion of girls from most varsity athletics, particularly those athletics which accord major prestige, serves to emphasize the questionable notion that men are superior and that women should not compete for certain positions. Many other positions are reserved for members of one or the other sex; in many colleges and schools, it is commonly expected the student president will be a boy and the secretary a girl.

Social Structure in Relation to the Curriculum

The "learner" role in a school or college is related in some respects, of course, to the social structure of the student group. Success or failure in learning a particular set of skills or body of knowledge may define the individual's position in the student group. At this point, the expectations of professors and teachers have significance in the definition of each position. The instructors and students jointly define the "A" student's position, as well as that of the failing student. Although elementary school teachers have deemphasized grades and other measures of achievement more than have secondary school teachers and college professors, the positions of "good student" and "poor student" are still clearly discernible in most elementary school rooms. Students are usually able to identify the person who occupies the position of the best reader; students themselves are able to tell which reading group is superior and which reading group is inferior. Students given "extended time" in a class are usually recognized as having failed. Reading groups are sometimes given special names in an attempt to disguise the fact that they are ability groups. Although steamboats are slower than airplanes, the first and second grade children know that the "steamboats" are better readers than the "jets." Whenever any sort of ability sectioning or grouping occurs, the positions of these differentiated groups are recognized by the students as well as the teachers. Membership in such groups carries with it certain expectancies and gives certain positions. Failure of a new teacher or any other member of the school society to recognize that Johnny Jones belongs to a superior reading group will not be permitted to continue long. Students who are placed in special education programs for learning problems often become identified as "slow." In several schools the authors have heard other students refer to these students as "retards," an unfortunate term.

In each classroom group, other more or less formal positions are established through the interaction of the students. In the early grades the tables at which the children sit may become the basis for a temporary structure. Within each seating group there may be such formally recognized positions as leader, cleanup detail, and messenger. These structures grow out of the activities of the learning situation. The teacher frequently formalizes such social groups through committee organization, with chairmen and similar positions.

As we have noted earlier, special curricula have a clear-cut relationship to the status structure of the community. Students taking particular courses or curricula may be assigned specific positions in the school structure. These are sometimes related to the community status and sometimes relatively independent of it. This is illustrated by one case in which the "overflow room" came to have a particular position in the school structure. In this school, the size of grades was such that overflow rooms were organized to take care of a few students from two or three elementary grades in which there were more than enough pupils for the regular classrooms in these grades. Each teacher was permitted to select the students to be placed in the overflow room. This resulted in the transfer of those students whom the teachers considered problems. The students then came to identify the overflow rooms as problem rooms. Those sent there were known as "dumbbells," "emotionally disturbed," or otherwise undesirable pupils.

In such situations, assignment to a certain room or teacher defines the positions which the students occupy in certain aspects of the school society. This pattern exists in larger schools at the junior high and secondary school level more extensively than at the elementary school level. In smaller schools, where there is a limited curriculum and all students may have to take the same courses with the same teachers, there may be little differentiation of this sort.

Frequently, students in a particular secondary school course occupy a special position. For example, algebra or physics students may have a status different from those in shop, general mathematics, or industrial arts classes. These rankings vary from one school to another. In one rural case, the vocational agricultural students, organized in a Future Farmers Club, occupy a high position and exert much power in the school group. In another urban school, it is the members of a dramatics club or the debating team who have higher status positions. Obviously, rural-urban variations and regional differences are important.

Friendships and Clique Structure in the School

An Elmtown high school teacher comments, "This school is full of cliques. You go into the hall, or the Commons Room (between classes or at noon) and you will find the same kids together day after day. Walk up Freedom Street at noon or in the evening and you will see them again. These kids run in bunches just like their parents. This town is full of cliques, and we can't expect the kids to be any different from their parents."[10]

Participation in friendship cliques occupies much of the time of adolescent as well as adult students. The size and nature of these informal groups vary considerably. Usually, these friendship groups tend to center around a dominant individual, and are always based on a symbiotic system of mutual relationships.[11]

Perhaps the most characteristic thing about the clique is the way its members plan to be together, to do things together, go places together. Within the clique, personal relations with one another involve the clique mates in emotional and sentimental situations of great moment to the participants. Confidences are exchanged between some or all members; often those very personal, wholly private, experiences that occur in the family which involve only one member may be exchanged with a best friend in the group. Relations with others outside the clique are discussed and decisions reached on the action to be taken by the clique, or by a particular member involved in a situation.

Membership is voluntary and informal; members are admitted gradually to a preexisting clique and dropped by the mutual consent of its participants. Although there are no explicit rules for membership, the clique has a more or less common set of values which determines who will be admitted, what it does, how it will censure some other member who does not abide by its values.

As the clique comes to be accepted by other cliques as a definite unit in a college or school society, it develops an awareness of self,

[10] Hollingshead, *Elmtown's Youth*, p. 204.

[11] Ibid., p. 207.

a "we feeling," sentiments and traditions which impel its members to act and think alike. Its members frequently identify their interests with the group in contrast to the interests of the family, other cliques, the school, and society. Generally clique interests come before those of the individual member or any outside group or interest. This attitude may result in conflicts between the clique and the family, between the clique and the school, or between the clique and the neighborhood. If this conflict element becomes the raison d'être of the group, the clique develops into what is commonly referred to as a gang.

The impact of clique controls on adolescent and adult students produces a sense of personal importance in his relations with other members, as well as with persons outside the clique, for the clique has a powerful emotional influence on him which he tends to carry over into outside social relations, using it to bolster his own conception of himself. Each member has a group status derived from perceived ability to achieve something or to contribute something to the well-being of the clique. This group-derived status is often valued very highly. Thus, the clique is a powerful influence in the life of the person, old or young, from its formation in the preadolescent years until death.

Outsiders, especially family, often fail to realize the meaning which the clique has for its members; consequently, there is a tendency for them to deprecate it. This may produce more resistance and withdrawal into the sanctuary of the clique on the part of the student, for, in a conflict situation, each of us tends to look to our friends for support. The individual, bolstered by a sense of belonging to a group that backs him or her, feels a sense of power, of belonging, of security, and consequently makes decisions in collaboration with his clique mates he or she would not make alone. Each member of the clique, reinforced by the presence of his or her friends and their agreement that some line of action is desirable or that something must be done or undone, produces a cohesive situation in which the clique acts as a unit. Controls operating in these cliques tend to produce uniformity of thought and action on the questions. Individuals who do not go along with the decision of the majority are coerced into acquiescence or ostracized. Adherence to the group code is guarded carefully by the clique's members, for cliques develop reputations and have favorable or unfavorable status attached to them by others.[12]

Clique Stability

We have only limited knowledge of the stability of clique groups. Certainly there is a stability in sociometric choices over short periods; however, it is obvious that friendship relationships do change to some

[12] Hollingshead, *Elmtown's Youth,* pp. 205–207.

extent from one grade to another. Changes in clique structure result from change in residence, shift from one major to another, loss of persons who achieve membership in a higher status clique, and changes in age. Changes in age are especially influential in cliques involving heterosexual relationships in the early adolescent years.

One may conclude that there is more evidence of change than of stability. Since the instructional staffs seldom make a conscious effort to change the clique structures, probably such changes occur without staff manipulation. Teachers' or professors' efforts to restructure cliques may not be effective anyway. Furthermore, any changes which they ostensibly effect may be the result of other forces within the student group.

Relation of Community Structure to Student Groups

Community and school analyses reveal that school cliques, as well as more formally organized school groups, are related to the structure of the community. The relationship between social class and curriculum, clique membership, and other in-school groups *has* shown this clearly. We italicize *has* because some evidence indicates that social class has been overemphasized as a factor in clique formation. This is not to say that social class is unimportant, but rather that other factors also significantly affect group association. As was noted earlier, many changes are taking place and have taken place in our educational system and in our total society. With the growing importance of education, students are, in some respects, less dependent on ascribed status than they once were. Whereas in the past a young person would typically assume an occupational role similar to that of his father, this no longer need be the case. On the contrary, many young people have moved up from the social class position of their parents by the completion of higher education. Of course, many others, particularly those from upper classes, have moved down. When schools are open and accessible to more and more people, achievement tends to become more important than family background. In our discussion of social class and education we indicated that social class frequently has been used as an explanatory variable when some other factor actually may be the cause for variation.

Too, the importance of athletics and other extracurricular activities in our schools and shifts in cultural norms regarding poverty have caused some decline in the importance of social class and family background. Social class lines are often crossed in friendship choices when individuals possess some skill or ability that others deem desirable.[13]

There is evidence that the clique structure in some schools and colleges is related to the ecological structure of the community. Students

[13] Coleman, *The Adolescent Society*, pp. 218–19.

who live together, walk back and forth to school, or ride in the same bus have many opportunities to develop friendly interpersonal relations. It should be apparent that this ecological factor is not independent of social class, and that what we may see operating is a natural pattern of people's choosing those they come to know rather than those who happened to be of the same social class background.

It is impossible to describe all types of informal cliques at this point because of their numbers and because they have not yet been adequately catalogued. We will, however, examine two types of groups with widely varying statuses in the student social structure: the elite and the "nobody" groups commonly found in schools and colleges.

Elite Groups

In every school and college which the authors have observed there exists some type of elite group given special attention by teachers and other students. Hollingshead found a girls' clique known as the "God We're Good Girls." In another school, the palace guard of elite girls was known as the "Big Four." In each of these is the phenomenon of a small group of students who are, in some respects in elementary and secondary schools, "teachers' pets." They receive special consideration in the enforcement of school regulations and are frequently selected to serve in various roles identified with the school staff.

Close association with the faculty gives such cliques access to much information not available to other students. Through this communication, they are frequently able to exert considerable power over other students. They may also be in a position to demand and to receive special consideration from teachers who cannot question the privileges the principal or higher-status teachers give this group.

Although no systematic study is available, it is probable that elite college and high-school groups are composed of middle- and upper-class students with economic and social resources and skill in human relations. In small undergraduate colleges and high schools, they are frequently members of elite clubs, honor societies, and sometimes editors or managers of school publications. Within the framework of graduate school departments, the elite tend to be those students who are engaged in some faculty member's research project. For example, a graduate student made the following statement in response to a questionnaire dealing with graduate school education in the United States: "There is a tendency for an elitist attitude to develop—a few students are given much attention by the faculty, and others are given none. The one way to get in with the faculty is to show that you are hell bent on research."[14]

[14] David Gottlieb, "The Socialization Process in American Graduate Schools." Ph.D. thesis, Chicago, University of Chicago, 1960.

The impact of contact with faculty is, of course, manifold and, as we shall note later, plays a vital role in the professional self-development of the student. For the moment, it is sufficient to point out that the elite may and often will benefit from the added attentions of the faculty.

In contrast, some data suggest that, among high-school teachers, academic ability and intelligence are not considered the sole criteria for elite group membership or for holding some valued school-sponsored office. Coleman asked 400 high-school teachers which of three boys they would prefer to have elected president of the senior class. Over 70 percent indicated a leader in extracurricular activities and fewer than 20 percent, a brilliant student. Fewer than four percent selected an athletic star. In explanation of their choices, the teachers stated that the activities leader would have leadership ability and be a responsible person. They suggested also that, unlike the brilliant student, the boy active in extracurricular activities would get along better with the other students. Coleman summarizes his analysis as follows: "In other words, the brilliant student is not seen as the appropriate background for class president, partly because he is not seen as having administrative ability, and partly because he is not 'close' to the other students and is not a focal point of attention for them."[15]

Additional support for the hypothesis that high-school teachers do not prefer creative or original students is found in the work of Getzels and Jackson, who suggested several years ago that the highly creative student tends to be rejected by teachers because these students fail to conform to the teachers' plans and expectations.[16] On the other hand, there are surely today a number of teachers who do prefer creative students. Teachers, like their students, are coming from very wide backgrounds, and while we have no proof, we think there are increasing numbers of teachers who value intelligence and creativeness.

"Nobody" Cliques

At the other end of the continuum of informal school groups there is generally a group of students at every age level, from first grade through graduate school, who are set off from others for opposite reasons. They are outcasts or blacklisted individuals. These students may be members of a "gang" or clique that frequently associates together, or they may be relatively isolated individuals. Such outcast students generally make poor grades and are otherwise unfavorably judged by teachers. In addition to being judged as inferior students, they may be considered

[15] Coleman, *The Adolescent Society,* p. 193.

[16] J. W. Getzels and P. W. Jackson, "The Study of Giftedness: A Multidimensional Approach," *The Gifted Student,* Cooperative Research Monograph No. 2, U.S. Department of Health, Education, and Welfare (Washington: United States Government Printing Office, 1960), pp. 1–18.

immoral, dirty, and "foul-mouthed," and are sometimes condemned by the high-status students. In other words, these are students whose behavior is unacceptable by the standards of the elite or near-elite groups.

The formally organized groups in school or college have varying levels of prestige. In a classic study over 40 years ago, Waller described the importance of participation in such groups as follows:

> There is distinction in these activities for individuals. That distinction rests in part upon the prominence which participation in them gives the individual in the eyes of the school at large, and in part upon the recognition which the adult group accords them. The variety of activities is almost endless, for each of the activities mentioned above has many subdivisions; these subdivisions are sometimes arranged in something of a hierarchy as in athletics, where the greatest distinction attaches to football, a little less to basketball, less yet to baseball and track. . . . It is noteworthy that a competitive spirit prevails in nearly all activities. Not all activities are really competitive, but the struggle for places may make them so, and the desirability of having some place in some school activity makes the competition keen. One "makes" the school orchestra or glee club quite as truly as one makes the football team.[17]

We believe that Waller's assessment over a half a century ago is still valid today.

Participation in formal groups or activities of high prestige is sought by those students who strive for recognition and higher status in student and communities society. The degree of recognition depends on the number of organizations to which they belong and the rating of the organization, as well as the positions which the student holds in each.

Athletic Teams

In most secondary schools, the football, basketball, baseball, and other athletic teams occupy highly rated positions. Occasionally the band or orchestra occupies a similar position, but generally it receives less student attention and acclaim than the athletic teams. It seems appropriate, therefore, to make a brief analysis of the internal social structure of the athletic team and its relationship to other segments of the school society.

Practically everyone has some impression of the social structure of athletic teams. The concept which the casual newspaper reader or the rabid fan has of the relationships existing within the squad may be quite different from the pattern with which the player or coach is acquainted.

---

[17] Willard Waller, *The Sociology of Teaching* (New York: Wiley, 1932), p. 112. Reprinted by permission.

The first factor in the structure of the group is that the coach or coaches are superordinate to the players. This dominance may be of various types. It may be of an authoritarian type, in which there is little or no informal interaction between the coach and the players. Or it may be of a "leader" type, in which the coach is the accepted and desired leader of the group. Of course, all degrees of variation between these two types of dominance may be found. Occasionally one finds a situation in which the coach is not the dominant individual. These are usually of short duration and occur when a team has an outstanding player who becomes the primary attraction.

Among the players there are two or more levels. There is always a difference in status between those who usually play and those who do not; the latter are included in the squad for use as substitutes and for competition in practice. This may become the basis for a distinction in terms. The term *squad* may be applied to the entire group of players, while *team* is applied to that group which participates in the games with other schools. On larger squads there may be several teams with varying degrees of status. Thus the role or status of the individual is determined by whether he is on *A*, *B*, *C*, or *X* team.

There are also variations resulting from the position played and the personalities of the players. In the football team the quarterback or other player who calls the plays has a role quite different from that of any other team member. He is dominant over all others during the game, and second only to the coach in control of the team. Here a leader who has the support of other members of the team is essential for success. While in other sports there are key men who have roles similar to that of the quarterback in football, in these it is not so much the position a man plays as it is how well he plays that position.

Other differences in role result from team position, though the relative ranking of each may be the same. This is noted especially in the difference between the line and backfield in football; the goalie and wing in hockey; the pitcher, catcher, infielder, and outfielder in baseball; and similar distinctions in other sports. It is necessary in any successful athletic team for each player not only to know his own role well but also to be able to take the role of another. It is only by this process that the interaction among the various players will culminate in the successful execution of plays. The nature of the clique structure and the relationship among cliques may be another factor affecting team roles. The off-team friendship groups may determine to some degree the relations among squad members. The "best" team may not always be composed of the most skillful players.

Team success is important because it is only through winning games that the members may satisfy the desire which caused them to join the group. Those players who cannot meet the standards of the team and thereby contribute to its success are either benched or dropped from the squad entirely, while those who contribute to its success because of a high level of performance become the core of the group. This process immediately distinguishes those who are "in" from those who are "out" of the group. It also has a strong centripetal or in-group effect on those who "make the grade."

The position of the athletic team in the total school society varies somewhat from one school to another and one sport to another, but teams in major sports are seldom ignored at either the secondary or undergraduate college level. Athletic awards and other forms of recognition tend to set the team members apart. Frequently, they have a higher status than that of fraternity cliques or the more select clubs in the school—although they often occupy these positions as well.

Student Values

A number of investigators and most of the population have attempted to understand the reasons for the "extensive" campus rebellion of the late 1960s. Student confrontations on high-school and college campuses have occurred in all parts of the world, in societies of every political persuasion and economic status. Campus life has changed and it would be trite merely to say that the values of students have also changed. The more difficult task is to assert in what ways and why they have changed their values.

Several scholars refer to the North American students of the 1950s as the "silent generation," the "privatistic generation," and the "cautious young men."[18] They are often compared with the "more politically aware," "socially critical," and "courageous" of the late 1960s and early 1970s.[19] Some scholars do not make this contrast, contending that privatized attitudes are still strong among most students.[20] Hoge's study of college students' values in 1952, 1968, and 1969 on two campuses suggests, to begin with, that recently students appear to feel more responsible for their future than formerly. Students of the 1960s were proportionately less likely to take a "let tomorrow take care of itself" attitude than students in the early 1950s. Students of today may also have less faith in human nature in general and "establishment" elders in particular.[21] Perhaps this feeling of personal responsibility is behind

[18] Dean R. Hoge, "College Students' Value Patterns in the 1950's and 1960's, "*Sociology of Education,* vol. 44 (Spring 1971), p. 171.

[19] Ibid.

[20] Ibid.

[21] Ibid., pp. 170–197.

the demands of some students to participate in decisions affecting their future.

The following case of Roslind in 1974 is characteristic of some middle-class students who have rejected passive roles and attitudes:

> Roslind is a white, 21-year-old junior with a major in art and psychology. She is the oldest child in a family of five girls and one boy. Roslind's father has a master's degree and works as an experimental engineer. Her mother has a master's degree and is a professional dietician. Roslind estimates her family income to be in the upper middle income range.
>
> In terms of student power, Roslind feels that students should have as much control as teachers and administrators. She would like to see students work through the democratic process to achieve their goals. If that does not work she suggests strikes and demonstrations. Roslind is not opposed to violence as long as it is a last resort.
>
> Politically, Roslind states that she is "almost a revolutionary." She has participated in demonstrations and has a strong desire to change the world situation. Although she admires the young revolutionary leaders, she feels that their goals are unclear and their tactics alienate too many people.
>
> In terms of family life, Roslind states that "children should be treated as adults as soon as they are born." Roslind feels that there was a great deal of parental surveillance on her when she was a child. She mentioned that her parents required her to go to church (Methodist) when she was young. Her parents also placed a heavy emphasis on religion. Roslind claims that even though her parents are conservative Republicans, politics are not stressed in her family as strongly as art, music, and literature.
>
> Roslind claims that while there is a fair amount of communication with her parents, there is definitely a generation gap. She especially avoids talking about political issues and drug use with her parents. Her parents also frown on her participation in demonstrations. On the whole, however, Roslind feels that her relationship with her parents is "not great but OK."
>
> Roslind believes she has changed her beliefs a great deal since entering college. Her beliefs were much more rigid when she was in high school. She states, "I see many shades of gray now, whereas in high school everything was black and white."
>
> In high school, Roslind had a profound admiration for President Eisenhower. She referred to him then as a "white knight type of person." Now, however, there is no one that she really admires. She states, "All of our idols have clay feet. I'm really looking for someone to admire." Roslind also had a strong dislike for Russians when she was in high school, though there was no one in particular that she disliked. Since entering college, she has overcome her specific dislike of Russians, but has strong negative feelings toward all politicians. She specifically mentioned her dislike for Nixon, Agnew, and the Kennedys. She believes

that politicians are "too mechanical" and are "run by big business." She feels that her attitudes toward politicians have had a strong negative influence on her thinking.

Roslind believes that the change in her views since high school is due largely to the influence of her college friends. She does not feel that her family or her old high school friends have had much impact on how she now thinks. Currently, her main goal in life is to finish school. After that, she is unsure as to what she would like to do.[22]

Tolerance of Others' Ideas

One particularly clear finding in Hoge's study of student values from 1952 to 1969 is the increasing tendency of students to be more tolerant of yesterday's "devils." The findings shown in Table 10–2 suggest that over 75 percent of the student body is willing to give anyone of any political, economic, social, or religious viewpoint a chance to be elected or speak out for their cause. Students of today, if Hoge's findings are generalizeable, are not nearly as likely to fear either the Catholic church or Communism as they did during the early 1960's.[23] Perhaps today's students are just as dogmatic and intolerant as yesterday's students. Perhaps their targets have changed and not their sense of validity.

Student Satisfaction

In examining the student social structure, it is important to observe the general satisfaction that students feel in their situation. Not only may their feelings of aversion or attraction to the student role, or their boredom, affect their performance levels, but also these may be related with retention in educational programs and disruption. There is evidence that unsatisfactory experience with education and its environment is a precursor to dropping out of school.[24]

While research is badly needed in this area, there is some knowledge and considerable speculation available concerning students' feelings toward their schools. As a matter of fact, schools and school programs are often organized with the express purpose of reducing the supposed alienation of students toward school. A number of researchers have, for instance, particularly focused on how the schools in our culture may be creating a pressure on students which is resulting in serious

[22] From a series of unpublished case studies of young people and their heroes conducted by Alan McEvoy and Edsel L. Erickson, Center for Sociological Research, Western Michigan University, 1974.

[23] Hoge, "College Students' Value Patterns," p. 183.

[24] Wayne E. Gregg, "Graduate Student Satisfaction." A paper presented at the American Educational Research Association meetings, New York, New York, February 1971.

TABLE 10–2
Attitudes toward Social Constraints (percent)

	Dartmouth						Michigan					
	1952			1968			1952			1969		
	A	*D*	*?*	*A*	*D*	*?*	*A*	*D*	*?*	*A*	*D*	*?*
It's unwise to give people with dangerous social and economic viewpoints a chance to be elected	36	48	15	12	77	10	42	47	11	18	73	9
Only people whose loyalty to the government has been proved should run for public office	42	43	15	15	76	10	52	39	9	12	78	10
People who talk politics without knowing what they are talking about should be kept quiet	31	61	7	14	80	6	27	67	6	20	72	9
Religions which preach unwholesome ideas should be suppressed	18	62	21	5	85	10	19	63	18	5	83	12
Steps should be taken right away to outlaw the Communist Party	30	56	15	5	85	10	36	50	13	11	77	11
Americans must be on guard against the power of the Catholic Church	30	56	14	8	86	7	20	68	12	13	76	11

A = "Agree," D = "Disagree," ? = "Uncertain."
Source: Adapted from Dean R. Hoge, "College Students' Value Patterns in the 1950's and 1960's," *Sociology of Education,* vol. 44 (Spring 1971) p. 183.

problems of alienation and "ressentiment." (Ressentiment is viewed as a feeling of impotence or powerlessness with attendant feeling of hostility.) While data are still not available to definitively assess the influence of schools upon such mental states, most educators and students believe that the student's sense of satisfaction with his educational environment is crucial to his conduct.

Recent research[25] has shown that among graduate students, the collegiality of faculty with students is a highly effective and consistent predictor of both academic and nonacademic satisfaction, regardless of sex, department size, school within the university, or degree objective. Interestingly, competitiveness among students for grades and status tends to have an inverse relationship to satisfaction among students—the more competitive the student environment, the less satisfaction students experience in school.

Many of our schools in Western culture have emphasized the value of competition and the maintenance of clear status differentials between students and teachers. Recently, however, several programs and rationales have come forth to challenge such beliefs. It may well be that maximum levels of achievement and satisfaction can be attained most efficiently by reducing the status differences between faculty and students. At this point, however, and in spite of the large number of studies on the effects of cooperation and competition, most of which favor cooperation, little can be definitively concluded.

Student Unrest

So far we have discussed primarily the attitudes of students on the assumption that such attitudes affect not only their roles, but also the structures of the total school. In Table 10–3, schools are divided between those experiencing violent protests and those experiencing nonviolent protests in the United States during the 1968–69 school year. The data suggest that the most clear cases of issues being associated with violence during those years were over the presence of Reserve Officer Training Programs, war-related research programs, student disciplinary measures and requests for amnesty, alleged administrative indifference toward community problems, minority group issues, police "brutality," administrative responses to previous protests, and student participation on committees. Instructional practices and social regulations concerning dress, drinking, sex, and so on, are more likely to be associated with nonviolent protests.

---

[25] See for a review of research: Robert D. Mandelsohn, Wilbur B. Brookover and Edsel L. Erickson, "Teacher Credibility and Parental Involvement in School Related Activities." Paper read at the American Educational Research Association meeting, Chicago, 1972.

TABLE 10–3
Protest Issues at Institutions Experiencing Incidents of Violent or Nonviolent Disruptive Protest: 1968–1969 Academic Year (weighted population estimates)

	Among Institutions Experiencing Violent Protests (N = 145)		*Among Institutions Experiencing Nonviolent Disruptive Protests (N = 379)*	
Protest Issue	*N*	*Percent*	*N*	*Percent*
1. U. S. military policy (e.g., Vietnam, CBW, ABM)	56	38.6	144	38.0
2. Selective service policy	40	27.6	88	23.2
3. ROTC programs	55	37.9	65	17.1
4. On-campus military or government research	43	29.6	40	10.6
5. On-campus recruiting by government or industry	52	35.9	114	30.1
Total, war-related issues (1-5)	71	49.0	194	51.2
6. Institutional services (e.g., food and medical services, housing and recreation facilities)	45	31.0	105	27.7
7. Institutional parietal rules (e.g., dress, dormitory regulations, drinking, sex, required attendance at school functions)	20	13.8	136	35.9
8. Institutional student disciplinary practices	67	46.2	102	26.9
9. Instructional procedures (e.g., class size, quality of instruction, grading system, student evaluation)	36	24.8	125	33.0
10. Tuition charges and fees	17	11.7	36	9.5
Total, services to students issues (6, 9, 10)	64	44.1	193	50.9
11. Special educational programs for minority groups (e.g., black studies, compensatory programs)	96	66.2	194	51.2
12. Special admissions policies for minority groups	55	37.9	97	25.6
Total, minority group students issues (11–12)	101	69.1	196	51.7
13. Civil rights (e.g., desegregation, voter registration	7	4.8	17	4.5
14. Labor problems (e.g., wages, benefits, unionization)	28	19.3	10	2.6
15. Administrative indifference or inaction concerning local community problems	61	42.1	29	7.6
Total, off-campus issues (1–5; 13–15)	102	70.3	214	56.5
16. Police brutality	37	25.5	13	3.4
17. Requests or demands for amnesty	46	31.7	50	13.2
18. Administrative indifference or inaction concerning previous protest grievances	63	43.4	106	28.0
19. Administrative response to previous protests	45	31.0	67	17.7
20. Mourning for students or others killed or wounded	22	15.2	34	9.0
Total, secondary issues (16–20)	96	66.2	157	41.4
21. Student participation in decision making (e.g., inclusion on committees)	78	53.8	147	38.8
22. Free expression (e.g., censorship of publications, exclusion of "controversial" speakers)	19	13.1	51	13.5
23. Faculty (e.g., academic freedom, hiring, tenure)	51	35.2	65	17.1
Total, student power issues (7, 8, 21–23)	113	77.9	283	74.7
24. Other	30	20.7	60	15.8
Grand total (1–24)	145	100.0	379	100.0

Source: Alan W. Bayer and Alexander W. Astin, "Violence and Disruption on the U.S. Campus, 1968–69," *Educational Record* vol. 50 (Fall 1969), p. 345.

Some would contend that students do not affect major decisions through violent and nonviolent protests. This contention is questionable in view of the data presented in Table 10–4.

TABLE 10–4
Immediate Outcomes of Protest Incidents on Campuses Experiencing Violent or Nonviolent Disruptive Protest: 1968–1969 Academic year (weighted population estimates)

	Among 145 Institutions Experiencing Violent Protests		*Among 379 Institutions Experiencing Nonviolent Disruptive Protests*	
Direct Results and Consequences	*N*	*Percent*	*N*	*Percent*
1. National Guard called in	2	1.4	0	0.0
2. Off-campus police called in	80	55.2	45	11.9
3. One or more persons killed	8	5.5	0	0.0
4. Some persons injured	45	31.0	0	0.0
5. Some protesters arrested	82	56.6	19	5.0
6. Some protesters indicted	37	25.5	10	2.6
Total, civil action against individual students (5–6)	87	60.0	24	6.3
7. Temporary restraining order or court injunction obtained	28	19.3	23	6.6
8. Classes suspended	60	41.4	42	11.1
9. National press or television coverage given to protest	69	47.6	143	37.7
10. Administration or faculty negotiated issues with demonstrators	90	62.1	316	83.4
11. Formal statement issued by faculty in support of protesters	43	29.6	67	17.7
12. One or more students dismissed or expelled	21	14.5	19	5.0
13. Some students suspended or put on probation	43	33.1	69	13.3
14. Formal student reprimands issued	32	35.8	41	10.3
15. Financial assistance withdrawn from some protesters	13	9.0	6	1.6
Total, major institutional discipline against individual students (12, 13, 15)	56	38.6	80	21.1
Total, either civil or institutional action against individual students (5, 6, 12, 13, 15)	109	75.2	84	22.2
16. Some faculty or administrators resigned as a result of the protest	13	9.0	2	0.5
17. Other	23	15.9	29	7.6

Source: Allan W. Bayer and Alexander W. Astin, "Violence and Disruption on the U.S. Campus 1968–69," *Educational Record*, vol. 50 (Fall 1969), p. 346.

The data indicate that, in both violent and nonviolent student protests, the schools reacted immediately and generally against the students. More importantly, however, the administration and faculty tended to negotiate immediately with the demonstrators. Table 10–5 suggests that the schools followed up their negotiations by making agreed institutional changes.

As Table 10–5 indicates, student demonstrations, both violent and

TABLE 10–5
Institutional Changes as Related to Major Incidents of Campus Protest, 1968–1969 Academic Year (weighted population estimates)

	As a Direct Result of Protest Incident				*Not as a Direct Result of Protest Incident*					
	On Campuses Experiencing Violent Protests (N = 145)		*On Campuses Experiencing Nonviolent Disruptive Protests (N = 379)*		*On Campuses Experiencing Violent Protests (N = 145)*		*On Campuses Experiencing Nonviolent Disruptive Protests (N = 379)*		*On Campuses Not Experiencing Violent or Nonviolent Disruptive Protests (N = 1818)*	
Changes	*N*	*Percent*	*N*	*Percent*	*N*	*Percent*	*N*	*Percent*	*N*	*Percent*
1. Establishment of black studies program or department	68	46.9	34	9.0	44	30.3	186	49.1	324	17.8
2. Institution of other curriculum changes	32	22.1	74	19.5	86	59.3	218	57.5	749	41.2
3. Institution of special admissions policies for minority group members	23	15.9	19	5.0	38	26.2	76	20.1	155	8.5
Total, changes in racial policies (1, 3)	80	55.2	42	11.1	61	42.1	202	53.3	424	23.3
4. Liberalization of parietal rules	8	5.5	47	12.4	78	53.8	156	41.2	448	24.6
5. Changes in institutional rules and regulations governing students	17	11.7	54	14.2	79	54.5	187	49.3	746	41.0
6. Provision to students of greater voice or representation on existing committees	33	22.8	69	18.2	81	55.9	194	51.2	823	45.3
Total, changes in student power (4–6)	37	25.5	118	31.1	104	71.7	258	68.1	1,062	58.4
7. Formation of new committees or study groups on campus	78	53.8	131	34.6	89	61.4	145	38.3	604	33.2
8. Termination of ROTC program	4	2.8	2	0.5	0	0.0	0	0.0	3	0.2
9. Changes in ROTC program, such as making it elective	16	11.0	14	3.7	4	2.8	16	4.2	19	1.0
10. Discontinuation of some campus research for the military	0	0.0	0	0.0	2	1.4	2	0.5	0	0.0
11. Prohibition of on-campus recruiting for some organizations	6	4.1	12	3.2	0	0.0	0	0.0	11	0.6
Total, substantive institutional changes (1–6, 8–11)	104	71.7	204	53.8	116	80.0	336	88.6	1,128	62.0
12. Other	13	9.0	31	8.2	5	3.4	5	1.3	36	2.0

Source: "Violence and Disruption on the U.S. Campus, 1968–69," *Educational Record*, Fall 1969.

nonviolent, have resulted in more changes than when student protests were absent. Students may not have the authority to effect changes in their environment, but they do have the power. It also appears that the power of students to effect such changes is related to the size of the school. Colleges under 1,000 seldom have disruptive demonstrations. One thousand seems to be a threshold for disruptive student actions to occur. There also is a positive relationship between whether the school is a two-year college, a four-year college, or a university. University students are much more likely to protest.

To what extent college students can attain power over their schools is only a guess. One thing is clear, however. The idea that the college student will sit at the feet of his professors and administrators absorbing without criticism is a thing of the past, at least for the foreseeable future. The credibility of a faculty member is easily eroded in a society where ideas find their way to students from many sources. Students learn about poverty, war, teaching techniques, and all domains of human values from television, leaders, friends, and a heterogeneous group of teachers. Students are less likely to believe something simply because their teacher said it was true. For many teachers and professors this presents a shock. For many students an air of newly won freedom is anticipated. What the outcome will be is difficult to tell.

A Generation Gap

During recent years one of the most popular explanations for student activism has been the worn phrase "generation gap." Obviously, among the youth of today there are value patterns not shared by many of their elders, but this would be true in any heterogenous society at any time. The term "generation gap," however, connotes much more than this; it connotes a generalized state of affairs in which the overall value systems do not agree. It further connotes that these differences are essentially a function of age.

Perhaps the generation gap notion has been exaggerated. Perhaps what generation gap exists is simply a function of some other condition and not an age difference phenomenon at all. Interestingly, while certain values among college students in the 1970s differ from their predecessors in the 1950s as discussed above, it is also true that there are many common beliefs and aspirations. The data in Table 10–6 show very few differences in occupational orientation between students in 1952 and 1969, at a college characterized by its share of student "radicalism." The only significant but modest differences concern working for private firms, organizations, and factories and working in the educational system. Apparently more students in the 1960s wished to be educators and fewer desired to work for private organizations, firms, or factories. However,

TABLE 10–6
Preferred Firm or Institution to Work in (Percent)

	University of Michigan, Percent	
	1952	*1969*
N =	*(396)*	*(376)*
Profit making:		
Own business or own firm	14	13
Own professional office	29	26
Family business or enterprise	3	1
Private firm, organization, factory	36	26
Nonprofit making:		
Educational institution	11	19
Social agency	1	3
Government bureau, office or agency	3	6
Military service	1	*
Other nonprofit organization	1	2
Other:	3	5

* Less than 1/2 percent.
Source: Adapted from Dean R. Hoge, "College Students' Value Patterns in the 1950's and 1960's," *Sociology of Education*, vol. 44 (Spring 1971) p. 176.

we believe that currently more and more college students are returning to business and other vocational majors. Similar proportions of students in each decade aspire to own their own businesses and firms or work for nonprofit-making groups outside of education. This similarity in occupational aspirations and particularly the finding that nearly all of the students in 1969 still preferred to work in traditionally accepted occupations does not reflect a drastic change in youth.

When students at Dartmouth and the University of Michigan were asked to indicate their expected sources of life satisfaction in 1952 and in the late 1960s, a period of considerable turmoil on campuses, we again get a picture of relative stability. Students of both decades overwhelmingly stated that they expected family relationships to provide their greatest source of life satisfaction (shifts were only 64 to 63 percent and 62 to 60 percent). Career or occupation was still second as an expected source of satisfaction, changing no more than 26 to 25 percent and 29 to 25 percent. Changes in the following areas of expected sources of life satisfaction were also small: religious beliefs, 2 to 3 percent in 1952 and 1 to 3 percent in the late 1960s; leisure time recreational pursuits, 4 to 6 percent in 1952 and 3 to 7 percent in the late 1960s; and community affairs, less than 1 percent in 1952 and 1 percent in the late 1960s. A slight increase was noted, however, for participation in activities directed toward national and international betterment as an expected source of satisfaction: 1 to 2 percent in 1952 to 5 to 7 percent in the late 1960s. It is clear from the data that expected sources of life satisfaction and career aspirations are much the same for most students today as they were for students 20 years ago. And yet certain values of students have changed.

There has been a decline in students' feelings of a need for some religious faith or philosophy, along with a decline in attendance at religious service; also, there are fewer students who believe in a divine God or creator of the universe.[26] And as discussed above, there are proportionately more students who have less faith in older leaders, political and business institutions, and human nature to make things turn out right. They feel more compelled to take responsibility for decisions affecting their personal futures. But do student values reflect a major division from their elders' values which is in turn a reflection of age? This is the crucial question.

We believe the answer is no. Basic value differences are more likely to be reflections of education and status for the vast majority of students and also for the elder generation. The fact that an increasing proportion of young people are becoming better educated and more aware of the nature of their society's problems may create some illusions of differences being dependent on age. These illusions can easily be adopted by both the young and old. What should be remembered, however, is that the political spectrum of beliefs spans all age brackets. Intolerance and ethnocentrism permeate all ages, as does respect and kindness. As a matter of fact, similarities in views are more likely to reflect a commonness of formal and informal education than it is age level.

The belief that the gap between generations is exaggerated is partially confirmed by findings in a study of adults views when attending Syracuse University in 1926 and their views in 1970, compared to student views in 1968. This study by George G. Stern and his associates[27] suggests a considerable sharing of views between students and their elders who attended their school 20 years earlier. The elders have tended to change their views over the 20 years in the direction of current student opinions on matters of college and social activities considered important.

Suggested Readings

Celia Morris, "On Being a Student in the 1950's: Learning the Hard Way," *Change,* 6, no. 6 (July-August 1974), pp. 46–48.

Theodore Newcomb and Everett Wilson, *College Peer Groups* (Chicago: Aldine Publishing Co., 1966).

Louise E. Silvern and Charles Nakamura, "An Analysis of the Relationship

[26] Hoge, "College Students' Value Patterns," p. 177.

[27] George G. Stern et al., "Added Perspective on the Nature of and Extent of Change in Students' Attitudes and the Generation Gap." Paper presented at the American Educational Research Association meetings, New York, February 1971.

between Students' Political Position and the Extent to Which They Deviate from Parents' Position," *Journal of Social Issues,* 29, no. 4 (1973), pp. 143–58.

Louis Vaccaro and James Thayne Covert, eds., *Student Freedom in American Higher Education* (New York: Teachers College Press, 1969).

Harry H. Vorrath and Larry Brendtro, *Positive Peer Culture* (Chicago: Aldine Publishing Co., 1974).

Daniel Yankilovich and Ruth Clark, "College and Non-College Youth Values," *Change,* 6, no. 7 (Sept. 1974), pp. 45–47.

part four

Learning in a Social System

11

Social Psychology of Learning

Two processes are the heart of education: teaching and learning. These interdependent processes are what schools, in large part, are all about. More generally, teaching and learning are at the center of much of man's existence, be it in the family, the military, the body politic or the formal school. Teaching and learning are part of our shifts in values, our changing dress codes, our purchasing of goods and services, our domination of others, and our submission to others. We are all teachers and we are all learners; we are involved in education regardless of our official affiliations with given school organizations.

When we consider education in this light, we cannot adequately explain what is learned in an educational setting by considering only the formal and informal aspects of the school itself. School social environments often make a difference in what is learned, but they are not the only influences. The learner is at the center of a matrix of a number of forces both in and out of the school. Some of these forces are organizational in character, others are normative, and others reside in the individual and in the interaction of the individual with others. No learner can be fully understood unless all of the social-cultural forces impinging upon and operating within the individual are considered.

One purpose of the educational system is to produce certain orientations, beliefs, and behaviors in the citizenry. These beliefs and orientations include views or knowledge such as the valued history and mythology of the culture and the development of attitudes and vocational skills. The schools exist, in part, to shape how we believe and behave. The educational system makes this effort through research programs to acquire knowledge, programs to allocate people to positions in society, programs to assist industry, government, religious and family institutions, and programs designed for the direct control of students. In common usage, we are talking about the school's role in teaching students to think, believe, and act. From the perspective of the sociologist, we are also talking about the maintenance and change of a society through the socialization of individuals, young and old, by the schools.

Although no one need assume that the school is the sole socializing agent, or even the most important one, it is clear that a significant portion of the process of teaching students, young and old, has been allocated to the educational system in modern society. While there are few precise expectations for what is to be taught by all schools in all societies, there are some agreements on some of the knowledge, skills, and other behavior patterns that students at various levels should learn, and we shall deal with these.

In this and the succeeding chapters, we examine the process by which schools and other features of culture affect learning among individuals. Although there are numerous intended and unintended outcomes of schooling, our primary concern in this and succeeding chapters is with the process by which schools produce in human beings certain knowledge, attitudes, skills, and behaviors. However, before we proceed, it may be helpful to first analyze the social-cultural context within which learning occurs.

The Social-Cultural Context of Learning

One important characteristic to note about the human learning process, both in school and in other social situations, is that cultural learning for any person involves other human beings. Certainly any teaching-learning process that occurs in a school setting is a social phenomenon. As a consequence, learning cannot be explained as a unique phenomenon, the result of the idiosyncratic characteristics of students alone. It is usually impossible to explain adequately why an individual learns what he or she does by taking into account only the characteristics of that person.

Unfortunately, the typical focus of attention on psychological traits frequently has put undue emphasis upon the characteristics of the learner and not enough on the characteristics of the social system in which learning occurs. For example, when a student fails to learn to read in school, the people concerned are likely to ask only what is wrong with the student. If facilities are available, he or she will be referred to a diagnostic center where psychologists, psychometrists, counselors, and other specialized personnel will study the individual in an effort to determine why he or she has not learned a certain behavior pattern, such as reading. Sometimes the analysis will refer to aspects of the school or cultural context, but generally the diagnosis will be concerned almost exclusively with characteristics of the failing student. The diagnosis typically involves some aspects of the student's cognitive ability, emotional status, or physical condition, and is accompanied by a vague prescription for remedying these difficulties or for adapting educational goals to the individual's presumed handicaps. Occasionally in this process an incompatibility between the student and the teacher is identified. But seldom is a thorough analysis made of the social system in which learning occurs.

We hasten to add that the characteristics of the individual learner are not irrelevant to the learning process. Certainly, each learner is an active member of that social network within which his or her learning occurs. One's perceptions, health, and physical and emotional state are all very important conditions in the learning process. However, these individual characteristics of students are not the only important conditions affecting learning. Classmates as well as teachers, other school staff, relatives, and friends are also likely to be active participants in the teaching-learning process of each student. The system of social arrangements within which we live are very important conditions indeed, affecting what we teach and what we learn. Formally, some of us are said to be teachers and others of us are designated as students. But regardless of our formal titles, as students we are informal teachers as well as learners, and, in turn, as teachers we are also continuously being taught. This interactive process among students with peers, teachers, and others is every bit as important in understanding what they learn as are the individual characteristics they bring to school.

If we accept the idea that the school social system functions to produce and reinforce attitudinal and behavioral patterns in individuals, the concept "behavior modification" which is currently being used among some educators and psychologists will not seem strange. In fact, the reinforcement model may contribute a great deal to our understanding of the learning process in certain school settings. But the original rhetoric of this model, drawn from research in the animal laboratory, may lead some to a misunderstanding of much that goes on in the school learning process. One danger is that the student may be perceived merely as a reactive subject whose behavior is totally shaped by external stimuli. Certainly, the stimuli provided by the learning context are a significant part of the learning process. But the student is not just a person reacting to the stimuli in his or her environment. Rather, students are significant actors in every school system and, as such, they often participate in deciding what they will learn. They commonly provide certain of the reinforcements for themselves as well as for other students. In short, the student is not a passive subject in most school learning. Teachers need the cooperative assistance of the students themselves every bit as much as they need the assistance of teacher aides, principals, school psychologists, and other so-called "helping" staff.

The students engage in operant or, if you will, decision-making behaviors which affect their and others' learning. The students are usually actively trying to program themselves and others at the same time that others are trying to program them. Because so much of our learning is dependent on our decisions, we believe it will be helpful if we examine the social-psychological processes by which our decisions develop—particularly those decisions we make regarding what we can and should learn. In order to understand these social-psychological processes, we must have a clear conception of the cultural processes through which all of us learn. To aid in this analysis, some concepts mentioned earlier require further elaboration: norms, rules, expectations, roles, perceptions of others, and self-assessments.

Norms, Values, Expectations

As in any other social system, within the school there are norms of behavior which define the boundaries of appropriate and permissible behavior. Such norms are closely related to the role expectations which persons hold for individuals behaving in particular social statuses such as teacher, student, or principal. Norms are expectations concerning how people should behave which apply to specific or general categories of persons. As an example of a general category, no one in the school system—teacher, principal, or student—is expected to run through the hall shouting at the top of his voice during the periods that school is in session. This applies to all participants in the social system. There are many such general behavioral norms in any school system. They are simply general definitions of the proper or appropriate behavior for all participants in given situations.

The application of punishment to school behavior that deviates from general norms or expectations probably occurs because many believe that punishment is an effective way of controlling behavior, because it is normative itself to use punishment, and because of the value commonly attached to educational traditions. Traditional behavioral norms in a school are likely to be maintained if both the participants in the school and influential persons outside of school commonly share the same values and perceived outcomes of traditional schooling. The high value many people place on traditional schooling in our society is reflected by the degree to which schooling is made compulsory, the vast extent of financial support and regulations provided, and the extensive controversy surrounding our schools as it is increasingly recognized that ours is a heterogeneous society.

In addition to the generalized or common expectations, there are varying and specific expectations for those in each of the specific status categories. We expect behaviors of older students and younger ones to differ. We also vary in our expectations for how students in any setting should behave in terms of other perceived social differences. Within the first-grade level, as within any age level, differing expectations are often found for students depending upon whether they are deemed slow or gifted, rich or poor, white or nonwhite, and emotionally disturbed or normal. Role expectations *define the appropriate behavior expected for each student occupying a particular status;* that is, role expectations specify how a student *ought* to behave or *should* behave because of his or her status in school. Such role expectations are communicated to students by others, both within and outside of the school system, through a variety of techniques. Once again, it is important to keep in mind that other students as well as teachers, professors, administrators, family, friends, and others are often, simultaneously, active participants in defining the appropriate role performance for each student. In a typical college or school, the level of learning expected of a particular student by any one other person or group of persons depends on a number of conditions, and of course may vary from culture to culture or even setting to setting within a given subculture.

Among the most common criteria associated with expectations for how given students should behave are evaluations of students' ability to learn particular kinds of behavior. These evaluations are commonly made by, but not restricted to, teachers, principals, psychologists, social workers, and other specialized personnel in the school system. One's peers and family also make evaluations. Evaluations of ability are generally transmitted among members of the social system including other students, parents, and teachers. When various members of the school, family, and peer systems evaluate a particular student's "ability" to perform in his or her role—as a student of mathematics, for example—this evaluation influences their role expectations for how the student should behave. The expectations held for how "slow" students should behave are affected by evaluations of ability to perform. In this society, expectations for students are very commonly dependent upon the presumed innate ability of students. This is not true in all industrialized societies.

Through the processes of communication and interaction with others in the social system, each student acquires conceptions of what teachers, students, and various others expect of him as a student in a particular classroom or particular area of learning. Each student also acquires a conception of others' evaluations of his or her ability to learn in this particular role. For example, we may believe that our teachers think we can and should learn history or geography but that we will not be able to learn algebra. All students have some conception of the evaluations that others make and of the level of role performance expected of them at a particular time in a particular school system. Much of the current emphasis on believed individual innate differences makes clear to students that some are expected to perform at much lower levels than others.

Through the same interaction processes, the student acquires a sense of the importance which others attach to a given role performance in his particular situation. Some students may learn that a high level of performance in the student role is not highly valued for them. The nature of the sanctions or rewards which teachers, parents, or other students provide for the behavior of any given student communicates not only a definition of appropriate behavior, but also the degree of importance attached to the role.

Cultural Perspectives in Ability

One of the paradoxical characteristics of educational rhetoric is the use of an emphasis on individual differences in innately structured and fixed learning ability as sufficient reason for teaching different levels of information and skill to children. This idea coexists with the practice of emphasizing different academic and vocational programs for children who differ in race, family position, income level, religion, ethnicity, and nationality—that is, in categories that do not take into account individual abilities except through false stereotypes. Unlike the commonly accepted norms for the socialization of *all* children in common patterns of behavior such as walking, talking, and feeding oneself, many educational norms are based on the agreement that each individual is unique in the school setting and should, therefore, not be taught the same academic and vocational skills as other children. Our emphasis on the norms and expectations of the social system may suggest that the school demands the same behavior from all students. But, as we have noted, this is true in only some types of behavior. The variations in student role expectations and the evaluations of students' ability to learn produce vast differences in the specific definitions of appropriate behavior for individual students. The considerable variation in student learning that does result is often the outcome of social differences and the interactions these social differences produce, and not simply of variations in genetically structured capacities.

Unfortunately, variations in level of learning and ability to learn have largely been attributed to genetic differences which were thought to produce a fixed intelligence. In this model, we answer the question "Why does Johnny learn more than Jimmy?" by reference to his superior innate ability, gifts, or intelligence. A considerable part of our school program is built on such explanations. As a consequence, intelligence and aptitude tests are used to pick out the children who are supposed to be better able to be taught. One false assumption of this view is that most people tend to perform up to or near their capacities. On the contrary, almost everyone can learn more complex skills than he or she has in his or her repertoire.

A second and perhaps false explanation for variations in learning assumes that most people are initially and essentially equal in innate learning capacities but that individuals acquire different levels of the skills and motivations necessary to learning. This, in a sense, is an extreme environmental position, which is opposite to the fixed intelligence concept. Of course, the assumption that all people are initially innately equal in learning capacities is not testable.

A third type of explanation, however, does not rest on the same kinds of untestable assumptions as do the first two explanations. This view holds that although there may be differences in heredity, such differences are largely irrelevant in explaining variations in the learning of most human activities.[1] One is not likely to conclude that the difference in speed of two typical cars traveling 25 and 50 miles an hour on the same street is due to differences in each car's maximum capacity for speed. In the same vein, people may learn rapidly or slowly, or even fail to learn for a variety of reasons, none of which has anything to do with their capacity. In this model, we assume that behaviors that may be considered very complex and abstract are within the range of most individuals' capacities to learn, if the right social conditions are present. Even retarded children learn Russian when they grow up in the USSR and associate with Russian-speaking people. Often they learn Russian better than "gifted" college students in American universities. The point is not that genetic differences do not exist, but that they do not make a discernable difference in many cases. For example, variations in the ability to see are present among all of us, but, even so, most of us can see well enough to carry on most activities.

Aside from the question of its scientific validity, the conception of fixed intelligence has had some very undesirable social consequences. Some people, including scholars, have used the fixed intelligence concept to justify racism, war, and various cultural myths. The myth of genetic differences has been and continues to be used to justify the subjugation

---

[1] See William H. Boyer and Paul Walsh, "Are Children Born Unequal," *Saturday Review*, vol. 51, no. 42, October 19, 1968, pp. 61–63, 77–79, for a discussion of these models and their implication. The paper is reprinted in Schuler, Hoult, Gibson, and Brookover, *Readings in Sociology*, 5th ed. (New York: Thomas Y. Crowell Co., 1971), pp. 55–62 under the title, "Innate Intelligence: An Insidious Myth?"

of people. All racial and ethnic groups include poor learners for whom no valid scientific evidence of a genetic deficit is available. We also have clear evidence of instances in which measured "slow" learners become "fast" learners.

Another common and false assumption about learning ability or intelligence concerns its generalizable nature. People are called "bright" or "dumb" with the same confidence that people are said to have blue eyes or brown eyes. It is true people with blue eyes tend to have blue eyes in most social situations over their lifetimes. The belief that learning ability is enduring over time and from one situation to another is much more tenuous. We generally take issue with the view that intellectual ability is fixed. A person's intellectual skills may vary from morning to night and from one social situation to another. We have known some individuals to become "brighter" on some tasks over time while others become less adept. Senility is not the only condition which can lessen intellectual skills. There is overwhelming evidence that many motivational and situational conditions affect learning ability.

Given the positions proposed here, learning abilities or intelligence can be acquired or lost. Learning ability is subject to modification. Although this is not to say that we can create the conditions necessary for anyone to become a genius, we do have, unfortunately, the skill to make "morons" or even "vegetables" out of nearly everyone. We can destroy the intellectual skills of anyone, and one of the points to be made in the following chapters is that often whole groups of people are intellectually denied and impeded. Furthermore, such impediments are often the unintentional consequences of otherwise dedicated educators and lay people—people equipped with the commonly held false belief systems about the nature of intelligence.

The differences in learning behavior which are frequently attributed to innate intelligence are often confused with clear differences in the social-cultural environment of the learner. The inappropriately used concepts, "culturally deprived," "cultural deficit," and "culturally different" all illustrate the confused situation in education. The conditions described by these concepts are frequently assumed to affect the student's ability to learn in school. Although many educators and lay persons recognize social-cultural origins of differences, they continue to operate the schools on the assumption that the differences are the result of individual differences in some innate ability to learn, and relate them to income, race, and the like. The unfortunate results of this paradoxical mythology are compounded.

In this and succeeding chapters, a sociological frame of reference is presented within which the learning of students in the school social system may be analyzed. This frame of reference does not imply that all human beings are identical in biological endowments. There may be significant differences in the organism that relate to school learning. However, this analysis is explicit in stating that race and other social categories are not inevitable causes of differences in achievement even though correlated in racist societies. The evidence for appraising the relative weight to be given to genetic and social category factors in accounting for differences is currently very limited and hardly a sound basis for explaining all school learning variation. Perhaps an examination of societal organization, the norms and expectations of the school, student role expectations and definitions, evaluations of students by others, and the individual's self-conceptions as a student will be helpful in gaining an expanded insight into the causes of variations in school learning. Furthermore, such examination may help us to explain why "race" in racist societies is correlated with school attainments. In similar vein, we may see why sex, income, and other social categories are also correlated with but not necessarily causes of attainment.

The Development and Functions of Self-Concept

In most of our discussion we have seen the student as being at the center of a matrix made up of the school, the family, the neighborhood, and other social conditions. The question which remains, however, concerns how the culture, the school, the norms, and the expectations of others become translated into action. To adequately deal with this problem, we must elaborate upon certain of our basic assumptions about man, learning, and behavior.

Learning has traditionally been referred to as the acquisition of new behavioral patterns. For example, when a student who does not appropriately calculate square roots begins to calculate them correctly, we say he has learned this academic behavior. As one might guess, learning specialists have gone on to make distinctions in types of learning. Some may distinguish between cognitive learning and motor learning, between rote memory and the acquisition of principles, and so forth. Students, of course, do learn academic skills. They also learn to have aversions from and attractions toward academic and social objects while at school. They acquire ideological values concerning politics, sex, clothes, school subjects, teaching—and about virtually everything else in their world. They may even acquire such behavioral patterns as stuttering, flinching, withdrawing, fantasizing, or being aggressive toward their teachers or peers. Students may learn to discard their racial or ethnic prejudices, or such attitudes may be reinforced. The point is that what is learned in school is considerable and varied. There are few students who fail to learn anything at all. Some may not learn their prescribed arithmetic lessons, but odds are they will learn something.

The wise teacher recognizes this. She recognizes that what students learn is as often by accident as it is intentional. Students frequently learn what neither they nor their teachers anticipated. And, of course, one of the tricks of the trade for effective teachers is occasionally getting students to learn what they had no intention of learning in the first place.

In this chapter we will focus our attention on that learning which is generally a function of the intentions or decisions of students. We believe that the academic subjects fall into this category. We believe that when students decide to learn mathematics, for example, they are much more likely to learn mathematics than when they are opposed to such learning. Conversely, we believe that when students decide, for whatever reason, they are not going to learn to square numbers, they usually will not. Many types of learning under certain conditions require the cooperation of students. We believe the academic subjects as currently taught in our typical colleges and schools are of this sort.

Student decision making is an important condition which we believe helps shape or determine academic achievement. We do not mean to suggest that the decisions of students totally determine their academic performance. As shown in Figure 11–1, there are many conditions which determine the final behavioral outcome. People often decide on courses of action which result in failure. Even so, students seldom learn the prescribed academic behaviors unless it is also their decision. As every effective teacher knows, the student's cooperation must be gained before the desired results can be achieved. Furthermore, when students decide to learn something often many of the otherwise mitigating conditions are lessened by the student's actions. Therefore, our focus in this chapter is on explaining what it is that shapes the decisions of students to learn prescribed academic tasks in school.

Decision Making

Life for all of us is a continuous series of decisions. We do not simply make a decision and then act on it. Rather, we construct a reality about what we and our situation are like and what responses are called for; we initiate action and, on the basis of perceived feedback, decide to continue or change our course of action. Decision making is an ongoing process that involves our continuous monitoring of ourselves and our situation. Decision making is not a mystical mental happening; rather, it is cognitive behavior which programs much of our subsequent behaviors. It is the cognitive behavior involved in selecting among alternatives and, more importantly, it involves the anticipation of how certain acts will turn out.

This cognitive completion of the act is a crucial concept in our theory

FIGURE 11–1
Schematic Representation of the Model of Sources and Functions of Self-Conceptions

Behavior of Significant Others →	*Monitoring* →	*Self-Concept Structure* →	*Plans* →	*Volitional Behavior* →	*Behavioral Act*
Actual Evaluations of Ability in Role →	Monitored Evaluations →	Self-Concept of Ability in Role			
		↕			
Actual Normative Expectations: Dispensation of Rewards and Punishments →	Monitored Normative Demands; Monitored Reinforcement Schedule →	Self-Concept of Instrumental Value of Role →	Specific Plan about Self in Future		
		↕	↕	Volitional Action (e.g., decision to study math) →	Behavior (e.g., act of studying mathematics)
Actual Communicated Values; Dispensation of Rewards and Punishments →	Monitored Values; Monitored Reinforcement Schedule →	Self-Concept of Intrinsic Value of Role	Other Plans about Self in Related Role		
	Monitored Prior Self-Concept Structure				
X ↗	X ↗	X ↗	X ↗	X ↗	

(where X represents other sets of unspecified variables which contribute to human action, e.g., hereditary factors, nutritional variables, environmental conditions, etc.)

of behavior which derives from George Herbert Mead[2] and others. Students who expect absolute failure in trying to learn mathematics are not likely to engage in attempts to learn mathematics; or, if they anticipate undesirable outcomes in terms of the possibility of punishment during the process of learning mathematics, they are also unlikely to make the intentional effort. We further posit that one's desires for the future are not as crucial as one's anticipations of outcomes. Put another way, we believe that people behave in terms of what they think are viable alternatives or probable outcomes, and not simply on the basis of their dreams. People do not decide to fly unless they see some probability of success. We present our propositions more formally as follows:

1. Voluntary decision-making behavior is a function of perceived probable outcomes of social acts.
2. The perceived probable outcomes of social acts are distinct from desired outcomes, as decision-making factors. Although aspirations and plans may at times be similar for an individual, these cognitive and affective constructs may be substantially different in content and in their functions.
3. If voluntary behavior is a function of aspirations, these aspirations tend to function within the limits set by one's view of the possible alternatives and what might be expected to happen in the future.[3]

TABLE 11–1
Additive and Independent Utility of Educational Plans and Educational Aspirations in Successful Prediction of High School-Dropout Rates

Desired to Leave School	*Planned to Leave School*	*Percentage of Successful Prediction of Dropout*
Yes	Yes	77
–	Yes	66
Yes	–	55

Source: G. E. Bryan, E. L. Erickson, and L. M. Joiner, "Forecasting Student Dropout Using Social-Psychological Data." Research paper presented to American Research Association, Minneapolis, Minnesota, 1970.

Table 11–1 presents research data demonstrating the relative validity of students' educational plans (decisions), and their educational aspirations in forecasting which students in eighth, ninth, tenth, and 11th

[2] George Herbert Mead, *Mind, Self and Society* (Chicago: University of Chicago Press, 1934).

[3] W. B. Brookover, E. L. Erickson, and L. M. Joiner, "Educational Aspirations and Plans in Relation to School Achievement and Socio-economic Status," *School Review,* vol. 75, no. 4 (Winter 1967), pp. 392–400.

grades will later drop out of school.[4] As was demonstrated, both aspirations and plans may be used to forecast high school-dropout. However, when student aspirations alone were used, the percent of successful predictions of dropout was 55 percent. When data on student plans were used to predict dropout, the rate of successful prediction increased to 66 percent. When both the students' plans and their aspirations were used to forecast dropout, the rate of successful prediction increased to 77 percent. These data on educational aspirations and plans were used to predict one to four years in advance which students would drop out; the success of the predictions provides considerable support for the relevance of students' plans or decisions to their later behavior.

Further support for the relevance of student plans has been developed. In follow-up research by Bryan and associates, it was found that educational plans added significantly to the accuracy of dropout prediction based on status, I.Q., and grade point average.[5] These studies and many other investigations[6] showing that the academic plans of students to achieve in school are associated with school achievement levels provide sufficient justification for attempting to determine those conditions responsible for student plans or decisions.

Before turning to antecedent conditions which influence a student's decisions, it is necessary to reiterate two important points which Herbert Blumer makes about the way individuals interpret their environment and selves.[7] Making decisions about one's self in relation to one's environment is essentially a process of interpretation. According to Blumer, this process has two distinct steps:

> First, the actor indicates to himself the things toward which he is acting; he has to point out to himself the things that have meaning. The making of such indications is an internalized social process in that the actor is interacting with himself. This interaction with himself is something other than an interplay of psychological elements; it is an instance of the person engaging in a process of communication with himself. Second, by virtue of this process of communicating with himself,

[4] Clifford Bryan and Edsel Erickson, "Forecasting Student Dropout," *Education and Urban Society,* August 1970, pp. 443–458.

[5] Clifford E. Bryan, Edsel L. Erickson, and Lee M. Joiner, "Forecasting Student Dropout Using Social-Psychological Data." Research paper presented to American Educational Research Association, Minneapolis, Minnesota, 1970.

[6] The research in this area is too numerous to list. For illustration see Brookover, et al., "Educational Aspirations and Plans in Relation to School Achievement," pp. 392–400; William G. Spady, "Status, Achievement and Motivation in the American High School," *School Review,* vol. 79, no. 3 (May 1971), pp. 379–403); and Edward L. McDill and James S. Coleman, "High School Social Status, College Plans and Interest in Academic Achievement: A Panel Analysis," *American Sociological Review,* vol. 28, no. 6 (December 1963), pp. 905–918.

[7] Herbert Blumer, *Symbolic Interactionism, Perspective and Method* (Englewood Cliffs, New Jersey; Prentice-Hall, Inc., 1969), p. 5.

> interpretation becomes a matter of handling meanings. The actor selects, checks, suspends, regroups, and transforms the meanings in the light of the situation in which he is placed and the direction of his action. Accordingly, interpretation should not be regarded as a mere automatic application of established meanings, but as a formative process in which meanings are used and revised as instruments for the guidance and formation of action.[8]

The point of Blumer's position for us is that decision making among students involves a considerable amount of internal communication. Students talk to themselves, as all of us do, and arrive at conclusions. Decision making is not an automatic reflex act. To modify the decisions of students, one must modify and have input into the communication processes where information about self is employed. Secondly, since the student is continually selecting information about self, checking on the information, suspending conclusions, and reinterpreting his information, no static model of input into the student will be adequate.

In the following section of this chapter our conception of a self-concept structure is presented. Actually, we will show we do not think of the self-concept as something or a trait which one has or possesses, but as a *defining behavioral process.* The self-concept, from our perspective, is a cognitive behavioral process. Put another way, people do not have self-concepts in the same sense as they have a nose or a mouth; they engage in self-conceptualizing behavior, defining themselves in the same way that they engage in other linguistic behaviors. We are concerned here with the self-conceptualizing behavior of students.

Self-Conceptualizing Behavior[9]

In order to explain the academic decisions of students and thereby account for their academic performance, it may be helpful to ask the more basic question: What is the best way to make sense out of the many ways people talk about themselves? People say many different things about themselves, and they often behave quite differently from one situation to another. The ways people think of themselves are not equally relevant in all situations. If we wished to account for the behaviors of a student in two or more different roles in school, what kinds of self-concept data would be most relevant and helpful? A female student in a statistics class, for example, might say and believe that she is loved by her friends, that she is pretty, that her teachers and friends

[8] Ibid.

[9] We are indebted to a number of our associates for helping us to clarify our thoughts on the self-conceptualizing process. We are particularly indebted to Robert Bilby, Lee M. Joiner, Shailer Thomas, and Ann Patterson. Many others have also contributed to a test of our ideas and will be reported elsewhere.

like her, that she is generally happy with her life, but that she is "dumb" in statistics. To effectively account for this student's behavior in statistics, we would need to focus on those self-conceptions directly related to the particular role in question, probably what she says about her ability to learn statistics.

Our problem then is how best to organize the role characterizations students have for themselves in each role we wish to explain. Our interest centers on specific and general academic roles and how best to explain student performance levels.

Students might say such diverse things as: "I hate statistics." I'm dumb in statistics." "This statistics test is keeping me from going on a date." "My dad does not care whether I learn statistics or not." "The statistics teacher is a bore." In the following set of theoretical propositions and statements we present a model for grouping these kinds of statements.

Even so, there is still the task of determining the relevance of people with whom the students interact which in turn shapes their views about themselves. We need a model which will help us to understand students in terms of their positions in social psychological contexts where their behavior is the outcome of their symbolic interactions with self (i.e., internal conversations) and their symbolic interactions with others. The following theoretical scheme presents our view of the process by which individuals interact with others to develop their self-conceptualizing behaviors which in turn help shape their decisions. These decisions, of course, reciprocally shape their interactions with others and the cycle is endlessly repeated.

Self-Concept: A Theoretical Scheme

As can be seen in Figure 11–2, the self-conceptualizing behavior of a student can be divided for analytical purposes into four major role categories:

1. Role requirements for self.
   a. In the specific role in question.
   b. In more general roles in the setting.
   c. In other roles currently engaged in and anticipated.
2. Self-concept of ability to carry out role requirements.
3. The intrinsic value to self of role performance.
4. The instrumental value to self of role performance.

Role Requirements for Self. We determine what we think are the appropriate behaviors for ourselves in each of our roles. We generally can state these requirements. For example, a person may identify his or her role by saying: "I am a teacher of the emotionally disturbed

FIGURE 11–2
Illustrative Determinants of Academic Decisions

Inputs	*Output*
Monitoring of Self; The Self-Concept Structure 1. Appropriateness of Role Act a. To classroom role: "Is this the kind of thing I should be learning in this class?" b. To general student role: "Do I need French to graduate?" c. To other roles: "Will I use French in college?" "Do my friends expect me to learn French?" "Will I ever need to know French?" 2. Ability to Carry Out Role Act "I can't learn French." "Foreign languages are easy for me." "I don't know if I can learn French or not." 3. Intrinsic Value of Role Act "I hate French." "I think French is fun." "I couldn't care less, one way or the other." 4. Instrumental Value of Role Act "My father will give me a new bike if I take French." "If I take French, I can't go out for golf, which I really want to do." "I won't get into college unless I take a foreign language, and French is easiest for me."	Volitional Behavior Decision to Study (e.g., to learn a French exercise)

in elementary school 'X'." This teacher will attach certain meanings to his or her role as a teacher of the emotionally disturbed, including norms for what he or her should or should not do in varying situations; e.g., "It would be wrong for me to hit my pupils," or "I should spank them when they get too disobedient." For persons who see themselves as students, the kinds of statements made could vary, for example, from "It is important for me to get all A's" to "All I need to do is get good enough grades to stay in school"; "The teacher knows what she is talking about" to "Miss Jones is a communist and I don't trust her"; or "It is important for me to learn how to read French" to "French isn't relevant." Each of these statements represents ways individuals conceptualize themselves in their roles. In other words, role expectations or prescriptions for self constitute one category of self-conceptions. Several sociologists and psychologists have gone on to analyze ways of organizing these kinds of self-assessments which each of us make in each of our roles. The following three types of self-assessments have their origins, in other words, in such analyses.

Self-Concept of Ability. Several years ago the senior author of this text elaborated a notion of "self-concept of ability."[10] This idea has many parallels in the social sciences. In psychology, the expectancy theories of J. W. Atkinson[11] and J. Rotter[12] are somewhat similar. The alienation concepts of power and powerlessness are also very similar.[13]

What we mean by *self-concept of ability* (SCA) in the performance of a role task is the individual's assessment of his or her competency to carry out the behaviors appropriate for the role. A self-concept of ability develops as one defines his or her ability in a role. This self-conception functions as a *threshold variable;* i.e., before an individual will attempt to carry out certain role behaviors, he or she must assume some probability that he or she will be successful to some minimal level. Individuals will not make parachute jumps out of airplanes or attempt to learn Spanish unless they feel there is some possibility that they will succeed in their aims. If individuals have a high degree of confidence in their ability to accomplish role tasks, then their self-concept of ability is not functioning to impede their efforts.

Simply because one believes that he or she is able to perform a task, however, does not mean that he or she will attempt to carry out the task. In other words, students with high self-concepts of academic ability will not necessarily be high achievers. But unless they believe they are able to be high achievers, they will not try to be high achievers. This is why we refer to self-concept of ability as a *functionally limiting threshold* condition. It functions to set minimal limits on what we decide to do. One's self-conceptions of ability in regard to various academic areas set limits on the kinds of subjects one chooses to register for and on the decisions he or she makes to study. Obviously, however, we will do things we did not decide upon which, in turn, affect our self-conceptions. Therein lies one key to understanding why we modify our self-assessments.

Instrumental Values to Self. A second kind of self-assessment in our model includes a person's cognitions or assessments of the rewards and costs to self associated with a given performance in a given role. The individual imaginatively "completes the act" of role performance

[10] Wilbur B. Brookover, "A Social Psychological Conception of Learning," *School and Society*, vol. 87 (Spring 1959), pp. 84–87.

[11] J. W. Atkinson, *An Introduction to Motivation* (Princeton, N.J.: D. VanNostrand, 1969).

[12] J. Rotter, M. Seeman, and S. Liverent, "Internal and External Control of the Environment, a Major Variable in Behavior Theory." In N. F. Washburne (Ed.), *Decisions, Values, and Groups*, vol. 2 (London: Paragon Press, 1962).

[13] Ibid.

and weighs the costs or rewards associated with the act. The use of this idea of instrumental value to self follows from a recognition of the fruitfulness of reinforcement notions employed by Homans,[14] Skinner,[15] and others. The costs and rewards considered may be in terms of tokens such as money or social approval, or in terms of achieving and maintaining desired relationships with others.

Intrinsic Values to Self. By "intrinsic value to self" we refer to an individual's cognitions about the worth, pleasure, or value involved in the act itself regardless of any "pay-off" from others, that is, any social or economic consequences. Here we are concerned with the way people place high value on, are neutral about, or reject doing things which go with certain roles. Some people may experience guilt in a role in which others experience pride. In similar fashion, we believe that some students like the idea of being students, some could not care less, and some find being a student a very repulsive identity and would only be students in order to achieve instrumental values such as avoiding pain or gaining rewards.

Here, we attempt to incorporate into our scheme the *internalized importance* of each role we play, conceptually distinct at any given time from the instrumental rewards and costs associated with the role behaviors. This emphasis reflects, among others, the work of Maslow,[16] Rogers,[17] and Coomb and Snygg.[18] It should be remembered that this description of three types of self-assessment does not disallow the possibility that the instrumental effects associated with a role can bring about a change over time in the intrinsic value for self which is associated with a role.

Self-Concept: Theoretical Propositions. So far, we have specified the major components of self-concept assessment. But we have not presented a set of explicit ideas about how the parts of our model function together to effect decision.

To explicate how self-assessments function, a series of examples in Figure 11–3 shows how students are likely to behave if they exhibit certain patterns of self-assessment. As will be noted, individuals could have a high self-concept of ability in a task which they value doing and which they think will have valued social consequences for them.

---

[14] George Homans, *Social Behavior: Its Elementary Forms* (New York: Harcourt Brace, 1961).

[15] B. F. Skinner, *Science and Human Behavior* (Glencoe, Ill.: The Free Press, 1953).

[16] Abraham Maslow, *Motivation and Learning* (New York: Harper and Brothers, 1954).

[17] Carl Rogers, *Client and Centered Therapy* (Boston: Houghton Mifflin Company, 1951).

[18] Arthur W. Combs and Donald Snygg, *Individual Behavior* (New York, Harper and Brothers, 1959).

For example, a mathematics student might feel that he is able to learn mathematics easily, that he values being a mathematician, and that others will reward him well for learning mathematics. In contrast, another mathematics student might feel that he cannot learn mathematics very well, that he hates the thought of working with numbers, and that others will penalize him if he does not learn mathematics. The reader should find it easy to project different outcomes for our two examples in a mathematics class. This is what we have done in Figure 11–3.

Our theory of self-concept is different from the traditional idea that people *possess* a self-concept in the same way that they possess green or blue eyes. People engage in the behavioral act of conceptualizing about themselves, and it is this behavioral *process* we are interested in.

A considerable amount of research has demonstrated the limited utility of attempting to measure self-concept as if it were a unitary phenomenon. Every global test of students' self-concept of which we are aware, groups all kinds of self-assessment information as if such diverse assessments referred to one self-concept, when factors analyzed have been shown to consist of multiple factors. Secondly, when used as a composite score, these global self-concept measures are not nearly as predictive of later achievements or performance as are the more task-specific self-concept instruments.[19] The implications of this finding are several. To begin with, it is simply inappropriate or inefficient to say a student has a low or high self-concept. Students conceptualize about themselves in many different areas, and it is important to specify which self-conceptions are being referred to and to determine whether these self-conceptions are relevant for the behavior in question.

Secondly, it is important to note that, like other behaviors, verbal behaviors by which people define themselves are subject to change. If the situation is appropriate, students can be conditioned and can condition themselves to view themselves as highly able in mathematics or as incompetent.

A third implication is that self-conceptions regarding any task may vary from morning to night, from day to day, or from one situation to another. However, the self-conceptions of individuals tend to be repeated; i.e., they are about as stable as most other behavioral patterns, and of course, some cognitions about self are more resistant to change than others. Individuals who assert a belief tend to assert their belief

[19] For example, see: Ellen V. Piers and Dale B. Harris, "Age and Other Correlates of Self-Concept in Children," *Journal of Educational Psychology*, vol. 55, no. 2 (Spring 1964), pp. 91–95; Ralph J. Nash, "A Study of Particular Self-Perceptions as Related to Scholastic Achievement," *Dissertation Abstracts*, vol. 24 (1964), 3837–3838. Ruth Wylie, "Children's Estimates of Their Schoolwork Ability as a Function of Sex, Race and Socio-Economic Level," *Journal of Personality*, vol. 31, no. 2 (1963), pp. 203–24.

FIGURE 11–3
Illustrative Hypotheses about How Students May Behave on the Basis of Their Profiles of Self-Assessments

Self-Concept of Academic Ability A	*Intrinsic Value of Student Role for Self* B	*Instrumental Value of Student Role for Self* C	*Illustrative Hypotheses: Predicted Outcomes*
(1) Positive	Positive	Positive	These students will attempt to carry out the behavior they think is appropriate for themselves as a student. They will attempt to have their performance under the surveillance of others who are also perceived to value student role and/or who are perceived to reward appropriate student behavior. However, inasmuch as carrying out the student role has intrinsic value for self (i.e., student's performance is reinforcing) surveillance and reinforcement by others is not essential for performances. Probably not many students like this.
(2) Positive	Neutral	Positive	These students will carry out their roles only to the extent they think others will provide "rewards" or sanctions. Hence, perceived surveillance by others who are in a position to reinforce student behavior is crucial. Students in this category are not likely to attempt academic achievements unless there is a "payoff" from others. This type of student is probably more typical in many of our high schools and colleges.
(3) Positive	Negative	Positive	This type of student will exhibit considerable tension as a result of role conflict. An example of this type would be a biology student who feels he should not learn the "theory of evolution because it is evil," but perceives high reward in doing so or considerable punishment should he fail to learn his biology lessons. Such a student will attempt to cope with the situation by becoming neutral about the value of being a biology learner or by removing himself from the surveillance of others in a position to reinforce his behavior (the latter coping behavior seems most likely). This profile is likely to be rare in most schools.

over time unless extinction or new learning takes place. It is also true that many of our beliefs about ourselves are made with a great deal of resistance to change, while other beliefs about ourselves are more readily modified.

A fourth implication is that what one believes about one's self does not have to fit with objective facts any more than does one's beliefs about the world. One may think the world is flat or that he or she cannot learn French and on both counts be wrong. However, as far as that person is concerned, he or she is not likely to venture forth around the world as did Columbus unless placed in irons (as were many of Columbus's crew) or attempt to learn French.

It is on the basis of our assumptions about ourselves in relation to our environment that we take certain postures toward our world. These assumptions about self provide a *frame of reference* for anticipating

FIGURE 11-3 (*continued*)

Self-Concept of Academic Ability A	*Intrinsic Value* B	*Instrumental Value* C	*Illustrative Hypotheses: Predicted Outcomes*
(4) Positive	Positive	Neutral	Will attempt to carry out student role without concern for surveillance of others. This type of student is very rare in our society which usually emphasizes learning as a means to achieve other values and not to be valued in itself.
(5) Positive	Positive	Negative	Will attempt to remove one's self in the performance of student role from the surveillance of others who are perceived to negatively sanction student behaviors he or she values for self. These students will attempt to be under the surveillance of persons who are perceived to value student achievement. If this is not possible, they are likely to devalue student role for self. A rare profile.
(6) Neutral (7) Neutral	Positive Neutral	Positive Positive	Will not stay in these profiles long and when they are, they will be very sensitive to cues indicating competency of incompetency to carry out appropriate student behaviors. However, neutrality about one's competency as a student is very rare in our society since most of us are taught early and regularly to accept some definition of competency in academic matters.
(8) Negative (9) Negative	Positive Neutral	Positive Positive	Will attempt to devalue or modify student role for self and remove one's self from student role or from surveillance of student role. If cues are provided that the person is competent they are likely to reinforce self-competency in student role. Generally, however, the basis for others reinforcing incompetency is likely to be present so this is not too likely. Such a student will perform at low levels and will stay in student role only insofar as it is forced upon him by others. He will drop out of school at the first opportune time.

and evaluating new experiences. A person's frame of reference can be classified into three categories: assumptions concerning fact, value, and possibility.[20] Each individual behaves in terms of how *he or she thinks things really are*. Each person also behaves in terms of how *he or she thinks things should be*. And in addition, each person behaves in terms of how *he or she thinks things could be*. In essence then, our life styles are partly a function of our frames of reference which are basically our assumptions about self in relation to our environment. The student's self-conceptions, therefore, influence the student's "style of behavior" as a student.

These theoretical implications, however, are merely conjecture unless there is evidence to back them up, and there is. Recent research by the authors and their associates show that self-concept of academic

[20] James C. Coleman, *Personality Dynamics and Effective Behavior* (Chicago: Scott, Foresman and Company, 1960), p. 58.

ability is significantly correlated with academic performance.[21] Students' self-concept of academic ability was found to account for a significant proportion of academic achievement when the analysis controlled for social class conditions, measured intelligence, the normative expectations of family, friends, and teachers, and past achievement levels. This research followed an entire class of approximately 1,500 students from junior high school through three years after high school. The major finding was that changes in self-concept of ability were followed by changes in academic achievement.

This finding has been verified in many situations in North America, Europe, and Asia. Several studies of the effects of self-concept of ability among retarded children have been conducted with the same results.[22] Similar findings have been found with delinquent institutionalized youth,[23] deaf and blind students,[24] school dropouts,[25] and junior college students.[26] An independent national study by Edgar G. Epps[27] of the achievement effects of self-concept of ability and other correlates among

[21] Wilbur B. Brookover, Ann Paterson, and Shailer Thomas, *Self-Concept of Ability and School Achievement:* I, *Cooperative Research Project No. 845* (East Lansing, Michigan: Michigan State University, 1962); Wilbur B. Brookover, Jean M. LePere, Don E. Hamacheck, Shailer Thomas, and Edsel L. Erickson, *Self-Concept of Ability and School Achievement,* II, *Cooperative Research Project No. 1636* (East Lansing, Michigan: Bureau of Educational Research Services, College of Education, Michigan State University, 1965); and Wilbur B. Brookover, Edsel L. Erickson, and Lee M. Joiner, *Self-Concept of Ability and School Achievement,* III, *Cooperative Research Project No. 2831* (East Lansing, Michigan: Educational Publication Services, Michigan State University, 1967).

[22] Richard E. Towne and Lee M. Joiner, *The Effect of Special Class Placement on the Self-Concept of Ability of the Educable Mentally Retarded Child.* Report on U.S. Office of Education grant 32-32-0410-6001 (East Lansing, Mich.: College of Education, Michigan State University, 1966), and Kenton T. Schurr and Wilbur B. Brookover, *The Effect of Special Class Placement on the Self Concept of Ability of the Educable Mentally Retarded Child* (East Lansing, Mich.: Publication Services, College of Education, Michigan State University, 1967).

[23] David Haarer, *A Comparative Study of Self-Concept of Ability Between Institutionalized Delinquent Boys and Non-Delinquent Boys Enrolled in Public Schools.* Ph.D. Dissertation, Michigan State University, 1969.

[24] Lee M. Joiner and Edsel L. Erickson, *Scales and Procedures for Assessing Social-Psychological Characteristics of Visually Impaired and Hearing Impaired Students,* U.S. Office of Education Cooperative Research Project No. 6-8720 (Washington: U.S. Government Printing Offices, 1967); Lee M. Joiner et al., "Predicting the Academic Achievement of the Acoustically Impaired Using Intelligence and Self-Concept of Academic Ability," *Journal of Special Education,* vol. 3, no. 4 (Winter 1969), p. 425–431.

[25] Kenneth Harding, *A Comparative Study of Caucasian Male High School Students Who Stay in School and Those Who Drop Out,* Ph.D. Dissertation, Michigan State University, 1969.

[26] Kenneth Sproull, *The Relationship Between High School Self-Concept of Academic Ability and Subsequent Academic Achievement at the Community College.* Dissertation, Michigan State University, 1969.

[27] Edgar G. Epps, "Correlates of Academic Achievement Among Northern and Southern Urban Negro Students," *Journal of Social Issues,* vol. 25, no. 3 (July 1969), pp. 55–70.

black students provides another set of interesting results. Epps concluded that *self-concept of academic ability* and *conformity* are among the most powerful of predictors of academic achievement. This conclusion is in accord with the earlier findings of Morse,[28] who compared white and black eighth-grade students in Michigan.

In related research, Wamhoff found that indicators of one's vocational conceptions of ability obtained during the senior year in high school were related to vocational decisions two years later.[29] Gabel, in a study of college plans among high school students in a small Western community, obtained similar findings.[30] Gabel found that, of 247 seniors who planned to go to a four-year college or university, only 31 percent had medium to low self-concepts of academic ability. On the other hand, of 44 seniors who planned to go only to junior college, 82 percent had medium to low self-concepts of academic ability. Interestingly, Gabel did not find a significant correlation between a global measure of self-concept and college plans. Only the self-concept measure that focused on the student role was predictive of plans for the student role.[31]

Cross-cultural research also has been conducted demonstrating the relationship of self-concept of academic ability to achievement. In studies by Votruba[32] and Auer[33] in Germany of students in three different types of schools—the *Gymnasium,* the *Mitteschule,* and the *Volkschule*—self-concept of academic ability was found to be clearly related to achievement when social class background and type of school were controlled. Sidawi[34] in a study of Lebanese students also found self-concept of academic ability to be related to achievement. In summary, the importance of self-concept of academic ability has been well substantiated.

The other components of our model, however, have not been so comprehensively demonstrated to have utility in accounting for student behavior. Only recently has research been begun which simultaneously takes into account all dimensions of self-assessment included in our scheme. In recent research, we found that the instrumental and intrinsic

[28] Richard J. Morse, *Self-Concept of Ability, Significant Others and School Achievement of Eighth Grade Students: A Comparative Analyses.* M.A. thesis, Michigan State University, 1963.

[29] Carroll H. Wamhoff, *Self-Concept of Vocational Ability: Its Relation to Selected Factors in Career Development.* Doctoral Dissertation, Michigan State University, 1969.

[30] Peter Gabel, *A Study of the Self-Concepts of High School Seniors and Their Post High School Plans,* Doctoral Dissertation, University of Colorado, 1970.

[31] Ibid.

[32] James Charles Votruba, "A Comparative Analysis of a Social-Psychological Theory of School Achievement." Master's thesis, Michigan State University, 1970.

[33] Michael Auer, *Self-Concept of Academic Ability of West German Eighth-Grade Students.* Doctoral Dissertation, Michigan State University, 1971.

[34] Ahmad Sidawi, *Self-Concept of Ability and School Achievement in Lebanon.* Doctoral Dissertation, Michigan State University, 1970.

self-assessments attached to the role of student contributed to our ability to predict student decisions concerning their career programs.[35] At the same time, this study suggests that the intrinsic and the instrumental perceptions are not as powerful in predicting achievement as is self-concept of ability. Of course, it takes several years to develop powerful and valid instruments, and perhaps these conclusions are premature. As it stands, however, the limited evidence available to date is in accord with our scheme of the organization of the self-conceptions of individuals.

The evidence relating self-conceptions to the influence of others contains a number of implications for educational practice. The following questions highlight some of them:

1. Do we as teachers or professors sometimes (perhaps inadvertently) emphasize or reinforce instrumental values of the student role while ignoring the development of intrinsic values of student achievements? What strategies would be most effective for creating positive assessment of self in the student role? What strategies are likely to be self-defeating?
2. Can we make academic achievement its own reward or must we be totally dependent upon the "carrot" approach to school achievement?
3. Should parents be enlisted in educational programs to affect students' cognitions as to their academic competencies and the instrumental and intrinsic values of student achievement? If so, how should the parents be guided? What should be avoided?
4. How can we as professors or teachers most effectively help students to achieve desired self-conceptions of ability? Are there behaviors we sometimes engage in which inadvertently lead to low self-conceptions of ability on the part of our students?
5. Are there organizational or other features in our schools and colleges which, in spite of their goals, lead to students' devaluing their student role or their abilities? How about certain grouping procedures and the labels commonly given to students in these groups?

The Influence of Others

Each of the above questions raises concerns for how the modification or development of student self-assessments takes place. In Figure 11–4, it should be noted, several kinds of conditions shape one's self-concept

[35] Robert W. Bilby, Edsel L. Erickson, and Wilbur B. Brookover, "Characterizations of Self and Student Decision Making," *Review of Educational Research*, vol. 42, no. 4 (Fall 1972), pp. 505–524.

FIGURE 11–4
The Influence of Others on Self-Conception

Inputs		*Output*
Actual Evaluations and Behaviors of Others:	Monitoring of Evaluation:	
1. Evaluations of ability communicated Parent: "You are just like me. I could never read either." Teacher: "Come on John, you can do it." Friends: "You stupe!"	1. Monitoring of other evaluations of self: "My teacher thinks I am about average." "My father thinks I am dumber than my sister." "My friends tease me about being dumb."	
2. Feedback to student on performance: Teacher: "You did well but you can do better." Friend: "You were lucky." "You did poorly but as well as expected." Counselor: "You scored 68 out of 100."	2. Monitoring of self-behavior: "I couldn't finish the story before recess like the other kids." "I failed a grade." "I'm in the red book with the slow readers."	Self-Concept Ability (e.g., in 5th grade reading) e.g., "I don't read very well." "I can't learn like the other kids." "I'm a good reader."
3. Criteria for evaluating performance: Teacher: "You should be able to read this story in the next 15 minutes." Parent: "You should get A's if you're really a good reader." Classmate: "You should be in the blue book if you are a good reader."	3. Monitoring of Situation: "Miss Jones can't help me—nobody can." "I have to go home." "I don't have time to do my homework." "The stories are stupid—too hard."	
4. Information on resources and requirements: Parents: "I need you home to baby-sit." Teacher: "There are too many children in this class for me to answer your questions now." Classmate: "I'll help you."		

of ability in any given role. The scheme emphasizes that one's self-conceptions of ability are functions of various types of monitoring by the individual of others' reactions to him, his own behavior, and the conditions of the situation. We use the term *monitoring*, in preference to attending or perceiving, in accord with Carl J. Couch's recent work,[36] which recognizes that attending and perceiving have relatively static connotations. "Not only is monitoring selective but in most social encounters attention moves from object to object and back and forth among

[36] Carl J. Couch, "Dimensions of Association in Collective Behavior Episodes," *Sociometry*, vol. 33, no. 4 (1970), p. 459.

the same set of objects."[37] All human action that is guided by rational processes requires that persons monitor themselves and others. A person's decision to act or a person's decision as to his ability reflects his monitoring of himself, others, and his situation.

Note that in Figure 11–4 the actual evaluations of self provided by others are not necessarily the same as one's conceptions of those evaluations. Niles found that the perceptions reported by elementary students from low SES families of their parents' evaluation and expectations of them were significantly correlated (.36) with their parents' reported evaluation and expectations.[38] An appropriate idea here is the concept of *role-taking.* Couch states: "All forms of role-taking involve some minimal attempt to assess the standpoint of others."[39] In addition, one may or may not adopt the standpoint of another as one's own.[40] Our problem, of course, is to assess the conditions which facilitate one's adoption of the ideas of others.

We know, for example, on the basis of considerable research and theory, that others play an important role in how we view ourselves. Perhaps the following anecdote will illustrate our point better than any set of statistics:[41]

> A group of graduate students in a seminar in social psychology became interested in the notions implied in the interactionist approach. One evening after the seminar, five of the male members of the group were discussing some of the implications of the theory and came to the realization that it might be possible to invent a situation where the "others" systematically manipulated their responses to another person, thereby changing that person's self-concept and in turn his behavior. They thought of an experiment to test the notions they were dealing with. They chose as their subject (victim) the one girl in their seminar. The subject can be described as, at best, a very plain girl who seemed to fit the stereotype (usually erroneous) that many have of graduate student females. The boys' plan was to begin in concert to respond to the girl as if she were the best-looking girl on campus. They agreed to work into it naturally so that she would not be aware of what they were up to. They drew lots to see who would be the first to date her. The loser, under the pressure of the others, asked her to go out. Although he found the situation quite unpleasant, he was a good actor

[37] Ibid.

[38] Bradley Niles, *A Comparison of Students' Perceived and Parents' Actual Evaluation-Expectations in Low SES Schools With School Achievement Level and Racial Composition Controlled.* Doctoral Dissertation, Michigan State University, 1974.

[39] Couch, "Dimensions of Association," p. 463.

[40] Ibid.

[41] Reprinted from John W. Kinch, "A Formalized Theory of the Self-Concept," *The American Journal of Sociology,* vol. 67 (January 1963), pp. 482–483, by permission of the University of Chicago Press (Copyright 1963, University of Chicago).

and by continually saying to himself "she's beautiful, she's beautiful . . . ," he got through the evening. According to the agreement, it was now the second man's turn and so it went. The dates were reinforced by the similar responses in all contacts the men had with the girl. In a matter of a few short weeks, the results began to show. At first, it was simply a matter of more care in her appearance; her hair was combed more often and her dresses were more neatly pressed, and before long she had been to the beauty parlor to have her hair styled, and was spending her hard-earned money on the latest fashions in women's campus wear. By the time the fourth man was taking his turn dating the young lady, the job that had once been undesirable was now quite a pleasant task. And when the last man in the conspiracy asked her out, he was informed that she was pretty well booked up for some time in the future. It seems there were more desirable males around than those "plain" graduate students.

The perspective stressed in the social-psychological tradition espoused here is that one's monitoring of other's expectations—one's definition or perception of the situation—and not the actual expectations for self held by others, is the more crucial condition for understanding decision-making. Rather than the actual expectations and behaviors of others, the most important element in this process is the manner in which one defines and interprets others' expectations and behaviors.[42] Within this process, perception of the credibility of the other is an important factor.[43] Credibility poses minimal conditions of believability and acceptance concerning others' intentions and behaviors. In addition, the degree of credibility which we attribute to others also influences the likelihood of our initiating or maintaining reciprocal role relationships with them.

The concept of credibility has been the subject of considerable discussion and research in all areas of social science, usually under the rubric of attitude formation.[44] Many of these theories have been in the

---

[42] Blumer, *Symbolic Interactionism.*

[43] We are particularly indebted to Robert D. Mendelsohn for assistance in clarifying our perspectives of conditions affecting credibility which are presented here. A more elaborate statement can be found in Robert D. Mendelsohn, Edsel L. Erickson, and Wilbur B. Brookover, "Parental Assessments of Teacher Credibility and Parental Participation in School-Related Activities," Paper presented at American Educational Research Association Meetings, Chicago, 1972; Robert D. Mendelsohn, "Using the Concept of Teacher Credibility for Forecasting Student Decision-Making" (doctoral dissertation, Western Michigan University, 1973); and Robert D. Mendelsohn and Edsel L. Erickson, "Forecasting Student Course Entry on the Basis of Instructor Believability, Expertise, and Trustworthiness: An Analysis of the Credibility Construct in Social Psychology," Paper read at North Central Sociological meetings, Cincinnati, 1973.

[44] W. McGuire, "The Nature of Attitudes and Attitude Change," in G. Lindsey and E. Aronson (eds.), *The Handbook of Social Psychology,* vol. 3, 2nd ed., (Boston: Addison-Wesley Publishing Company, 1969), pp. 172–75.

cognitive consistency tradition exemplified by Heider[45] and Newcomb.[46] These theorists have generally viewed credibility as an attribute of communications processes. One of the more fruitful systematic attempts to elaborate on the concept of credibility was that of Kelman.[47] Kelman proposes three components of influence: credibility, attractiveness, and power. Each component is assumed to effect an attitude change in the receiver as a result of one or a combination of the following psychological conditions: *internalization* of the views and values of others; *identification* with others; and *compliance* with the expectations of others.

Obviously, much of academic role performance is compliant behavior. In a study by one of the authors,[48] and as shown in Table 11–2, when parents are perceived as making high academic demands the students tended to behave in accordance with those demands. Parental demands were assessed by three conditions: perceived parental classroom surveillance of self in the role of student; the specific achievement expectations of the parents; and the importance parents attached to their achievement expectations for their child.

Given the findings in Table 11–2, typical academic achievement does not seem to be as much a matter of compliance to friends' demands as it is to parents. There have been numerous other studies yielding other conclusions as to the relative influence of parents and friends. We will deal with this issue more thoroughly in the next chapter. At this point, it is only necessary to recognize that a considerable amount of academic behavior in most of our schools is of a compliant sort. Not many students would continue to study if offered the alternative of playing with their peers. What should not be overlooked, however, is the fact that, while much of academic behavior is compliant, the internalized beliefs and values of others as self-conceptions also play an important role. We will, therefore, continue to direct our attention to how others provide input into the developing self-conceptions of students.

Figure 11–5 further elaborates on this input into student self-conceptions. Similar to the model presented in Figure 11–4, student monitoring of others, self, and situation are important determinants of student self-conceptions.

---

[45] F. Heider, *The Psychology of Interpersonal Relations* (New York: John Wiley & Sons, Inc., 1958).

[46] T. Newcomb, *The Acquaintance Process* (New York: Holt, Rinehart and Winston, 1961).

[47] H. Kelman, "Compliance, Identification and Internalization: Three Processes of Attitude Change," *Journal of Conflict Resolution,* vol. 2, no. 1 (1958), pp. 51–60.

[48] Edsel L. Erickson, "A Study of the Normative Influence of Parents and Friends Upon Academic Achievement." Doctoral dissertation, Michigan State University, 1965.

TABLE 11–2
Number of Parents and Friends Perceived as Making High or Low Academic Demands upon High and Low Achieving Students with Normal or Higher Intelligence

	Number of Parents Perceived as Making:			*Number of Friends Perceived as Making:*		
	High Academic Demands	*Low Academic Demands*	*No Academic Demands*	*High Academic Demands*	*Low Academic Demands*	*No Academic Demands*
High Achievers (GPA 3.5–4.0) N = 67	61	0	6	26	3	38
Low Achievers (GPA 0.0–0.75) N = 35	3	14	18	2	6	27

All subjects had I.Q. 91 or higher, which was within one standard deviation of the mean I.Q. = 103.59, SD = 12.69.

All low achievers are two or more standard deviations below the mean GPA = 2.26, SD = .76.

Source: Adapted from Edsel L. Erickson, "A Study of the Normative Influence of Parents and Friends Upon Academic Achievement." Doctoral dissertation, Michigan State University, 1965.

Figure 11–6 illustrates a similar pattern. There is an interactive process between the environment and the condition of an individual which is characterized by a monitoring process. The consequences of this process are cognitions as to the value for self of any behavior one thinks he might engage in. Cognitions of intrinsic value, instrumental value, and ability then interact to produce decisions which are stimuli to further decision processes.

FIGURE 11–5
Determinants of Instrumental Value

Typical Inputs		*Output*
Actual Environmental Situation:	*Student Monitoring of Others:*	*Self-Conception:*
1. Actual Expectations for Students	Expectations of parents, peers, teachers and others. "My mother wants me to learn French."	Self-concept of ability (to learn French) ↕
2. Reinforcement Structure Provided Student	Rewards and sanctions others attach to their expectations. "Will I get yelled at?" "Will I get a new bike?" "Will they like me better?"	Instrumental value attached to role-act (of learning French) ↕
3. Surveillance of Student	Surveillance by others of self. "Will they know if I don't learn?" "When will they find out?" "Who will know?"	Intrinsic value attached to role-act (of learning French)
4. Prior Behavior and Cognitant Patterns of Student		

FIGURE 11–6
Determinants of Intrinsic Value

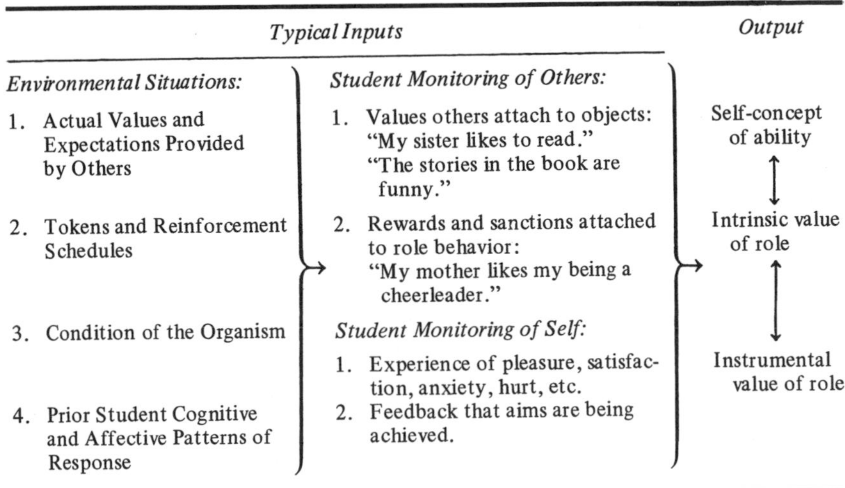

Language and Learning

So far, we have examined models for self-concept development which begin to relate the individual to his social and social-psychological context. In each of these models there is an implicit notion of the power of language. In one instance, the individual communicates with self and comes to characterize self often with the language of his or her culture. If one's culture has the concept *retarded,* one may come to use the label to describe self—and act accordingly.

Language is also implied in each of the models because it is through shared symbols that most expectations, values, feedback, and reinforcements are provided the individual. One concept which may help us to understand this phenomenon is the phrase "cooling the mark out." Goffman[49] used this phrase to describe a process by which a social system gets an individual or group to accept failure or inferior treatment. A "mark," a term borrowed from illegal confidence games in which "marks" were swindled out of their possessions, is a person who once viewed himself as having a skill, talent, or possession and as capable and deserving of the attribute, learns that he is without such assets. Goffman's early illustration was that this person was the object of a con game.[50] The following discussion illustrates how we may all participate to "con" students into accepting failure.

[49] Erving Goffman, "On Cooling the Mark Out" *Psychiatry,* vol. 15, no. 4 (Fall 1952), pp. 451–63.

[50] Ibid.

Labeling Processes: An Illustration[51]

The public school with its open-door policy, accompanied by a dedication to the maintenance of academic standards, is a likely environment in which to find "marks." Children go to school expecting to complete whatever is required of them. Some, however, do not adequately perform the academic tasks deemed important—tasks which Dexter[52] has said are necessary for passage from child to adult status in our society. Nonperformance of these tasks often entails removal from the regular program, an action which causes the child to realize that he is deficient in important ways. This creates a need for redefinition of the self. In brief, the student is designated as "educable mentally retarded"; he is accordingly placed; he recognizes failure; he becomes a mark who requires cooling out.

While there are other aspects of this process, only the classification problem and its implications will be discussed here. For the student, designation or labeling as retarded serves as a means for locating him in an intellectual hierarchy. He attains a formal, comparative rank in the eyes of the others.

One possible result of such classification is that the *abstract character of the category* to which he is formally assigned results in what Gutchen[53] termed *misplaced concreteness.* In the instance of educable mental retardation, the meaning of designation EMR begins to expand beyond the set of school-related behaviors which define the category. Once designated, the child is thought of by others as "*being*" educable, an "educable person" rather than a person who performs in a particular way under certain conditions.

Thus, whatever "educability" means to someone, regardless of accuracy of connection with immediate behavior, that person's expectations and interpretation of the behavior of the child will be affected by his definition of what *this kind of person* is supposed to be like. Vague feelings and observations about the individual's behavior become anchored to the concept. *A social object* is created through the development of a cognitive category which serves to connect or interrelate many disparate characteristics. The *social object* takes on authenticity, since the observed behaviors become defined as causal conditions in explaining the genesis of the behavior. The individual's inept performance of an

---

[51] Excerpted by permission of the authors, Lee M. Joiner, Richard C. Towne, and Edsel L. Erickson, "A Sociological Analysis of Separate and Special Education for the Educable Mentally Retarded." Unpublished manuscript, Bureau of Educational Research, Michigan State University, 1965.

[52] L. A. Dexter, "A Social Theory of Mental Deficiency," *American Journal of Mental Deficiency,* vol. 62 (Fall 1958), pp. 920–28.

[53] Robert A. Gutchen, "On the Classification of Human Beings," *Indian Journal of Social Research,* vol. 4 (January 1963), pp. 42–48.

important task is explained by defining him as a member of a subset of individuals who are supposed to behave this way by definition.

This process is made clear by Heider,[54] who, in discussing social perception and phenomenal causality, suggests that causes of failure are rarely connected with situational circumstances, but are seen more directly as an outgrowth of personal inadequacies or deficiencies. Again, the person who behaves in any given set of circumstances in any prescribed fashion is seen as the kind of person who would be expected to do such things. From the act of failing is born the failure.

Another concern of practical importance is the human tendency to recruit members for abstract categories. Becker[55] claims that once an abstract category is created, there arises the need to fill it with examples. Insofar as there are few, if ever any, unfilled openings in special classes, we are led to wonder if this results from a real need or from our heightened awareness of the category (educable mentally retarded) and the subsequent search for children who fit within the defined human subset.

Our second area of discussion deals with the cooling out process itself. Once a person has experienced the disappointment of a reasonable expectation or finds himself in a situation wherein he or she has defined him or herself in a way which the social facts come to contradict, he or she must be supplied with a "new framework in which to view and judge self." This process of redefining the self along defensible lines is what Goffman[56] calls *cooling out*. The person who instigates the process and carries it along is the "cooler."

In a con game "it is good business for one of the operators to stay with the mark in order to talk him or her into a point of view from which it is possible to accept a loss." The "cooler" exercises the "art of consolidation" upon the mark and "gives instruction in the philosophy of taking a loss."

Much the same process occurs in the public schools. As Goffman[57] explains, one of the typical situations that occur in the social life of the failure is the "dramatic process by which persons who have died in important ways come gradually to be brought together into a common graveyard that is separated ecologically from the living community." This special, homogeneous, segregated class may be viewed as an ecologically separate common graveyard for school failures. It is there that so-called educable mentally retarded students are cooled out to accept the idea that they will never be given the major rewards of society.

---

[54] Heider, *Psychology of Interpersonal Relations.*

[55] Howard S. Becker, *Outsiders: Studies in the Sociology of Deviance* (Glencoe, Ill.: The Free Press, 1963).

[56] Goffman, "On Cooling the Mark Out."

[57] Ibid.

The structure of the separate class itself provides for cooling out, since it facilitates exposure to "ability comparables." According to Festinger,[58] exposure to "ability comparables" allows people to obtain an accurate evaluation of their ability. In theory, therefore, the homogeneous nature of the special class should reduce frustration, rejection, and unsatisfactory social interaction.

Placement in a special homogeneous group should also relieve the sense of similar failure and encourage comparison with others having similar problems. Edgerton and Sabagh[59] discuss the positive benefits of such comparisons for the self-conceptions of high-grade defectives in a state institution for the retarded; here it was discovered that the "high grades" took on the attitudes toward the "low grades" which the normals took toward them. This stratification and comparison process furthered the "aggrandizement" of self among the "high grades." It must be remembered, however, that such aggrandizement took place, not in our world vis-a-vis all people, but in a restricted world vis-a-vis "lesser" social objects.

Wolk's[60] survey of curriculum practices for the educable mentally retarded further illustrates methods devised with educational goals in mind which, in a real sense, "cool the mark out." Since the educable mentally retarded are defined as lacking the talents and abilities that make culturally defined goals accessible to them through conventional means, the culturally defined goals are deemphasized. Rather than providing alternate means for approaching the commonly defined goals, the cooling process alters the goals themselves. The special class teacher encourages her students to accept the idea that academic skills and other common indicators of school success are not as important for them as they are for others. The educable mentally retarded are often encouraged to do anything, regardless of whether or not society views their accomplishments as being worth while.

Another means whereby the mark is cooled is the creation of *modified success*. Weiner[61] emphasizes this when she states that the school is responsible for preventing failure in young people labeled educable mentally retarded. She suggests that the emphasis should be shifted

---

[58] L. Festinger, "A Theory of Social Comparison Processes," *Human Relations*, vol. 7 (Winter 1964), pp. 117–140.

[59] Robert B. Edgerton and George Sabagh, "From Mortification to Aggrandizement: Changing Self-Concepts in the Careers of the Mentally Retarded," *Psychiatry*, vol. 25, no. 3 (Summer 1962), pp. 263–72.

[60] Shirley M. Wolk, "A Survey of the Literature on Curriculum Practice for the Mentally Retarded," *American Journal of Mental Deficiency*, vol. 62 (Fall 1958), pp. 826–39.

[61] Bluma B. Weiner, "Essential Features of a Pre-School Program for Young Mentally Handicapped Children," *American Journal of Mental Deficiency*, vol. 50 (Winter 1954), p. 58.

from commonly held conceptions of school success to more restricted goals having the immediate objective of socialization, language, concept development, and recreational skills. This view, however, ignores the fact that what Bredameier and Toby[62] call "standards of worthiness" have been defined for us by the society in which we interact. The new simplified goal or success experience becomes recognized as only relevant to activities performed by particular social types, in this case the educable mentally retarded. Such an outcome is shown in Clark's[63] study, wherein regular grade students described the activities of educable mentally retarded students in special classes as "play" and "arts and crafts." In spite of so-called modified success, however, the educable mentally retarded remains a mark in the eyes of other children in the school.

The general stance taken by those who cool out those labeled as having less capabilities is the "mental hygiene" or "psychiatric" approach discussed by Goffman in *Stigma.*[64] The individual is told that he or she is first of all a human being who, at worst, is somewhat different in only one small area of life.

Since his or her affliction is nothing in itself, he or she should not be ashamed of it or of others who have it; nor should he or she compromise by trying to conceal it. On the other hand, by hard work and persistent self-training, one should fulfill ordinary standards as fully as one can, stopping short only when the issue of normification arises; that is, where one's efforts might be given the impression that one is trying to deny his or her differentness.

Further, do not feel "bitter," "resentful," or "self-pitying." Instead, cultivate "a cheerful, outgoing manner." If one does this, one is considered "adjusted," "has a strong character," and has developed a "deep philosophy of life." One also will have developed a way of behaving in keeping with typical educational definitions and labels of the educable mentally retarded: a prognosis of minimal academic achievement, minimal social adjustment, and minimal occupational adequacy.

Finally, what are the consequences of being cooled out as it occurs for those labeled educable mentally retarded or otherwise different? Findings such as those of Johnson[65] and Clark[66] provide evidence of

---

[62] Harry C. Brademeier and Jackson Toby, *Social Problems in America: Costs and Casualties in an Acquisitive Society* (New York: John Wiley and Sons, Inc., 1960).

[63] Edward T. Clark, "Children's Perception of a Special Class Placement for Educable Mentally Retarded Children," *Exceptional Children,* vol. 30, no. 7 (September 1964), pp. 289–295.

[64] Erving Goffman, *Stigma: Notes on the Management of Spoiled Identity* (Englewood Cliffs, N.J.: Prentice-Hall, Inc., 1963).

[65] O. Johnson, "Special Education for the Mentally Retarded—A Paradox," *Journal of Social Research,* vol. 29 (Winter 1962), pp. 62–69.

[66] Edward T. Clark, *Children's Perception of a Special Class Placement.*

depreciations directed at special-class students by children in the regular grades, and that special-class youngsters will accept such depreciated judgments and, thereby, conceptualize themselves as inferior individuals.

A further problem is that the techniques utilized to cool the mark out serve to establish aspiration boundaries which, according to Faris,[67] "serve to lower demands and expectations rather than serving some functional or preventative purpose." The expressed concern by educators that even medium-level goals are not meant for so-called educable mentally retarded students denotes the establishment of such boundaries. It is assumed by definition that the educable mentally retarded will fail to achieve any such "unrealistic goals." Interestingly enough, such aspiration boundaries have created the need for another definition and label, "pseudoretardation," to explain all those cases in which initially labeled "retardates" subsequently manage to achieve beyond the aspiration boundaries set by their labelers or perform on a higher-than-expected level.

A person becomes, in part, educable mentally retarded when one is socially defined as such. And the definition will stick as long as there are repeated performances of the acts which suggest the role along with continued failure to contradict the defined role by roles or stories of a different category. But once the individual does not perform as expected, one becomes something else, in this case a "pseudoretardate."

Do the educable mentally retarded ever contradict their expected role? Generally not when grouped and treated as retardates. Observations of special classes often show that the educable mentally retarded child has little opportunity to demonstrate anything other than the expected behavior. Little is demanded of him in such areas as leadership. His influence upon the course of events within the school is inconsequential. Segregation from the rest of the school, except during recreation or other secondary activities, provides little opportunity to contradict his or her image as a failure, "mark" or "fool." His or her role in the school becomes that of a "living object lesson" serving, as Coser[68] suggests, both to define what is normal and to arouse the community to the consequences of breaking one of its norms.

Allied to this is the situation wherein classification as educable mentally retarded is an important step toward ensuring minimal existence in a society which emphasizes technological and academic skills. Since low level occupational attainment is predicted and encouraged, it is almost always realized. Although it may be argued that low level employment is a necessary consequence of low intelligence, it can also be thought

---

[67] Robert E. Faris, "Reflections of the Ability Dimensions in Human Society," *American Sociological Review*, vol. 26, no. 6 (June 1961), pp. 835–43.

[68] Lewis A. Coser, "Some Functions of Deviant Behavior and Normative Flexability," *American Journal of Sociology*, vol. 68, no. 2 (February 1962), pp. 172–81.

to stem from what Reynolds[69] terms *base rate* thinking. Base rate thinking means that low level prediction is the safest prediction for the future adjustment of the individual who deviates significantly from the norm in any way. The outcome is the creation of a recruitment pool for low level occupations; occupations which Becker and Strauss[70] contend are the most difficult to fill and are filled by failures, "to whom they are almost the only means of survival."

A friend recently related an example of this which occurred while some so-called educable mentally retarded students were preparing for a trip to the library to survey occupational folders. The teacher said, "Look kids, let's face it . . . You're not too smart so don't be looking up jobs like foreman. Look up jobs like car washer, sweeper, and bus boy. These are the kind of jobs you're going to get."

Differential goals, substitute success, and the reality rhetoric have been observed along with base rate thinking and low level expectation. Such concepts remain important influences upon the behavior of the educable mentally retarded even though we are turning away from the idea of human mental ability as something fixed in the psychological sense and are beginning to view it as a flexible and pliable attribute.

In summary, our brief analysis of the social psychological situation of the students who are labeled as retardates in special classes has been presented from the point of view of symbolic interaction theory and Erving Goffman's "Cooling the Mark Out."[71] Influences such as base rate thinking, role behavior, self-concept, behavioral expectations, differential goals, and substitute success have been presented as aspects of a total interaction situation. The behavior patterns caused by these influences are hypothesized to result in less than optimal achievement and adjustment in the school or in later life. Research has begun in this area, but we must strive further to find ways in which the interaction situation can be structured and an educational setting devised in which the social penalties paid for being given special help will not negate the opportunities of the more ideal educational setting. We may then be better able to attain the superior results expected of various grouping practices.

Strategies to Enhance Learning

A considerable amount of discussion and evidence has been presented suggesting that our traditional norms, values, and structures are responsi-

[69] Maynard C. Reynolds, "The Social Psychology of Exceptional Children," *Exceptional Children,* vol. 26 (Fall 1960), pp. 243–47.

[70] Howard S. Becker and Anselm L. Strauss, "Careers, Personality, and Adult Socialization," *American Journal of Sociology,* vol. 62, no. 3 (March 1962), pp. 253–63.

[71] Goffman, "On Cooling the Mark Out."

ble for much of the failure in school. In a similar fashion, there has been a tradition in social science, education, and the popular literature in which academic failure has been mistakenly treated as the inevitable outcome of social class, parental indifference, and race.

Social scientists themselves have been guilty of assuming that the correlations of our times, such as between father's socioeconomic status level and child's educational attainment, are of necessity causal. Fortunately, we are finally obtaining evidence and insight into more fundamental associations and processes than detected by surveys of social class factors alone. We know, for instance, that the upper peninsula of Michigan is composed of many communities of lower socioeconomic status in which the achievement levels of the schools are among the highest in the state and country. The authors are currently doing research to assess differences among other schools which rank among the highest and lowest in achievement levels. We are also examining certain upper-class, all-white, suburban schools which have significantly lower achievement levels than are typical of such schools. Four of the schools we studied were all-black, inner-city schools, where poverty was prevalent. Two of these all-black schools are now among the higher-achieving schools in the state, while ten years ago they were among the lowest. What accounted for their dramatic improvement? At this point, we are not sure. However, we know enough to know that the climates afforded by schools and their communities are very important. We will discuss this in more detail in subsequent chapters. We also know that fundamental beliefs about the educability of children must be changed in order to change the children's conceptions of themselves.

Recently, we conducted a series of experiments[72] for working with parents to help them change their conceptions of their children and to help them modify their children's conceptions of themselves. These experimental studies were designed to test specific strategies for enhancing low-achieving students' self-concept of academic ability and thereby result in an increase in academic achievement. One experiment, a counseling experiment, was designed to counteract the effects of parents who held low expectations and evaluations for their children by having the counselor provide assessments of adequacy and competance for the students. A second experiment, also designed to counteract the effects of parents who held low expectations and evaluations for their children, involved the use of "experts" from a university to meet regularly with students to communicate to the students that they were able to achieve at higher levels in school. Our third experiment had two phases to it, each involving a different method of working directly with parents. One parent treatment program was based on a "nondirective approach" in

---

[72] Brookover et al., *Self-Concept of Ability and School Achievement* II (1965).

which the parents discussed their problems with the school as they pictured the situation. The second parent treatment program began by placing the responsibility for their children's failure or success in school in the parents' hands.

Unfortunately, three of the programs were unsuccessful in modifying students' self-concept of academic ability or achievement levels. The counseling program, the "expert" approach and the "nondirective," personal-problem-oriented, parent program all failed to attain their objectives. We should, perhaps, point out that there were a few unintended successes. For one, the counselor program resulted in some long-term relationships between counselor and students which helped the students when they later experienced psychological and social difficulties. Their achievement in school, however, was not improved nor were their academic self-conceptions. No discernible effects in any area could be attributed to the university "experts" working directly with students. The nondirective parent program did have a few positive consequences. A more favorable attitude toward school in general and toward teachers, counselors, and administrators in particular was attained. Secondly, these parents became more interested in school problems. Parenthetically, two of these parents entered school politics and ran for board of education positions as a result of their involvement in the experimental program. However, in spite of the parents' newly acquired positive attitudes toward education, the children continued their failing performances in school and retained their low self-conceptions of ability.

In the one experiment, in which the parents and students altered their conceptions and the students enhanced their achievement levels, the parents were initially made hostile toward the experimenters. Perhaps this was due to the fact that during the first two meetings, which were held monthly for an entire school year, information was presented to them that they were the ones who were most responsible for their child's past failing performance levels, that teaching deficiencies could be overcome by them. Perhaps the success of the program lies in the fact that the parents were given a set of rules and procedures and taught how to implement them in working with their children. The parents were told not to reward any negative statements their children might make about their academic ability. They were told to avoid even such statements as "I wasn't good in reading either." The children were to be told often and regularly in as subtle a fashion as possible that they were academically able and ought to do better in school. Any positive statement of ability or achievement, no matter how small, was to be rewarded with commendatory remarks, tokens, or prizes. The parents were told to expect that small gains would occur and to make increasingly higher demands on the student. Negative behavior or low achievement was to be overtly ignored. The feedback to the parents was an increasing level of performance on the part of their children and a sense that they were responsible for their children's new accomplishments. Needless to say, the parents became less and less hostile toward the experimenters, and showed greater and greater appreciation.

One very interesting feature of our parental experiments was that, as far as could be determined by the investigators, neither the students nor their teachers were aware that an experiment was being conducted. The parents were told to avoid letting their children know that they were being talked about. The parents, as far as their children were apparently concerned, were merely at the university to discuss school-community problems.

The implications of these experiments and several replications by independent researchers are several. Most importantly, they show that simply being aware of a need to change things and the enthusiasm to work at modifying one's world is not sufficient. There have been many compensatory programs, for example, which have failed to attain their objectives. But some have been successful, and it would be absurd to indict the idea of creating more effective schools simply because most programs have failed.

Many so-called new programs are not new at all. They are merely more of the same. If we are to move ahead to attain higher levels of performance, then it is necessary that the few successful programs be analyzed very carefully. Strategies must be developed for working not only with students, but with their teachers, parents, and community as well.

Suggested Readings

Sarane S. Boocock, *An Introduction to the Sociology of Learning* (Boston: Houghton-Mifflin Co., 1972).

Wilbur B. Brookover and Edsel Erickson, *Society, Schools and Learning* (East Lansing, Mich.: Michigan State University Press, 1973).

Wilbur B. Brookover, Shailer Thomas, and Ann Paterson, "Self-Concept of Ability and School Achievement," *Sociology of Education,* 37, no. 5 (Spring 1964).

Seymour Epstein, "The Self-Concept Revisited: Or a Theory of a Theory," *American Psychologist,* 28, no. 5 (May 1973).

Chad Gordon and Kenneth J. Gergen, *The Self in Social Interaction* (New York: John Wiley & Sons, 1963).

David W. Johnson, *The Social Psychology of Education* (New York: Holt, Rinehart and Winston, 1970).

Alan C. Kerchoff, *Socialization and Social Class* (Englewood Cliffs, N.J.: Prentice-Hall, 1972).

William W. Purkey, *Self Concept and Achievement* (Englewood Cliffs, N.J.: Prentice-Hall, 1970).

Darwin L. Thomas, David D. Franks, and James M. Calonico, "Role-Taking and Power in Social Psychology," *American Sociological Review,* 37, no. 5 (October 1972).

Shailer Thomas, Wilbur B. Brookover, Jean M. LePere, Don E. Hamachek, and Edsel Erickson, "An Experiment to Modify Self-Concept and School Performance," *Sociological Focus on Education,* 3, no. 1 (Autumn 1969).

12

Significant Others and Learning[*]

We do not learn directly from such abstractions as *society* or *culture.* Rather, each of us learns his culture from particular groups and persons. If each of us has a unique set of experiences with others, each of us is bound to be unique in outlook and behavior. Conversely, if each of us shares experiences with others, each is likely to be similar to others in outlook and behavior. Hence, to understand the unique and common characteristics of students involves a knowledge of the groups and persons with whom students interact.

The Importance of Grouping

In this chapter, we shall turn our attention to those persons and groups most likely to affect the behavior of students: significant others and reference groups.

Ascribed and Achieved Membership

One way of classifying groups is by distinguishing between ascribed and achieved or voluntary groups. Membership in ascribed groups is not by choice of the members. An ascribed group is best illustrated by age and sex groups. All females in a given society are ascribed members of a broad category of persons simply because they are female.

[*] This chapter draws heavily on "Group Norms and Expectations," Chapter 4 in *Schools, Society and Learning* (East Lansing, Michigan: Michigan State University Press, 1973), by the same authors.

Likewise, identification as a male ascribes a person to another category or group.[1] The conception of these ascribed statuses may of course change from time to time.

Although not as sharply defined, age is also a basis for ascribed group membership, particularly in our schools. The exact time at which we cease to be a child and become an adolescent or cease to be an adolescent and become an adult is not precisely identified. However, in our schools we often have very clearly established standards of behavior and attitude which are expected on the basis of year and month of birth. Intelligence tests, standardized achievement tests and even personality tests are often interpreted on the basis of age norms. We often specify age as the main criterion for entry into school and for assessing mental ability. Individuals are often assessed as slow, normal, or gifted on the basis of their age in reference to their peers. Even with the advent of so-called nongraded schools, age is unlikely to become less than a very important basis for identifying and grouping individuals in school.

On a broader, more general level, age is also implied in such concepts as "generation gap" and "adolescent culture." Later in this chapter we will challenge some of the implications associated with reference to "adolescent subcultures." Certainly, adolescent groups are not of the same kinds of structure as are other subcultures, such as the Amish.

In addition to grouping students on the basis of their age, sex, and other physical and assumed mental properties, we have also emphasized the fact that educators group students on the basis of class, ethnicity, race, previous schools attended, and parents' educational level. Further, we group others and we group ourselves on the basis of perceived idiosyncracies. We group on the basis of what we believe to be unique interests, talents, and proximity. Grouping and living in groups are essential acts of human existence. Sociologists, in studying this grouping phenomenon, have developed a number of concepts, such as *reference group,* to describe the processes by which we come to characterize ourselves in terms of others. These concepts contribute significantly to an understanding of the educational process.

Reference Groups

There have been two ways in which the concept of reference groups has been used.[2] One refers to those groups which provide us with our values and beliefs. The other refers to those groups which provide us

[1] See Richard Dewey and W. J. Humber, *An Introduction to Social Psychology* (New York: The Macmillan Company, 1966), pp. 104–121, for an analysis of groups and significant others.

[2] Robert Merton, *Social Theory and Social Structure* (Glencoe, Illinois: The Free Press, 1957), pp. 253–54.

with standards with which to compare our own characteristics and attainments; i.e., comparison groups. Although a given group may serve both of these functions, individuals nearly always take the standard of some particular group by which to evaluate or judge themselves. An individual, for example, may adopt a group's criterion as to what is handsome or beautiful in assessing his or her own handsomeness or beauty. A group whose standard the individual adopts is one of the individual's reference groups.[3] A group may be both a membership group and a reference group to a particular person, but need not be both, and one can be a member of a group which is not a reference group. The latter case is illustrated by a high school student who is a member of one clique in his or her school but uses the standards of another clique to judge himself or herself. The distinction emphasizes the fact that the persons with whom an individual observably is associated are not necessarily the ones that most strongly affect his or her behavior.

Significant Others

The concept "reference group" is closely related to, although not synonymous with, the concept "significant other." "Significant other" is used in the singular to identify real or imaginary persons who influence our beliefs about ourselves and our world. In this sense, the two concepts have similar meanings, although "reference group" has a group denotation and "significant other" more commonly has an individual connotation.

The relevant reference group or significant other may vary from one situation to another. For example, in the development of students' occupational aspirations, the parents may be the ones the perceived expectations and evaluations of whom are of most concern to the child. In another area of behavior, for example, students' dating partners, schoolmates, or peer groups may be the most significant sources of influence. In some areas of behavior, the expectations of two or more reference groups or significant others may be perceived as equally valid. In such instances, one set of expectations may reinforce the other, but in some situations the expectations may be perceived as incompatible. In the latter case, the person must attempt to resolve the perceived conflict in some manner. Situations in which two or more significant others are perceived to hold incompatible expectations are generally identified as one form of role conflict.[4]

---

[3] G. H. Mead used the concept "generalized other" to refer to the abstract group to which the individual referred for evaluation. This is similar in meaning to the concept reference group. See *Mind, Self and Society* (Chicago: University of Chicago Press, 1934).

[4] See Chapter 6 for a discussion of role conflict.

Adolescent Groups

People do not always make a clear distinction between subsocieties and the social aggregates or groups which make up the subsocieties. The members of one subsociety or stratum frequently perceive other subsocieties as if there were no differentiated groups within that subsociety. Some white persons in the United States, Canada, and Mexico, for example, frequently classify all American Indians as essentially alike. In fact, however, there are many subsocieties or subcultural groups within the broader American Indian population. The Amish in the United States are also frequently perceived as a relatively small, homogeneous subsociety. This is correct in the sense that there are common cultural patterns of behavior among the various Amish communities. In the total Amish subsociety, however, there are many groups or communities that easily can be differentiated in terms of the norms of behavior and the type of religious beliefs which are maintained.[5] An analysis of the behavior and patterns of socialization within the Amish communities would necessitate a recognition of the differences among the numerous Amish groups. Although outsiders may not recognize these differences, the members of the various groups readily distinguish members of one group from those of another by particular behavior patterns and symbols. The symbols frequently involve variations in clothing and language usage.

The distinction between a subsociety and a group is relevant to our discussion at this point, because we have chosen to analyze the school "society" and its attendant cultural patterns as one of several possible student groups. This approach is not in accord with the views of several scholars who have identified adolescents as making up a subsociety with divergent cultural patterns.[6] Others have further subdivided the high-school and college societies into what might be termed "subsubcultures." Such classifications are based on the fact that it is possible to identify differences in values and behavior between the adolescent and adult segments of communities. Although we concur in the differentiation of peer and adult influences, we believe the differences have been somewhat exaggerated. It may be inappropriate to label adolescent groups as representing a subculture. "Subculture" has generally included a means of socializing persons into and maintaining membership in the subculture. The adolescent stage is a transitory stage involving socialization to wider community or subcultural practices and beliefs. The ques-

[5] See John Hostetler, *Amish Society* (Baltimore: Johns Hopkins Press, 1963), for an excellent analysis of the Amish.

[6] Among these is James Coleman, *The Adolescent Society* (New York: The Free Press of Glencoe, 1961); *The Adolescent and the School* (New York: Basic Books, 1965).

tion remains, however: what is it that adolescent and other groups contribute to student socialization?

Identifying Significant Others

Two major questions are relevant: (1) Who are the significant others and reference groups of students? (2) What are the students' perceptions of these significant others and reference groups? That is, what do the students think their reference groups expect of them as students? There is increasing literature designed to answer these questions for the high-school and college age groups in America, but there is very little sound evidence on which to answer such questions concerning younger elementary-age students. This lack of information may result from the assumption that parents are by and large the most significant others for the elementary age group and that teachers function largely as parent surrogates in the elementary classrooms. These may be accurate assumptions, but we are not in a position to verify them with very much sound research evidence.

Much research on the secondary school, and to a lesser extent on the college level, has assumed that students' age-grade peers provide the dominant point of reference for these categories of students. Coleman, for example, assumes that age-grade peers are the dominating source of influence on adolescents.

> This setting-apart of our children in schools—which take on ever more functions, ever more "extracurricular activities"—for an ever longer period of training has a singular impact on the child of high-school age. He is "cut off" from the rest of society, forced inward toward his own age group, made to carry out his whole social life with others his own age. With his fellows, he comes to constitute a small society, one that has most of its important interactions *within* itself, and maintains only a few threads of connection with the outside adult society. In our modern world of mass communication and rapid diffusion of ideas and knowledge, it is hard to realize that separate subcultures can exist right under the very noses of adults—subcultures with languages all their own, with special symbols, and, most importantly, with value systems that may differ from adults.[7]

Coleman here implies that the norms and expectations of the adolescents not only are different from those of adults, but also control the academic behavior of adolescents.

Although the peer group provides a significant portion of social interaction, students also have extensive contacts with other segments of

---

[7] Reprinted from Coleman, *The Adolescent Society*, p. 3, by permission of the Publishers (Copyright 1962, The Free Press of Glencoe).

society through both mass communication and personal face-to-face contacts. In fact, children and adolescents in North American schools probably maintain greater contact with adults, particularly family members, outside the school than do students in those European societies where boarding schools are more common.

In an earlier rural society with limited means of transportation and communication, children and youth of school age interacted with a relatively narrow circle of associates. There was a continuous interaction with parents and siblings, and frequently with other family members, as well as with a small circle of neighbors. In general, the circle of others with whom the student interacted held similar expectations for their behavior. This was also true of the teachers, who usually came from the same community or a similar one nearby. Thus, the child in school had a small circle of interaction with people who held a relatively homogeneous set of expectations. In contemporary industrialized society with its high degree of specialization, the child interacts less continuously with parents, but the child has contact with a much wider circle of adult associates. Such wide interaction may involve people from different groups and subsocieties who hold varying expectations for them. Accordingly, it is not easy to determine which of the several groups and individuals is the more relevant. At times, the age-grade peers may, indeed, be the most relevant referent. In other circumstances, teachers, parents, other adults, or even distant individuals may be the student's guiding influence.

With little foundation on which to base a conclusion, some writers dealing with the adolescent period have assumed that the adolescent peer group is the dominant and perhaps the only significant group affecting the behavior of adolescent boys and girls, regardless of the behavior in question.[8] Numerous studies have shown, however, that not only is it inappropriate to characterize the adolescent period as a subculture,[9] but that family and other adults, in some circumstances, may have influence equal to or greater than the peer group.[10] In societies with an extensive range of interaction such as we have in Canada and the United States, the significant group or persons often varies greatly from one

[8] See Coleman, *Adolescent and the Schools*, particularly Chapter 2.

[9] See for example Oral Callahan and Stanley Robin, "A Social Systems Analysis of Preferred Leadership Role Characteristics in High School," *Sociology of Education*, vol. 42, no. 3 (Summer 1969), pp. 251–60.

[10] Lee Joiner, Edsel L. Erickson, and Wilbur B. Brookover, "Socio-Economic Status and Perceived Expectations as Measures of Family Influence," *Personnel and Guidance Journal* (March 1969), p. 665; Herbert L. Smith and Robert Horton, "The Influence of Family, Peer Groups, Self-Image and the School Subculture," paper read at the Michigan Academy of Arts and Sciences, spring meeting, Ann Arbor, Michigan, 1967; William S. Spady, "Lament for the Letterman: Effects of Peer Status and Extra Curricular Activities on Goals and Attainment," *American Journal of Sociology*, vol. 75, no. 4 (January 1970), pp. 680–702.

situation to another. For example, the adolescent may employ peer group values in his evaluation of himself as a dancer. This same student may also use the standards of his parents or other adults to appraise his performance in algebra or history.

Persons Perceived to Be Important and Concerned

The authors and their colleagues have sought to identify the significant others for academic behavior. For a population of students in junior and senior high schools in a Midwestern city of over 100,000 population partial information on this problem was obtained by asking the students to respond to the following questions each year while in grades eight through 12:

> There are many people who are important in our lives. In the space below, list the NAMES of the people who you feel are important in YOUR life. Please indicate who each person is.

and:

> There are many people who are concerned about how well young people do in school. In the space below, list the NAMES of the people you feel are concerned about how well you do in school. Please indicate who each person is.

These questions were intended to elicit identification of persons who were perceived as generally important to the respondent and also those who were particularly oriented to the area of academic behavior in school. The answers of 561 students who responded to these questions each year, beginning in the eighth grade, are presented in Tables 12–1 and 12–2.[11]

Almost the entire class named parents as being important in their lives and concerned about how well they performed in school throughout their junior and senior high-school years. Although one might question the formulation of the questions used and the assumption that students will give valid answers rather than the expected answers, there is little indication that the age-grade friends of the respondents are the dominant influence. The proportion who named one or more age-grade friends varies somewhat from one year to another, but at no time does it approximate the proportion who named parents in response to either question. This casts some doubt on the assumption that adolescents are the most important influence on students' behavior.

Other investigations of student indications of persons whose judgment they value with regard to clothing, musical interests, and other adoles-

[11] W. B. Brookover, Edsel Erickson, and Lee Joiner, *Concept of Ability and School Achievement III.* Report of Cooperative Research Project 2831, Bureau of Publication Services (East Lansing: Michigan State University, 1967), pp. 107–109.

TABLE 12–1
Percentage of the Same Students at Each Grade Level Who Name at Least One Person in Each of the Following Categories of Significant Others as Being *Important in Their Lives* (Males = 255 and Females = 306)

Categories of Others *"General Significant Others"*	*Sex*	*Grade 8* %	*Grade 9* %	*Grade 10* %	*Grade 11* %	*Grade 12* %
Parent (s)	Males	97	96	96	95	93
	Females	99	98	96	98	98
Age Level Relatives	Males	62	60	46	52	57
	Females	76	75	70	78	75
Adult Relatives	Males	38	40	27	35	31
	Females	55	57	47	53	52
Friends, Same Sex	Males	44	48	26	33	27
	Females	54	68	46	62	53
Friends, Opposite Sex	Males	15	18	14	22	26
	Females	30	32	33	57	25
Local Adults	Males	19	20	15	20	24
	Females	27	32	23	23	16
Teachers in General	Males	38	37	24	20	18
	Females	34	34	12	16	16
Other Academic Persons: (Counselors, coaches, principals)	Males	9	9	6	13	15
	Females	12	6	3	7	7
Unclassified: (e.g., God, famous people, dogs, me, etc.)	Males	28	22	18	25	16
	Females	12	17	13	15	12

TABLE 12–2
Percentage of the Same Students at Each Grade Level Who Name at Least One Person in Each of the Following Categories of Significant Others as Being *Concerned About How Well They Do in School* (Males = 255 and Females = 306)

Categories of Others *"Academic Significant Others"*	*Sex*	*Grade 8* %	*Grade 9* %	*Grade 10* %	*Grade 11* %	*Grade 12* %
Parent (s)	Males	96	97	96	95	96
	Females	99	99	98	98	97
Age Level Relatives	Males	19	30	20	26	29
	Females	24	38	29	42	45
Adult Relatives	Males	30	37	31	29	27
	Females	45	55	41	52	31
Friends, Same Sex	Males	5	8	6	10	11
	Females	11	21	17	30	39
Friends, Opposite Sex	Males	4	7	5	13	21
	Females	4	9	16	31	16
Local Adults	Males	4	5	5	7	10
	Females	6	11	7	14	19
Teachers in General	Males	60	53	44	34	26
	Females	63	50	35	35	29
Other Academic Persons: (Counselors, coaches, principals)	Males	29	27	33	33	18
	Females	37	33	33	33	32
Unclassified: (e.g., God, famous people, dogs, me, etc.)	Males	35	23	24	30	25
	Females	37	30	32	22	25

cent-oriented activities indicate that age-grade friends are somewhat more likely to be named by high-school students when concerned about these types of behavior than are parents. However, the vast majority of students also named parents as significant others in reference to these areas of behavior.

Also, as indicated in Tables 12–1 and 12–2, a large proportion of students identify others in addition to their parents and friends as being generally important in their lives. These findings reflect the considerable range of student interaction with people whom they perceive as important and concerned about their academic performance. Although these findings do not measure the student's reference groups directly, it seems reasonable to conclude that for many secondary school students the family, neighbors, and other adult groups may all contribute to the criteria by which the students determine what is appropriate to learn as well as to assess their competencies to learn. Others have concluded likewise.[12] Certainly there is no reason to conclude that only one person or one reference group is solely responsible for all of a student's perceptions of self as a student.

The student in school not only interacts with a wide range of people, but also functions in numerous roles or statuses in the process of interaction. The roles include those of a son or a daughter, a brother or a sister, a student in a particular grade or school, a child in the neighborhood, a playmate, a boy friend, or a girl friend. The average child, adolescent, or adult student is also a member of various informal cliques or crowds within which he performs particular roles. In addition to the family and student roles, the student may function in various school-related or nonschool groups such as 4H Clubs, Boy or Girl Scouts, college sororities or fraternities, and numerous recreational activity groups. In each of these groups, the child, adolescent, or adult student functions in relation to the expectations which relevant others hold for them in their particular roles. On numerous occasions, more than one group may hold varying expectations for each student. Although the expectations of the parents or spouses for students may take precedence in the student's role as a son, daughter, or spouse, it is clear that the expectations held by other adults and other members of the family are not usually irrelevant for a student's behavior in his or her role as a student. Several people usually hold expectations for the individual as a student in school. The same may be said of almost any role in which a person functions.

The multiple role expectations may require the student to behave in terms of two or more roles at the same time. Thus, the same significant other or reference group may expect the student to be both a good

---

[12] T. Kemper, "Reference Groups, Socialization and Achievement," *American Sociological Review*, vol. 55, no. 1 (January 1968), pp. 31–45.

student and an obedient son or daughter at the same time and in the same kinds of circumstances. At another stage, the parents may expect a son to function as a good student and a good athlete at the same time.

The multiplicity of roles and of persons and groups which hold expectations for the student has led to a considerable discussion of the possible similarities and conflicts in these expectations and the relative importance of each of them. One gets the impression from the literature on adolescence that the expectations of adults and the adolescent peers vary greatly and are frequently in conflict.

We believe the assumed conflict in family and friendship expectations has been extrapolated far beyond sound data. The fact that adolescent norms and behavior can be differentiated to some extent from those of adults has led to presumption that adult expectations are in conflict with the expectations of the adolescent peer group. The adolescent peer group's emphasis on athletics, fun, good personality, and a variety of other behaviors has led to the conclusion that students do not anticipate or expect their peers to perform to certain minimal levels in school, while teachers and parents hold such expectations for them. Evidence does not clearly support the conflict thesis.

It is an oversimplification to speak of either parents, friends, or teachers as having more or less general influence on students' behavior. As stated in the discussion of reference groups, friends may well have more influence on students' dating patterns, while parents may be the most significant others affecting how their children evaluate their career opportunities. The general influence of others on career choices may vary by age of children, ability to communicate, extent of surveillance, and many other factors. For example, the parents of deaf, institutionalized high-school children seem to have less influence on their children's self-concept of academic ability than do parents of non-hearing-impaired children in public schools.[13]

Relative Impact on Self-Evaluations

In order to assess the impact of others' expectations and perceived evaluations on a person's behavior, we should know what these others desire of the student, how they evaluate his or her ability, and how they reward or punish, if they do. Even more important, we should know the student's perceptions of expectations and evaluations of others. If significant others act as if the student is capable of performing in accord with their preferences for him, the student is likely to carry

[13] Lee Joiner and Edsel Erickson, *Scales and Procedures for Assessing Social Psychological Characteristics of Hearing Impaired Students,* USOE Cooperative Research Project No. 6-8720 (Washington, D.C.: U.S. Government Printing Office, 1967).

out their desires. While there is evidence that students' perception of others' expectations and evaluations for self are highly correlated with the actual expectations and evaluations of these others, there is, however, some communication failure. Thus, it is important to remember that individuals behave in terms of what they perceive of others and not solely in terms of the actual expectations and assessments that others hold.

In a recent study of public school students, in grades seven, eight, nine, and ten, it was concluded that the parental evaluations of students' academic ability were more highly related to students' self-conceptions of academic ability than were friends' evaluations of students.[14] In grade 11, the parents and friends seemed to have an equal impact on students' self-concept of ability. In grade 12, the evaluations of friends in contrast to parents were slightly more related to students' self-concept of ability. From grades seven through 12, the impact of parental evaluations on self-concept of ability was greater than that of teacher evaluations. We must be careful, however, in the way in which we interpret these findings. First, no conclusion is warranted that one or the other group has no influence or cannot increase its influence. The evaluations of all three groups, parents, friends, and teachers, accounted for some of the variation in students' self-concept independent of one another. In addition, parents, friends, and teachers often shared the same evaluations of students, so that the importance of one group or another cannot be readily discerned.

Conditions Affecting Influence

Another problem in understanding the relative influence of others' expectations and evaluations on students concerns an adequate assessment of the conditions which modify the impact of these evaluations and expectations.

Parents and Peers

It is quite possible that a parent may communicate to his son that he ought to get Bs in school but, more important, that he ought to make the first string of the varsity football team. Another parent may communicate to his son that he ought to get Bs in school and that getting Bs is more important than anything else he might do in school. In other words, the relative importance that others attach to their expectations of students can influence the impact of those expectations.

[14] Brookover et al., *Self-Concept of Ability and School Achievement* (1967), pp. 107–109.

Another factor which may affect the influence of expectations is the extent to which the individual perceives that others will be aware of whether or not he carries out their expectations. Two sets of parents can both desire that their children receive Bs. They can place equal importance on getting B grades in school, but one set of parents may not have their child's school behavior under close surveillance while the other parents may be much aware of what and how well their child is doing in school. The parents who are more aware of how their child is doing in school are in a position to reinforce through approval or sanction the desired academic behavior.

The comparison of the expectations of parents and friends concerning a particular activity is not likely to provide valid evidence of the relative influence of these groups unless the degree of importance and surveillance attached to the expectations by each are also examined. Parents may tend to prefer certain achievement levels on the part of students which may or may not differ from friends' preferences for students. If they do differ, it is rather "far-fetched" to infer that there is any meaningful-conflict on the part of the student, or that one group's expectations are more relevant than another group's, unless one knows that there are conditions of importance and surveillance attached to these expectations. Importance and surveillance are conditions which tend to obligate the individual to carry out the expectations of others. If others do not place much importance on their desires for the student or are perceived to be unaware of whether or not these desires are met, there is no social obligation to carry out their desires.[15]

Without questioning the fact that peers may exert considerable influence in many areas, the assertion that parents are not an important influence on the academic achievement of students is unfounded. The relationships of students to friends are not as likely to involve obligations for achievement as are their relation to parents. Friends are simply not likely to make a particular level of academic achievement a condition for continued friendship. Parents, on the other hand, are likely to emphasize the importance of achievement at some level, even though it may be only a passing grade.

The absence of extensive conflict in the expectations held by parents and high-school friends is further indicated by a study of tenth graders in a Midwestern city. Only eight out of 942 students in this group reported that parents held high academic achievement expectations while friends held low achievement expectations or vice versa, under conditions in which they felt obligated to fulfill the expectations of both parties. More than one-fourth of these students felt that their parents considered

[15] Ibid., Chap. 9, pp. 191–204; and Edsel Erickson, *A Study of the Normative Influence of Parents and Friends on Academic Achievement,* doctoral dissertation, Michigan State University, 1965.

the expected level of achievement important and kept a close surveillance over them. Less than ten percent felt that their friends placed such conditions of obligation on their achievement expectations. The academic expectations which these students perceived that their parents and friends held for them were similar for all but eight students. Less than one percent of these high school students were faced with academic role conflict between parents and friends in which they felt obligated to perform in accord with different expectations.

Social Class. We have noted the wide range of people who may be significant points of reference with whom the student of every age may interact. The failure of many students to achieve at a high level has led various scholars and educators to suggest that some one group or significant others are responsible for the low achievement. Teachers and professors frequently indicate that lower-class parents have low expectations and aspirations for their children while parents from higher status levels may expect too much from their children. This suggests vast differences in the school achievement expected of school-age children. Although our evidence is meager, we believe that the presumed conflicts and differences have been greatly exaggerated. Most parents at all socioeconomic levels, we believe, desire that their children do well in school. Recent research by Bilby[16] and others has shown that the parents of lower-class children do not desire less for their children. Lower-class parents, however, may not see high academic attainments as a possibility for their children, and therefore do not sanction and reward academic behaviors as much as middle- and upper-class parents. Similarly, we do not believe that most high school adolescents desire their peers to fail or to do poorly in school. Even if it is true that the academic achievements of students are less relevant to friends than to parents, this is hardly a basis for asserting parent-friend conflict.

Language Skills and Self-Concept. Parents clearly have an important role in what their children learn in school. For example, where the language of the school differs from that of the home, Hess and Shipman have demonstrated the obvious: the child does not have the same advantages in learning the different and standard language of the school as do those students who have had school-valued training at home.[17] Even so, the school can, if properly organized and if the expectations and the ability to relate to parents are there, assist parents in helping their

---

[16] Robert W. Bilby et al., "The Rights and Obligations of Students From the Perspectives of the Parents," and John A. Vonk et al., "Characteristics of Parents Who Hold Their Children Under Academic Surveillance." Papers read at the American Educational Research Association meetings, New York, 1971.

[17] Robert Hess and Virginia Shipman, "Early Experience and the Socialization of Cognitive Modes in Children," *Child Development*, vol. 36, no. 4 (December 1965), pp. 869–86.

children. In a recent experiment it was found, for instance, that poor parents, regardless of race, could be involved and taught how to help instruct their children.[18] Experimental research demonstrating that programs have been developed for successfully teaching parents how to positively affect their children's self-concept of academic ability also has been done.[19]

Surveillance. An important part of the social-psychological model for self-concept development is the monitoring we do of others. One focus of this monitoring of others, which is extremely important, is our monitoring of others monitoring us; i.e., our perceptions of their surveillance of ourselves. We are particularly sensitive about the surveillance of those whom we value or who are in a position to provide us with rewards and sanctions. One's surveillance or monitoring of others, of course, is an important condition affecting group behavior.[20] Research has shown that both actual parental surveillance of student performance[21] and students' perception of such surveillance[22] are related to the effects parental achievement expectations have on student achievement.

Stability of Family. There is some research that indicates a relationship between stability of a family—one- or two-parent—to performance in school. Despres found that the presence of one or both parents was related to standard language fluency in school, after controlling for socioeconomic status, race, and type of school curriculum.[23] There is also some evidence of a negative statistical association between one-parent families and dissonant attitudes of students toward teachers and other authority figures.[24]

The position that the one-parent family structure is associated with adverse effects among students is also supported by data obtained on

[18] Edsel L. Erickson, *Experiments in Head Start and Preschool Curriculum Structure.* Final Report, OEO-4150, Office of Economic Opportunity, 1969.

[19] Wilbur B. Brookover, et al., *Self-Concept of Ability and School Achievement,* II. Cooperative Research Project No. 1636 (East Lansing, Michigan: Bureau of Educational Research Services, College of Education, Michigan State University), 1965; and Wilbur B. Brookover and Edsel Erickson, *Society, Schools and Learning* (E. Lansing, Michigan, Michigan State University Press, 1973), pp. 107–113.

[20] See for example Carl Couch, "Dimensions of Association in Collective Behavior Episodes," *Sociometry,* vol. 33, no. 4 (December 1970), pp. 457–71.

[21] John A. Vonk, Edsel L. Erickson and Clifford E. Bryan, "Parental Surveillance as a Variant of Contextual and Social Psychological Conditions." Paper read at the American Educational Research Association meetings, New York, 1971.

[22] Erickson, *Normative Influence of Parents and Friends.*

[23] Ann Despres, "Forecasting Classroom Adjustment: The Utility of Language Adjustment." Master's thesis, Western Michigan University, 1970.

[24] Martha Bullock Lamberts et al., "Family Structure and Rejection of Teacher Authority." Paper read at the Ohio Valley Sociological Association Meetings, Cleveland, Ohio, 1971.

families of schizophrenics,[25] unwed mothers,[26] delinquents,[27] and school dropouts.[28] However, we should be careful before assuming that it is merely the presence or absence of parents that causes the difficulties. Nye and his associates[29] have provided considerable evidence that it is not the presence or absence per se of the parents which is most relevant in many cases. They found that adolescents from broken homes were better adjusted than those from unhappy but intact families. It seems probable that a climate of norms and values are more easily reinforced by two parents than one, given that they are in accord with one another. The dyad—two-parent families—given appropriate and reinforcing personalities, is probably the more favorable situation for providing academic and social monitoring with support and affection than is a single-parent family. A single adult, other things being equal, probably has a tougher task than two adults.

Our point, however, is that many two-parent families are characterized by differences in values and orientations toward child rearing, and sometimes such differences may be reflected in school behavior. Another point is that both one-parent and two-parent families can cripple their children's performance in school in a number of ways. Certainly, anyone who has taught school has experienced many tragic cases which are the result of family conditions. The consequences of such cases do not stop with the student in question. A socially or emotionally disturbed student or teacher, regardless of background causes, can be very disruptive to the total school scene. Inevitably, what goes on in the family affects what goes on in the school.

Involvement. The data of one recent study, while not clearly establishing causal direction, clearly depict an association between parental involvement and the achievement level of the school, after controlling for social status. "For example, almost two-thirds (65 percent) of the highly involved parents had children attending high achieving schools, whereas less than half (39 percent) of the less involved parents had children in high achieving schools. Similarly, the majority of parents who were low in involvement (61 percent) had children in low achieving

[25] Theodore Lidz, Alice R. Cornelison, Stephen Fleck, and Dorothy Terry, "Schism and Skew in the Families of Schizophrenics," in Norman W. Bell and Ezra S. Vogel (eds.), *A Modern Introduction to Family* (New York: The Free Press, 1968), pp. 595–607.

[26] Clark B. Vincent, *Unmarried Mothers* (New York: Free Press of Glencoe, Inc., 1961).

[27] Harry Manuel Shulman, *Juvenile Delinquency in American Society* (New York: Harper and Row, 1961).

[28] Daniel Schreiber, "Drop-Outs—Causes and Consequences," *Encyclopedia of Educational Research,* 4th ed. (New York: Macmillan,1969).

[29] F. Ivan Nye, Joseph B. Perry, Jr., and Richard Ogles, "Anxiety and Antisocial Behavior in Preschool Children,"in F. Ivan Nye and Lois Wladis Hoffman (eds.), *The Employed Mother in America* (Chicago: Rand McNally and Company, 1963).

schools while only about one-third (35 percent) of the highly involved parents had children attending low achieving schools."[30] In other words, parental involvement is associated with the achievement levels of schools.

However, the openness of educational systems to include parents is probably not an important value for many educators, regardless of their rhetoric about local control and parent support. Parent-teacher groups are often shaped and carefully controlled by school administrators. Community and lay involvement in education seems to strike agony into the heart of many an educator. Parents are often informed about their children at very superficial levels and then only days, weeks, or months later—unless, of course, the student's behavior is very disruptive. Whether such an attitude is appropriate to high achievement is a matter of debate. We do know, however, that the openness of schools to parent involvement has been found to be related to the extent to which parents are academically significant others to their children.[31] This finding suggests, in accord with an open systems perspective, that the effectiveness of parents and the effectiveness of schools are each facilitated or impeded by what the other does. Schools can help or hinder parents and vice versa. Neither institution exists apart from the other. To expect changes in one without changes in the other is unrealistic.

This conclusion, however, raises the question of what structural components of school and family are necessary for each institution to facilitate the other. The school can provide sufficiently detached feedback to parents about the nature of their children's school experience so that parents can more appropriately reinforce desired school behaviors and achievements. The school can also communicate to parents positive expectations and evaluations of their children and suggest strategies for parental assistance. However, whatever the school intends to communicate, the effects must be a function of credibility, an attribute not always given to educators.

Teachers' Expectations. The impact of teachers' expectations on students at all levels has been popularized by Rosenthal and Jacobson[32] and supported by numerous other researchers.[33] The results of research generally support the view that students tend to behave in terms of others' expectations and that teacher expectations are associated with

[30] Robert D. Mendelsohn, Wilbur B. Brookover, and Edsel L. Erickson, "Teacher Credibility and Parental Involvement in School Related Activities." Paper read at the American Educational Research Association meeting, Chicago, 1972.

[31] Michael H. Walizer, "Boundary Openness and Interpersonal Outcomes in Schools." Paper read at the Southern Sociological Society, Miami, May 1971.

[32] Robert Rosenthal and Lenore Jacobson, *Pygmalion in the Classroom* (New York: Holt, Rinehart, 1968).

[33] For a review of research see Ray Rist, "Student Social Class and Teacher Expectations," *Harvard Educational Review*, vol. 40 (1970), pp. 441–51.

student achievement. We believe it is reasonable to conclude that the expectations of teachers as well as those of other adults and students affect the student's school performance.

Recent concern with adolescent society and emphasis on individualized instruction have caused some to overlook the norms and expectations held for students by teachers and other adults. Although the adult definitions of appropriate behavior vary somewhat from one school to another and for particular students, some consensus is clearly present. For example, school authorities and teachers generally expect most children to learn basic reading, writing, and arithmetic skills. Although there has been much criticism of the failure of schools to achieve their goals, it is clear that a high proportion of students attain a minimum level of skill in these areas.

In addition to these basic skills, certain aspects of natural science, history of the nation, and various other areas of knowledge are considered important by nearly all teachers and other adults connected with the school. Although schools may differ somewhat on the knowledge students are expected to acquire in each, the teachers do set certain norms of skill and knowledge which they apply to essentially all students at various ages. The frequently expressed concern about a school's inadequacy or failures is generally stated in terms of these norms.

At the upper-grade levels, the teachers and other adults differentiate extensively between the behavior expected of some students and that expected of others. This differentiation occurs to some degree in the early elementary grades, but it becomes more pronounced in the secondary grades when the students are assigned to different curricula. Through the processes of differentiation, the students come to understand that the society, including teachers and other school officials, does not expect the same behavior of all of them. They learn that the school provides alternate patterns of formal learning as the larger society does in other areas of behavior.

A particular alternate curriculum is not required of everybody and the specific areas of knowledge required of students enrolled in a given curriculum may vary considerably from time to time and from student to student. As we have noted earlier, one of the functions of the school is to classify and select students for particular kinds of learning and through this to enable them to assume various positions in society.

The norms of the society and the teacher's expectations reflect this function. Teachers generally feel that it is not appropriate for everyone to learn advanced mathematics and science or senior English, which characterize most college preparatory curricula. Both the teachers and out-of-school adults believe it is quite appropriate for a significant proportion of the students to learn quite different types of knowledge and skills in the secondary school. This differentiation in function is highly valued and the quality of education provided by a school is currently rated, in part, according to the range and variety of curriculum opportunities available. The secondary schools and colleges are seldom, if ever, rated on their success in teaching all students the same knowledge. However, the early elementary school is often judged on its success in teaching all students to read.

In addition to performance in terms of the formal curricula, there are many other types of student behavior that are considered appropriate by adults. Male and female students at all age levels are expected to learn to behave in the appropriate manner for their sex. Many other culturally required behaviors are taught in an informal manner by the teachers in every school. Although such subjects may not be specified in the course schedule, it is not difficult to identify a wide range of behaviors which teachers expect children and adolescents to acquire. We have thought of athletics as a student-valued behavior and we shall recognize it as such in the following section, but athletics are also very much a part of the adult culture in Canada and the United States. Both teachers and other adults continually socialize the students into this athletic complex. It is not surprising, therefore, that various types of athletic behavior have been introduced into the school in both the formal curricula and in extra curricular activities. The emphasis on athletics in the colleges and secondary schools results from community as well as student interest. In this instance, the interests and values of the students and school staff often converge.

However, sometimes overt and latent conflicts between students and school staff lead observers of the school culture to minimize the teachers' effectiveness in socializing students in the areas of behavior which teachers value. In emphasizing these failures, we have sometimes conveyed the impression that teachers' or professors' expectations are irrelevant to students and are ignored by them. Although many older students would not identify teachers as their most significant others, few students fail to understand that certain types of behavior are expected of them, and nearly all acquire a minimum level of the knowledge and skills expected by the staff. Some observers have been so concerned about the norms of the student groups that they have ignored the extent to which students learn to behave as their teachers expect them to. For example, Coleman states: "A shock awaits the adult who makes his first venture into the present day world of adolescence. He finds it populated with jazzed-up autos, athletic stars, and 'the group,' that most powerful agent in a teenager's life, which calls him to go for a ride, or to go down to the snack bar, or just to come and 'hang around.'"[34]

Coleman analyzed the value expectations of the high-school adoles-

[34] Coleman, *Adolescent and the Schools,* pp. 18–19.

cents in parts by identifying what the students considered necessary to get into the leading crowds in the high schools which he studied. He then answered the question, What does it take to get into the leading crowd in these schools?

> According to the adolescents themselves (and we asked all of them this question) it takes a lot of things; but academic success is not one of them. It takes athletic prowess, knowing how to dance, owning a car, having a good reputation, or liking to have fun. It takes being a good date, liking parties, and often not being a prude (for girls) or a sissy (for boys). Good grades and intelligence are mentioned, but not very often and not as often as any of the other items.[35]

In spite of the report that academic success is not valued, Coleman also indicated that all members of the leading crowds in the schools studied were college-bound students. This indicates that high-school students recognize that they must acquire certain kinds of behavior expected by adults, including a degree of competence in the formally prescribed curriculum. The school dropouts and the poorer students who do not learn the prescribed patterns of behavior reasonably well are seldom in the leading crowds. The contest between the students and their professors or teachers may tend to lead the students to minimize the importance of the adult-expected behavior; but the students do not ignore their teachers or professors, for they at least seek to achieve the minimum levels of performance acceptable to them.

It should be recognized also that the types of behavior identified by the students as essential for participating in "leading crowds" are valued by the school staff and community as well. Athletic prowess, dancing, owning a car, having a good reputation, and acceptance by the opposite sex are quite as highly valued in society as they are in student societies.[36] Failure to mention academic achievement may simply reflect the students' desire to avoid emphasizing the behavior constantly demanded by those who control the institution.

However, the norms of the high-school age reference groups do differ in some respects from those of the adult groups. Vocabulary, types of music preferred, clothing styles, and a variety of other activities perceived as appropriate and expected by students at all age levels are in some degree divergent from those of nonstudents. It does not follow, however, that the teacher or professor expectations are irrelevant in the lives of the students. We maintain that students in school and college,

---

[35] Ibid., p. 19.

[36] See for an illustration of the relevance of extra curricular involvement on school achievement and self-concept, William G. Spady, "Status, Achievement and Motivation in the American School," *School Review,* vol. 79, no. 3 (May 1971), pp. 379–96; and Terry Schurr and Wilbur B. Brookover, "Athletics, Self-Concept and Academic Achievement," *Medicine and Science in Sports,* vol. 2, no. 2 (Summer 1970), pp. 96–99.

regardless of age level, learn to behave in terms of the expected behaviors associated with many roles.

Elementary, secondary, and college level students come to behave in terms of the role expectations held by their family, peers, and teachers, as well as many other persons and groups, whose expectations they value as important. The questions asked in some research in this field assume that the values of one group or another must take precedence in their effect on the student. For example, Coleman based much of his analysis of adolescent high school society on forced-choice questions such as this: "If you could be remembered here at school for one of the three things below, which one would you want it to be? Brilliant student; athletic star; most popular."[37] In response to this forced-choice question, 31 percent of the boys said brilliant student, 44 percent said athletic star and 25 percent said most popular.[38] Although a larger proportion of the boys in the high schools studied gave athletic star preference over brilliant student, there is no evidence that they did not value both. Similar questions were asked of students in a large Midwestern school system, but they were given the opportunity to indicate if they would like to be both a good student and a good athlete as well as one or the other. In the three high schools in the system, 87 percent of the boys indicated that they would like to be known both as a good athlete and a good student.[39] Most of these boys do not consider academic success undesirable. Rather, doing well in academic work as well as athletics is valued highly by nearly all high-school boys. They may devalue behavior that emphasizes brilliance to the exclusion of any other kind of activity, for the student who overdisplays his brilliance is identified as a "square." This is further demonstrated by Tannenbaum's study of the acceptability of ascribed traits among high-school students.[40] He asked the students to rate eight different types in order of acceptability with the following results:

1. Brilliant, nonstudious, athlete.
2. Average, nonstudious, athlete.
3. Average, studious, athlete.
4. Brilliant, nonstudious, nonathlete.
5. Brilliant, studious, athlete.
6. Average, nonstudious, nonathlete.
7. Average, studious, nonathlete.
8. Brilliant, studious, nonathlete.

[37] Coleman, *The Adolescent Society.*

[38] Ibid., p. 134.

[39] This was part of a larger study by the authors and associates on *Self-Concept of Ability and School Achievement.* These data were analyzed by Nelson Goud.

[40] Abraham J. Tannenbaum, *Adolescents' Attitudes toward Academic Brilliance.* Unpublished doctoral dissertation, New York University, 1969.

Athletes are rated higher as a whole than nonathletes, but it should also be noted that the brilliant student is rated higher than the average student when described as nonstudious. The nonstudious student is always rated above the studious one with brilliance and athletics controlled. This suggests that the characteristic most disliked is studiousness. We do not know exactly what this implies to high-school students, but it probably suggests a person with a limited range of interests and an exclusive concentration on study. The most acceptable person was the brilliant athlete who was not studious.

The general conclusion derived from these studies is that high-school students value both athletics and good academic performance. They do not, however, like their peers to display their studiousness. Perhaps they would also dislike athletes who displayed their "athleticness" constantly without other characteristics. The norms of the student group include a wide range of behavior. Some are strictly adolescent, but other behaviors valued by students are also valued by teachers and parents. These norms include good academic performance if it is not displayed to the exclusion of the athletics or other activities which the adolescents also value.

Credibility. Closely associated with teachers' or professors' expectations and with positive family involvement in education is the family's assessment of the teacher's credibility.[41] The extent to which teachers at all age levels are perceived as being trustworthy, expert in their views, and having similar value orientations is associated with the way families approach the school, both directly and indirectly, through their children. A tentative inference one may make is that if the schools or colleges desire greater support from student parents or spouses, then they should consider ways of increasing the credibility of teachers to the parents and spouses of students. Based on a review of the research literature, Mendolsohn[42] developed several hypotheses relevant to the development of credibility among college teachers which may also hold for teachers at elementary and secondary levels:

1. Teacher credibility is dependent upon the educational environment; i.e., students and parents will be more likely to attribute credibility to teachers within the school and classroom than anywhere else.
2. Credibility occurs when high status is accorded a source to the extent that the receiver is aware of that status; i.e., families and students who define the teaching profession as high in status are likely to attribute more credibility to teachers than others.
3. Credibility is a function of the receiver's reference group's defini-

[41] Mendelsohn et al., "Teacher Credibility and Parent Involvement."
[42] Ibid.

tions of the source; i.e., parents and students are likely to attribute credibility to the same teachers as do their significant peers.

4. Credibility is a function of the receiver's perceptions of the objectivity of the source; i.e., parents and students who perceive their teachers as impartial are likely to attribute credibility to them.

5. Credibility is a function of the reliability of the source; i.e., the more consistent the teacher is in his role performance, the more likely the parents and students will attribute credibility.

6. Credibility is affected by the personality systems of the source and receiver; i.e., the more a parent or student likes a teacher, the more likely they will attribute credibility to that teacher.

7. Credibility is a function of the degree of "social distance" between the source and the receiver; i.e., the more frequently parents and students have the opportunity to interact informally with a teacher, the more likely they are to attribute credibility to that teacher.

8. Credibility is affected by the uniqueness of the message; i.e., parents and students are more likely to attribute credibility to those teachers who present them with new and unusual ideas.

9. Credibility is a function of period of time during which interaction is maintained between the receiver and the source; i.e., the more courses and/or the longer the time period during which a student has interacted with a teacher, the more likely credibility will be attributed.

10. Credibility is affected by the shared activities which occur between the source and the receiver; i.e., parents and students who work *with* rather than *for* teachers are more likely to attribute credibility to the teacher.

11. Credibility is a function of ideology; i.e., parents and students are more likely to attribute credibility to conservatively oriented teachers if they (parents and students) are conservatively oriented, liberal if parents and students are liberal, etc.

Each of the above hypotheses concerning credibility has relevance for how people come to influence others by providing them with beliefs and attitudes about themselves and their world.

Societal Context. In summary, teacher-student relationships are affected not only by what goes on in the home or school; they are also affected by general role relationships in the society.[43] For example, in a society where black-white institutionalized conflict occurs, "the general (racial) hostility occurring in the social context of the society at large becomes translated into conflict in the classroom."[44] How is this possible? "It is held . . . that a teacher's racial identity is a symbol

[43] See Gordon DeBlaey, "A Comparison of Teacher Role Between Parochial and Public Schools." Doctoral dissertation, Western Michigan University, 1970.

[44] Karen VanWagner, "A Cumulative Effect of Teachers' Racial Identity on Black Students—An Eight Year Study," master's thesis, Western Michigan University, 1972; and Bradley Niles, "Selecting Teachers as Role Models: Differences Between White and Black Students," master's thesis, Western Michigan University, 1972.

which is conveyed to the student; and on this basis of previous cumulated knowledge . . . the student attaches meaning to this symbol of racial identity in his or her present relationship. . . ."[45]

Race, like income level, nationality, and numerous other identities, is a secondary characteristic of individuals; and secondary characteristics affect what is taught and learned by students and teachers alike. For example, as shown in Table 12–3, the way students viewed their white teachers in an urban inner city school is a function of students' race.

TABLE 12–3
Differences between White and Black Elementary Students' Perceptions of White Teachers in an Inner City School*

	Percent	
Students Indicated:	*Black (N = 56)*	*White (N = 154)*
1. Teachers were:		
a. Concerned for Students	9	13
b. Fair	38	64
2. Would ask teachers for help	34	42

* The same pattern was observed when controlling for sex, age, and socioeconomic status.

Source: Bradley Niles, "Selecting Teachers as Role Models: Differences between White and Black Students." Master's Thesis, Western University, 1972.

This is not a one-sided phenomenon. In a study of black and white teachers' evaluations of the same behaviors exhibited by white and black students, race was again found to be a factor. Gottlieb found that white teachers rated the same "deviant" behaviors as more desirable when exhibited by white students than by black students.[46] Black teachers did not devaluate black students as much as did white teachers.

We hope that the condition of teachers' taking into account students' race and students' taking into account teachers' race is disappearing from the scene in European-spawned cultures. But such disappearance will not occur as long as the cultural context of the school instills fear and mistrust among different cultural groups. It is not inevitable that teachers and their students should respond to one another on the basis of such secondary attributes, but they often do. It is a common phenomenon. The tragedy experienced by people every day because of too long or too short hair, the wrong color of skin, the wrong nationality, the wrong race, the school attended, the wrong family name, the wrong sex, the wrong clothes, the wrong address, and so on ad infinitum is played out in nearly every social arena.

[45] VanWagner, "Effect of Teachers' Racial Identity on Black Students."

[46] David Gottlieb, "The View of Negro and White Teachers," *The Sociology of Education,* vol. 27 (Summer 1964), pp. 345–53.

Teachers respond on the basis of their cultural heritage and so do students and parents. The mythology of the culture inevitably affects what is taught, how it is taught, and what is learned in school.

Suggested Readings

Robert E. Cleary, "The Agents of Political Socialization," Chapter 5 in *Political Education in the American Democracy,* (Scranton, Pa.: Intext Educational Publishers, 1971).

June A. Hamblin and Robert L. Hamblin, "On Teaching Disadvantaged Preschoolers to Read: A Successful Experiment," *American Educational Research Journal,* vol. 9, no. 2 (Spring 1972), pp. 209–12. An interesting experiment involving students in the reward structures to teach reading.

Ronald W. Henderson and Angela B. Garcia, "The Effects of Parent Training Program on the Question-Asking Behavior of Mexican-American Children," *American Educational Research Journal,* vol. 10, no. 3 (Summer, 1973), pp. 193–201.

David C. Hughes, "An Experimental Investigation of the Effects of Pupil Responding and Teacher Reacting on Pupil Achievement," *American Educational Research Journal,* vol. 10, no. 1 (Winter 1973), pp. 21–37. Presents evidence that regular positive teacher reactions to pupil responses facilitate student achievement.

T. D. Kemper, "Reference Groups, Socialization and Achievement," *American Sociological Review,* vol. 33 (January 1968), pp. 31–45.

F. Musgrove, *The Family, Education and Society* (London: Routledge and Kegan Paul, 1966). Chapters 1 and 2 of this book provide an interesting discussion of the changing role of parents, substituting influence for power.

T. M. Newcomb, "Attitude Development as a Function of Reference Groups," in Proshankey and Seidenberg (eds.), *Basic Studies in Social Psychology* (New York: Holt, Rinehart and Winston, 1965), pp. 215–25.

Kenneth Polk and Walter Schafer (eds.), *Schools and Delinquency* (Englewood Cliffs, N.J.: Prentice-Hall, 1972). An excellent set of readings showing how the allocation and labeling processes engaged in by teachers and students affect achievement and deviancy.

M. C. Sherif and C. Sherif, *Reference Groups: Explorations into Conformity and Deviation of Adolescents* (New York: Harper and Row, 1964).

Frederick Williams, Jack L. Whitehead, and Leslie Miller, "Relations between Language Attitudes and Teacher Expectancy," *American Educational Research Journal,* vol. 9, no. 2 (Spring 1972).

13

School Social Organization and Learning

WITHOUT any clues in advance as to its identity, most people would recognize the social organization of almost any school and correctly identify it as a school. Although schools have many organizational characteristics in common, they also differ in the way in which the various positions or statuses are defined and the interrelations among the various positions. In some schools teachers function as counselors, while in other schools the counselors teach; in still others the counselors do not teach and the teachers do not counsel. The duties or activities of the teacher can be organized and divided into almost infinite varieties of roles. Teaching aides in some schools are given direct teaching responsibilities and function much like regular classroom teachers. In other schools, teachers aides may run errands, collect milk money, take attendance, and engage in a variety of other nonteaching activities. Similarly, in some schools students are expected to assume some teaching responsibilities, while in others any student cooperation may be condemned as cheating. Some schools and classrooms are characterized by strictly ordered procedures or patterns of interaction, while in others students may move about freely and at their own direction. In this chapter we want to examine the extent to which variations in the way schools are organized affect the outcomes or learning of students within the school.

In the following chapter we analyze the relation of the school climate to the outcomes in cognitive achievement and other types of student behavior. The effect of norms, expectations, and related cultural characteristics of the school, which we have identified as climate, are not always separated from the effect of various structural characteristics of the schools such as those identified in this chapter. The climate of the school may be in part at least a function of the organization. For example, the norms of academic achievement may vary with patterns of interaction between children of more highly educated and less educated parents as determined by the schools' integrated or segregated structure. Although we have sought to distinguish between the two sets of variables in our analysis, this and the following chapter should be viewed as complementary to each other.

In addition to the interrelations among the various positions or statuses in the social system of the school, as in other organizations, there is a system of authority and the distribution of rewards for functioning in an appropriate manner within the organization. Each of the various status-roles are related to others in some hierarchy of power and authority through which much of the material as well as social rewards are distributed. This stratified order includes not only the administrative hierarchy, but also definitions of differential status and power among teachers and the positions of students within the system as well. As noted in a previous chapter, rewards and power are differentially allocated to students on the basis of age, type of program in which enrolled, sex, and a variety of other attributes.

In the previous chapters we have examined the interactionist theory of school learning and noted the importance of the groups of persons with whom the student interacts in defining his self and the expectations for him. The nature of the formal organization is relevant in defining the arena of interaction for many students. The closed, self-contained classroom provides a quite different arena of interaction from that of the open classroom. The segregated black school or white school provides a range of possible interaction considerably different from that available in a school in which students, black and white, are mixed. The interactions with teachers are potentially quite different in a teaching team organization and in a single-teacher classroom. It is therefore possible that the organization of the school social system encompasses crucial factors both in defining the goals of the school and in affecting the behavior that is learned in the arena of interaction.

Organizational Variation in Contemporary Schools

We previously examined the relation of some organizational variations in schools to the stratification and allocation processes in society. We have also examined some aspects of the organization of school management and the social control of schools. In each of these, we have touched on some aspects of the relation to school outcomes. In none, however, have we examined the outcomes of the various types of school organization proposed and established to enhance learning or for other reasons.

Americans often think that there is consensus concerning the learning anticipated in any type of school organization, but different forms of organization often are proposed to achieve different goals and not merely as new ways to achieve the same objectives. The differing philosophies of school organization also involve differing assumptions about the nature of learning, successful techniques of teaching, and the rights and obligations of teachers and students.

Each school program which has been advocated in recent years has carried with it a distinct philosophy of education and assumptions about the nature of man and learning. Some programs deemphasize the importance of teaching academic subjects to children; others place considerable stress on the mastery of certain intellectual skills. These programs also implicitly differ with regard to the conception of what society should be like. Some school programs, for example, have proposed to maintain a given system of eliteness based on family and class affiliations. Others are designed to grant greater power to the masses. Some programs are designed to gain acceptance for retarded children, while other programs have as their objective the eradication of retardation. Some programs are designed to cool out parents and students from a sense of failure in school, while others place active responsibility on the parents. The list of objectives, often unstated, for the many school programs and organizations offered is extensive; it is nearly as extensive as the many competing social philosophies that exist in the larger society.

These differences in assumptions about man and society and differences in beliefs about children provide bases for debate and conflict over the school and its organization. In the recent years there have been many modifications of school organization and programs presumably designed to affect the outcomes. In fact the contemporary style in American education is to experiment with various types of school organization. These involve preschool programs, whether or not to have a comprehensive school (with or without a tracking system) or a separate vocational school or career center. These various modifications are seriously contested among educators and their publics.

This interest in types of experimental school organization is not a new phenomenon. More than a half a century ago, educators developed a junior-high-school organization. In this innovation they used some arguments that are now being used to condemn the junior-high-school organization and to advocate middle school organization. Similarily, we abandoned the one-room school on the basis that it was much more effective to have children in a single age level taught by a single teacher. Advocates of a return to the multigrade level organization are promoting the return to essentially the same type of classroom organization that existed in the one-room primary school. In the decade of the 20s and the 30s many American cities established separate vocational high schools. Subsequently, nearly all of these vocational high schools were abandoned only to see a revival of a similar model in the 70s under somewhat different nomenclature, such as career centers. Many of these organizational changes have been made with little or no systematic evaluation of the differences in outcome, if any, resulting from the organizational variations. This practice of making collective decisions without careful prior assessment continues, and many are currently advocating separate vocational career education on the assumption that such organizational systems and programs will prevent dropouts and alienation from the school. There is little if any evidence to support such claims.

It is impossible at this time to examine all of the detailed variations in elementary, secondary, or college organization in relation to student outcomes. There are few or no data on the outcomes of many types of organizations, and the variety is too great for analysis here. Below, however, we will examine to a limited extent the relation of types of organization to learning. We will examine the impact of segregated versus integrated schools, the various types of homogeneous and heterogeneous groupings as well as the related nongraded schools and tracking, the contemporary middle school organization and team teaching in contrast to junior-high-school and single-teacher classrooms. Recent assessments of the outcomes of "open" versus more traditional school organization will be reviewed. In many cases research has not been done and there are wide differences in goals for various types of organization. We will, however, try to examine academic achievement outcomes as well as noncognitive kinds of student behavior. Where possible we will assess the effects of students' perceptions of themselves and of their relations with other people as well as the extent to which the school organization may be productive of favorable attitudes toward education or of alienation from the school and society. In the following examination of variations in school organizations we will assess the extent to which they may or may not achieve their stated objectives and we will appraise their impact on academic achievement and other aspects of student learning.

Learning in Various Organizational Models

The crucial test of the value of various organizational models in education is the effect that such organization may have on the student's learning. Various types of school organizations in contemporary schools have generally been advocated on the basis that they will make some difference in the outcomes of the educational process. Although there is much variation in the exact outcomes desired from the school, most agree that children should acquire certain cognitive skills and knowledge of the world around them. In recent years a number of scholars have examined the outcome of school organization in terms of the student's integration into the school and the larger society. But Green, for example, builds a very strong case that schools are not focused on educating students, but rather on certifying, sorting, and selecting in such a manner that it interferes with effective teaching.[1] He maintains that many schools do not exist to teach students to comprehend themselves and their society and to prepare for life work roles. As a consequence of the certifying and selecting and sorting phenomena to which we referred in an earlier chapter, students become alienated from school. Thus one of the outcomes of education may be continual hostility toward school and alienation from both the school and the larger society. Some observers maintain that students thus come to value credentials and grades that are emphasized in the school rather than learning about themselves and their world.[2]

Another set of outcomes that has been emphasized in recent years is the effect of the school on the student's feelings about himself and on his efficacy in functioning in the society about him. The relation of the school to the student's self-esteem or other aspects of his self-assessment has been the subject of much research and discussion.[3] The demonstrated relationship between self-concept and student's sense of control to school academic achievement has led to much examination of the relation of school organization to these outcomes as well as the more traditional cognitive skills and knowledge.

It is important to recognize that school organizations may be advocated for reasons quite different from the presumed effect on children's learning. As we have noted, schools function to maintain the stratification system in the society and allocate students to various statuses and positions in the society. Organizations having these consequences may also affect the types of behavior children learn, incidental to the primary function of social allocation. Other types of school organization may be designed primarily for the convenience and satisfaction of the teachers, the administrators, or the parents rather than for the effect on children's learning. All these differences in objectives tend to complicate and confuse the analysis of the relationship of the school organization to student learning.

---

[1] Thomas F. Green, *Work, Leisure and the American School* (New York: Random House, 1968), pp. 147–56.

[2] Edgar Friedenberg et al., *Influence of Ressentiment on Student Experience in Secondary Schools.* Cooperative Research Project 1788, Brooklyn College, New York, 1968.

[3] Grace Gist Henderson, "An Analysis of Self-Concept of Academic Ability as Related to Social-Psychological Variables Comprising School Climate in White and Black Elementary Children within Different School Settings" (Ph.D. dissertation, Michigan State University, 1973). Gives a comprehensive review of the literature on the school and student self-concept of ability.

Segregated versus Integrated Schools

No question regarding school organization is of more concern to Americans in this period than the question of segregation versus integration of school populations. As we noted in Chapters 5 and 6, large proportions of American students are segregated by race, socioeconomic status, and ethnic or religious origin. It is clearly demonstrated by a large variety of studies that students in segregated black, lower socioeconomic status, Puerto Rican, or chicano schools achieve at significantly lower levels than students in white middle-class schools. There is further evidence that academic achievement of poor and black students is somewhat higher in desegregated schools with predominantly white students than in segregated schools.[4]

Although the difference in academic achievement between racially segregated or socioeconomically segregated schools is very clear, it is still difficult to identify the causal factors involved in producing these differences. The family and the neighborhood social background of the students as well are inextricably interrelated with the effect of the school environment on the students' performance. Furthermore, the various aspects of the school environment are difficult to isolate. As we shall note in the following chapter, the school climate or social norms are intimately associated with composition of the school and, thus, with its organization as a segregated or desegregated school. The effect of school segregation/integration on outcomes is summarized by Mayeske as follows:

> The influence of the school is bound up with the social background of the students that they get initially. Very little influence of the school can be separated from the social background of the students, and very little of the influence of social background can be separated from the influence of the schools. The schools as they are currently constituted produce more learning and foster greater motivation when they have a high proportion of students who: (1) come from the higher social economic strata rather than from the lower social economic strata; (2) have both parents in the home rather than only one or neither parent in the home; (3) are white or oriental-American rather than Mexican-American, Puerto-Rican or Negro.[5]

[4] James Coleman et al., *Equality of Educational Opportunity* (Washington, D.C.: Government Printing Office, 1966); and Thomas Pettigrew, "The Case for the Racial Integration of the Schools," in Edgar A. Schuler, Thomas Ford Hoult, Duane L. Gibson, and Wilbur B. Brookover, *Readings in Sociology* (New York: Thomas Y. Crowell Company, 1974).

[5] George Mayeske et al., *A Study of Our Nation's Schools*, mimeographed (Washington, D.C.: Office of Education, U.S. Department of Health, Education and Welfare, 1969).

The composition of the school as well as the family background of the students is thus clearly related to the segregated organization of the schools, and at this point we are not in the position to separate adequately the effect of these factors on the student's performance. Studies of students who have moved from segregated to desegregated schools indicate that the achievement of black students generally improves while the white students either improve or remain the same.[6]

The effect of segregated parochial school on school achievement has been the subject of some research. In a study of the education of Catholic Americans, Greeley and Rossi sought to determine whether the commonly held assumption that Catholic education led to lowered levels of educational and occupational achievement were true. "Exactly the contrary finding emerged; Catholics who went to Catholic schools were more successful than Catholics who did not. Even though the association was rather weak, it stubbornly persisted in the face of a battery of controls. In fact, the association became stronger for those respondents who themselves had more education and made higher scores on the general knowledge index."[7] This finding is based upon the portion of students going on to college and their subsequent occupational index rather than upon standardized tests of school achievement. But it suggests that contrary to some assumptions the academic outcomes of students attending Catholic schools are not inferior to the outcomes of Catholic students attending integrated schools.

The relation of segregated-integrated organization to other educational outcomes is difficult to isolate from other aspects of the school environment. An analysis of the data from the Equality of Educational Opportunity study indicated that black students' self-concepts were higher in segregated schools than in desegregated ones. There were no significant differences in self-concepts between white students in segregated and desegregated schools.[8] Studies also indicate that black students in upper elementary grades have somewhat higher self-concepts of academic ability than white students in predominantly white schools when the socioeconomic status of the schools is controlled.[9] These differences in self-concept between blacks and whites in segregated schools and between blacks in integrated and segregated schools is in contrast to the differences in the sense of control of the black students in school situations. Coleman found that blacks in racially mixed schools felt that they had more control over their school success than similar students in segregated schools.

[6] Pettigrew, "Case for Racial Integration of Schools."

[7] Andrew Greeley and Peter Rossi, *The Education of Catholic Americans* (Chicago 1968), pp. 147–56.

[8] Coleman et al., *Equality of Educational Opportunity.*

[9] G. Henderson, "An Analysis of Self-Concept of Academic Ability."

Another study of elementary students in predominantly black and predominantly white schools indicate that the black student's sense of control is decidedly lower than that of the white students.[10] Although other aspects of the school environment may be relevant to this area, the data suggest that a segregated school organization has an unfavorable impact on black students' sense of control of their environment. To the extent that this is true, it may account for the lower level of achievement in these schools.

There is little evidence concerning the impact of segregated schools on the possible alienation of the students from both the school and the society in general. Greeley and Rossi found, "Catholic school Catholics are just as likely to be interested in community affairs, have non-Catholic visitors, neighbors and co-workers as are public school Catholics. However, Catholics who had a 'mixed' educational experience are more likely to have non-Catholic friends and to be involved in community affairs than either of the other two groups—though the difference is minor."[11] This suggests that attendance at Catholic schools does not isolate Catholics from other people in their community and may indicate that students in Catholic schools are less alienated than their peers in integrated schools. Although we have no similar data for racially segregated and integrated education, there is some indication that students in black segregated schools are more likely to drop out and not continue into higher levels of education than are black students in integrated schools. This may or may not indicate alienation from the school, however.

The effect of segregation and integration on the outcomes of school vary with the particular type of segregation involved. A comprehensive study of the effect of such variation in organization with other factors controlled has not been done. Our conclusions, therefore, concerning the effect that this aspect of school organization per se has on the outcomes of education cannot be conclusive.

The Learning in Tracks and Ability Groups

In most American schools and other Western countries, students are classified and placed in some type of differentiated tracks or groups based upon some assumed differences in learning ability, interests, or

---

[10] Ronald Henderson, "A Comparative Analysis of Social-Psychological School Climate Variables in White and Black Elementary Schools with Socio-Economic Status and Achievement Controlled" Ph.D. dissertation, unpublished, East Lansing, Michigan State University, 1972; and Wilbur B. Brookover, Richard Gigliott, Ronald Henderson, and Jeffrey Schneider, *Elementary School Social Environments and School Achievement,* College for Urban Development, Michigan State University, East Lansing, 1973.

[11] Greeley and Rossi, *Education of Catholic Americans,* pp. 136–37.

aspirations. Although the organizations commonly identified as tracking and as homogeneous in ability grouping have many similarities, a distinction can be made between these two types of organizations. Generally speaking, tracking refers to the arrangements in which students are placed in different curricula with somewhat different long-term goals for their learning. These are illustrated by what is commonly called college-bound and non-college-bound curricula in American secondary schools. Another illustration of tracking is the assignment of students to different types of mathematics at the junior-high-school level so that some students may take algebra while others are enrolled in a "general math" course of some sort. We thus have the algebra track mathematics and the non-algebra-track mathematics. These frequently are associated with the college-bound and the non-college-bound track in the high school. Similar patterns are identified as streaming in British schools. The decision concerning the choice of tracks is commonly based upon some prior measure of achievement or presumed differences in aptitude. But the tracks are distinguished by the fact that the outcomes intended for each group are quite different. Although the non-algebra-track student may have some exposure to elementary algebraic concepts, there is no intent of having him or her achieve competence in algebra.

In contrast to tracking is the widespread classification and assignment of students to different ability groups within the same general curriculum. This type of organization generally begins in the early elementary schools and frequently continues throughout the educational career. It is illustrated by the various reading groups that are common in early elementary grades. Assignment is frequently based upon the presumed level of reading skill at a particular time. The goal in all groups, however, is to have the child learn to read. There may be great differences in the time and period at which reading skill is expected to occur, but the goal for all students is similar, if not essentially the same.

The differences between tracking and grouping make evaluation of the effectiveness of the two types of organizations quite different. In the case of grouping, the intention of producing similar kinds of learning makes it relatively convenient to compare the outcomes of "homogeneously" grouped students and "heterogeneously" grouped students. Since the purpose of tracking, however, is to produce different kinds of learning in the different tracks, it is not appropriate to examine the effectiveness of the tracking organization by comparison of the outcomes in the same areas of learning. As a consequence of this difference there have been many studies of the effect of homogeneous grouping on learning outcomes but few comparing the outcomes of nontracking and tracking systems. The effect of tracking organization on school learning must be assessed in other ways.

One of the few general evaluations of the relative achievement of students in schools that are highly tracked grows out of an analysis of the Equality of Educational Opportunity data. Smith's reanalysis of these data indicated that students in schools in which the teachers reported that a high proportion of the student body were in the academic or college-bound tracks had significantly higher achievement than students in schools with lower proportion reported in such tracks when family, socioeconomic-status, and other school variables were controlled.[12] These data indicate that the organization of schools into several tracks with a high proportion of the students in the lower or nonacademic track tends to reduce the level of achievement in the type of cognitive skills and knowledge measured in the Equality of Opportunity study. As we shall note in the following chapter, this may not be the direct result of the organizational scheme, but rather of school climate or norms that tend to be associated with school organization.

It must be recognized, however, that such differences in academic outcome are clearly intended and it would be quite surprising if the differences in organization in the different curricula tracks did not affect the learning that occurred in the school.

The tracking organization is based upon the assumption that the school should provide the training specifically oriented to different kinds of occupational roles and that some students do not have the necessary qualities to acquire the academic skills and knowledge. As a result of these assumptions, attempts are made to identify the genetically talented children and provide them with high levels of academic training. Those who are not deemed to be intellectually superior are then assigned to various kinds of vocational programs in agricultural commercial, and industrial skills, or a non-college-oriented general program. Many schools diagnose the students' performance early in their school career, generally at the end of the sixth grade, and place them in three or more levels or tracks such as: (1) college-bound with a strong emphasis upon academics; (2) general, with less emphasis upon academics; (3) a basic track which has the least emphasis upon academics and most emphasis on vocational skills and social adjustments. In a separate school or a distinctly separate portion of the comprehensive school, a fourth kind of track may be identified for the mentally retarded.

We have noted in Chapters 5 and 6 that the assignment to tracks is highly correlated with the social class and racial background of the students and that one of the—perhaps unintended—consequences is to maintain the social class system through this differentiated tracking organization of the school.

Analysis of the tracking practices in two Midwestern school systems demonstrates the function of tracking in the maintenance of socioeco-

---

[12] Marshall Smith, in Daniel Moynihan and Frederick Mostellar, *On Equality of Educational Opportunity,* (New York: Vantage Books, 1972).

nomic differences.[13] Kariger found that the student's socioeconomic status level was an important determinant of class placement over and above that accounted for by his school achievement level. The data shown in Table 13–1 indicate that only 47 percent of the lower-class

TABLE 13–1
Students Eligible by Achievement Level for Upper Track and Their Placement

Socioeconomic Level	*Number Qualified for Top Track N*	*Qualified for Top Track and Placed in Top Track, Percent*	*Error of Placement, Percent*
Upper Class	333	80	20
Middle Class	894	65	35
Lower Class	408	47	53

Sources: Unpublished study by Wilbur B. Brookover, D. J. Leu, and R. H. Kariger, "Tracking," mimeographed, (1965); and R. H. Kariger. "The Relationship of Lane Grouping to the Socioeconomic Status of the Parents of Seventh-Grade Pupils in Three Junior High Schools" (doctoral dissertation, Michigan State University, 1962).

students who were qualified, by virtue of their achievement test scores for placement in the upper or academic track, were placed there. Students from the upper third of the socioeconomic strata who were qualified for the top track were placed there in 80 percent of the cases. As indicated in Table 13–2, only two percent of the upper-class students

TABLE 13–2
Students Eligible by Achievement Level for Lower Track and Their Placement

Socioeconomic Level	*Number Qualified for Low Track N*	*Qualified for Low Track and Placed in Low Track, Percent*	*Error of Placement, Percent*
Upper Class	22	2	98
Middle Class	187	63	35
Lower Class	283	85	15

Sources: Unpublished study by Wilbur B. Brookover, D. J. Leu, and R. H. Kariger, "Tracking," mimeographed (1965); and R. H. Kariger, "The Relationship of Lane Grouping to the Socio-Economic Status of the Parents of Seventh Grade Pupils in Three Junior High Schools (doctoral dissertation, Michigan State University, 1962).

whose test scores qualified them for the lower track were placed in that track, while 85 percent of the lower-class students with similar

[13] Roger Hugh Kariger, "The Relation of Lane Grouping to the Socio-Economic status of Parents in Three Junior High Schools." Doctoral dissertation, Michigan State University, East Lansing, 1962.

test scores were placed there. These data demonstrate that there were significant differences in the student's track placements associated with the socioeconomic level of his or her family and clearly indicate that one of the likely outcomes of the tracking system is the perpetuation of the social class differentiation. This is particularly true since less than one percent of the students were transferred from one track to another in this school system during the year of the study. Since students in the lower track were provided different math programs than those in the upper track, it is clear that the many students in this system were not going to learn algebra even though their elementary math achievement indicated that they might well do so. In similar fashion, placement in differentiated reading tracks is likely to affect other areas of achievement as well as reading. A child placed in low track reading is not only likely to read less well than a similar nontracked student, but will not have the opportunity to learn literature or social science available to upper-track students.

It is clear that some students may move up or down from one track to another in some school systems. The data obtained from the court-subpoenaed track-placement schedules of another Midwestern school system indicate that there was considerable movement from one track to another.[14] In this system, the track placement of each student was traced over a three-year period. This made it possible to determine (1) the distribution of students among tracks for each year, and (2) the extent of mobility from year to year. The racial identity of each student had been indicated on the school record used to make placements. Students who were not enrolled in the school for all of the three years were excluded from the analysis. As the school officials testified, there was considerable degree of mobility from one track to another for both black and white students. Although this mobility is present, it is clear from examination of data in Table 13–3 that the movement from track to track over the three-year period tended to widen the gap between black and white students in this school system. It will be noted that there was an equal distribution of black students in the three tracks; academic, 32.4 percent, general, 34.3 percent, and basic, 33.3 percent at the seventh-grade level. The white students were predominantly placed in the academic and general track. Thus, more than twice as large a proportion of black students was placed in the lower track than white students. By the ninth grade the proportion of blacks in the highest or academic track had declined from 33 percent to 10 percent, the proportion of whites in the upper track in the ninth grade has also declined, but by decidely less than the black students. The

[14] James A. Jones, Edsel Erickson, and Ronald Crowell, "Increasing the Gap Between Whites and Black: Tracking as a Contributory Source," *Education and Urban Society*, vol. 14, no. 3, May 1972.

TABLE 13–3
Original Placement of Black and White 7th Grade Students and How They Were Distributed by Track in the 8th and 9th Grades

Same Class at Each Grade Level		Track			
		Academic %	General %	Basic %	Total %
7th	Black	33	34	33	100
	White	44	41	15	100
8th	Black	20	34	46	100
	White	47	38	15	100
9th	Black	10	31	59	100
	White	30	32	38	100

Source: James D. Jones, Edsel Erickson, and Ronald Crowell, "Increasing the Gap between Whites and Blacks: Tracking as a Contributory Source," *Education and Urban Society,* 4, no. 3 (May 1972), pp. 339–49.

overall effect of the tracking system here was to decrease the proportion of students who had achieved in the academic curriculum. This was decidedly more marked among black students than among white.

As we noted in Chapter 5, the federal courts have recognized that tracking is a denial of equal protection of the laws.[15] Tracking is, of course, a vehicle for grouping children and setting boundaries on the type of curriculum and learning opportunities provided students. In essence, whatever the intention, the allocation of students to varying programs on the basis of assumed ability to learn will influence what students are taught and what they learn. Learning ability is a function of what one previously has learned as well as other variables. If we group the poor and the socially disadvantaged together and fail to teach them the skills required for participation in some social strata, we assure their failure to succeed in such statuses. Tracking based on presumed differences in interests and abilities clearly structures the nature of the student's learning opportunities and his or her actual achievement in the school system.

Systems, like tracking, are generally based on some criteria of intelligence, ability, or achievement level. Since these homogeneous and heterogeneous groups commonly have similar curricula and curriculum goals, there has been very extensive research on this relative effectiveness. Like tracking, ability grouping is typically related to socioeconomic background of the student's family. Many would argue that "ability grouping is simply a means of making respectable the procedures whereby people from lower socioeconomic and racial or ethnic minorities

[15] Hobson *vs.* Hanson, 269 F. Supplement, 401 (1967).

are relegated to the slower and 'nonacademic' programs and provided basically inferior education. Observers of racially mixed schools frequently find that ability grouping is a means by which peoples are resegregated within the school."[16] In this respect, however, it serves the purpose of allocating students to differential curricula or tracks and through this to differential positions in society. Many will argue that these potential outcomes are overweighted by the presumed improvements in the individual achievement and affective outcomes among the students. An examination of the research on the outcomes of homogeneous and heterogeneous grouping organizations is therefore essential.

Although there are many studies of homogeneous grouping, it should be recognized that some of them do not meet sound criteria of carefully designed research. There is considerable variation in the findings with regard to academic achievement and other outcomes of education. An extensive survey of ability grouping research prior to 1960 summarized significant conclusions as follows:

> (1) ability grouping in itself does not produce improved achievement in children. (2) Contrary to statements in previous summaries of the research on the effects of ability grouping on children's achievement . . . , more research evidence seems to indicate that ability grouping actually may be detrimental to children in the average and lower ability groups. (3) Research evidence in the area is quite meager, but what is available does not support the prevalent assumption that college achievement is improved by ability grouping. (4) The evidence is fairly conclusive that grouping practices in a school can assist in developing social situations that influence the student's perception of self, his sense of dignity and worth, and his attitudes toward other children. In view of this, grouping practices should be concerned with furthering the establishment of social climates that will encourage the intellectual and personal development of EVERY child without detrimental effects on the individual child.[17]

After an extensive review of the research on ability grouping through the decade of the 60s, Findley and Bryan concluded:

> Briefly we find that ability grouping as defined above shows no consistent positive value for helping students generally, or particular groups of students, to learn better. Taking all studies into account, the balance of findings is chiefly of no strong effect either favorable or unfavorable. Among the studies showing significant effects, the slight preponderance

[16] A. Harry Passow, *Toward Creating a Model Urban School System: A Study of the Washington D.C. Public Schools,* New York Teachers College, Columbia University, 1967.

[17] Maurice J. Eash, "Grouping: What We Have Learned," *Educational Leadership,* vol. 18, pp. 429–34, April 1961.

> of evidence showing the practice favorable for the learning of high ability students is more than offset by evidence of unfavorable effects on the learning of average and low ability groups, particularly the latter. There is no appreciable difference in the effects at elementary and secondary school levels. Finally, those instances of special benefit under ability grouping have generally involved substantial modification of materials and methods, which may well be the influential factors wholly apart from grouping.[18]

It is clear from the examination of the wide range of research studies that the cognitive or academic achievement outcomes of the homogeneous grouping can hardly justify such organization of the school.

In the absence of clear advantages in the cognitive domain, support for a tracking or grouping organization of the school would necessarily have to be found in other outcomes. The research in this area is much less extensive than that concerned with the academic achievement. Some educators have argued that the placement of lower-achieving students in heterogeneous groups makes them more academically successful but destroys their self-esteem or self-concept of ability. Borg found that ability grouping was generally associated with less favorable self-concept scores for all samples and at all levels in a longitudinal study of students in the United States.[19] Auer, in a study of German students of junior high school age found no significant difference in self-concept of ability among *Gymnazium, Mittelschule,* and *Volksschule* students when social class background of the students was controlled.[20] The effect of self-concepts of academic ability on the placement of educable mentally retarded students in special classes seems to vary over time. Towne and Joiner[21] and Schurr and Brookover[22] found that self-concept of academic ability responses increased slightly immediately after placement in EMR classes, but positive effect leveled off over a longer time. The self-concepts of a small group of students who were returned to regular classes declined somewhat after this replacement. These data suggest that self-concept may vary with the group with which the student is comparing himself. Such changes in reported self-concept may not reflect

[18] Warren G. Finley and Miriam Bryan, *Ability Grouping: 1970.* (Athens, Georgia: Center for Educational Improvement, University of Georgia, 1971).

[19] Walter Borg, *Ability Grouping in the Public Schools,* 2nd ed. (Madison, Wisconsin: Dembar Educational Research Services, Inc., 1966).

[20] Michael Auer, "Self-Concept of Academic Ability of West German Eighth-Grade Students," dissertation, Michigan State University, 1971.

[21] Richard Towne and Lee Joiner, *The Effect of Special Class Placement on the Self-Concept-of-Ability of the Educable Mentally Retarded Child,* (East Lansing, Michigan: College of Education, Michigan State University, 1966).

[22] Terry Schurr and W. B. Brookover, *The Effect of Special Class Placement on the Self-Concept of Ability of the Educable Mentally Retarded Child* (East Lansing, Michigan: Educational Publication Services, College of Education, Michigan State University, 1967).

any change in self-assessment based on a constant comparison group. It seems unlikely that the students who are identified as retarded by the school social system over a long period of time will maintain high assessment of their ability to learn the common academic tasks in the school.

There is some evidence of the effect of placement on dropout rates which may be an indication of alienation from the school. There is a popular notion that the placement of students in vocational schools or curricula reduces materially the dropout from secondary schools and their alienation from the school. The evidence to support this notion is meager, if any exists. Most of the opinion is based upon testimonials by persons with an interest in vocational education. Analysis of the school records of two high schools indicated that students in the lower academic or nonacademic tracks are more likely to drop out of school than students in the higher or academic tracks when SES and ability are controlled.[23] It seems unlikely, therefore, that grouping or tracking favorably affects alienation from school, self-concept or other noncognitive outcomes. In summarizing the findings of the wide range of research on affective development of children, Finley and Bryan said:

> The findings of impact of ability grouping on the affective development of children are essentially unfavorable. Whatever the practice does to build the egos of children in the high groups is overbalanced by evidence of unfavorable effects stigmatizing average and low groups as inferior and incapable of learning.
>
> In the absence of evidence of positive effects on learning and personal development of children, and in the light of negative effects on the scholastic achievement and self-concepts of low ability groups, the tendency of ability grouping to separate children along ethnic and socio-economic lines must be deemed to discriminate against children from lower socio-economic classes and minority groups. The mechanism may be said to operate primarily by denying the lower groups the scholastic stimulation of their more able peers, and by stigmatizing the low groups as inferior and incapable of learning in their own eyes and those of their teachers. . . .
>
> The evidence simply indicates that ability grouping *per se* tends to be ineffective and do more harm than good. Any procedure that involves ability grouping and correlary ethnic separation must be justified in terms of other strong evidence of likely beneficial effects.[24]

In spite of the lack of conclusive evidence of superior cognitive or affective outcomes from tracking or ability grouping, this remains a widespread practice both in the United States and the other Western

[23] Walter E. Schafer and Carol Olexa, *Tracking and Opportunity* (Scranton, Pa.: Chandler Publishing Co., 1971).

[24] Finley and Bryan, *Ability Grouping: 1970.*

countries. The reasons for this persistence are probably found in the preference of teachers for teaching in differentiated tracks and ability groups and in the overall desire of the dominant interests in the societies to maintain the stratification system.

Middle Schools versus Junior High Schools

One of the contemporary types of public-school organization is the "middle school." This is the organization of the middle years of the elementary and secondary school in a somewhat different pattern from that of the more common junior high school. The extensive movement to change to some middle-school type has resulted in a variety of types of organization of these school years. The change has sometimes been accompanied by a shift to team teaching rather than self-contained classrooms and use of teacher aides, or other types of diversified instructional staff. Systematic evaluation of the impact of each of these organizational changes has not occurred. Much of the change to middle-school organizations has been based upon a belief in the desirability of such change rather than any sound evaluation of the outcomes. In preparation for a study of the extent to which middle schools have achieved the stated objectives and their impact on teacher, parent, and students compared to the traditional junior high school, Bryan and Erickson reviewed the literature which stated objectives and anticipated outcomes of the middle school. The generally stated goals for middle schools as compared with the junior high school were: (1) deemphasize the emulation of senior high school; (2) combine the best features of the elementary and secondary school; (3) include grade levels six, seven, and eight; (4) encourage each student to work at his own level of ability; and (5) limit school population to 700 to 800 students. These middle school organizations were most clearly distinguished from junior high schools by the grade levels generally included. Junior high schools have been typically seventh and eighth grade or seventh, eighth, and ninth grade, while the middle school has generally started with the sixth grade, although sometimes fifth, sixth, seventh, and eighth are included.

Bryan and Erickson's review of the literature also identified the proponents' anticipated outcomes of middle schools for teachers, students, and parents. The most commonly anticipated outcomes for teachers are: (1) greater job and role satisfaction; (2) more likely to function as role models for students; (3) more likely to be informed about student's progress in other classes (4) more satisfied with the decision-making process; and (5) more satisfied with relationships with colleagues particularly if assigned to teacher teams. The goals or anticipated outcomes for the students include: (1) more likely to select a staff member as an academic significant other; (2) less likely to feel peer pressure for grades; (3) more likely to feel their parents are well-informed about what they do in school; and (4) more likely feel that they "belong" to their school.[25]

In the same study, the outcomes anticipated for parents were identified as: (1) their being more likely to state that their children have a favorite teacher; (2) more likely to indicate that the children feel that they "belong" to their school; (3) more likely to feel that their children are working at their own capacity; and (4) more likely to deemphasize the importance of grades in the school.

Perhaps the most striking thing to be said about this list of goals and anticipated outcomes of middle-school organization is the absence of any mention of improved academic achievement. The middle school advocates have based their arguments on the presumed effect of the structure on other kinds of outcomes and have not emphasized improved learning in traditional academic areas. Perhaps because of this emphasis, there is little evidence of the relative impact of middle school organizations on academic achievement. One would hazard the speculation that, after reviewing the impact of school organization or other school factors on academic achievement in this and the following chapter, little if any difference in achievement could be attributed to the middle-school organization per se.

Among major areas of anticipated outcomes of the middle school were those concerned with the relationships between students and teachers. In their comparisons of middle-school and junior-high-school types of organization Bryan and Erickson[25] found the middle-school teachers were more likely than the junior high teachers to be viewed as approachable by both the students and their parents. The middle school teachers were also more likely to be satisfied with the students. On the other hand, contrary to the goals and hoped-for outcomes held by the proponents of middle-school organizations, junior-high-school students were more likely to (1) be somewhat happier and satisfied with the school setting, (2) to have a favored teacher or teachers, and (3) to perceive that their teachers held higher expectations for them regarding future formal education.[26] It is not entirely clear how these findings should be interpreted, but certainly there was no evidence to indicate that middle school results in less student alienation from the school. Although middle school teachers seem to be more easily approached by students, the students in junior high schools had more favorite teachers. This may result from the fact that there were team-teaching operations in the middle school in contrast to the junior high school. At the same

[25] Clifford Bryan and Edsel Erickson, *Structural Effects on School Behavior: A Comparison of Middle School and Junior High School Programs* (Grand Rapids, Michigan: Center for Educational Studies, 1970).

[26] Ibid.

time, these differences may be accounted for by factors other than the differences in organizations. The higher expectations which the junior high school students believed their teachers held for them may derive from the middle-school philosophy in which scholastic rewards or grades are presumably deemphasized. It also suggests that it is possible that the junior-high-school organization is more likely to produce high academic achievement as a result of the high expectations. In contrast to this, students in the middle schools perceive that their peers place greater emphasis on their academic skills than students in the junior high school. The students in the junior-high organization seem to have a different perception of the academic norms than would be expected from the middle-school philosophy.

The parents of middle school students were more likely to evaluate positively their children's relationship with the teachers than were parents of junior high school students. Middle school parents also were more likely to feel that their children were working up to their capabilities, but they did not expect their children to go as far in school as did the junior high parents even though the middle students perceived that their parents placed greater emphasis on achievement than those in junior high school. There was little difference between the two groups of parents in their emphasis on grades; however, the teachers in the middle school were more likely to be satisfied with the cooperation and help which they received from the parents. Although the majority of the parents of both schools favored student involvement in school policy, the junior-high-school parents were more likely to advocate the students' having such a voice than were the middle school parents. They also felt or were more apt to feel that the children should have a right to express their feelings on social issues.

There were a number of areas in which there was no difference between the perceptions of the middle-school student's parents and the junior-high-school student's parents. Both hold similar educational and behavioral expectations for their children and had similar opinions of how they were informed concerning their children's conduct in school. About one-third of the parents in both situations felt that they were not well enough informed. About 70 percent of the parents in each group thought that their children were being helped to become responsible citizens, and there was little difference in their definitions of the school's role. There was no preponderance of evidence that the type of school organization related significantly to any general pattern of parents' evaluation or their relation to the school.

Middle school teachers seem somewhat more likely to be satisfied with their positions and their relations to other members of the staff. For example, compared with junior-high teachers they were (1) more satisfied with the attitudes of the faculty toward students than before,

(2) more satisfied with the cooperation and help received from guidance personnel, (3) more likely to be satisfied with methods employed in making decisions on curriculum matters, (4) satisfied with teaching students at the middle-school level, (5) more likely to accept the opportunity to remain in their present settings, and (6) satisfied with being able to follow what other teachers were doing with the students they teach. Junior high school teachers, on the other hand, were slightly more satisfied with their administrators. In other areas, there was little difference between middle and junior high school teachers, and both preferred their respective school organization and their philosophies. Both desired greater participation in school curriculum decisions, but both were reasonably satisfied with teaching as a profession and did not want to leave for a higher-paying position. In general, there was no significant difference in the teachers' feelings of satisfaction with the way the students behaved and the way the schools operated. Both groups of teachers were satisfied with the school organization in their school.[27]

Although the Bryan and Erickson study does not provide a definitive analysis of the effects of school organization, the findings suggest that the establishment of a formal middle-school organizational structure does not guarantee the achievement of the intended objectives and outcomes. It is entirely possible that the presumed changes in organization did not result in significant changes in the patterns of interaction and role relationships within the school. The middle-school teachers, staff, and students may not have behaved any differently than those in the junior high school organization. It is also possible that such structural changes in the school organization are not relevant to the goals or outcomes anticipated. The study of middle school compared to junior high school suggests that we are, as yet, unable to predict accurately how these changes in organization will affect the learning of the students involved.

Team Teaching versus Single Teacher Classroom

The development of middle schools is sometimes associated with team teaching or other multiple staff for a given group of students. Team teaching is probably more frequently found in the middle or junior high school years than in the elementary and secondary schools. There are two general types of team teaching with some variations found within each. One involves an hierarchial arrangement with a supervising teacher in charge of a staff of two or more certified teachers and perhaps some interns or teachers' aides responsible for teaching 100 or more students. The other general type involves several "coequal" teachers' working together to plan and operate the program of instruction, guid-

[27] Ibid.

ance counseling, and all the instructional services of a group of students. The number of students, of course, varies with the number of teachers in the team. In some cases the cooperative effort is limited and does not have the complex interrelation of fully developed teams of teachers functioning as a single unit. Some of these teacher teams are little more than two or more teachers taking turns teaching a particular group. A team, however, can function as an athletic team in which members play a different role, but the various members are simultaneously teaching for common goals.

Perhaps the most significant outcome of the team-teaching organization involves the change in the role of the teachers and their relation to each other. The single-teacher classroom gives each teacher a great deal of autonomy to determine the method of instruction and the teaching relationship with the students. Single-classroom teachers may informally interact with each other and exchange ideas, methods, and information, but a team-teaching organization requires a different type of relationship. If it is a hierarchial type, the supervisor present most of the school day has more direct control over the behavior of other team members than is common in a single-teacher classroom. In both types of teams there is greater division of labor and differentiation of roles. Frequently the teachers in each team have competence in different subject areas and cooperate in sharing knowledge of the students in their group. They typically meet to make plans and jointly supervise each student's progress. Their instructional tasks may be assigned on the basis of each teacher's competence and interest or on the basis of each teacher's relationship to the students. Advocates maintain that a multiple teacher staff with the accompanying variation in interaction among teachers and pupils produces a superior instructional program. Brownell and Taylor[28] maintain that the lack of opportunity for students to take part in teaching-team situations has undesirable consequences because students do not have the opportunity to interact with more than a single adult at a particular time and have a variety of patterns of interaction. If the student fails to develop a satisfactory relationship with one adult he may develop a more satisfactory one with another member of the team. In single teacher classrooms, they claim, students may develop feelings of isolation and may reject the adult role, whereas the team-teaching milieu reduces feelings of isolation and increases the student's identification with the school.

Although its advocates claim that superior outcomes result from team teaching, the evaluations do not consistently support such conclusions. Team students may do as well as those in single classroom programs on the typical standardized tests, but proponents of team teaching fre-

[28] J. A. Brownell and H. Taylor, "Theoretical Perspectives and Team Teaching," *Phi Delta Kappan*, vol. 43 (1963), p. 30.

quently reject this kind of evaluation. They insist that such tests do not measure adequately the outcomes of team-teaching organizations.[29] Although the proponents of team teaching feel that such classroom organization provides a superior learning environment, there is little evidence to support the claim that academic achievement is either enhanced or damaged by team teaching.

Systematic studies of the other outcomes of team teaching as compared with the single classroom have been very limited, but one study examined the relationship of the team teaching organization to student alienation.[30] Three types of teaching systems were investigated: (1) an organized teaching team system in a middle school; (2) a traditional one-teacher classroom in a middle school; (3) and a one-teacher system in a junior high school. The teaching teams were of the coequal cooperating type in which several teachers work together to plan and operate the instructional program. Each team of teachers had 150 students and was composed of eight teachers of different subject areas who cooperated in sharing knowledge of students in the group. They met to plan for each student's work and to organize the instructional activities.

The single-teacher classroom organization in the middle school operated in the same school building, while the junior high school single-teacher system was in another building. The students of the same age were brought together for each class under the administration of a single teacher in both schools. Each teacher took care of the records, taught one or more subjects, and operated as a traditional one-teacher classroom. The students were assigned to their respective groups on a random basis, but the administrators and the teaching teams claimed that the students in the single-teacher classrooms included a disproportionate share of the behavioral problems. It was anticipated, therefore, that the team-teaching students would be even less alienated from the school than would result from the organizational structure alone.

The evidence did not support the hypothesis that team-teaching students would be less alienated. In fact, the evidence was just the reverse: middle school students assigned to the traditional non-team-teaching approach had the highest sense of pride in their school, followed by the junior high school students assigned to the traditional non-team-teaching classroom. The students in the teacher teams of the middle school showed the least amount of pride in the school. When the variables of race, socioeconomic status, and sex were controlled, the middle school students assigned to teacher teams who were thought to have

---

[29] Harold S. Davis, "Team Teaching," *The Encyclopedia of Education* (New York: Macmillan and The Free Press), vol. 9, pp. 89–94.

[30] Theophilius O. Odetola, Edsel Erickson, Clifford Bryan, and Lewis Walker, *Organizational Structure and Student Alienation* (Kalamazoo, Michigan: Center for Sociological Research. Western Michigan University, 1971).

fewer behavioral problems consistently exhibited the lowest degree of school pride.

This study of single teacher and team teaching is of course not definitive. It is possible that the teacher team system in this school was unrepresentative of team teaching. It is possible that the teachers in these teams were not responsive to the student's needs and they may not have functioned as the ideal team is supposed to function. It is possible, also, that the teachers in the team may have a tendency to become less knowledgeable about their students and develop a secondary and less personal type of relationship with the larger group of students. The single teacher in a classroom may have closer, more primary types of relationship with the students, who in turn feel more identified with the teacher and the school. The students, therefore, may find more satisfying relationships with the single adult in the classroom in which social psychological security is provided to the middle-school-aged students.

In spite of the extensive literature advocating team teaching and the rather popular movement to organize schools in this fashion, there is little evidence to justify this development. The evidence does not indicate that team teaching is superior in either cognitive achievement or in the affective domain. Such assessments must be very tentative, for we know little about the dynamics associated with team teaching.

Nongraded Schools

As the name indicates, the nongraded education refers to an organizational pattern without grades by age level. This plan is based upon the theoretical assumption that every child is different in his intellectual, physical, social development and that the job of the school is to provide a specifically identified program of learning experiences presumably tailored to fit his or her individual interests and educational needs. In its presumed ideal form, all systems of promotion from kindergarten through third grade in the primary schools would be eliminated. This sometimes results in what is described as a continuous progress school. The proponents of the nongraded school maintain that it is not merely an organizational model, but an approach which is based on the value of individual differences and individualized instruction. This organizational system presumably, then, is associated with a highly flexible and adaptable curriculum in which each student is carrying on a program of studies planned jointly by the teacher and the student.

At the high school level, the nongraded school is based upon a similar conception that students are not ready for the same academic experiences at the same age. The nongraded program at the high school level is likely to be composed of several curricula or learning situations which vary with the achievement level and social background of the students.

Proponents claim to strive to avoid the negative aspects of social status and psychological expectations commonly present in ability grouping and the track system. In fact, however, the curricula or tracks established in a nongraded high school are difficult to distinguish from a traditional tracking system. The various phases of a "nongraded" high school are quite similar to criteria for placement of students in a particular track. For example, in one school these are described as follows: "Phase one. Designed for students who are quite deficient in the basic skills and who require much personal attention; Phase two, designed for students who are somewhat deficient in basic skills and who would profit from additional help in developing these skills; Phase three, designed for students who are average achievers and are capable of certain amount of self direction; Phase four, designed for students who wish to study a subject in great depth; Phase five, designed for students who wish to take a college-level course in high school."[31] The continuous progress model of educational program in the high school is much less common than the sort of phasing or grouping characterized above. Both types may, of course, operate relatively simultaneously. Both depend upon a diagnosis of the presumed level of achievement characterizing the student and the prescription of a presumably suitable academic environment based upon that diagnosis.

Although there have been some efforts to evaluate the nongraded elementary and secondary schools, the proponents very reluctantly indicate that there are difficulties involved in comparative evaluation of the nongraded schools and the traditional graded organizations. This stems from the fact that the goals or outcomes at a particular time are not standard for all students in the nongraded school. As in the traditional tracking system described above, it is not possible to compare outcomes directly because it is not intended that all students should have achieved a knowledge of algebra, for example. There are reports by teachers and students in nongraded secondary schools which indicate that the participants in such schools believe that the results are quite favorable.[32] They maintain that achievement is raised, dropout rates are lowered, students' allegiance to the school is improved, and generally the atmosphere at the school is more desirable. Jenkins, however, adds, "There is little evidence as to their ultimate worth." An examination of the Melbourne, Florida, nongraded high school indicated that there were no statistically significant differences between the nongraded high school and a control group in attitudes toward school, achievement in primary academic discipline, or ability to think critically.[33]

---

[31] John M. Jenkins, "Non-Graded High Schools," *Encyclopedia of Education*, vol. 6, pp. 587–93, 1971.

[32] Ibid.

[33] Sydney L. Besvinich and John Crittenden, "The Effectiveness of a Non-Graded School," *School and Society*, 96, no. 2305 (1968), pp. 181–84.

The evaluations of elementary level nongraded schools produced similar findings. McLaughlin, reviewing the research completed prior to 1966, concluded that nongrading appeared to make little difference in the academic performance of children at any level.[34] Neither is there evidence that students from nongraded classes exhibit social or classroom adjustments superior to those of children from graded classes. The proponents of nongraded schools tend to reject these findings because they are comitted to the superiority of the individualized programs of instruction and cannot accept the possibility that superior learning does not result. Comprehensive evaluation of nongraded organization are not likely to occur (1) because of both the methodological and political difficulties in comparative evaluation when the goals are different and (2) because the teachers in nongraded schools generally object to holding themselves or their students accountable for any specific level of learning. The basic philosophy of individualized instruction and individual differences maintains that the student should proceed at his own level and set his own objectives of achievement. If one operates in this context, it is quite inappropriate to hold teachers accountable for achieving any level of learning among their students. Whatever an individual student learns is defined as acceptable because this is what he has indicated he wants to learn and is apparently what meets his particular needs at the particular time. Some proponents maintain that the aggregate of such learning would be superior to that achieved in graded schools. They also argue that quality of a nongraded program can only be evaluated in terms of the extent to which individual students achieve what they want.

Open School Organization

The development of open school organization has been somewhat parallel to the nongraded classroom and is based on similar assumptions about individual differences and the desirability of giving students a wide range of alternate activities and freedom of movement. Schools may exhibit varying degrees of openness from the one in which all students engage in the same activities at a given time and march from place to place together under the teacher's direction to one in which all students engage in widely varying activities of their own choosing at any time or place. The recent emphasis on humanistic education has been associated with a trend toward the open type of school organization. The outcomes of such open schools may be somewhat different from those in the traditionally ordered school organization.

McPartland and Epstein have undertaken to assess the relationship

[34] William P. McLaughlin, *The Non-Graded School: A Critical Assessment* (Albany: The University of the State of New York, the State Department of Education, 1967).

between degrees or types of openness in the social environment and the outcomes of the schools in the public schools of Harvard County, Maryland. Their definition is: "An open-environment school is one in which many alternative activities for students are permitted, in which the alternatives available correspond to important differences among students in their interests and needs, and in which students share some responsibility for selecting assignments, supervising progress, and setting goals."[35] From this conception of the open school organization, McPartland and Epstein developed measures of "(1) variety of activities permitted, (2) individualization of tasks, (3) sharing of responsibility for selecting assignments, (4) sharing of responsibility for supervising programs, and (5) sharing of responsibility for setting goals."[36]

Since open school patterns of student-teacher and student-student relationship may produce different outcomes from those in schools with more traditional organization, a range of possible student behavior was considered as outcomes. These were: (1) the students' positive-negative reactions to school work, teachers, and general school environment; (2) the students' self-reliance or ability to act in situations without direction, supervision, or social support; (3) the students' ability to make realistic judgements and assessments of themselves; (4) the students' achievement on standard tests of academic performance.

McPartland and Epstein hypothesized that the effects of the schools' organization on students would depend on earlier experience. For example, student reactions to open environments were hypothesized to be more positive if earlier experience had been in open organization, and the impact on self-reliance would be greater if students had not previously experienced open environments.

Preliminary results of this study indicate that the relationship between measures of school openness and student reactions to school varies from one grade level to another in this sample of schools. At the eighth-grade level there is a generally positive relation between openness and general satisfaction with schools, interest in schools, and reactions to teachers. Among sixth graders, school openness is not consistently related to reactions to school. The relationship at the 11th grade varies with the length of experience in open schools and family style.

The preliminary results indicate that "the experiences in open schools have effects on the development of student self-reliance, although the effects are small compared to other factors and probably require extended experiences in open schools over more than one year."[37]

---

[35] James M. McPartland and Joyce M. Eqatein, *Interim Report: School Organization and Student Outcomes* (Baltimore, Maryland: Center for Social Organization of Schools, The Johns Hopkins University, 1973).

[36] Ibid., p. 4.

[37] Ibid., p. 37.

The effects of open school organization variables on student judgement and academic performance have not yet been determined, but McPartland and Epstein predict no relationship between openness and academic performance. If this hypothesis is supported, it will further indicate that organizational variables may have little direct effect on school academic learning, although they may significantly affect other outcomes.

Earlier studies of effects of teacher-pupil relations on student achievement[38] indicate that classes characterized by more openness, as measured by more sharing of authority, achieve less or are not significantly different from those in which teachers direct the activities.

The impact of organizational openness as defined here, on various behavior learned in school, has certainly not yet been determined. It seems likely that whatever impact it has may be indirect and may vary with numerous other factors such as previous experience, length of exposure and the cultural norms that prevail concerning achievement. The current interest in open school organization is great, and further assessment of its relation to outcomes is certain to occur. This interest is reflected in the following discussion of various types of alternate schools which usually exhibit high degrees of open organization.

Alternate Schools. The final type of school organization that we wish to discuss is variously identified as the open school, the alternate school, or the free school. Although there are many variations in the individual school organizations, these are generally identified as alternates to the traditional public or private school organizations. In concept, the alternate school is the antithesis of organization: it grows out of the belief that the structure or organization of the traditional schools has alienated or "turned off" the students. Accordingly the intent of the alternate school is to provide an environment in which the student can direct his own activities with a minimum of adult supervision. Each student is presumably provided an opportunity to "do his own thing." The goals and objectives of the school are or may be different for each student or each small group of students, but are decided by the individual student or the group in consultation with other students and staff.

The history of alternate schools in the United States suggests that such "nonorganized" schools have a relatively short life span. Although both teachers and students are attracted to the schools because of the apparent freedom of choice in activities, the schools tend to break down because there is no agreement on what the outcomes should be. Neither is there any agreement on how the differentiated goals should be

[38] Wilbur B. Brookover, "Social Factors in Schools' Achievement," *Journal of Experimental Education,* 1943; and Kenneth S. Parr, *The Social Relations of Teachers as Related to Teaching Competency,* thesis for the Degree of M.A., Michigan State University, East Lansing, 1967.

achieved. Few such schools have survived for more than three or four years. This internal lack of agreement and outside opposition from educational traditionalists reduce the life span of most alternate schools.

The central theme of the alternate or free school movement is based upon what its proponents identify as a radical theory in which freedom is the central virtue.[39] This theme of freedom often is identified with rejection of the traditional public and private schools, which are perceived to represent a denial of free choice. It follows that all major characteristics of the public school organization and method are opposed: the standardized curriculum, the teacher-led groups, the emphasis on discipline, the system of evaluation, and a variety of other characteristics of the school. This extreme concept of free schools, however, is a distortion because it is based upon the assumption that there is no direction, no order, no norms of behavior.

> In visiting many of the rural free schools in the course of these two years, my wife and I repeatedly asked ourselves this question: Why is it, in so many of these self-conscious, open and ecstatic Free Schools for rich children, everyone boasts that he is doing his "own thing" but everyone in each of these schools, from coast to coast, is doing the same *kind* of thing? Why is it, we ask, that "free choice" so often proves to mean that weaver's loom, tie-dyed and macrame, and that "organic growth" turns out in every case to mean the potter's kiln? How come it doesn't ever mean that passionate and searching look into the origins of unearned wealth that makes this segregated Free School possible? How is it that it never pertains to danger, choice, or confrontation?[40]

Although the alternate school development is in one way or another a reaction to the structure and program of the traditional public and private schools, we must recognize that alternate schools are simply alternate social organizations that have their own boundaries and their own limitations and definitions of appropriate behavior. Although each student may do "his own thing" that is somewhat different from what he might do in the traditional school, these students are also limited by the possibilities provided by alternate social situations. The boundaries and limits of behavior vary from one type of alternate school to another. The middle class well-to-do alternate high schools are very different in process and goals from the street academies for poor minority youth such as the Benjamin Franklin Street Academy in Harlem. In the latter case there is an atmosphere of staff discipline, although students do not perceive it as the same disciplines as experienced in

[39] Allen Graubard, "The Free School Movement," *Harvard Educational Review*, vol. 42, pp. 351–73, August 1972.

[40] Jonathan Kozal, "Politics, Rage and Motivation in the Free Schools," *Harvard Educational Review*, vol. 42, pp. 414–22, August 1972.

public schools. The emphasis is upon acquiring the necessary skills and knowledge for the black people to make the grade. The middle-class or so-called free secondary schools are not motivated by the same pressure to achieve upward mobility. A secure status is taken for granted, and it is assumed that the students' status will not be destroyed by participation in a youth culture with a radical perspective.

The absence of standardized outcomes or norms of achievement makes evaluation of the outcomes difficult. Since one of the purposes of such schools generally is to provide an alternate school setting for students who have become alienated from the traditional, school success in overcoming alienation is one possible basis for evaluating them. The levels of achievement in the standardized skills, areas of knowledge, and competence in inquiry are potential bases for evaluation. There have been few studies of the outcomes of such alternate schools, but limited evidence has accumulated.

A recent study of open schools in Minneapolis gives some indication of the learning outcomes.[41] The results of this two-year observation and study of open schools in Minneapolis indicate that fourth-, fifth-, and sixth-grade-aged groups became more estranged and alienated from school than they were before attending open schools. Their parents also indicated that the academic achievement of this age group of students was less satisfactory in the alternate school. The older students of secondary school age seemed to like the freedom of the alternate school and to some extent felt they benefitted by the opportunity to participate in such school environment. Their alienation and rejection of the educational program was reduced. There is also some evidence that their academic achievement improved in the open school setting. This study, therefore, indicates that there may be differences in outcomes depending upon the age of the students who had either dropped out of the more structured school organization or were close to dropping out. Any experience which tend to continue their education would be considered an improvement over the situation from which they had withdrawn or were withdrawing.

Although a systematic evaluation of the outcomes of the alternate schools is difficult, some indication of their thrust may be obtained by noting the trends in their development. The decade prior to 1965 witnessed the establishment of a few schools that might be identified as free schools. Since 1965, there has been a rapid increase in the number of schools established each year. Complete figures are not available, but Graubard indicates that perhaps 200 schools opened in September 1971. Most of these schools were small, with the modal population in the 30s.[42] Although alternate schools do not tend to survive

[41] Lee Joiner, *Open Schools,* Unpublished manuscript, 1973.

[42] Graubard, "Free School Movement."

survival may not reflect their importance in the educational scene. The rapid acceleration in the number of schools may have significant impact on the programs and structure of the public and private school organizations. It is not possible at this time to indicate the extent of such influence.

The General Impact of Organization on Learning

Our analyses of the impact of various types of social structure or organization on school learning indicate that the evidence is limited and very spotty for most types of organization. The paucity of evaluation of organizational types may reflect the fact that organizational changes are frequently advocated because it is the fashion or because of political ideology rather than to improve the quality of school achievement. As we have noted, social change in educational methods or organization seems to follow patterns of style or fads. After a time in which a particular form of organization such as the nongraded school increases rapidly, it frequently declines and returns to previous patterns of organization. Some movements may leave a residue of effect on school organization, but others produce little or no long-term change. It would be difficult, for example, to find any significant impact of the widespread movement for core curriculum which was the style of the early 1950s. The adoption of such organization and of program fads is seldom based on systematic evidence that they produce significantly different outcomes. Examination of the literature on types of organization initiated in the early 70s reveals little systematic evidence of their learning outcomes. Advocates of these organizations ignore any evidence that does not indicate a superior outcome and frequently maintain that research on the outcomes is either impossible or inappropriate until the particular model which they advocate has been firmly established in the school system.

Changes in organization may be advocated for reasons other than the improvement of the student learning outcomes. Teachers and administrators, for example, like the type of staff relations and staff roles that is characteristic of the nongraded classroom better than that of the traditional age-graded classroom. If this is true and parents believe that the nongraded school is a satisfactory arrangement, it may persist regardless of the relative outcomes in student learning.

As we have noted, the differences in goals identified with various organizations make comparisons of a single outcome debatable. In fact, several of the organizational models proposed in recent years are based upon the philosophy that standardized learning outcomes are undesirable. The alternate schools, the nongraded classrooms, and a number of other contemporary models emerge from a belief in a wide range of individual differences and the belief that students should not be expected to learn any common standard curriculum. This belief converges with a contemporary humanistic movement which emphasizes the happiness of the child and focuses on the damage which grading or other types of evaluation may have on the child's self-fulfillment. This general movement in American education is contrary to a parallel movement which emphasizes school accountability for achieving certain levels of learning. The latter supports efforts to evaluate or assess the outcomes of the educational programs and to hold the school administrators and teachers accountable for achieving a minimum level of learning in the accepted skills and knowledge. This, of course, involves some common objectives and the development of common measures of those outcomes. To the extent that the movement for state and national school assessment and accountability prevails, it would be possible to examine the relative effects of various types of school organization. If, however, the countermovement for highly differentiated educational program with an emphasis upon nonstandardized patterns of learning prevails, it may be impossible to achieve any systematic evaluation of various organizational models.

We have alluded to the idea that the formal organization of the school may not always be important in the determination of learning outcomes. It is apparent that children learn many different kinds of behavior in many different social settings. Certainly the one-to-one relationship between the child and mother or father is a significant social interaction model in the acquisition of human behavior. The informal friendship group including students of varying ages is also the scene of much learning. We maintain that the many varieties of human behavior can be and are learned in many different systems of social interaction. The particular type of behavior and the level of behavior learned are probably much more determined by the definitions of the situation within the social setting than by the organization that prevails. As will be noted in the next chapter, the norms of behavior, the expectations which the others hold for the students, the evaluations which are made of the student, and the students' feeling that it is possible for them to learn may all be much more relevant in determining the nature and extent of learning that occurs. Homogeneous groups can be devised in which every student is expected to learn at a high level. The differences between learning among students in different tracks are not necessarily the result of the tracking organization, but the result of the definitions of what is appropriate and expected in the different tracks. Similarly, everyone may be expected to learn at a high level in either a nongraded or graded school. Both the nongraded and graded organizations may also be associated with low levels of expected achievement.

In contemporary education, however, some types of social structure may be associated with characteristic social norms or climates for learning. For example, homogeneous ability grouping, tracking, nongraded, and segregated school organizations are generally associated with the belief in vast differences of ability and the expectation that outcomes will vary greatly among children. Particular types of organization may lead to and facilitate difference in outcome because they are designed to achieve such differences. In another society or at another time, similar organizations might be associated with norms for other outcomes. In contemporary American society, however, it is difficult to have a segregated lower-class black school produce the same level of achievement that a middle-class white school produces. Similarly, a nongraded school with emphasis upon individual differences is not likely to produce common levels of achievement among all students in contemporary schools.

As different types of organization are now associated with particular types of school norms and school climate, the establishment of a new set of norms may tend to produce a particular type of school organization. The establishment of mastery learning norms in a school, as advocated by Bloom and his associates,[43] is compatible with a heterogeneous non-ability-grouped classroom organization. The mastery learning model assumes that all children can master a certain set of skills or body of knowledge and encourages any organization designed to produce such results. An organization which emphasizes differentiation and a wide range of outcomes is not likely to be associated with mastery.[44] Similarly, an individualized instructional model such as the nongraded school is not compatible with the norms of mastery.

Systematic analyses of the interrelation between organizational types, school climate types, and levels of school achievement have not been extensive. In the next chapter, we will examine the relation of culturally oriented aspects of the school social environment to achievement. This, of course, has some relevance for patterns of school organizations. The two chapters, therefore, should be recognized as a unit.

Suggested Readings

Kenneth Clark, "Alternate Public School Systems," *Harvard Educational Review,* 38 (1968), pp. 100–13.

Nan Coppock, *Middle Schools: School Leadership Digest* (Arlington, Va.: National Association of Elementary School Principals, 1974).

---

[43] James Block, *Mastery Learning in the Classroom: An Overview of Research* (Santa Barbara, California, 1973); and Benjamin S. Bloom, "Learning for Mastery," *Evaluation Comment,* vol. 1, no. 2, 1968.

[44] William Spady, "A Sociologist's View of Mastery," paper presented at A.E.R.A., New Orleans, 1973.

Urban S. Dahllof, *Ability Grouping, Content Validity and Curriculum Process Analysis* (New York: Teachers College Press, 1971).

Geneva Gary, "Exploring Verbal Interactions in Desegregated Classrooms," *Educational Leadership,* 31, no. 8 (May 1974), pp. 727–30.

Christopher Jencks et al., *Inequality* (New York: Basic Books, 1972), and Symposium Review of Jencks, *Inequality,* in *The American Educational Research Journal,* vol. 2, no. 2 (Spring 1974), pp. 149–69.

Frederick Mosteller and Daniel Moynihan, *An Equality of Educational Opportunity* (New York: Vintage Books, 1972). An assessment of the Coleman report.

Walter E. Schafer and Carol Olexa, *Tracking and Opportunity* (Scranton, Pa.: Chandler Publishing Co., 1971).

Dee Schofield, *Class Size: School Leadership Digest* (Arlington, Va.: National Association of Elementary School Principals, 1974).

Marvin Shaw, "Changes in Sociometric Choices Following Forced Integration of an Elementary School," *Journal of Social Issues,* 29, no. 4 (1973), pp. 143–58.

14

Social Context, Social Climate, and School Learning

The level of learning varies from one school to another. Much research in recent years demonstrates the great variation in mean achievement in various categories of schools. As we have noted earlier, many striking differences in elementary and secondary schools are related to the racial, ethnic, and social class composition of the schools. The curve of reading achievement, for example, in New York City schools is bimodal. The schools largely composed of black or Puerto Rican students have mean achievement levels averaging two and one-half years below grade level. The other predominantly white schools have an average modal reading achievement of two and one-half years above grade level.[1] The average child in the predominantly black and Puerto Rican schools is approximately functionally illiterate after completing the first eight years of schooling, while the average middle-class white child reads at the high school level. This variation in reading achievement among schools also can be reproduced on other achievement measures. The differences between black or Puerto Rican student bodies and the predominantly white school students increase as they move through school.

The variations between schools at the elementary and secondary level can probably be duplicated among universities and colleges. Although we do not have adequate measures of the outcomes in academic or other types of achievement by which to compare colleges and universities, it is widely assumed that students who graduate from the high prestige institutions such as Harvard, University of California-Berkeley,

[1] Annie Stein, "Strategies for Failure," *Harvard Educational Review,* vol. 41, no. 2, May 1971, pp. 158–204.

Oberlin, or Kalamazoo College are decidedly different in achievement from students who graduate from lower-rated teachers' colleges, municipal universities, or struggling private liberal arts colleges. It is possible that the differences in outcomes, if any, are essentially explained by differences in the students who enter these institutions. But the desire to enter the elite institutions is based, in part at least, on the assumption that the education received there is superior to that in other institutions.

In examining all these differences, we can appropriately ask the question, What makes the difference? Why are some elementary schools or secondary schools producing significantly higher levels of achievement than others? Why are some colleges, professional schools, graduate schools, if it be so, producing superior products? American educators at all levels, but particularly in the elementary and secondary schools, have commonly attributed the differences in achievement to students' individual characteristics for which the school was not responsible. Such characteristics may be classified as genetic differences or environmental differences which occurred prior to and outside the school. Although we recognize the possible importance of both categories of differences originating outside the school, we are concerned here with those characteristics of the school environment which may explain some of the variance. In discussing the vast differences in achievement level between predominantly black and Puerto Rican schools on the one hand, and the predominantly white higher socioeconomic schools on the other in New York City, Stein commented:

> This is a massive accomplishment. It took the efforts of 63,000 teachers, thousands more of administrators, scholars and social scientists, and expenditures of billions of dollars. . . . Perhaps an even greater achievement of the schools has been their ability to place the responsibility for this extraordinary record of failure upon the children themselves, their families, and their community. Social scientists engage in learned disputes as to whether it is heredity or environment that makes the child of poverty an inferior form of human kind—but the assumption of his inferiority is not disputed except by the parents and the child himself.[2]

The differences in schools are recognized by both educators and laymen, but they have been more clearly documented by the Equality of Opportunity survey[3] and other recent studies (Michigan Assessment Program, 1970, 1971, 1972).

The evidence that measured intelligence scores are significantly correlated with the family socioeconomic status and racial identification has been cited as evidence that lower-status white and black boys and girls

[2] Ibid.

[3] James Coleman et al., *Equality of Educational Opportunity*, HEW Office of Education, U.S. Government Printing Office, 1966.

are genetically inferior to the higher-status white children.[4] As the extended discussion of this issue indicates, there is no completely valid evidence as to the extent of the genetic determination of learning ability.[5] Without experimentally controlled studies it is not possible to separate entirely the effect of social environment and organic factors on learning. The evidence indicating changes in I.Q. and other measures of learned behavior with changes in social environment suggests that some characteristics of the latter are relevant considerations. Jensen recommends that the school programs be adapted to the differences in presumed levels of genetically structured ability. This already common practice tends to fulfill the predictions that are based upon presumed differences of ability and to create a school social environment designed to enhance the differences in learning. This conception of the school is transmitted to members of the social system including students, parents, and teachers, as well as persons outside the school.

Because of the evidence which indicates that the level of school achievement is significantly related to the social status and racial background of the children's families, it has frequently been assumed that family background and related out-of-school factors determine the success of students in school and elsewhere.[6] The Equality of Educational Opportunity study attributed a major portion of the variation in school achievement to such family background factors.[7] Such contentions are based upon the assumption that what has happened to the child prior to entering the school and in out-of-school situations is of such overpowering impact that the school can have little or no effect in modifying the differences that occur among children. The limited success of compensatory education efforts in overcoming the educational disadvantages of lower-class minority group children have been used to support this contention.[8] The failure of the schools to overcome the disadvantages of many lower-class children has led some to a variety of explanations of the differences in families as well as genetic differences that may explain the achievement of such children. Differences in language[9] and

---

[4] Arthur R. Jensen, "How Much Can We Boost I.Q. and Scholastic Achievement?" *Harvard Educational Review,* vol. 39, Winter, 1969, pp. 1–123.

[5] Richard Lewontin, "Race and Intelligence," *Bulletin of Atomic Scientists,* vol. 26, March 1970, pp. 2–8. Reprinted in E. A. Schuler, T. E. Hoult, D. L. Gibson, and W. B. Brookover, *Readings in Sociology,* 5th ed. (New York: T. Y. Crowell Company, 1974).

[6] Christopher Jencks et al., *Inequality: A Reassessment of the Effect of Family and Schooling in America* (New York: Basic Books, Inc., 1972).

[7] Coleman et al., *Equality of Educational Opportunity.*

[8] Jensen, "How Much Can We Boost I.Q?"

[9] Basil Berstein, "Social Class and Linguistic Development: A Theory of Social Learning," in A. H. Halsey, Jean Floud, and C. A. Anderson, *Education, Economy & Society* (New York: Free Press of Glencoe, 1961).

possible differences in cognitive styles[10] have been advanced as primary explanations of such differences. Both genetic and family background may contribute to the level of achievement which occurs in school and accounts for some of the great differences among children. All these, however, tend to shift the focus of attention away from the possible effect of the school social environment on students' learning.

In the previous chapter we examined the relation of several types of school organization to academic achievement and other school outcomes. This examination reveals that little of the great differences in outcomes is currently explained by the organizational variables considered. Educators have assumed in the past that the differences resulted to a large extent from the quality of the school facilities, instructional material, teacher-pupil ratio, and other factors associated with expenditures for education. Recent research indicates that such factors account for little of the difference in school achievement.[11] In contrast, these and other studies indicate that some other aspects of the school social environment may substantially affect the performances of the students.

School Social Context and School Climate

The social aspects of school environment could be classified in several ways. We have used three concepts to refer to different aspects of the social environment—social organization, social context, and social climate. These are not independent categories; variation in one may be and frequently is associated with variation in one or both of the others. In the previous chapter we identified a number of organizational variables that may be related to the behavioral norms, expectations, and other aspects of the school climate or culture. The climate variables may in turn be related to the social context or social composition of the school.

The concepts of social context and social climate as they relate to the school situation have frequently been used interchangeably. This has resulted in some misinterpretation of the factors which affect school performance. The social context of a school refers more precisely to the characteristics of the students that compose the student body. Thus, a school composed of all black or nearly all black students would be characterized as a school having a black student social context. Similarly,

[10] Margaret Bachman, "Patterns of Mental Abilities: Ethnic, Socioeconomics and Sex Differences," *American Educational Research Journal*, vol. 9, pp. 1–12, 1972.

[11] Coleman, *Equality of Educational Opportunity;* Frederick Mosteller and Daniel P. Moynihan, *On Equality of Educational Opportunity* (New York: Vintage Books, 1972); and George Mayeske et al., *A Study of Our Nations Schools,* (Washington, D.C.: U.S. Department of Health, Education and Welfare, 1969).

a middle-class white school would be so identified by the composition of the student population. In considering the impact on school performance we therefore refer to presumed effects of the predominantly black or middle-class white student body on the behavior of particular students. The attributes of the students—such as race, social-economic status, age, sex—in the aggregate would define the social context in which the students' achievement occurred. The context of the student body is directly related to some aspects of organization. Racially segregated school organizations, for example, at the same time determine one aspect of composition but SES composition may vary greatly in segregated schools.

School climate or the school subculture refers to the attitudes, beliefs, values, and norms that characterize the social system of the school. The climate or culture is determined by the aggregate attitudes, beliefs, norms, and expectations of the persons who make up the school social system.

In many schools, the nature of the school climate or culture is closely related to the composition of the student body. Thus, the socioeconomic or racial composition of the school student body is typically related to the aggregate attitude of both students and teachers. For example, the socioeconomic composition of the student body is generally related to the educational aspirations of students. In a similar fashion, the academic norms and the expectations which teachers hold for students are related to social composition. The Equality of Educational Opportunity study and other research have demonstrated that the proportion of a student body from families of higher socioeconomic status, the proportion white and the proportion enrolled in college preparatory curricula are significant predictors of school achievement. These findings do not demonstrate, however, that these social context factors are the actual causes of the differences in achievement. Variant attitudinal or social climate factors which are associated with the context variables may more directly account for the differences in achievement. To the extent that these two sets of variables are highly correlated, regression analysis does not provide a means for separating the effects of various factors. Efforts to statistically sort out the effect uniquely attributable to different sets of interrelated variables in the school environment have not been very successful.[12]

Although it is difficult to separate the effects of the aggregate social context and the social climate variables on school achievement, it does not follow that the norms and other aspects of the climate are automatically produced by the social context or composition of the school. Although the correlation between the social class composition and the

[12] Mayeske et al., *Our Nation's Schools.*

teachers' expectations of the students may be quite high, it is not inevitable that high SES schools will be characterized by high levels of expectations or that low SES schools are necessarily characterized by low levels of expectations. Both aspects of the social environment—social context and the school social climate—may independently affect achievement as well as interact to affect achievement.[13]

The Relation of School Performance to Social Context

Since the composition of the school is related to the school culture or climate, an examination of the major evidence showing the relation of the social context to the school achievement and other aspects of the school performance is essential to an understanding of the relationship of climate to achievement.

The most comprehensive study of the effects of the school social context on school achievement is provided by the Equality of Educational Opportunity study. This national study revealed that "attributes of other students account for far more variation in the achievement of minority group children than do any attributes of school facilities and slightly more than do attributes of the staff."[14] Although the school characteristics including the student body composition account for less of the variance in the achievement of white students than in that of minorities, the characteristics of the white student body also account for more variance than any other school characteristics. These conclusions are based on the analysis of the data in which the effect of family background on school achievement had already been removed. The comparative effects of various school factors on school verbal achievement of the sixth-, ninth-, and 12th-grade students is shown in Table 14–1. It will be noted that the percentage of the variance accounted for by the student body quality is significantly greater than that accounted for by the school and teacher characteristic variables. The proportion of the variance attributable to student body characteristics is, in some cases, greater than the amount attributable to all of these school factors acting in common.

Further analysis of the Equality of Opportunity data indicates that differences in the socioeconomic composition of the student body were the most significant student body factor accounting for variance in achievement. Thus, the social composition or social context of the student

[13] Sarane A. Boocock, *An Introduction to the Sociology of Learning* (Boston: Houghton-Mifflin Company, 1972).

[14] Coleman et al., *Equality of Educational Opportunity*, p. 302.

TABLE 14–1
Percent of Variance in Verbal Achievement Uniquely Accounted for by One Variable Representing Each of: School Facilities (A), Curriculum (B), Teacher Quality (C), Teacher Attitudes (D), Student Body Quality (E), at Grades 12, 9, and 6

	Joint		*Unique*				
	ABCDE	*Common*	*A*	*B*	*C*	*D*	*E*
Grade 12							
Puerto Ricans	21.83	11.93	1.00	0.01	0.44	0.89	8.55
Indian Americans	10.60	3.56	.31	.52	0	2.77	3.44
Mexican Americans	15.70	7.45	.22	.20	.27	.42	7.14
Negro, South	11.06	2.80	0	0	.01	.18	8.07
Negro, North	7.59	3.58	.13	.04	0	.17	3.67
Oriental Americans	1.18	.44	.03	.03	.18	.09	.41
White, South	3.02	.25	.02	0	0	.24	2.34
White, North	1.58	.25	.02	0	0	0	1.31
Negro, total	12.43	5.58	.02	1.01	.02	.03	6.77
White, total	2.52	.50	.01	0	0	0	2.01
Grade 9							
Puerto Ricans	14.46	2.95	.13	.23	.05	.31	10.79
Indian Americans	8.69	2.39	.89	.16	.19	.30	4.76
Mexican Americans	9.22	3.88	.05	.19	.28	1.18	3.64
Negro, South	8.84	3.40	0	0	.07	.02	5.35
Negro, North	3.37	1.38	.07	.01	.01	.24	1.66
Oriental Americans	3.79	–.34	.05	.20	.27	.13	3.48
White, South	2.05	.15	.03	.03	.01	.05	1.78
White, North	1.23	.01	.01	.12	.08	.01	1.10
Negro, total	8.21	3.99	.01	0	.08	.08	4.05
White, total	1.88	–.06	.02	.08	.06	.09	1.69
Grade 6							
Puerto Ricans	12.01	4.07	.01	.02	.03	.02	7.86
Indian Americans	9.14	2.28	.54	.09	.40	.34	5.49
Mexican Americans	12.91	4.91	0	.01	.10	.22	7.67
Negro, South	9.48	3.22	.05	.03	.06	.04	6.12
Negro, North	4.81	.87	0	.05	.19	.01	3.69
Oriental Americans	4.99	1.39	.15	.42	.08	.04	2.91
White, South	2.13	–.02	.03	0	0	.01	2.11
White, North	4.56	.02	.15	0	.08	0	4.31
Negro, total	9.38	2.85	0	.03	0	.01	6.49
White, total	4.37	–.06	.03	0	.05	.09	4.26

Source: James Coleman et al., *Equality of Educational Opportunity,* HEW Office of Education, U.S. Government Printing Office, 1966, p. 303.

body as measured primarily by characteristics of socioeconomic status is more highly related to school achievement than any other school characteristic.

The extent to which the racial composition of schools accounts for variance in achievement has been the subject of considerable debate. Both the original analysis of the Equality of Educational Opportunity data and the subsequent analysis indicate that the difference in achievement among black students attending segregated and integrated schools is associated with differences in socioeconomic-status composition of the student bodies.[15] A subsequent and independent analysis by the U.S. Commission on Civil Rights (1967) indicated, however, that racial composition was associated somewhat more with differences in achievement than the earlier analysis suggested. More significant, however, than the racial and ethnic differences were the clear differences in achievement of children from varying levels of socioeconomic status in society. These differences in outcomes were in turn related to the socioeconomic composition of the schools.

The Coleman findings and subsequent analysis that the achievement of lower-class white and black students is slightly higher in racially-mixed schools, and that middle-class white students learn just as well in racially-mixed schools as they do in segregated middle-class schools, has provided support for desegregation proponents.[16] Although the data are not adequate at this time to verify such conclusions, many believe that integrated schools have other desirable outcomes such as better human relations in American society.

School Climate and Learning

School climate has been defined in various ways but generally refers to some characteristics of school social systems. A range of variables from strictly personal characteristics of students to general cultural characteristics of the school have been used as indexes of school climates.

One of the early applications of the concept "climate" to educational organizations was made by Pace and Stern.[17] For them, organizational climate included both individual needs as identified by the personality characteristics and values of the members and the organizational pressures on student and adult participants which they termed "press." Astin and Holland assumed that the organizational pressures were largely dependent upon the people within that environment.[18] Organizational climate was therefore defined as the personality orientations and characteristics of the major portion of the students within the school. Michael generally concurred in the Astin and Holland conception, but Boyle included both structural characteristics of the school and the characteris-

[15] Jencks et al., *Inequality.*

[16] Thomas F. Pettigrew, "The Case for Racial Integration of the Schools," in E. A. Schuler, T. F. Hoult, D. L. Gibson, W. B. Brookover (eds.), *Readings in Sociology* (New York: T. Y. Crowell Company, 1974), pp. 373–85.

[17] C. R. Pace and G. G. Stern, "Approach to the Measurement of Psychological Environments," *Journal of Educational Psychology,* vol. 49, pp. 269–77, 1959.

[18] A. W. Astin and J. L. Holland, "The Environmental Assessment Technique: A Way to Measure College Environments," *Journal of Educational Psychology,* vol. 52 (1961), pp. 308–16.

tics of the students.[19] Somewhat later, Bachman and Secord elaborated their definition of climate to include three kinds of variables: first, personality characteristics, motives, educational plans, and past experiences of the students; second, the norms, values, role requirements, and other similar characteristics of the school social system; and third, the values and norms of the informal organization of the school.[20] They recognized in the latter condition that large institutions such as universities or large high schools include varying norms or climates for different segments of the student body.

In the social-psychological frame of reference in which we examine learning, the school social climate encompasses a composite of variables as defined and perceived by the members of the group. These factors may be broadly conceived as the norms of the social system and the expectations held for various members as perceived by the members of the group and communicated to members of the group.[21] Johnson conceived of norms as "the common beliefs of an evaluating type that make explicit the forms of behavior for members of a social system."[22] The role expectations involve both the definitions of behavior expressed by others in the system and the perception of these as understood by members. The role expectations may be general in the sense that they are applied to all members of the particular category such as students, or they may be more specific as applied to different categories of students or individuals. The impact of the norms and perceived role expectations depends upon the extent to which the incumbent considers the role important to him and the extent to which the norms and expectations are enforced. Enforcement of the norms and expectations depends on the quality of surveillance by the social system.[23] This refers to the extent to which someone in the social system is checking on the performance of other members. In addition, conformity to the norms and expectations is reinforced by appropriate approval and awards and failure to conform results in the withholding of the rewards or sanctions.

[19] J. A. Michael, "High School Climates and Plans for Entering College," *Public Opinion Quarterly*, vol. 25, pp. 585–95, 1961; and R. P. Boyle, "The Effect of High School on Students' Aspirations," *American Journal of Sociology*, vol. 71, pp. 628–39, 1966.

[20] Carl W. Bachman and Paul F. Secord, *A Social Psychological View of Education* (New York: Harcourt Brace & World Inc., 1968).

[21] Bradley Niles, *A Comparison of Student Perceived and Parents Actual Evaluations-Expectations in Low SES Schools with School Achievement Level and Racial Composition Controlled.* Ph.D. Dissertation, Michigan State University, 1974. An analysis of the convergence of students' perception of expectations with parents' expressed expectations.

[22] David W. Johnson, *The Social Psychology of Education* (New York: Holt Rinehart and Winston, Inc., 1970).

[23] Edsel Erickson, *A Study of Normative Influence of Parent and Friends Upon Academic Achievement.* Doctoral Dissertation, Michigan State University, 1965.

Schools' norms and role expectations define the appropriateness of a wide range of student behavior. These may include such matters as running in the corridors, tardiness, dress behavior, hair style, and many other behaviors as well as the level of academic performance. Some of the norms and expectations apply to all students and all teachers in the system while others may apply to all those occupying specific roles. Thus, 12th-grade students are expected to behave in certain ways that may not apply to freshmen.

While norms and expectations define many types of student behavior (they should not run in the halls, should not arrive late to class, should not be absent).[24] We are concerned here primarily with the norms and expectations which define the academic climate of the school.

Norms. Conformity to pressure or group norms has been studied by social psychologists.[25] Numerous studies indicate that individual members tend to conform to the majority opinion or behavior. Others have been concerned with the identification of the obligation or "ought" quality of the norms. Both dimensions, the actual conformity of behavior and the obligation to behave in certain ways, are characteristic of the norms and, no doubt, operate to produce some conformity to the majority pattern that is deemed appropriate or necessary.

The extent of the conformity to the group norms varies somewhat with the saliency or importance of the group as a reference for the students involved. If the norms are for a group which an individual considers irrelevant or a group whose members' good opinion is not valued, the individual is less likely to conform to the group's norms. A student's conformity to the school norms depends to some extent on the importance he attaches to the school group's opinion and his membership in it.

The importance or saliency of the norms of a particular reference group may vary from time to time. Charters and Newcomb found that the religious norms of a group of Catholic students were made more salient by discussion of the basic assumptions of the Catholic faith and opinions.[26] A group of students who had engaged in such discussions responded quite differently to attitudinal questions concerning matters for which their religious faith was relevant than a similar group of students who had not engaged in such discussion. There were no differences between the groups' attitudes on matters that were not related

[24] Robert Dreeban, *On What is Learned in School* (Reading, Massachusetts: Addison-Wesley Publishing Company, 1968).

[25] Johnson, *Social Psychology of Education.*

[26] W. W. Charters, Jr. and T. M. Newcomb, "Some Attitudinal Effects of Experimentally Increased Silence of a Membership Group," in G. E. Swanson, T. M. Newcomb, and E. L. Hartley, *Reading in Social Psychology,* 2d ed. (New York: Holt, Rinehart and Winston, 1952).

to the Catholic faith. Thus, the degree of conformity to the norm was affected by the saliency of that group and the immediate application of the norms to the situation at hand. This evidence indicates that a person must be aware of the group norms before he can conform. Even though the teachers may feel that academic achievement is important in the school and some students may be equally committed to high levels of learning, such norms are not likely to influence other students unless the behavior is made salient and important to all students.

The extent of conformity to group norms also depends on the surveillance of the group to whose norms the individual may be conforming. If the group cannot determine whether or not an individual is conforming or if it does not check up on him in any manner, the individual is less likely to conform to the norms of that particular group. Of course, if the group has surveillance over the members, the conformity may depend on the possibility that sanctions of some sort may be applied to members who deviate from the norm. One sanction in many informal school groups is the denial of membership in the group to those who do not conform. In similar fashion, students who do not conform to certain norms are sometimes expelled from high school or college student bodies. This extreme measure, however, may be no more important to students than the good opinion and acceptance of an informal clique or subgroup within the student body.

A group's norms may influence people who are not observable members. A student who aspires to membership or who wishes the approval of a group with norms of high academic performance may be influenced to achieve at the group's level. If a student is certain that he cannot achieve membership in a particular group, regardless of the degree of his conformity, he is not likely to be greatly influenced by its norms. A lower-class student, for example, who is certain he will not be admitted to the college-bound curriculum or an academic-oriented group, is not likely to conform to the academic behavioral norms of this college-bound group.

Some individual personality characteristics may also directly or indirectly affect conformity to the group. Some evidence indicates that dependency or self-confidence may influence the degree to which particular individuals conform to certain groups. Generally, however, relevant groups have significant influence on behavior. When the group opinion is important to the individual, he may tend to conform to what appears to be the group's judgment even though it is clearly in error or contrary to facts.[27] Such findings emphasize the importance of group norms for school performance. If the norms of the school social system define the display of superior academic performance as undesirable, a student

[27] S. E. Asch, *Social Psychology* (Englewood Cliffs, New Jersey: Prentice Hall, Inc., 1952).

may sometimes give incorrect answers even when he knows they are incorrect. This also suggests the possibility of incompatible or conflicting norms. A student's parents and teachers may expect him to excel in classroom recitation, but the student group norms may condemn such behavior. When the norms of a school group are not congruent with the family norms or expectations for him, the student must decide to which norms he will conform or find another solution to the dilemma. The degree to which a student conforms to the classroom norms may be affected by the degree to which they are congruent with the norms of other groups to which he refers himself.

Student Role Expectations. The norms of a social group are largely composed of the common expectations which members of the group hold for each other. The school social system is composed of a variety of different roles. The teachers, of course, occupy quite a different position from that of the students. Among both the teachers and the students there are also identifiably different positions which carry with them different role expectations. As a school group interacts, some individual variations in the role expectations develop for members of the same age group. Someone may come to occupy the position of the clown or player of jokes; others may be expected to be serious at all times. In this manner a school group may define varying expectations with respect to academic achievement for the students in a classroom. Although expectations may vary for particular students, a general level of behavior is expected of all and the range of expectations as well as the typical or median level of achievement in one school may be somewhat different from those in another school.

In a study of the social class characteristics of urban elementary schools, Herriot and St. John examined the images and expectations which teachers and principals held for their students. In a national sample of 187 urban elementary schools, they found that "in the average school of highest socioeconomic status, nine percent of the pupils, according to the principal and 14 percent, according to the teachers, were not interested in learning. But in the average school in the lowest socioeconomic category, 22 percent and 29 percent, respectively, are felt to be uninterested."[28] The principals in these schools were also asked, "What percentage of the students in your school will probably drop out before they graduate from high school?" and "What percentage of students in your school will probably go to college?" In the highest quartile, according to socioeconomic status of the school, the principal expected 64 percent of the children to go to college and only 7 percent to drop out before finishing high school. In the lowest socioeconomic status quartile, they expected seven percent to go to college and 44

[28] Robert Herriot and Nancy St. John, *Social Class and the Urban School* (New York: Wiley, 1966), p. 44.

percent to drop out before they finished high school.[29] To the extent that principals and teachers can define the role expectations for students in the elementary school, these data suggest that there are vast differences in the expectations held for students in various schools. It is likely that the teacher's and principal's expectations for the students are related to the evaluations which they make of the student's ability to learn.

Rosenthal and Jacobson examined the effect of reporting high intelligence test scores to the teachers of a random sample of elementary school children on their subsequent achievement and intelligence.[30] The hypothesis of this "Pygmalion" study was that teachers who thought that some students had high measured intelligence would expect higher levels of performance and that their expectations would be fulfilled. Although there are some variations in the results, this study provided support for the hypothesis, particularly for early elementary students. It is important to note that the study did not examine whether or not the expectations of teachers were actually changed. It is possible that some teachers, particularly those in the lower elementary grades, were more likely to accept the report of the investigators that a sample of their students were spurters or rapid learners. The credibility of the researcher probably varied from one teacher to another and his information was probably more likely to be accepted by teachers of early elementary classes than those of upper elementary classes. Furthermore, teachers were probably more likely to accept the reported intelligence changes for students in the "average ability" sections than for students who were clearly identified as students of superior ability or low ability. Since Rosenthal and Jacobson did not examine the extent to which teachers accepted the reported IQ data and thus modified their expectations of these children, it is only a tenable hypothesis that these variations affected the extent of the difference in achievement and measured intelligence among experimental students and the control students in the classrooms.

College Climate. Most of the earlier studies of the organizational climate were focused on college and university environments. Generally such studies have assumed differences in student achievement among various colleges.[31] After review of the literature on the effect of colleges on students, Jacob concluded that only a relatively few colleges had a major effect on the values which the students held.[32] The effect of

---

[29] Ibid., p. 53.

[30] Robert Rosenthal and Lenore Jacobson, *Pygmalion in the Classroom* (New York: Holt, Rinehart and Winston, 1968).

[31] R. H. Knapp and J. J. Greenbaum, *The Younger American Scholar: His Collegiate Origins* (Chicago, University of Chicago Press, 1952).

[32] P. Jacob, *Changing Values in College* (New York: Harper & Row Publishers, 1957).

the college climate on students' behavior is not precisely identified in most of these studies, however. Many colleges that are selective in their student bodies attract students who already behave essentially in the manner that they try to produce in their graduates. This, plus the self-selection in which students engage, has the effect of matching the student's precollege values and behavior to the college environment. In such circumstances little change should be expected. Furthermore, many of the studies have examined values and attitudes which the college is not intended to change. In instances where these conditions do not exist there is some evidence that the college environment does affect significantly the behavior of students. Newcomb found that upper-middle-class girls who attended Bennington College acquired more liberal political and social attitudes in the Bennington social environment.[33] This suggests that there are significant changes in behavior in those areas in which the college focuses particular attention. Most of the studies of changes in college have not examined the acquisition of academic knowledge and skills which are presumably the primary focus of the college environment.

School Climate and Academic Achievement. In previous paragraphs, we have examined some of the research on norms and role expectations which provides the foundation for studies that more specifically focus on school climate and the achievement of students in school. We specifically ask how this complex of variables which we have identified as school climate is related to school achievement. In each of the studies reviewed below, attempts are made to separate the effect of social context or social composition factors from the effects of school climate factors. We are thus able to identify to some degree what it is about a typically higher SES school that produces higher levels of achievement than in typically low SES schools.

In a recent study, McDill and his associates developed a measure of the normative secondary school climate and examined the effect of the complex of variables thus identified on school achievement.[34] In their analysis, the socioeconomic composition of the school and the relevant family background and other variables were controlled. McDill and his associates developed a questionnaire for both students and teachers on which both served as reporters of the general academic climate of the school social system.

Factor analysis of the student and teacher responses to 35 items identified six factors in the school climate. These factors were labeled: (1) academic emulation; (2) student perception of intellectualism and

---

[33] T. M. Newcomb, *Personality and Social Change: Attitude Formation in a Student Community* (New York: Dryden Press, 1943).

[34] Edward McDill and Leo Rigsby, *The Academic Impact of Educational Climates* (Baltimore, Maryland: The Johns Hopkins University Press, 1973).

aestheticism; (3) cohesive and equalitarian aestheticism; (4) scientism; (5) humanistic excellence; and (6) academically oriented student status system. These six factors thus became "indicators of the normative influence of different school climates." A level of school achievement in the schools was measured by a mathematics achievement test.

The analysis indicated that the composition of the school with respect to socioeconomic status was related to the achievement of the students but that each of the climate dimensions except factor 4 was more strongly related to achievement than SES context. The first factor, academic emulation, explained more than twice the variation in math achievement than that explained by social-status composition. Furthermore, with the effects of socioeconomic context as well as ability and family background controlled, the six climate dimensions accounted for more than 40 percent of the variance in math performance. The first factor, academic emulation, accounts for more of the variance in mathematics achievement than any of the other factors, but each contributes a significant amount to the total climate effect on achievement.

Although academic climate factors, particularly academic emulation, are correlated with the socioeconomic status context of the 20 high schools, the correlation is largely explained by the schools in the top and bottom quartile of both social-status composition and academic emulation. There is no relationship between SES context and climate among the schools in the middle range of social-class composition. Since the school climate factors account for most of the variance generally attributed to social class composition, it is clear that normative climate factors identified here are significantly better predictors of academic achievement in mathematics than is the socioeconomic composition of the student body.

Although this study involved only 20 white high schools, it contributes significantly to our understanding of the climate factors which may explain differences in achievement in schools in different socioeconomic and racial composition. The findings of this study are significant as background for a subsequent study by the senior author and his associates of the social climates of elementary schools.[35] The findings of the two studies, although different in design, must be examined in relation to each other.

The latter study was also designed to separate the effects of socioeconomic and racial composition from those of school climate. The design of the latter study might be described as an ex post facto experiment. Instead of selecting a sample of schools from a larger population at random, certain specific deviant schools were identified to compare with

[35] Wilbur B. Brookover, Richard J. Gigliotti, Ronald P. Henderson, and Jeffrey M. Schneider, *Elementary School Social Environments and Achievement* (East Lansing, Michigan: College of Urban Development, Michigan State University, 1973).

more typical schools. With the cooperation of the Michigan State Department of Education, the socioeconomic composition, racial composition, and mean fourth grade school achievement data for all elementary schools in Michigan were identified. These data provided the basis for selecting a sample of matched pairs of schools with similar socioeconomic and racial composition, but significantly different levels of school achievement. Table 14–2 indicates the distribution of schools selected. The study

TABLE 14–2
Characteristics of Schools Selected for Study: Race, Mean S.E.S., Mean Achievement Level, Urban-Rural Type, and Number of Students and Teachers in Each School Sample

School	*S.E.S. Level*	*Achievement Level*	*Percent White*	*N Students*	*N Teachers*
		White			
01	Higher–55.1	Higher–59.6	85.0	140	6
02	Higher–55.2	Lower–48.1	100.0	173	6
03	Higher–58.2	Higher–54.4	100.0	224	9
04	Higher–54.9	Lower–47.8	100.0	202	7
05	Higher–50.1	Higher–58.0	100.0	88	3
06	Higher–49.4	Lower–43.6	97.7	67	2
07	Lower–43.2	Higher–56.7	100.0	104	4
08	Lower–44.9	Lower–44.6	100.0	88	3
09	Lower–46.6	Higher–55.1	97.7	151	6
10	Lower–46.8	Lower–43.7	95.1	81	3
		Black			
11	Higher–61.3	Higher–55.1	30.0	276	6
12	Higher–52.9	Lower–47.2	01.0	406	12
13[a]	Higher–50.0	Higher–51.8			
14	Higher–49.2	Lower–37.3	00.5	149	6
15	Lower–43.8	Higher–47.2	00.8	116	6
16	Lower–46.7	Lower–38.0	13.8	105	6
17	Lower–47.0	Higher–49.6	09.5	105	4
18	Lower–46.7	Lower–39.6	05.3	384	11
		Rural			
19	Higher–53.2	Higher–58.1	100.0	16	2
20	Lower–44.6	Higher–58.4	100.0	13	2
21	Lower–42.9	Higher–58.2	100.0	18	1
22	Lower–44.3	Higher–60.6	87.6	55	3
23	Higher–50.7	Lower–50.2	100.0	62	3
24	Lower–47.8	Lower–45.6	100.0	40	2
25	Lower–37.8	Lower–42.5	100.0	9	1

[a] Chosen as part of the original sample, but not permitted to collect data.

was designed to reveal as nearly as possible the differences in school social climate that might explain the difference in achievement between schools with similar composition, but significantly different achievement. Pairs of high and low SES white schools as well as high and low SES black urban schools and some rural schools were studied. Since the social class and racial composition of the schools were controlled, we were asking, What differences in "treatment" occurred in these schools to produce the differences in achievement?

Deriving their items from the social psychological conception of school climate elaborated in this chapter, Brookover and his associates developed both a student and a teacher questionnaire which were administered to the fourth, fifth, and sixth grade students in each of the elementary schools selected. Separate factor analyses were done for the teacher and student questionnaires. The factor analyses produced four factors describing school academic climate as perceived by the students and six factors as reported by the teachers.

Student Factors. The four factors which emerged from the student data were identified as: (1) student perceptions of the present evaluations-expectations of "others" in their school social system; (2) student perceptions of the future evaluations-expectations of "others" in their school social system; (3) student perceptions about the level of feelings of futility permeating the social system of the school; and (4) student perceptions of those academic norms stressing academic achievement which exist in their school and social system.

The evaluation-expectations variable is composed of two separate school climate factors. The first included those items which concentrated upon the expectations and evaluations of "others" (parents, teachers, friends), as well as the students' own "self-concept of academic ability" from the *present* through the completion of high school. This was named Student Perceived *Present* Evaluations and Expectations.

The second factor dealt with student perceptions of the beliefs of "others" (parents, teachers, friends) concerning the subject's chances of *future* academic accomplishments and the student's future oriented "self-concept of academic ability" and self-evaluation. More specifically, this factor includes those items related to the reported beliefs and perceptions of beliefs about college attendance and success. It was identified as Student Perceived *Future* Evaluations and Expectations.

The third factor included a modification of the "sense of control" questions used by Coleman and several items which reflected the student's perceptions of the teachers and, to a lesser extent, other students' feelings of hopelessness or lack of caring about academic achievement.[36] This was identified as the Student's Reported Sense of Futility.

The last student factor included items assessing the student perceptions about the amount of pressure placed upon achievement by members of the school social system and school bureaucracy. Items reflected the student perception concerning the evaluations and expectations of their principal, the general normative academic push of the school environment, the amount of student perceived competition-cooperation

[36] Coleman et al., *Equality of Educational Opportunity.*

within the environment, and the importance of the student role. This factor was identified as the Student Perception of School Academic Norms.

Teacher Factors. A second factor analysis identified six factors from the teachers' responses to 49 questions. These were: (1) teacher present evaluations-expectations; (2) teacher future evaluations-expectations; (3) teacher perceptions of parent-student push for education achievement; (4) teacher-reported push of individual students; (5) teacher satisfaction; (6) teacher perceptions of the social system belief in student improvability.

Just as in the case of the student factor analysis, the teacher data revealed the emergence of two separate evaluation-expectation factors; those items more oriented to the present time and those having a more future orientation. Items forming the Teacher Present Evaluation and Expectations factor generally referred to teachers' evaluations and expectations of students in the immediate present and through the high school period.

The Teacher Future Evaluation-Expectation factor included items dealing with teachers' evaluations and expectations about their students in the future, specifically with the possibility of the students' gaining entrance into and finding success in college.

The items comprising the fourth teacher factor were designed to measure the amount of push that teachers were willing to exert upon individual students in order to encourage performance greater than the teacher expectations. It was identified as the Teachers' Reported Push of Individual Students. Another factor emerging from the factor analysis consisted of three items designed to assess the degree of teacher satisfaction with his present school and with teaching in general. It was identified as Teacher Reported Feelings of Job Satisfaction.

The factor labeled Teacher Perception of Student Academic Improvability was based upon items designed to report teachers' perceptions of whether or not students in the school could overcome past academic failure. Specifically, this factor represents the belief within the school social system that hard work will result in improved student academic performance.

A regression analysis of the amount of variance in mean school achievement accounted for by the ten student and teacher factors revealed that four factors made significant contributions. The results of this analysis which first eliminated that portion of the variance accounted for by the demographic factors of SES, race, and urban-rural community type are shown in Table 14–3.

Socioeconomic and racial composition account for less of the variance in achievement than is normally the case because the design controlled most of these effects. This analysis clearly demonstrates that by far

TABLE 14–3
Findings of Least Square Add Linear Regression Analysis of the Variance in Mean School Achievement Accounted for by Ten Student and Teacher School Climate Variables

Variable	*R*	R^2	*Prob.*	*Percent Added to the Prediction of Achievement*	*Significance of B*
S.E.S.					
Race					
Urban-Rural					
Interaction.	0.5056	0.2556	0.109		
Student Sense of Futility . .	0.8395	0.7048	<0.0005	.4492	<0.0005
Teacher Future Evaluations-Expectations	0.8962	0.8031	0 0.008	.0983	<0.0005
Teacher Reported Push Individual Students.	0.9225	0.8559	0.023	.0528	<0.0005
Student Present Evaluations-Expectations	0.9418	0.8995	0.052	.0336	<0.0005

the most important of the ten climate variables was the students' reported sense of futility which accounted for 44.9 percent of the variance in achievement. Other variables significantly contributing to the higher mean school achievement were: higher teacher-reported future evaluations-expectations, less teacher-reported need to push individual students, and higher student-perceived present evaluations-expectations. These four school climate variables predicted slightly over 63 percent of the achievement variations in our sampled schools. Thus, significant differences in social psychological climate factors do appear to exist between high and low achieving schools when the effects of SES and racial composition and urban-rural community type are controlled.

Since the "students' reported sense of futility" accounted for a high proportion of the difference in school achievement, the effect of the other nine factors on its variance was analyzed. The results of this analysis after the effects of SES and racial composition and urban-rural type were removed are shown in Table 14–4.

This analysis indicates that over 40 percent of the variation in student sense of futility among the fourth, fifth and sixth grade students in 24 schools is accounted for by three significant academic climate variables. First, a low sense of futility is found in those schools which also have a high teacher present evaluation-expectation. Secondly, schools with a lower student-reported sense of futility also have a more positive student perception of the presence within the school environment of norms stressing academic achievement. And thirdly, there exists high student perceptions of the present evaluations-expectations of student achievement. All of these variables appear to exercise an important indirect relationship on the mean school achievement.

TABLE 14–4
Least Square Add Linear Regression Analysis of the Variance in the "Sense of Futility" Accounted for by Nine Other Climate Factors with S.E.S. and Racial Composition and Community Type Controlled

Variable	*R*	R^2	*Prob.*	*Percent Added to the Prediction of Achievement*	*Significance of B*
S.E.S. Race Urban-Rural Interaction.	0.6320	0.3994	0.015		
Teacher Present Evaluations-Expectations	0.8069	0.6511	0.002	.2517	<0.0005
Student Perceived School Academic Norms	0.8569	0.7343	0.029	.0832	<0.0005
Student Present Evaluations-Expectations	0.8906	0.8147	0.042	.0804	<0.0005

This study indicates that several dimensions of school climate directly or indirectly affect the level of achievement occurring in elementary schools when both racial and socioeconomic composition are controlled. The students' feeling that he cannot master the school social system and that teachers do not care about whether he succeeds or not, as identified in "students' sense of futility," clearly distinguishes between high and low achieving schools and accounts for much of the variation in mean school achievement. Both the students' perception of the evaluation-expectations held for them and the teachers' evaluations-expectations of the students contribute significantly to explaining the variance in mean school achievement. These data show that the pattern of evaluations and expectations that characterize the school significantly influences the students' beliefs about himself and the possibilities of his success. Although much more definitive research needs to be carried on, the data from the study by McDill and others as well as the research of Brookover and others indicate that the social psychological characteristics of the school climate explain much of the differences in levels of school achievement.[37] Further analysis of the elementary school data indicates that the students' feeling of futility and their perception of the evaluation-expectation held for them in the school also distinguish between black and white schools. Furthermore, the students' perception of academic norms are clearly different in higher and lower SES schools when the effect of race is controlled. These findings suggest that the differences in the climate factors characterizing the elementary schools may explain much of the difference commonly attributed to racial and

[37] McDill and Rigsby, *Academic Impact of Educational Climates;* and Brookover et al., *Elementary School Social Environments and Achievement.*

socioeconomic-status composition. This would support the findings from the McDill study of secondary schools at the elementary school level. Although in somewhat different frame of reference and involving a different research design, the study by Brookover and others tends to substantiate the Rosenthal and Jacobson emphasis upon expectations as a factor affecting student achievement.[38] A further study of school climates in a random sample of elementary schools is currently being carried out by the senior author.

Summary

In this and the previous chapter, we have examined the effects of school organization, social context, and school climate on the achievement of students in school. The evidence has now clearly demonstrated that the complex of composition and climate factors has a significant affect on the level of achievement of students in school. The separation of the effects of various context and climate variables has not, however, produced clear conclusions. Recent studies indicate that much of the difference in school performance that has been attributed to the racial and socioeconomic composition of the school may be more directly the result of the differences in the school climate. This raises the question of whether or not it is possible to create a favorable academic climate in schools with predominantly lower-class or predominantly black student bodies. The few exceptions to the common pattern of low achievement in lower SES and black schools suggest the possibility of creating such favorable climates. However, this would be a very large task, given the condition where there is a tendency for favorable academic climates to be associated with middle-class white schools and unfavorable academic climates with lower SES black schools. We will examine the importance of this in American society in the following chapter.

Suggested Readings

Wilbur B. Brookover, Richard Gigliotti, Ronald P. Henderson, and Jeffery M. Schneider, *Elementary School Social Environments and Achievement* (East Lansing, Mich.: College of Urban Development, Michigan State University, 1973).

David W. Johnson, *Social Psychology of Education* (N.Y.: Holt, Rinehart and Winston, 1970).

David Kamens, "Colleges and Elite Formation: The Case of Prestigious

[38] Rosenthal and Jacobson, *Pygmalion in the Classroom.*

American Colleges," *Sociology of Education,* 47, no. 3 (Summer 1974) pp. 354–78.

Edward McDill and Leo Rigsby, *The Academic Import of Educational Climates* (Baltimore: The Johns Hopkins University Press, 1973).

Stephan Riches, "Programme Composition and Educational Plans," *Sociology of Education,* 47, no. 3 (Summer 1974) pp. 337–54.

Robert Rosenthal and Lenore Jacobson, *Pygmalion in the Classroom* (N.Y.: Holt, Rinehart and Winston, 1968).

part five

Conclusion

15

School Learning in American Culture

In the two previous chapters we have found that the social norms or climates of the school are important in the definition of what is learned and who learns it in the school setting. We noted, however, that it is difficult to isolate the effects of the school climate from those of the family, neighborhood, and other aspects of the larger society. In this final chapter, we want to examine in broad perspective the interrelation of school learning with the general cultural norms of the society and the definition of the school's function in the society. Since the school operates as an integral part of the larger society which defines the boundaries within which the school social system may function, it is clear that the educational social system interacts with a wide range of other social institutions in defining the type of teaching and learning appropriate to and required of the school.

Throughout this volume we have examined the school and particularly the learning process which occurs in the school as a social phenomenon. The children who are sent to the school to learn certain types of behavior are not isolated learning mechanisms. Every child functions in a social system and interacts with an expanding range of adults and children in that social system. What behavior is to be learned and who learns it are usually defined by the people with whom the child interacts. This arena of interaction, of course, includes people both within the school and outside the boundaries of the school. But learning is a social process regardless of where it occurs.

The importance of education in American society is indicated by the fact that educational questions have become major political issues in contemporary America. National, state, and local elections are contested over issues concerning who shall go to school with whom, and who shall learn what types of behavior in these schools. The "busing issue" in American society is, of course, not a busing issue at all. The underlying issue is the maintenance of the segregated, differentiated, educational programs for boys and girls from different racial and socioeconomic categories. Demand for the maintenance of segregation is based upon the demand that some children learn to behave in different ways and should have a differential arena of interaction in which this learning will occur.

The pervasiveness of the educational issues of a society is illustrated by a recent recommendation of a regional planning commission. In identifying urgent needs in planning for people this commission reflected the prevailing middle-class emphasis upon differentiated education for different groups of children. With little regard for evidence, the planning commission, in criticizing college educational emphasis said, "This constant emphasis on college academics tends to alienate many students and disillusion them with school. Schools must emphasize that there are fields and skills just as important as going to college. Then through career and vocational training the school can prepare individuals for the world of work."[1] Although the Commission cites no evidence that students in college preparatory curricula are more likely to become alienated from school, it clearly supports the prevailing belief that some children should be provided education that directs them into positions and statuses for which a college education is prerequisite, but others should be educated in a manner that directs them into positions prior to college. This commission is the direct arm of the municipalities and units of government in the region involved. It perceives education, apparently, as one of the areas of planning essential to the development of the region.

The public's interest in maintaining and expanding differentiated education is also reflected in our policies concerning the transportation or busing of students. Our society resists busing to integrate students in order to enhance the possibility of quality education for the disadvantaged, but expands busing to segregate and differentiate learning facilities. The development of career centers or vocational schools in recent years reflects the desire to provide differentiated types of education for various lower income groups of students and usually involves busing to these schools.

These widespread cultural patterns are undergirded by the almost universal acceptance of the belief that the ability to learn various types of behavior is widely varied and distributed in a bell-shaped curve.

[1] Tri-County Regional Planning Commission for Clinton, Eaton, and Ingham Counties, *12 Urgent Planning Needs of the Tri-County Region* (Lansing, Michigan, 1973).

Although the concept of the normal curve with the assumption of limited and fixed ability to learn is most exemplified in the American educational system, it has wide acceptance in the larger society. Although we believe in equality of educational opportunity, the belief in inequality of ability dominates in American culture. The concept of fixed and limited ability, identified as intelligence and distributed according to a bell-shaped curve, is almost a sacred norm in American culture. This belief is seldom questioned and anyone who does so is condemned for denying a sacred principle. The adaptation of instructional programs and the norms and expectations of the school to this conception of human learning is essentially a requirement in American education and in many other aspects of life. The adaptation of educational programs and expectations to the normal curve conception of abilities leads to a self-fulfilling prophecy in American education. Children are defined as unable to learn or not ready to learn or with limited ability to learn and programs of instruction are adapted to these conceptions so that the outcomes inevitably conform to the predicted result. In American culture limited levels of learning are defined as appropriate for a large portion of the populace. We have, therefore, designed the educational system to conform to the cultural norms.

There are areas of human behavior for which we socialize essentially 100 percent of all children. As Linton pointed out 40 years ago, there are universal patterns of behavior in every society.[2] These are the patterns of human behavior that all people in the society learn. At about the same time, Allport demonstrated that much of human behavior is not distributed in the bell-shaped curve but in what he termed a J-shaped curve.[3] In this manner, Allport described the fact that essentially everyone in a society learns those types of behavior common to the culture and conforms to the cultural norms. The performance of such behavior is therefore distributed in a J-shaped fashion rather than the bell-shaped curve. This is illustrated by the fact that almost 100 percent of Americans learn to drive on the right-hand side of the road and almost all Britishers learn to drive on the left-hand side of the road. At a more abstract and verbal level, we recognize that almost 100 percent of the children in every society of the world learn to speak and communicate in an abstract, complex set of verbal symbols which we call language. The acquisition of these universal patterns of behavior demonstrates that the concept of limited ability distributed in a bell-shaped curve is not applicable to a wide range of human behavior. The acquisition of such behavior demonstrates that society defines the level of ability

[2] Ralph Linton, *Study of Man* (New York: D. Appleton Century Co., Inc., 1936).

[3] Floyd Allport, "J Curve Hypothesis of Conforming Behavior," *Journal of Social Psychology,* 1934, pp. 141–181.

and learning which will be achieved.[4] Almost all children can and will learn whatever is defined as appropriate and required in the culture and will fail to learn those types of behavior that society defines as inappropriate, improper, or not expected of them. The nature and extent of behavior in any arena acquired by young people in the society is defined not by the child himself, as an isolated learning mechanism, but by the norms and expectations of the culture of which he is a part.

As we noted in the previous chapter, the norms and expectations as defined in the climate of American schools assume that a large proportion of American children cannot, will not, and should not learn many types of behavior taught in those schools. Such climates, of course, typically characterize schools composed of students of lower socioeconomic status, or minority group students. They also, however, define the learning that is appropriate for various individuals in all schools. The conception of limited ability distributed in the bell-shaped curve justifies a widespread differentiation of learning in the school, and our testing technology confirms the results. This conception of human learning and human abilities is so fixed in American culture that the validity of an aptitude or achievement test is determined, in part at least, by the extent to which the test scores conform to the bell-shaped distribution. The educational process is defined as improper and inadequate if the learning resulting from the process is not distributed in this fashion.

Unlike our demand that all children learn to speak the language, our educational system demands that some children not learn algebra or physics and a wide range of other behavior. The result of this conception of human ability and human learning and the educational practices based upon it is a school system that produces widely varied types of achievement in student groups classified and labeled as different in ability, interests, and needs.

The almost universal belief in limited learning abilities and in the appropriateness of highly differentiated levels of achieving much human behavior causes many to believe that American education cannot and should not be modified to enhance the achievement of students labeled as slow learners. The current emphasis upon individual differences and the resulting individualization of educational programs based on presumed differences in ability are not likely to produce change that will enhance the learning of all. Most proposals for the improvement of American schools are firmly based on this concept of wide differences in ability to learn and the design of widely differentiated and individualized programs of instruction. Treatments and educational reform based upon this perception are almost certain to enhance the differences in learning rather than maximize the learning of all.

---

[4] Robert Faris, "The Ability Dimension in Human Society," *American Sociological Review*, vol. 26, pp. 835–42, December 1961.

Contemporary efforts to improve the quality of education and learning of children in school have been far from successful. Changes in the organization of the classroom and the school social system without parallel changes in the cultural norms have produced little significant change. Emphasis upon increased individualization of instruction has not produced significant improvement unless it is accompanied by changing norms and expectations of learning. The deviant schools composed of low SES or black students that are achieving at high levels demonstrate that the poor and disadvantaged children can learn. The development of mastery learning procedures also demonstrates that all or nearly all children can learn at essentially the same level.[5] These schools have demonstrated their success and the mastery learning experiments are operated on the assumption that children can and will learn. These assumptions lead to the creating of a school climate in which learning by all is the normative expectation. Such educational environments are the exception in the United States and most of the Western world. They assume a J-shaped distribution of the ability to learn and the mastery of various types of behavior. Mastery of complex subject matter by nearly all students is not likely to occur in situations in which the "normal" curve of achievement is the criterion of appropriate outcomes.

The likelihood of increasing the level and the quality of outcomes in American schools depends on the extent to which a high level of learning is accepted as the norm in American culture. If the predominant powers in American society continue to define human ability as drastically limited and accept the bell-shaped curve of achievement as the valid outcome of educational programs, the schools will produce a wide range of performance and continue to enhance the differences in educational achievement among the students. If, however, the current demands of minorities and poor that the schools improve educational performance come to characterize the dominant educational expectations in the American culture, significant improvement in school performance may be achieved. Educators could then abandon the concept of limited ability and normal distribution of learned behavior and society would hold the schools accountable for mastery levels of achievement. Such outcomes are not likely to occur so long as the contemporary American beliefs that only a limited proportion of the students can learn school subject matter prevails. We generally expect the schools to differentiate among students; and assign them to different curricula or levels of achievement.

[5] Benjamin S. Bloom, "Learning for Mastery," *Evaluation Comment,* vol. 1, no. 2, 1968; and James Block, *Mastery Learning in the Classroom: An Overview of Research* (Santa Barbara, California 1973); and James Block (ed.), *Mastery Learning, Theory and Practice* (New York: Holt Rhinehart Winston, Inc., 1971).

Suggested Readings

Ronald Corwin, *Education in Crisis* (New York: John Wiley and Sons, 1974).

Lewis Anthony Dexter, *The Tyranny of Schooling* (New York: Basic Books, 1964).

Robert L. Green, "The Awesome Danger of Intelligence Tests," *Ebony*, August 1974.

Jerome Hellmuth, ed., *Compensatory Education: A National Debate*, vol. 3 of *Disadvantaged Child* (New York: Brunner/Mazel, 1970).

Milton Schwebel, *Who Can Be Educated?* (New York: Grove Press, 1968).

Index

Index

A

B

P

R

This book has been set in 10 point and 9 point Caledonia, leaded 2 points. Part numbers and chapter titles are 18 point Scotch Roman italic; part titles and chapter numbers in 18 and 36 point Scotch Roman. The size of the type page is 27 × 45½ picas.